AF905584

Design and Diagnosis for Sustainable Organizations

José Pérez Ríos

Design and Diagnosis for Sustainable Organizations

The Viable System Method

Springer

Prof. José Pérez Ríos
Universidad de Valladolid
Campus Miguel Delibes
47011 Valladolid
Spain
rios@uva.es

ISBN 978-3-642-43707-6 ISBN 978-3-642-22318-1 (eBook)
DOI 10.1007/978-3-642-22318-1
Springer Heidelberg Dordrecht London New York

Softcover reprint of the hardcover 1st edition 2012

Printed on acid-free paper

Springer is part of Springer Science+Business Media (www.springer.com)

To my parents José and Hortensia
(in memoriam)
To my wife Irene
To my sons Alexandre and Xavier

Foreword

The appearance of the book *Design and Diagnosis for Sustainable Organisations* is propitious both for the theory of the organisation as well as for its application. It represents a bridging of the gap between, on the one hand, the urgent need to find solutions to problems resulting from the ever-increasing dynamic complexity faced by managers today and, on the other, the inability of traditional organizational theory to meet that demand.

Fortunately, during the last few years a new and powerful theoretical corpus has been developed which allows such complex problems to be dealt with. Its origins can be found in Cybernetics, the science of communication and control of complex systems. However, the significantly abstract degree of this theory makes it difficult to put into practice. For this reason, we deem it of the utmost importance that its theoretical bases be developed and translated into the language of entrepreneurship.

Design and Diagnosis for Sustainable Organisations meets both necessities. First of all, it re-examines the status quo of applied research, and it also shows the body of conceptual knowledge in a perfectly intelligible way. The text demonstrates the author's deep understanding of both the life of an organisation with its colossal challenges, as well as of the theory and its great heuristic potential.

José Pérez Ríos continues the tradition established by Stafford Beer, the pioneer of Organisational Cybernetics. He extends the master's scientific legacy, in line with the models proposed by the latter, developing them and adding cybernetic innovations. Amongst these we will mention the creation of new software facilitating the application of Organisational Cybernetics to the study of specific issues.

The book is an important contribution to organizational science, whilst helping readers to understand the potential of cybernetic models and methods. It shows those wishing to develop this potential how to proceed, providing the key for competent applications to improve the adaptability, intelligence and viability of organisations.

This book is a masterpiece! Whoever reads it will benefit greatly, whether it be for widening their knowledge or honing their efficiency and, in general, for the progress and enhancement of their organisations. Therefore, I hope this book will be widely read, which it deserves to be.

Markus Schwaninger
Professor of Management,
University of St.Gallen, Switzerland
June 2011

Preface

In the last few decades the world has changed dramatically. The diverse factors that have played their role in this change, together with their inter-relationship, have also led to a formidable complexity implicit in such a situation. Some examples of aspects involved here are the high degree of inter-dependence among different world economies (let us consider the impact of North-American sub-prime mortgages on the rest of the, mainly Western, world), the globalisation phenomenon, increases in the price of oil, the increase in the use of fossil fuels, or the impact of economic growth in countries like India and China on both the supply of products as well as on the demand for raw materials, energy and other components, etc. To this we can add the as yet uncertain but all the same worrying effects of possible climate change, migratory pressure towards developed countries, and security problems (threats of biological or nuclear terrorism, etc.). To these far-reaching problems that are affecting both humanity in general as well as organisations and companies, obviously we could add many more. Also, the fact that many of these problems are inter-related adds a further difficulty in terms of their study and possible solution.

We may summarize this state of affairs by maintaining that we are facing highly complex problems. Consequently, if our aim is first of all to understand them and then endeavour to improve their diverse facets, we need the appropriate means for this purpose. Managers in companies or organisations, politicians in their different areas of responsibility and, in general, any person who has to take decisions, should have at their disposal the necessary tools for tackling the problem facing them. At the start of the seventies, Conant and Ashby had argued, in the famous theorem which bears their name, that "a good regulator of a system must be a model of the system". But this model and, as a result, the regulating system with it, should possess a degree of variety (complexity) in accordance with that of the system they are trying to regulate (manage). For example, a light switch with only two positions (for instance, on and off) is unable to regulate multiple lighting intensity as it lacks sufficient variety, in this case, lighting options.

For this reason, we need models of problematic situations containing such corresponding variety, that is to say, ones that are able to give a response to the diverse situations raised. Nevertheless, very often the models employed simply lack sufficient variety.

One of the aims of this book is to show some of the methodological and technical tools that so-called Systems Thinking has developed over several decades since its dissemination around the middle of the twentieth century. These tools provide us with the possibility of constructing models with sufficient variety (the capacity to deal with complexity) to attempt to deal with current problems.

Since the first studies by Betalanffy or Wiener, etc., in the middle of the last century, until nowadays, many schools and approaches have appeared within the general framework of Systems Thinking. Consequently, in this book I will limit myself to dealing mainly with the development of Cybernetics and, in particular, Organisational Cybernetics (OC) of S. Beer. OC offers a wealth of conceptual elements which are extremely useful in terms of their application in designing and managing any type of organisation (company, institution, etc.). In this book, we will look in detail at two of its most important components, namely, the Viable System Model (VSM) and Team Syntegrity (TS).

The number of applications of both methodologies is very large. Nevertheless, the knowledge that managers and academics have in relation to them is still inadequate. One of the reasons given, especially in the case of the VSM, is that it is difficult both to understand and to apply. A further reason put forward is the lack of support for facilitating its use, such as specialised software to act as a guide in its application. The wide dissemination of other systemic methodologies such as Forrester's Systems Dynamics, is attributed in part to the appearance of specialised software, which has helped enormously to construct and visualise the models designed with this methodology. Another purpose of this book is, in fact, to highlight the VSMod® software created with the specific intention of at least partly addressing these shortcomings.

In general, I hope that those who read this book find the following of use:

- Recognising the magnitude of the problems faced by managers of any organisation and the means of assessing it, albeit in an approximate way.
- Recognising the existence and utility of the systems approach for dealing with certain problems facing society and organisations.
- Gaining familiarity with the basic concepts of Organisational Cybernetics.
- A sufficient knowledge of the principal components of the Viable Systems Model for carrying out a preliminary diagnosis of an organisation's viability.
- The ability to recognise some of the pathologies commonly showing up in organisations, as a prior step to dealing with them (diagnosis) or preventing their appearance (design).
- Learning of the existence and basic elements of Team Syntegrity, in order to judge whether its deployment is worthwhile.
- Gaining familiarity with the main aspects of VSMod® software, thereby attaining a better understanding of the Viable System Model.
- Increasing awareness of conceptual approaches to dealing with complexity, and acknowledging the role of the manager as the person responsible for dealing with it.

Structure of the Book

One of the main aims of this book is to deal with those aspects referred to above, related to the difficulty of increasing the dissemination of OC and the VSM among managers and academics. Hence, I will first of all endeavour to clarify the concepts contained in OC and the VSM by taking a look at its main components, and then go on to provide guidelines for using them in both the diagnosis and design of organisations. The other aspect covered in the book is a description of the software created with the special aim of facilitating the application and understanding of the VSM.

The book consists of six chapters. In the first, beginning with an introduction concerning the need to apply the systems approach, a relatively detailed account is given of the essential content of OC and the VSM. Chapter 2 is devoted in its entirety to showing how the VSM can be applied in both diagnosing and designing any organisation. For this purpose, structured and systematic VSM operational procedures are described, and each and every one of its essential components is considered.

Once familiarised with the application of the methodology, in Chap. 3 we will see some of the pathologies which most commonly occur as a result of non-compliance with the necessary requirements proposed by VSM theory. A knowledge of these pathologies and certain of the recommendable elements for dealing with them may help managers to understand the problems affecting the organisations they are trying to run.

Chapter 4 deals with the second of the limitations mentioned above, concerning the availability of specialised software to facilitate the application of OC and the VSM. I present the VSMod® software created for this purpose. This software is the result of over a decade's work for which I have been responsible at Valladolid University, aiming to develop software tools that could facilitate the application of various systemic methodologies, particularly OC and above all VSM. In this chapter we look at the principal components of VSMod® software and the way it is used. I should add here that, besides the version described in the book (version 1.3), other variants of this software are currently being developed which cover aspects not dealt with in this particular version. Such is the case, for example, with a collaborative version of VSMod® that allows several people to work on the same VSM study via Internet, and also an advanced version that includes additional design and diagnostic tools and methodological guides (both currently in the trial period).

Chapter 5 is concerned with the conceptual bases of the latest of S. Beer's innovations, termed Team Syntegrity. We show the main application protocols in its basic form and comment on the areas in which the use of TS might be recommended.

Chapter 6 makes a final reflection on the book as a whole and suggests some ideas for future work.

The book has two appendices. The first presents the complete version of the *laudatio* I had the honour of giving S. Beer during his investiture as Honoris Causa by the University of Valladolid (October 26, 2001). The reason for its inclusion is the detailed account I give of the whole of Beer's work, which I believe may contribute to providing a wide and reasonably in-depth view of the scope of his intellectual production and activity. Appendix II includes the Aphorisms, Organization Principles, Theorem, Axioms and Law devised by Beer as a synthesis of the content of the VSM. Obviously, the complexity involved obliges the reader to consult the complete sources (Beer's own books) to find their justification.

Acknowledgements

In a book like this, the list of people I have to thank for their manifold contribution is a long one.

My first expression of thanks must go to Stafford Beer, with whom I was most fortunate and honoured to share long conversations during the days prior to the act of investiture as Dr.Honoris Causa by the University of Valladolid in October of 2001. Those days were of incalculable value for me in terms of knowledge sharing. In our conversations, dedicated to preparing the Spanish version of his investiture speech, we could not imagine that this speech would be the last he would give in public. Stafford died in August of the following year, 2002. My special thanks also go to his partner Allenna Leonard, who took part in all those conversations, enriching them and helping me to interpret different aspects of Beer's OC.

I owe particular gratitude also to my dear colleague M. Schwaninger, with whom I have had the satisfaction and honour of sharing joint research work since 1994. His enthusiasm, drive and wealth of ideas have been a constant stimulus for me.

I would also like to express my gratitude to Raúl Espejo, for honouring me with his friendship and his valuable comments on Organisational Cybernetics. His generosity in sharing first-hand information on OC application both in Chile and later in various other countries is something for which I am particularly thankful.

I also want to thank Maurice Yolles for sharing with me his thoughts on methodology, with reference to both the VSM and OC as well as to other matters and to Nikitas Assimakopoulos for inviting me to contribute to his excellent activity in the promotion of these systemic approaches in Greece. Similarly, I extend my gratitude to Malik Management Zentrum St. Gallen, and in particular to my dear old friends and colleagues Martin Pfiffner and Peter Stadelman, for giving me the company's support in my research projects. I would also very much like to thank Fredmund Malik and Constantin Malik for their support, interest and friendship.

I would also like to express my gratitude to my dear department colleagues Cesáreo Hernández, to whom I owe so much and whose uninterrupted stimulus over more than 20 years has been my gift, and Pablo Sánchez Mayoral, for sharing with me so many intellectual concerns and interests. Without his help also in releasing me from numerous administrative and academic tasks, it would have been difficult for me to maintain a reasonably constant professional activity. I would also like to thank Pablo Sánchez and Iván Velasco for the stimulus provided in the questions they have asked me relating to the content, interpretation and application difficulties of the VSM, and who have encouraged me to write this book in order to give not only a verbal but also a written response to the diverse problems posed by the VSM and its application. I hope that the explanation given in the book is useful to both students and researchers or VSM users in general. My thanks also to my dear colleagues Adolfo López and Javier Pajares who so succesfully continue the expansion and diffusion of systems thinking approaches in our university. Thanks also to Rubén Herranz and to the book production team at Springer for their friendly and professional support throughout the project. Special thanks go to Michael Bursik who handled so smoothly and sucessfully this project.

To this list I would like to add four people who have also had a large influence on my work. One is my doctoral thesis supervisor José María Bueno Lidón, who introduced me to the systems dynamics field and opened university doors to my career. I am most grateful for that. Also I wish to thank my old friend Zenón Jiménez-Ridruejo for his enormous help during my preparation of the doctoral thesis. His deep knowledge about economic theory was extremely useful to me. Another person is the eminent doctor and very old friend Luis Fernando Márquez, always present despite geographical distance, and whose conversations on the relationship between psychiatry (his speciality) and systems thinking have been so stimulating for me. And the fourth person is the urban architect and professor Xosé Lois Martínez, with whom almost five decades of friendship, providing hundreds of hours of conversation (testing the patience of our respective wives), have enabled us to reflect on both the significance of systems thinking and its application to town planning and society in general, as well as to so many other issues.

I am particularly indebted to David Rixham for his help in translating my spanish texts into english and to John Peck for his wonderful, intelligent support in matters of language.

Finally, I want to thank my dear wife Irene for her patience and help in reading the different versions of the manuscript and for her vital support, and also my sons Xavier and Alexandre for their assistance with the formal aspects of the book and suggestions relating to content.

Valladolid, May 2011 José Pérez Ríos

The author would like to express his thanks to the Ministerio de Ciencia e Innovación, Gobierno de España, Plan Nacional de I + D + i, for its financial assistance. REF: CSO2010-15745.

Contents

Chapter 1
Systems Thinking, Organisational Cybernetics and the Viable System Model

1.1 Introduction

The profoundly rapid changes occurring in the operating environment for organisations in general and companies in particular are making it essential, if their viability is to be guaranteed, for the provision of tools that can deal with the kind of complexity inherent in such changes.

Over the last decades, many theoretical developments have occurred in the field of the organisation and management of both companies and organisations in general. In this context we should pay special attention to the progress achieved in the area of Systems Thinking (Pérez Ríos 2007a).

The need for an approach like that supplied by Systems Thinking for the study of complex problems has been accentuated as a result of the changes the world has undergone throughout the twentieth century, a need that is seen to be even more acute with the diverse events shaping the beginning of the twenty-first century. Systems Thinking provides an intellectual framework of tremendous utility for dealing with the numerous problems affecting both humanity (ecological disasters, the unequal distribution of wealth, threats of biological, chemical and nuclear terrorism, corruption, the absence of a suitable global judicial system, massive migratory movements, climate change, etc.) as well as organisations and firms. These are all problems of great complexity (variety), and they require tools in keeping with that fact. However, the models that are still being employed to understand them have not always kept pace with the complexity of the problems to be addressed. As already pointed out by Conant and Ashby (1970) in their well-known theorem maintaining that "a good regulator of a system should be a model of the system", we need models of problematic situations with requisite variety, that is to say, with the capacity to respond to diverse particular situations. Unfortunately, in many cases the models employed are obviously lacking in such variety.

This new era, initiated during the last century and called by Ackoff (1999a, 1999b) "The systems era", as opposed to "The machine era" appropriate to the industrial revolution, is characterised by the complexity, turbulence and diverse

J. Pérez Ríos, *Design and Diagnosis for Sustainable Organizations*,
DOI 10.1007/978-3-642-22318-1_1,

points of view concerning the question of how to face serious problems at every level, from the individual one to that of organisations, societies or the natural environment. Such problems are particularly suited to being addressed by Systems Thinking. The dominant approach in the machine era for dealing with problems was to divide them into parts in order to facilitate their study. For thinkers applying the systems approach, attention is not focussed on parts as such, but fundamentally on the interrelationships they have both among themselves and with the environment, and on how properties emerge that characterise the whole and which none of the parts possesses.

The tradition of Systems Thinking has a long history, but it was not until the end of the 40s and start of the 50s that it became a discipline, especially as a result of the work of Wiener and Bertalanffy. The decades spanning the 50s and the 70s represent the period of maximum influence for this current in management sciences, as well as in many other fields (Pérez Ríos 2004). Since the 70s, the traditional systems approach has come in for growing criticism, especially with regard to its usefulness when dealing with badly structured problems, and in situations where it was not easy to agree on a common goal or in which there were opposing interests.

As a result of such criticism, the end of the 70s and the following decade saw the appearance of alternative systems approaches capable of dealing with these problematic issues. More recently, critical currents have surfaced relating to the way those approaches, and science in general, were applied, giving rise to what is known as the emancipatory or critical movement.

The systems methodologies of the first years, such as Systems Analysis and Systems Engineering, were useful when studying simple and unitary problems (clearly identified and agreed-upon goals). Nevertheless, the excessive emphasis on mathematical models of systems as the object of study revealed their insufficiency when dealing with complex problems (difficult to model mathematically) and contexts involving pluralistic decision-making or conflictive situations (multiple goals and lack of agreement). This situation encouraged the appearance of new approaches more suited to these problems, such as Stafford Beer's Organisational Cybernetics. OC does not entail searching for the mathematical model for the problem based on its surface manifestations, but rather identifying the deep foundations for viability. The positive approach gives rise to a structural one, and the focus of interest shifts from simple systems to adaptive complex systems. The interest in facilitating decision-making in pluralistic and conflictive contexts gave rise to what are called "soft systems" and emancipatory systemic approaches.

The interpretive systemic approach is also known as "soft systems thinking" because it places people at the centre of the study, as opposed to technology, structure or organisation, and makes perceptions, beliefs, values and interests its main concern. It takes as its starting point the consideration that there are multiple perceptions of reality. Therefore, it attempts to help decision-makers work in a pluralist context. Now, the important thing is to identify the different "world views" (Weltanschauungen) or "appreciative systems" people use in order to understand and construct social reality (Churchman 1968, 1971, 1979). The issue therefore becomes a search for "accommodation" among the different groups in the coalition that an organisation represents.

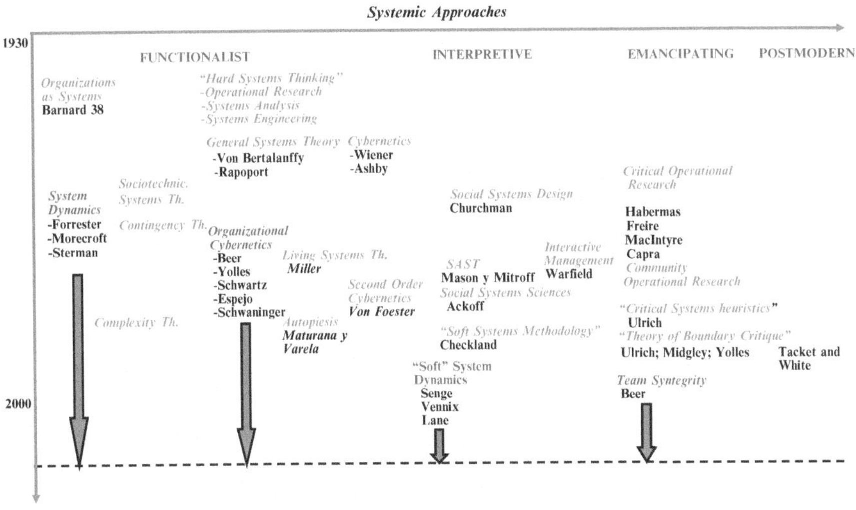

Fig. 1.1 Several representatives of different systemic approaches and approaches included in this book

During the 80s and 90s, more and more systems thinkers began to question the use of technical instruments without, however paying attention to the interests they serve. Based on the critical tradition existing in philosophy and sociology, the aim was to hone an emancipatory systemic approach (Ulrich 1994). This evolutionary process has also been accompanied in the last few years by the use of several methodologies in the same study (Pérez Ríos and Schwaninger 1996), resulting in a growing interest in methodological pluralism (Schwaninger and Pérez Ríos 1996). Figure 1.1 shows several schools belonging to the trends termed *functionalist, interpretative, emancipatory* and *post-modern*, with certain researchers whose work is related to these. The aim of this figure is to show the possible setting for the systemic approaches which I include in this book: Organisational Cybernetics, Team Syntegrity and Systems Dynamics.

The recent appearance of new ways of studying complex problems, such as Agent-Based Modelling, which seek to understand the emerging behaviour of a system as a result of the behaviour of the individuals of whom it is comprised, and their interactions among themselves and with the environment in which they operate, by means of a bottom-up approach, serves as a complement to the top-down approach widely used up to now (Pérez Casares et al. 2008; Pajares et al. 2003; López Paredes et al. 2002; López Paredes and Hernández 2008; Hernández and López 1999; Hernández 2004). This approach allows us to draw conclusions about observed generalities and to arrive at explanations of how the macro-behaviour is generated out of the individual inter-relationships and their micro-motives. This joint consideration of micro and macro issues raises new, thought-provoking questions of enormous interest for systems thinkers. Its capacity for dealing with aspects related to the behaviour of agents, depending on the environment and the rules of interaction by which they are conditioned, is a new and promising challenge for Systems Thinking.

I am including these considerations in order to give an idea of the large diversity of tools developed over the last few decades within the sphere of Systems Thinking. In this book mainly I will use of the Organisational Cybernetics (OC) of S. Beer, and within this the Viable System Model (VSM) in particular, to show how they can be employed in the diagnosis or design of organisations. The intention is to see whether, in the case of already existing organisations, they comply with the conditions established by the VSM as being necessary and sufficient for viability, that is, for having the capacity to maintain an independent existence and adapting to the changes taking place within their environment.

Certain of the systemic methodologies mentioned above have become quite widespread. This is the case, for instance, with Systems Dynamics. However, others have failed to reach this level of dissemination. Among these we must include OC. One possible reason for this is the difficulty involved in both understanding and applying it, together with the lack of tools to support its use (e.g., specialised software).

The aim of this book is, as I have said, to help, at least in part, to address such shortcomings. I will show in detail how the relevant concepts of OC can be applied, and how to use the VSM in practice, in both the design of a new organisation and the diagnosis of an already existing one. In both cases it is important to remember that the aim is to make the organisation in question capable of meeting the purpose for which it either has been or will be created.

1.1.1 The Systemic Approach

I said before that both OC and the VSM form part of what is called Systems Thinking. Consequently, I will first of all comment briefly on the essence of this overall approach.

If we consider a system as a set of elements in dynamic interaction, the first thing we must realise is that this represents a whole which cannot be divided into parts without the corresponding loss of its essential properties. In a system these essential properties belong to the system as a whole, none of whose parts possesses them. For this reason, when we divide and separate the parts, they no longer possess the properties of the whole unit from which they derive.

This has important methodological implications, for if we intend to design a new system or understand an existing one, we cannot apply only the "*analytical*" approach, which is concerned simply with breaking down the object of study into parts and then analysing each of these parts in order to explain its behaviour and properties, to finally combine this information to explain the whole system.

We need the *synthetic* approach, which first of all lets us identify the whole (system) of which the object of our study forms part. Next, we arrive at an explanation of the behaviour and properties of the whole, by means of which we can finally make sense of the behaviour and properties of the object of our study, in terms of the role or function it plays inside the containing entity.

Consequently, I have mentioned on the one hand analysis and on the other synthesis. It is not a matter of deciding which of the two is the most important, since each performs different functions and both are necessary. In an analytical approach, the subject in question is dealt with as a whole to be divided into two or more parts. In the synthetic approach, the thing being explained is a part of the whole to which it belongs. One allows a description of the object of study and the other an understanding of its function and justification. The "*systemic*" approach proposes a combination of synthesis and analysis. In order to design a new system (for example, a university, a judicial system, a new rail link, a hospital, a vehicle, a computer application, a town plan, a company, etc.), the first thing we need to do is identify the larger system which contains it and then define what its function within that larger system will be.

If we take the example of a new railway connection, it is appropriate to bear in mind that a passenger normally wishes to reduce travelling time between home and some final destination. This wider view of transport, which includes journeys from the passenger's home to their departure station, and from their arrival station to their final destination, obliges the designer to include in the study all additional aspects in order to achieve the aim. The implications of this inclusiveness for the design of the (complete) transport system may be significant.

Once we have clarified the function of our system as the object of study, and have taken note of the environment in which it will operate, we can proceed with the detailed design of the parts of the new system. This will basically constitute the sequence that we will apply when using OC. First, however, we must explain what is understood by OC.

1.2 What Is Organisational Cybernetics?

Before attempting to answer this question, we will begin by clarifying the meaning of the term *cybernetics*. When we speak of the difficulties faced by organisations in the current turbulent environment, we normally use the term *complexity* to characterise the different situations or problems to be dealt with. The reason for the existence of managers is directly related with the existence of such complexity, and their work basically consists of dealing with this factor. To that end, they will need to employ their knowledge and specific problem-solving models in order to bring about the desired result in the evolution of the problem. In doing so, managers in fact "govern" the organisation for which they are responsible, therefore trying to ensure that the goals established for the organisation are achieved. This action is associated with the term "cybernetics", whose etymology returns us to the Greek *kybernetes*, which referred to steersman placed at the helm of a ship so as to steer it to the desired destination. This word was transformed by the Romans into "gubernator", which finally takes us to the term "governor" or "government". As a consequence, when we speak of organisational "cybernetics", the main term in fact signifies the organisation's "director", its governor or steersman.

Thus, cybernetics can be understood as the science dealing with control, in the sense of governing (managing) an organisation (Pérez Ríos 2008a).

Regarding OC, (Pérez Ríos and Schwaninger 2008), this is one of the systems approaches which, deriving from the Cybernetics created by Wiener (see the seminal book *Cybernetics: Control and Communication in the Animal and the Machine,* 1948), applies the principles associated with "Communication and Control" from Cybernetics to organisations. OC was developed from both a theoretical and methodological point of view by S. Beer (1959, 1966, 1979, 1981, 1985). For an in-depth overview of the extent and scope of the work of S. Beer, consult Beer's *laudatio* (Pérez Ríos 2001) at his investiture as Dr. Honoris Causa by the University of Valladolid in 2001; this is included as Appendix I at the end of this book.

OC has been applied to a very wide range of problems, sectors, companies and organisations of diverse sizes and ownership. Two instances of recent application in Spain may be consulted in: Almuiña et al. (2008), in which OC is employed to explore the "Impact of the new information and communication technologies in media companies"; and in Pérez Ríos and Martínez (2007), where it is applied as an element of the strategic planning in a Spanish public university.

In this book I will not give a detailed account of the components of OC, although I will comment on those essential elements I deem it fundamental to be familiar with. Amongst these we will examine the concepts of variety and viability, Ashby's Law, the Conant-Ashby Theorem, together with other essential aspects of OC, such as the convenience of intrinsic control and information in real time, as well as the implications of the redundancy of potential command. I will end this survey of OC with an account of the most significant aspects of the Viable System Model.

1.2.1 Variety

I referred previously to the concept of complexity to highlight the fact that the task of managers directly involves how to deal with it. Let us see how this can be characterized and its dimension assessed.

Among the various alternatives available for qualifying complexity – among others, distinguishing between computation-al, technical, organisational, personal and emotional complexity (Yolles 1999), or between static, structural and dynamic complexity (Cambel 1992), or between dynamic complexity and detail complexity (Senge 1990) – here we will use the term to characterise the potential of a system for adopting multiple states of a different nature. In the case of social systems, that potential also includes possible forms of behaviour.

Regarding an evaluation of the diverse degrees of complexity, we will make use of the concept of *variety*. The latter has been employed by Ashby to reflect the degree of complexity in a system (organisation, company, etc.). It equals the number of possible states and real or potential forms of behaviour that may arise from a given situation or problem. We will use this concept not to accurately measure its value in each case but in order to clarify the size of the problem faced by managers when trying to run their organisations. Just to give some idea of the size it may reach, take the example in which the number of possible relations in a group consisting of *n* elements (for instance, people) is $n(n-1)/2$, when there is only one type of possible relation between two components of the group. It is easy to see how the number of relations increases exponentially with the number of individuals. Therefore, in a group of 30 people, we find that there are 435 possible relations; if the group consists of 300 people, then the result would be 44,850 possible relations. In view of such figures, it is hardly surprising that in more or less large groups (university committees, parliaments or simply various types of commissions with many members), it is hard to exchange ideas in an exhaustive and productive way. In parliament, the frequent image of conversations which are "practically monologues" is an example of this difficulty.

The task of managers and, in general, decision-takers in organisations is more or less difficult depending on the complexity (variety) with which they are faced. If there is very little complexity, the problem is trivial.

For a system (an organisation, company, etc.) to be viable it must be capable of coping with the variety (complexity) of the environment in which it operates. From the cybernetic point of view, managing complexity is the essence of a manager's activity. Controlling a situation means being able to deal with its complexity, that is, its variety.

If, on the one hand, the manager's function is to ensure that the organisation he runs is capable of achieving its goals and staying alive (in other words, being viable) in the environment in which it operates; and if, on the other hand, the complexity of the latter is huge (we may think about the diversity of clients, individual preferences, products, suppliers, competitors, legislation, public authorities and the multitude of potential interactions among these elements and others which have their place in the environment of any company), then how can the manager face such complexity? In the following Sections I will attempt to answer this question.

1.2.2 Ashby's Law (Law of Requisite Variety)

In order to understand the mechanisms available for dealing with complexity, we will employ, in addition to the previously mentioned concept of variety, R. Ashby's (1956) so-called "Law of Requisite Variety". This establishes that "only variety destroys (absorbs) variety". What this basically means is that to come to terms with a certain degree of variety (complexity), the system in question (for instance, a regulatory system, organisation or manager) should be capable of deploying an equivalent amount of variety. For an understanding of this law, let us imagine, for example, a light switch in a room. If we have simply a switch with two positions – on or off – it will be impossible to have various types of lighting – high-medium-low-off.

From the viewpoint of "management", this law implies that in order to face the enormous amount of variety to be found in the environment in which their organisation operates, as well as in the production operations for which they are responsible, managers should be able to develop the variety required. Notice that managers are placed at the narrow end of a funnel within a three-tiered cascade. That is, the variety in the environment is enormously greater than that of the productive system which provides it with the products or services, whilst the variety in the productive system is in turn far greater than that available in the management system controlling it. Generally speaking, therefore, the problem facing an organisation attempting to deal with the complexity of its environment is how to meet the requirements of Ashby's Law of Requisite Variety (Ashby 1956) when, as a rule, the variety to be found in any organisation or its managerial team is always by necessity much less than the huge variety of the environment. The answer to this problem comes through two sets of options provided by Organisational Cybernetics.

1.2.3 Vertical Unfolding of Complexity

The first of these operates in what we may consider a *vertical dimension*, and consists of the environment being divided into sub-environments, smaller ones inside the original, and these in turn into other, even smaller sub-sub-environments, and so on; in this way, each of these sub-environments has its corresponding smaller organisations within the initial organisation, in order to reduce the complexity to be dealt with by these "parts" of the company or organisation, making it more manageable. These "parts" are not fragments of the initial organisation; however, they must possess all the requisites for being fully operative units similar to the original organisation, but with a more limited area of activity. Espejo (1989) calls this process of vertical division the "unfolding of complexity" (Fig. 1.2). By means of the figure, one can appreciate how the organisation at level 0 deals with its corresponding environment. In the example given, this global organisation has three sub-systems (sub-organisations), each of which is responsible for a part of

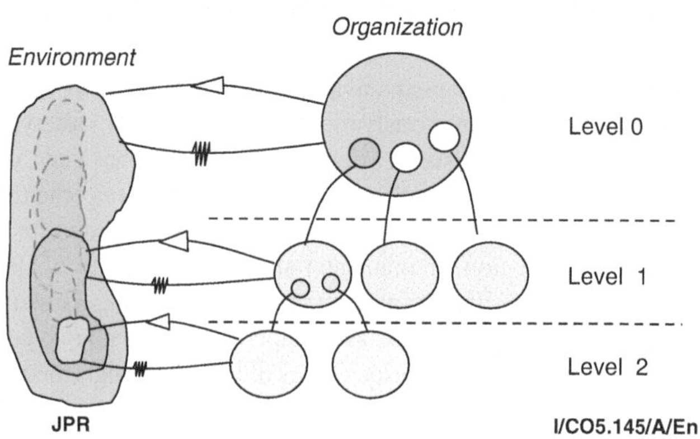

Fig. 1.2 Unfolding of complexity (Vertical dimension)

the general environment, as we can see in level 1. Similarly, one of the level-1 organisations contains two sub-organisations, which in turn are responsible for other smaller parts of the previous environment (level 2).

Depending on the organisation in question (an association of companies, a particular firm, the state educational system, a particular university, etc.), the number of vertical levels will be greater or smaller. This ratio will be determined by both the complexity of the initial environment and the organisation we are dealing with.

1.2.4 Attenuators and Amplifiers

The second group of possible actions for dealing with variety (complexity) operates basically in what we may regard as a *horizontal dimension*, where another set of mechanisms can be encountered for managing complexity. In this dimension the components exist at a specific level, and basically are: the environment, the organisation itself and the organisation's management team. Once again, the variety of the environment (clients, markets, products, competition, technologies, legislation, etc.) is far greater than that available within an organisation, whilst that of the organisation is in turn much greater than that available in the managerial team. To comply, then, with the previously-mentioned Ashby's Law, we need mechanisms that make possible a balance among all of them, that is, that equip each element with the ability to manage the complexity (variety) affecting it.

These mechanisms are, on the one hand, "*Attenuators*" of variety and, on the other, "*Amplifiers*" of variety. The first kind selects, from the huge variety existing in the environment, only that which is pertinent to our organisation, namely, related to aspects which the system (organisation) will have to deal with in order to maintain its viability. One example of an attenuator would be the selection, as a company's target market, of only one spatially limited geographical area.

Unlike "Attenuators" which reduce variety, "Amplifying" mechanisms allow us to enlarge an organisation's capacity (for example, by means of widespread publicity) in relation to the environment, or its managerial capacity in relation to the company or organisation itself (by means of mechanisms like delegating, etc.). We may take media companies as an example (press, television, etc.), where an increasingly common case of amplification expands the number of information "addressees" themselves, such as readers of digital newspapers who redirect an item of news to other people (friends, family, etc.) with whom they share it, and these in turn may do the same, redirecting it to others, and so on (Almuiña et al. 2008, pp. 253–265). Such effects, generated by new ways of using technologies, represent real amplifiers, making it possible for an item of news to reach a far greater number of "addressees" than that reached by the medium first mentioning the item (for instance, the newspaper in which it was published).

Figure 1.3 represents an organisation inside the environment in which it operates. Figure 1.4 shows the "management" or managerial team of an organisation as part of this organisation, likewise positioned inside the environment in which it is active.

In Fig. 1.5 these three elements (Environment-Operations-Management) are shown separately in order to make it easier to explain their inter-relationships, as I will do later on.

An important point to bear in mind is that not all the relevant variety should be attended to by the organisation, since part of it may be absorbed by elements of the

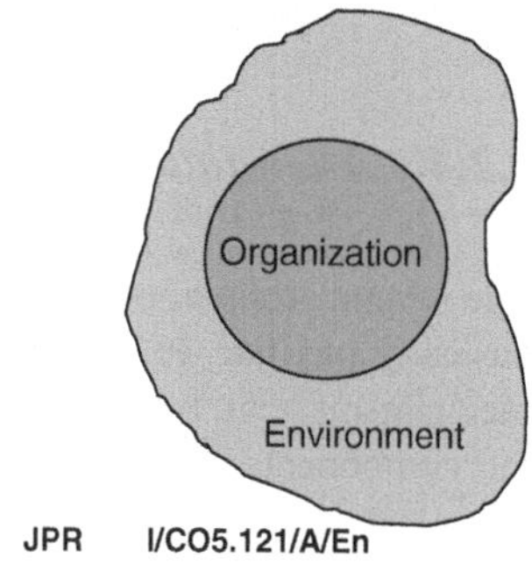

Fig. 1.3 An organisation in its environment

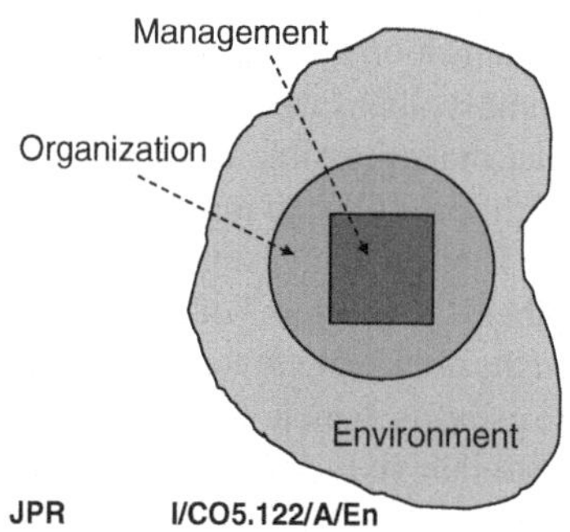

Fig. 1.4 The "Management" responsible for the embedded organisation and this in its environment

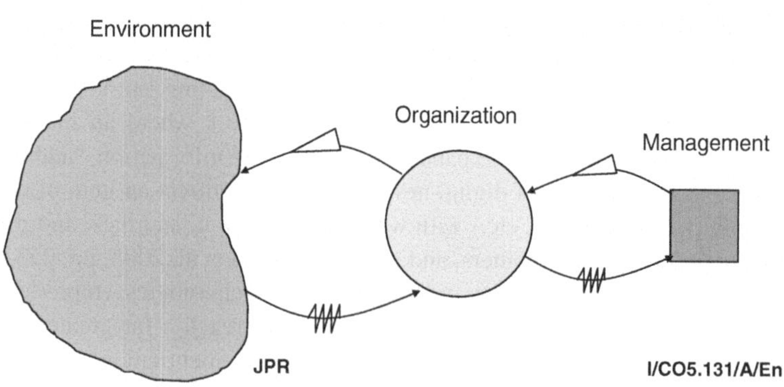

Fig. 1.5 A company or organisation system: environment, operations and management

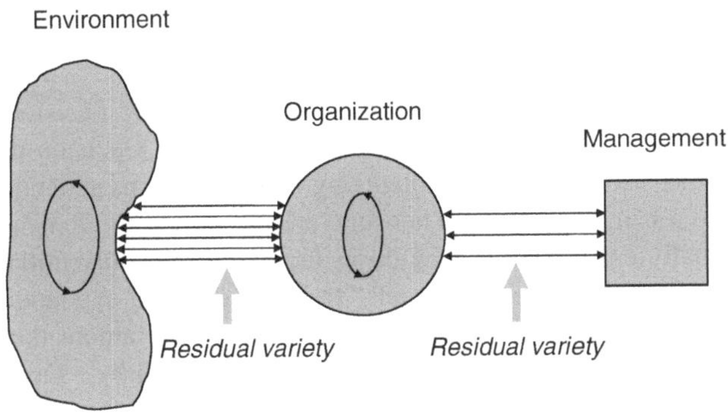

Fig. 1.6 Residual variety

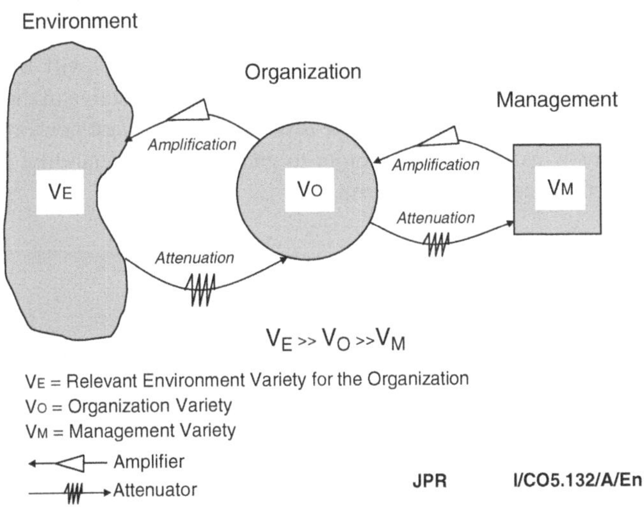

Fig. 1.7 Amplifiers and attenuators (Environment-Operations-Management). Horizontal dimension

environment itself (which is what occurs, for instance, when car dealers resolve technical questions with buyers instead of the manufacturers); as a result, the organisation will need to deal only with what Espejo (1989) refers to as *residual variety* (Fig. 1.6).

We can put ourselves in a better position to face complexity by coming up with an appropriate design for the mechanisms mentioned above, first in terms of the vertical dimension by means of unfolding complexity, and in the horizontal dimension through mechanisms that both attenuate and amplify variety. The diverse tools at the disposal of managers for dealing with complexity (variety), and with the ways in which these can be employed, form part of what Beer has termed *Variety Engineering*. These tools constitute an essential part of the work of managers in any kind of organisation (Fig. 1.7).

1.2.5 The Conant-Ashby Theorem

A third component of OC refers to the "models" used by decision-takers (for example, managers) to tackle the problems facing them. Decision-making must somehow be able to meet these problems by studying them, generating possible alternatives, assessing the latter, choosing among them, implementing one or several and finally ensuring that they do in fact work, not only initially but also over time. The need for suitable "models" had already been expounded, as I said before, by Conant-Ashby (Conant and Ashby 1970), in the famous theorem which bears their name. In this theorem, deriving directly from Ashby's Law, it says that "*A good regulator of a system must be a model of that system*". If the aim of managers is to regulate, that is, to govern their organisation or firm, they should have at their disposal suitable "models" of the firm within its problem environment. The quality of their work will depend on the quality of such models which, in turn, should possess the variety required by the problem they are trying to solve. In this regard, the cybernetic model, and in particular the VSM which I will describe later, are, I believe, appropriate tools for this task. The ultimate objective of the VSM is to help managers (in both public and private institutions) to design new organisations or diagnose already existing ones in order to guarantee their viability. Let us now have at look at the meaning of this term.

1.2.6 Viability

By viability we understand the capacity of a system (organisation, company, etc.) to maintain a separate existence (that is, to survive) over time, and to do this despite ongoing changes in the environment (even if these have not been foreseen). The term commonly employed in medicine to refer to the foetus from the moment when it is capable of existing independently of the mother, serves also to illustrate a similar characteristic in organisations or systems in general.

The new being has a different *identity* from the mother and, in the case of organisations, from other organisations. Of course, links between the infant and its mother, family, etc., will remain throughout its life, in spite of its having a separate identity. The same may be said of an organisation or company. By maintaining this identity, an organisation shows, through the regulatory process applying to the whole organisation, that it will survive, in other words, that its *identity* will persist through processes of learning, adaptation and evolution. This concept of identity should be understood in a sense that transcends the mere survival of the organisation, one that aims at "viability beyond survival" (Schwaninger 2006, p. 65). Therefore, the idea is that the organisation will still retain its identity while undergoing such radical transformations as, for instance, changing its sector of activity and with it much of its apparent character, acquiring a radically different type. The example of phase-change in zoology can help here:

the pupa becomes a butterfly while the individual insect persists, just as an organisation can pass through a radical "materialisation" or metamorphosis, substantially altering its physical forms and means of existence.

1.2.7 Intrinsic Control

As I have said, cybernetics deals with governing the system (or organisation), in other words, controlling its functioning in such a way that this is self-sustainable, regardless of the changes taking place in its environment. The best type of control in the cybernetic sense is incorporated in the very process of going out of control, making control instantaneous. The aim therefore is to achieve intrinsic control. Within the organisation and its processes, we should already have incorporated the mechanisms that can detect (if possible, instantaneously) any deviation from the desired behaviour, thereby intervening to redress the balance.

The concept of intrinsic control is directly related to other components of cybernetics, such as the concept of viable systems with its recursive character, the availability of information in real time and the redundancy of potential command. All these factors are related to the objective of attaining systemic control of the organisation, which among other aspects implies having decision and action points, placed as near as possible to information sources (decision) and to where intervention is necessary (action). Certain concepts frequently used in the literature on the theory of organisation and management are nothing more than specific cases and drastic simplifications of these cybernetic concepts. Two examples would be, first, "empowerment", that is, increasing the capacity for decision-making and intervention in elements of the organisation, and second, "the design of more horizontal organisational structures", by means of shortening the chains of command in order to accelerate decision-making.

Moreover, the concept of intrinsic control is also deeply associated with the aim of amplifying the variety (Ashby's Law) of management. If an organisation makes full use of its potential by activating the capacity of staff at every organisational level, it will be better prepared to achieve its purpose on a stable basis over time, in other words, to be viable. For this purpose we must design the processes, information systems, communication channels and the organisation's recursive structure so as to deal with the total complexity (variety).

Also related to the concept of intrinsic control is that of *ultra-stability*, deriving from the work of Ashby. We have already seen that the aim behind applying the principles of organisational cybernetics is to ensure that the organisation we wish to design or run is viable, that is to say, that it is self-sustaining or capable of surviving in the same way that a human being is viable when he can survive outside the womb. This does not signify total independence (since nothing is totally independent), but it does imply autonomy within the defined limits of the particular physiology. This capacity for survival means being able to deal with the changes that will inevitably take place in the environment in which the organisation (system) operates. However, some of these changes will be unknown and unpredictable. How, then, is it possible to ensure that our system (organisation) will be able to respond to these and survive? The answer comes from the design of ultra-stable systems. It is a matter of incorporating into the design those change-detection systems that the system itself considers to be warning signals for its survival and which, when activated, set in motion previously built-in emergency mechanisms. A system may be deemed ultra-stable when it is capable of resuming normal functioning after having undergone a disruption unforeseen by the designer.

1.2.8 Information in Real Time

In the previous Sect. 1.2.7 mentioned the convenience of intrinsic control. For this to materialise, it is obvious that the diverse functions of the system (or organisation) must have information at the precise moment when one must decide and take appropriate measures. Many of these decisions and actions require information in real time. Should it come late to the decision point, then it may be useless or, what is worse, counter-productive. We may consider what would happen to a human being if their decisions related to functioning (for instance, moving) were taken with delayed information. Let us imagine starting to cross a street with heavy traffic when our information (on the number of cars, the direction of the traffic, speed, etc.) came a few seconds or, worse still, minutes or hours later. Obviously, a human being would not be viable in such an environment.

Similarly with organisations, it is easy to imagine the effects if the information supplied cannot be used in real time. Depending on the type of decision, the consequences for the organisation may be quite negative, if not lethal.

When we consider the Viable System Model and its information requirements, we will have occasion to highlight this model usefulness as a conceptual reference framework for designing and managing organisational information systems. The need for information in real time must be kept in mind when identifying which functions and decisions require it, so that it is incorporated accordingly in the requisite features relating to design and management.

1.2.9 Redundancy of Potential Command

"Authority does not lie in the chains of command, but in the relevance of the information"

(Beer 2001: "Vital Aspects of Viability: The Viable System Model in Management", Keynote address for the *First International Conference On Systemic Management*, Vienna, May 1st 2001).

Another aspect also directly related to the availability of information for taking the right decisions is the cybernetic principle referred to as *redundancy of potential command*. This concept was formulated by the American cybernetician Warren McCulloch. It refers to the capacity to take control of a particular situation at a given moment by a sub-group within the organisation which, at that particular moment, possesses the information pertinent to the situation. The principle of redundancy (see Beer 1966, p. 196) was identified by Von Neumann as the basic trick employed by the human brain for the trustworthy processing of signals (combined signals) from untrustworthy elements (connections between neurons).

In terms of organisational design, the principle of redundancy of potential command manifests in the tremendous utility and capacity for taking correct decisions that rests with the sub-groups in an organisation. This simply means that in the process of taking a particular decision at a given moment, those in the organisation who have the necessary information for that particular case should be the ones to intervene. These sub-groups need not coincide (in fact, they rarely do so) with the ones designed in the organisational chart. The centre of command continually changes in accordance with the person who has the relevant information at the required moment. A potential centre of command, in this context, is any group of individuals related through the information applying to the case. In simple exemplary terms, let us consider who in an organisation really takes such a decision as selecting and purchasing a technologically sophisticated and costly piece of equipment: the young engineer with the technical skills for assessing the different alternatives available, or the managing director responsible for "taking the decision" by giving approval to spend the money?

Once we have understood what is meant by the concepts of variety, viability and other essential components of Organisational Cybernetics, as well as what is implied by Ashby's Law and Conant-Ashby's Theorem, we are in a position to examine the Viable System Model. But before we itemise its main elements, let us see how it came into being. To this end, I include here part of the *laudatio* of S. Beer which I delivered (Pérez Ríos 2001) on the occasion of his investiture as Doctor Honoris Causa by the University of Valladolid. (The whole document, also part of this book, gives an overview of Beer's work, describing the emergence of Organizational Cybernetics and the Viable System Model, together with Beer's latest innovation, Team Syntegrity). Examining the content of Beer's books in the sequence in which they appeared will help us to comprehend his impressive work in the field of OC, in particular the genesis of the Viable System Model.

1.2.10 Genesis of Organizational Cybernetics and the Viable System Model

[...] After this necessarily rapid overview of Professor Stafford Beer's biography, let us take note of some of the most outstanding aspects of his monumental production, for which the recent comments made by Dr. Beer himself regarding his work in the Kybernetes journal will be very useful.

The upheaval facing humanity due to the dramatic events taking place and the multitude of problems affecting it (world terrorism, pollution, climate change, poverty, lack of equality among and inside countries, migratory movements, etc.) and growing economic globalisation, means that ever greater attention is being paid to the systemic nature of the world in which we live. There is a growing awareness, albeit dramatically, of the inter-relationship among such phenomena. Classical institutions are of no use for controlling the new state of affairs, by which is meant the appropriate functioning of the system. The problems are global but the institutions are not, or at least not global enough. The question is how to design them. It is here where we can best appreciate the work of Dr. Beer.

Following the success of the inter-disciplinary workgroups (eventually referred to as Operational Research groups) during the Second World War, in resolving problems transcending the particular area of each individual group, the employment of such groups extended, once this conflict was over, to dealing with non-military problems. One was created by Norbert Wiener in Mexico, which recognised the essential unity of a series of problems related with communication and control, both in the machine and in living beings. His work, as well as that of scientists such as Warren McCulloch, Walter Pitts, Ross Ashby and Grey Walter among others, gave rise to a new view concerning the interaction of complex systems and human responses to these. It was Wiener who gave the name *Cybernetics* to the new science, which he defined as the **science of communication and control in the animal and the machine**. In the post-war years numerous articles and books were published on this issue, and an international community began to develop an interest. During this period Stafford Beer comes into contact with the central group behind this trend, and in fact becomes part of it.

The ideas contained in Wiener's *Cybernetics* are put into practice by Stafford Beer in the British Steel company. Throughout the 1950s, he is responsible for several publications, seminars and talks until, in 1959, he publishes *Cybernetics and Management*.

With this book is born **management cybernetics**, that is, the application of the principles of cybernetic science to the study of organisations. In it Beer gives a historical review of the origin of cybernetics as a science, and proposes the system concept as an alternative to the reductionist approach then dominant in western culture. The description of complex systems as black boxes and the notion that systems with a purpose are defined by the product coming out of the black box (and not by desires or intentions) were responsible for Dr. Beer's famous statement: "the purpose of a system is what it does".

The book is a defence of "holism", through the study of whole systems, as opposed to the reductionism prevalent in the scientific method. Although nearly 50 years have passed since this call for applying a systemic approach to the study of complex problems, and despite the global nature of problems affecting humanity, the reductionist approach is still dominant in scientific, academic and medical environments as well as in the social sciences. Therefore, it is appropriate to remember what Dr. Beer proposes in the introduction to the book, when he argues that similarly to science's search for the original source of energy in the physics of the sun itself, that is, the liberation of energy in the basic process of transformation represented by the fusion of hydrogen-helium, science should now balance such findings by searching for the original source of control in the cybernetics of natural processes, in the evolution of the nervous system itself and the brain. The importance of research into control increases on a daily basis, as do the uncontrolled forces. This book sets out, for the first time, the possibility of scientifically designing an organisation as a system equipped with the capacity of learning, adapting and evolving.

In 1966, Dr. Beer publishes "*Decision and Control*", which deals with "management" and the way in which science may be employed to resolve problems of decision and control. "Management" is regarded as a profession responsible for the future of firms, countries and even the world, and one which requires a suitable language. Herein resides one of the book's chief aims. Old ideas and words are of no use when it comes to creating new approaches, and without these new approaches to new problems we will be condemned to suffer undesired consequences. For this reason, he once again proposes a holistic approach in contrast with the fragmented and partial nature of the then prevailing orthodoxy in the field of "management".

Since its origins at the start of the II World War, the aim of Operational Research was to be able to face extremely complex problems and increase the likelihood of effective decisions being taken in situations of extreme uncertainty. Hence, Dr. Beer has formalized the Operational Research approach with the following definition:

"Operational Research is the attack of modern science on complex problems arising in the direction and management of large systems of men, machines, materials and money in industry, business, government and defence. Its distinctive approach is to develop a scientific model of the system, incorporating measurements of factors such as chance and risk, with which to predict and compare the outcomes of alternative decisions, strategies or controls. The purpose is to help management to determine its policy and actions scientifically."

Decision and Control aimed to clarify these propositions in the context of "management". As Dr. Beer himself points out, the book is not the result of an academic research, but rather of real experience over more than 20 years in applying the principles contained therein whilst in charge of operational research activities in the then largest steel-producing company in Europe.

Stafford Beer considers this orientation towards problem solving to be vital for society, and he proposes cybernetics as the most powerful approach available for building multi-disciplinary models. The development of "academic" interests has, however, meant that operations research has become a type of applied mathematics, distancing it from creative problem solving. Although Professor Beer considers mathematics useful as a powerful language for discussing models and has, in fact, used them in some of his most innovative studies, he believes that models do not necessarily need to be mathematical. One of the most outstanding aspects of the book is precisely the way he deals with the appropriate methodology for selecting and using models.

The density of the book *Decision and Control* and the wish to render it more accessible to managers in general is what prompted the appearance in 1968 of *Management Science: The Business Use of Operational Research*. In this work he insists on differentiating between what is a scientific knowledge of "management" based on the theory of systems, and the consideration of the science of management as a collection of topics (an understanding of human factors, market research, cost analysis, balances, leadership, etc.) no matter how interesting and useful they might be, since its objects of study are complex, probabilistic systems considered as a whole.

The publication, in 1972, of *Brain of the Firm* marks the appearance of the first book in Dr. Beers' trilogy dedicated to explaining the Viable System Model (VSM). Employing the epistemology expounded in *Decision and Control*, the VSM is conceived on the basis of the necessary and sufficient conditions that should be met by any system for it to be viable.

The book creates a description of the firm (or any other organisation) based on reflections deriving from the study of the human nervous system. The structures of the brain and "management" are continuously clarified and compared until they give way to a theory of effective organisation. This is not an analogy but rather a question of deducing the fundamental principles according to which viable self-organised systems are constructed.

The purpose of this book is stated by Dr. Beer when he maintains that the main discovery of cybernetics is identifying fundamental control principles applicable to all large systems. It is oriented towards a study of the contribution that cybernetics (the science of control) can make to "management" (the profession of control). Control is not something to be encountered in a place or a specific element of the firm (or organisation), but rather the function of control is shared by the whole of the firm's architecture. Control is what helps systems to go on functioning.

The model identified by Stafford Beer distinguishes five sub-systems, each of which carries out a systemic role. These are continually interacting so as maintain the system in a state of homeostatic equilibrium, in other words, under control. The entire regulatory process aims to ensure the system's survival, both in the short and long term, by means of learning, adaptation and evolution. Moreover, the five sub-systems cannot be isolated from one another because they form a whole in constant interaction.

In the second edition of *The Brain of the Firm*, published in 1981, Professor Beer adds a description of an application of the VSM and cybernetic principles to the case of Chile. It is tremendously interesting to see how in a short period of time it was possible to incorporate in the model two thirds of the country's social economy, as well as the diverse innovations that were applied to the system of control. More specifically, the orthodox information systems were replaced by a computerised system in real time, based on Kalman filters and Bayes' probabilities theory. Communications by microwave and automatic statistical filtering of information were used, and ergonomically designed operations rooms were created, as spaces for decision taking. Economic information at all levels, from production plants to the presidential cabinet itself, and which was never more than 24 h old, was filtered with a view to identifying the important aspects. In spite of the whole complexity of the control system, the informatics system was organised so as to decentralise authority.

After the work undertaken in Chile during the years 1971–1973, Dr. Beer was sought after by a multitude of organizations and institutions in several countries. One of these was Canada, where as a consequence of intense activity for various organisations and governmental departments, the Canadian Broadcasting Corporation invited him to give the 1973 Massey Lectures. These were a series of talks broadcast on the radio each year to the whole country, and were given by an important person in the world of science or culture. All the lectures delivered by Professor Stafford Beer were included in the book entitled *Designing Freedom* published in 1974. The purpose of the broadcasts, as well as that of the book, was to explain to the general public some of the fundamental concepts of cybernetics. Emphasis is placed on the need to design new institutions that can make use of science as well as information and communication technologies for the benefit of mankind, in order that ongoing processes of instability may be controlled.

Dr. Beer's dedication to studying problems of a global nature affecting mankind and society increased in the 1970s. An indication of his intense activity during this period are more than 15 inaugural talks or plenary sessions he gave during the year 1970, to audiences as diverse as the Operational Research Society, the Pierre Theilard de Chardin Association in London, UNESCO, the Institute of Management Science, and the Society for General Systems Research in the U.S.A., etc. To prepare the content of such a wide range of activities, he decided to take on a more far-reaching project, namely, a book in which he would give his ideas on the relevance of this new science of cybernetics for holism, proposing it as a new world view. At the same time, whilst developing different concepts he would apply them to the pertinent problems of the various audiences. This context supplies the origin of the book *Platform for Change*, published in 1975.

It is a hugely original book in both form and content. Stafford Beer himself maintains that it is "a new kind of book for a new kind of world". It is structured around a thesis, named total system, which represents a world philosophy set forth in a simple systems diagram.

The main idea of the book focuses on the urgent need to reconsider all our social institutions, for which it offers a conceptual framework. Many questions are dealt with, such as global threats to humanity, overwhelming complexity, systems and meta-language, the use of science for studying organisations and society, and that of computers to manage information. Different colours and text layouts are employed to differentiate the arguments from the meta-systems in which they are included.

In 1979, he publishes *The Heart of Enterprise*. When Stafford Beer designs the neuro-cybernetic model of the firm as a viable system in *Brain of the Firm* (1972), he suggests that the human nervous system allows us to identify the rules according to which an organisation is able to survive, that is to say: it is regulated, it learns, it adapts and it evolves. Many considered the model to be an "analogy", in which case its validity on different specific occasions would be debatable. Nevertheless, as Dr. Beer himself has repeatedly argued, the model "is not an analogy".

This signifies that it ought to be possible to identify the nature of viable systems and create this model from basic principles, regardless of the source from which the cybernetic considerations are drawn (in the case of *Brain of the Firm*, from neurophysiology). This is precisely the purpose of the book *The Heart of Enterprise*. The reason for including the term "heart" in the title is Professor Stafford Beer's awareness that man has to be placed in the centre of "management". In this work, he makes it clear that cybernetic concepts can be applied to all kinds of organisations (not only firms).

The book begins with a discussion regarding the meaning of the word system and its subjective and relative nature. After debating the question of measuring a system's complexity and how variety flux determines the latter's dynamic complexity, he considers how systems can be regulated. The answer constitutes the central axis of the book: by means of organisation. The book deals with organisational cybernetics: the science of effective organisation. Following the initial concepts he manages, by a deductive process, to identify the five sub-systems regarded as fundamental when it comes to guaranteeing the viability of any system.

The third book in the trilogy dedicated to the VSM is published in 1985 and is entitled *Diagnosing the System for Organizations*. Due to the complexity of the two previous books (*Brain of the Firm* and *The Heart of Enterprise*), Stafford Beer decides to write a book to facilitate the application of the principles contained in the VSM. All the same, this work is not restricted to aiding implementation but also constitutes the definitive formalisation, in graphic form, of this model. The origins of the VSM go back to a mathematical model of the brain published in 1960. Nevertheless, both the model, based on the theory of sets, and the mathematical notion of recursion, were not all that accessible to the general public on account of their difficulty. For this reason, he decided to represent the mathematical model in terms of rigorous diagrams, in this way fully maintaining the model's mathematical validity.

In 1994, he publishes his last book: *Beyond Dispute*. In all viable systems there are two sub-systems with very different functions, which he calls System Three and System Four. In simple terms, we may say that the former is responsible for the "here and now", that is, for ensuring functioning in present time, whilst the latter is responsible for the "exterior and the future", in other words, for trying to create the future of the organisation. Interaction between both is generally very conflictive due to diverse interests, but it is vital that they function properly for the system to survive as it depends on them for adaptation. This is one of the reasons why Dr. Beer has, throughout his last years, been interested in how to facilitate this interaction. The result of this is his invention of Team Syntegrity. We might say that this is a method designed to facilitate normative, strategic and operational planning, allowing us to capture the essence of an organization in a non-hierarchical and non-political way.

In its original format, it takes its inspiration from an icosahedron (a regular 20-sided polyhedron), in which each of the 30 edges represents a person and each vertex one of the topics into which the object of debate has been broken down; the latter could be symbolically situated in the centre of the icosahedron. All the edges are identical. There is no hierarchy. There is no top, bottom, right or left. Besides, the functioning protocols guarantee that the information circulates freely throughout the whole group, becoming more extensive and enhanced along the way until becoming totally diffused. Therefore, a group organised in this way is said to represent the greatest expression of participatory democracy, as each role is, structurally speaking, not distinguishable from the others. Finally, I will add that the agenda is not established previously, but that it is generated by the members of the group themselves whilst the progress is in motion.

Apart from the utility of this tool for guaranteeing that the homeostat formed by Systems 3 and 4 works properly, it may also be extremely useful in the resolution of conflicts. (Pérez Ríos 2001).

In the next section a description is given of the most significant aspects of the VSM. This explanation will be vital for understanding, in Chap. 2, how the VSM can be used both for the diagnosis and design of viable organisations, and for identifying, in Chap. 3, some of the pathologies that commonly jeopardise the viability of organisations.

1.3 The Viable System Model (VSM)

Now that we have seen the beginnings of the VSM detailed in the previous section, let us look at its fundamental components.

As Beer highlights in *The Brain of the Firm*, the main discovery of cybernetics is the identification of the fundamental principles of control applicable to all large systems. The VSM concretely exemplifies the contribution that cybernetics (the science of control) can make to "management" (the profession of control). Control is not something to be encountered in a place or a specific element of the firm (or organisation); rather, the control function is shared by the whole of the system's architecture. Control is what helps systems to exist and to go on functioning.

The VSM distinguishes five sub-systems, each of which undertakes a systemic role. They remain in continual interaction so as to maintain the system in a state of homeostatic equilibrium, that is, under control. The entire regulating process aims to ensure the system's survival, both in the short and long term, by processes of learning, adaptation and evolution. Furthermore, the five sub-systems cannot be isolated from one another, as together they constitute an entity in continual interaction.

The VSM establishes the necessary and sufficient conditions for an organisation to be viable. Compliance with these conditions is possible only if the organisation in question possesses the five functions or sub-systems identified as being essential. Beer simply calls these five sub-systems System 1, System 2, System 3, System 4 and System 5. Each corresponds in a drastically simplified way (and, due to their explaining very little, only as an indication) with the functions of Implementing, Coordinating, Integration, Intelligence and Policy. To these is added System 3* (e.g., Channel auditor) as a complement to System 3. The VSM model is

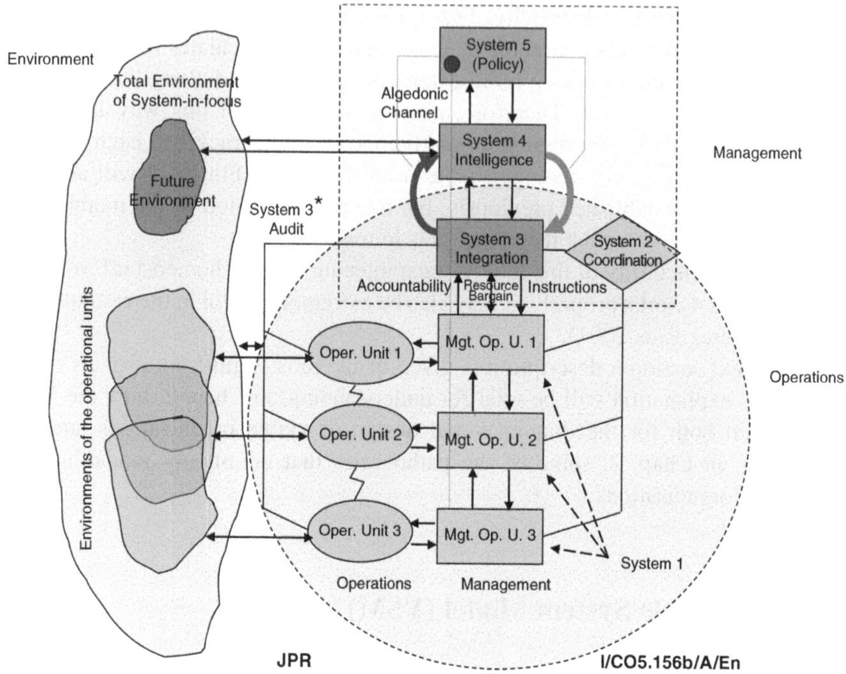

Fig. 1.8 Viable system model (Adapted from Beer 1985)

represented in Fig. 1.8. We can see the five sub-systems together with an example of system 1 made up of three divisions (operational units) in a firm or organisation.

1.3.1 System in Focus

When explaining the concept of viability, I pointed out that a system is viable when it can maintain a separate existence. I also argued that this does not mean not having relations with others, since in the same way that an individual, despite having his own identity, remains in contact with his mother and family, etc., an organisation or firm may also maintain a relationship with the organisation or mother company (whatever the case) to which it belongs. For this reason, when we design a new organisation or study an already existing one, we must make clear both what it is and what its limits are (let us imagine, for example, that the object of our particular study is a car manufacturing company or a university faculty). We must identify also the viable parts of which it is composed (which in our example would be, in the case of the automobile manufacturer, the different production units of different models or types of vehicles, or, in the case of the faculty, the different academic degrees taught), as well as the viable larger unit in which the organisation is contained (the global organization of the automobile firm or the university on which the faculty depends).

Such an exploration of the containing entity and what it contains is common when we are dealing with systems. Every system is contained in systems that include it, and the system in turn has sub-systems which are also systems; and so the containment process continues. If, for instance, we take the individual as the system-in-focus, we can work backwards via the family, community, town, country, etc., until we reach the universe; and, in the opposite direction, we can go down to the cell, etc., and all the way to the nucleus of the atom or the basic particles of which it is composed.

Because we can change the focus of our attention, it becomes necessary to clearly identify our system (organization) under study and the limits separating it from the environment surrounding it. So that we may remain constantly aware of the level we are considering and the system or organisation on which we are working, the latter is termed *system-in-focus* or *organisation-in-focus*. Obviously, we can use many dimensions for going forwards or backwards from the system in focus; our focus may be regarded as the centre of a sphere whose diameters would be the different dimensions (Fig. 1.9). Regarding the multi-dimensional recursive characteristic of the VSM, it is interesting to consult the works of Beer (1994,

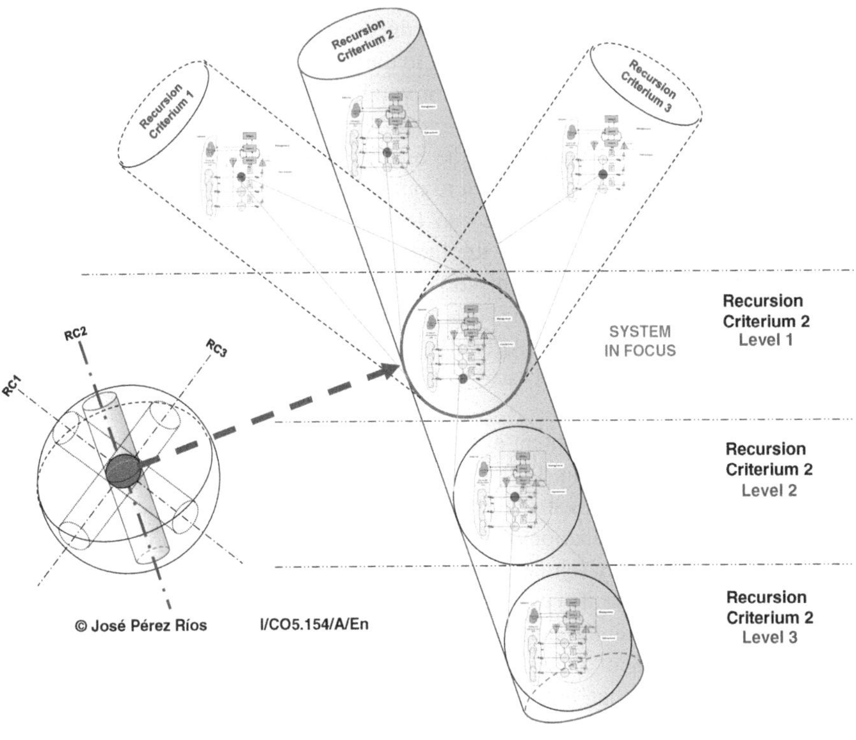

Fig. 1.9 The system in focus as the crossing of multiple dimensions (criteria and recursion levels) (Pérez Ríos 2008e)

pp. 227–255), Leonard (1989, p. 176) and Schwaninger (2006, p. 87). I will return to this point in the chapter dealing with the design and diagnosis of organisations.

These three levels we have just mentioned (the level including the organisation we are studying, the level of the organisation per se and the level comprising the other organisations contained in it) are known as *recursion levels*. This term from mathematics here indicates that, despite there being three different levels, the structure and composition of the organisation corresponding to each one is always the same. This particularity is one of the strengths of cybernetics: when we know the necessary and sufficient characteristics for an organisation to be viable, we then know them also for all viable organisations, whatever their size, sector, scope, purpose, etc.

In accordance with the above, the VSM is a recursive model in the sense that a viable organisation will need to possess the five functions or sub-systems mentioned at all the levels comprising the organisation. A viable organisation is made up, as has been shown, of other likewise viable ones, and is itself a part of others which are also viable. In Chap. 2, which looks at the design and diagnosis of organisations, we will see how this structural conception is employed.

In the following section we will examine the content of each of these functions or systems – Beer's Systems 1, 2, 3, 4 and 5 – which every viable organisation must possess. Given that the conception of the VSM is recursive, we can focus our attention on any of the many levels contained in the global organisation we are studying. The organisation corresponding to the level with which we are concerned, either within the chain of organizations or within organisations, is called, as I have said, the *system in focus* or *organisation in focus*, by that we mean the object of our analysis. Of course, we may change the organisation in focus in accordance with our convenience or interest. To return to our example of the auto company; When applying the VSM to its study we can focus our attention either on one of its factories in a specific place, or all the factories in a country or all the production units in the world, etc. The organisation corresponding to the level at which we pause (for example, all the factories in a particular country) will be our organisation in focus (or system in focus). After the following sections on all the functions/systems comprising the VSM, we will again consider the implications of the model's recursive nature.

Let us now survey the content of the VSM and the characteristics of each of its principal components. In Fig. 1.10, we can observe a representation of the model in which the three basic elements (Environment, Organisation/Operations, Management) and the essential functions can be distinguished. On the left side of the figure there is an organisation (circle), containing its own "management" (rectangle) which in turn are inside its environment (amoeba-shaped). In the central part we can see the same three components (amoeba, circle, rectangle) but separated for a better visualisation of their inter-relations. On the right side the same three elements are included but with the content of each shown.

In fact, in the VSM representation of any organisation we will always find the three basic components: Environment, Organisation (also called "Operations" or *System*) and "Management" (also known as *Metasystem*) of the organisation.

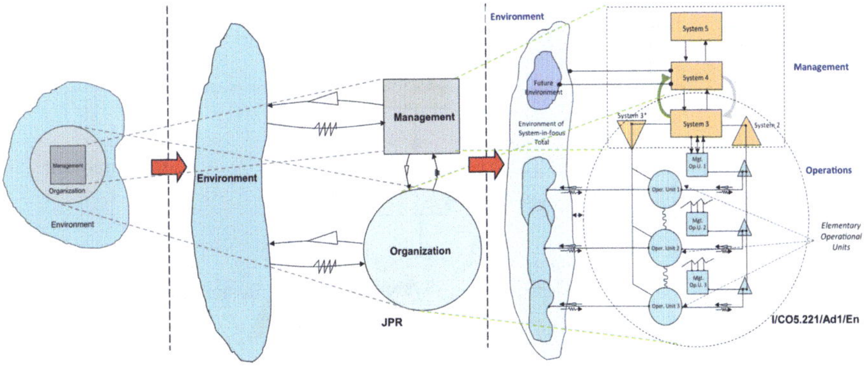

Fig. 1.10 Environment/Operations/Management set and complete VSM (Adapted from Beer 1985 [Pérez Ríos 2008a])

The Organisation or Operations contains the so-called System 1, System 2, System 3 and System 3*. The "Management" of the organisation contains Systems 3, System 4 and System 5. As we can appreciate, System 3 appears in both elements (System and Metasystem). The significance of this duality will be explained later.

In Fig. 1.11 we have an example representing the VSM with the software VSMod® (Pérez Ríos 2008c).[1] Let us now consider the principal components of the VSM.

1.3.1.1 System 1

System 1 is responsible for the production and delivery of the organisation's goods or services to the pertinent environment (market, etc.). System 1 is made up of operational organisational units (complete viable systems), each of which is responsible for a line of activity or product, etc. It is these units which "produce" what the organization is supposed to produce.

In Figs. 1.12 and 1.13 we have an example in which System 1 is composed of three basic operational units. These are units which possess a high degree of autonomy in order to adapt to the changes in their particular environment. The figure shows some of the relationships of System 1 with other components of the whole organisation, as well as others encountered among the basic units of which System 1 is comprised. These relationships will be examined in more detail later on.

Defining the units which make up system 1 is the task of high-level managers, who must bear in mind that these should comply with all the viability requisites demanded of the organisation to which they belong. In fact, they are the only units

---

[1] VSMod® is a software developed specifically to facilitate application of the VSM (www.vsmod.org). For a detailed description of how it works, see Chapter 4 of this book and Pérez Ríos (2003, 2006b, 2008c and 2008e).

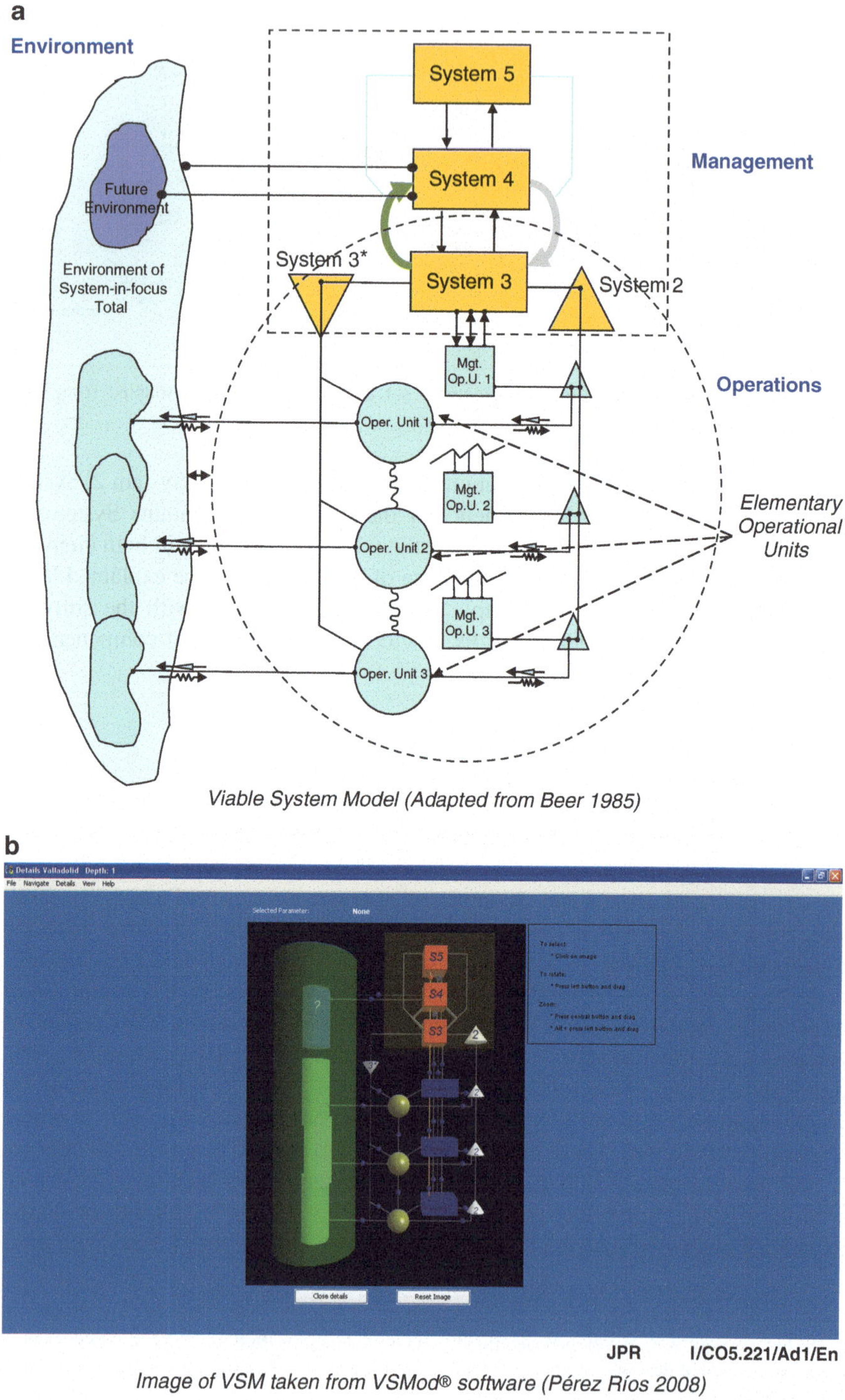

Fig. 1.11 Representation of the viable system model by means of software VSMod® (Pérez Ríos 2008c)

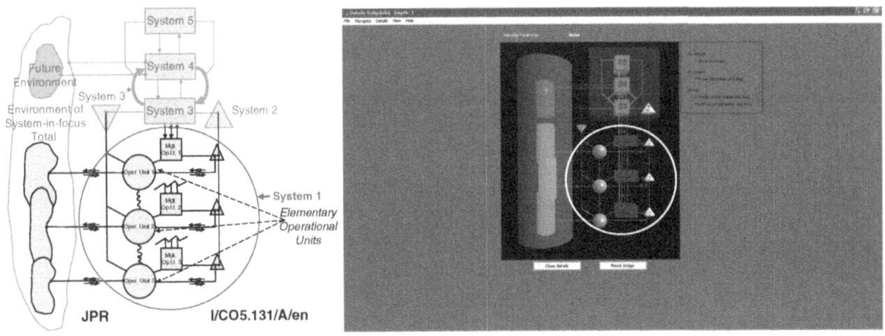

Fig. 1.12 System 1 (Adapted from Beer 1985 and image taken from VSMod® [Pérez Ríos 2008c])

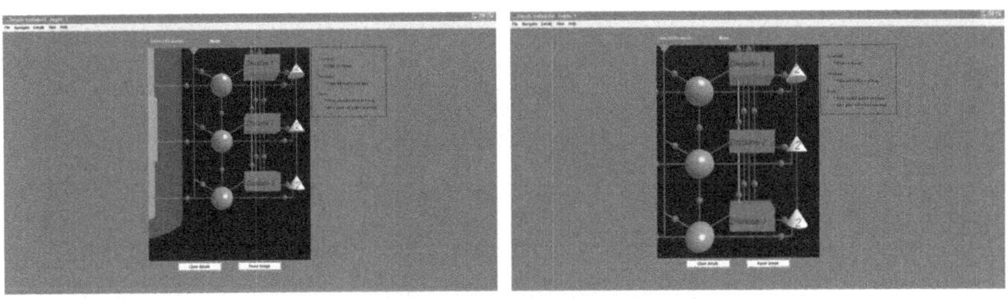

Fig. 1.13 Enlarged images of a System 1 taken from VSMod® (Pérez Ríos 2008c)

within the organisation that are viable. The others, constituting the entire organisation according to the VSM, are non-viable regulatory units; in other words, they are incapable of existing independently outside the organisation, unlike system 1 units. The fact that they can be independent does not mean that they are so, as they form part of a whole, namely, the organization to which they belong. Yet despite their dependence relationship with management, they must have the necessary degree of autonomy, in compatibility with the cohesion of the whole organisation, for responding to the requirements of their pertinent environment (market, scope of activity, etc.).

Each operational unit consists of the three elements that play a part in any organisation: environment, operations and management. Besides these components, each unit also possesses an element of coordination (system 2) or regulatory centre, whose function I will address at a later stage (Figs. 1.14 and 1.15).

Each operational unit making up System 1 is related to corporate or "senior" management (System 3), on which it directly depends (Fig. 1.16).

Apart from the relations with System 3 on which it depends, the management of each elementary operational unit also comes into contact with the other elementary

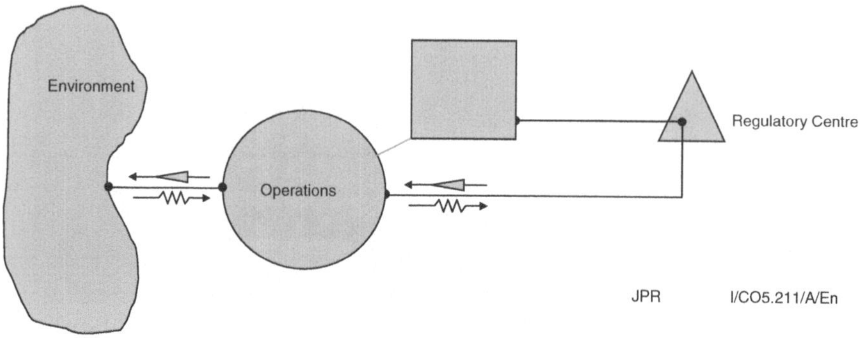

Fig. 1.14 Elementary operational unit for System 1

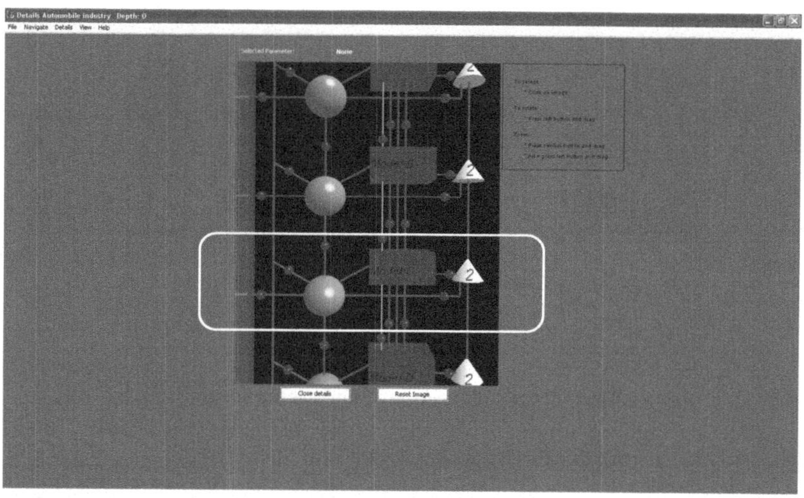

Fig. 1.15 Image of an elementary operational unit taken from VSMod® (Pérez Ríos 2008c)

units comprising System 1 of the organisation (organisation-in-focus). In all, each operational unit in System 1 has the following relations:

1. With corporate management (System 3) via the three kinds of fundamental relations (Fig. 1.17) represented by: "receiving instructions and guidelines", "accountability" and "resources bargaining",
2. With its specific environment comprising, amongst others, its market or the addressees of the services offered by the unit,
3. With its regulatory unit (System 2),
4. With the auditing function (System 3*: special information channel),
5. With the other operational units (System 1 components),
6. With the various managements of the other operational units and, finally,

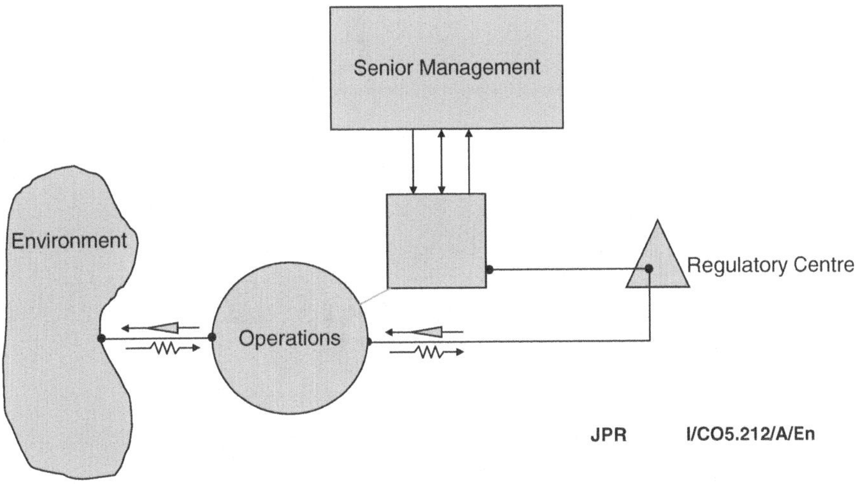

Fig. 1.16 Elementary operational unit making up System 1 and relationship with System 3 (Corporative or "senior" management)

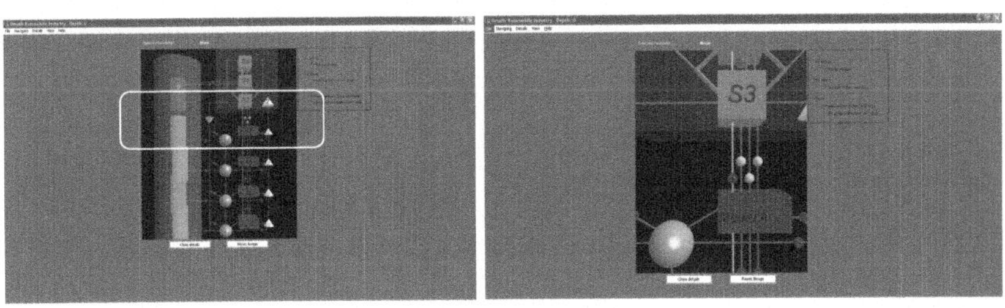

Fig. 1.17 Images of the relations between a elementary operational unit and System 3 taken from VSMod® (Pérez Ríos 2008c)

7. With the metasystem via the algedonic channel. At the end of the section on information needs and communication channels, which we will see later, an explanation is given of the purpose of this special channel.

1.3.1.2 System 2

This system is intended to make the set of organisational units which comprise System 1 (Fig. 1.18) function harmoniously. These units may be related by production processes and supply chains, or simply compete for the organisation's common resources and even clients or suppliers, etc., which might lead to conflict as a result of each one attempting to achieve its own goals (the delivery of the assigned

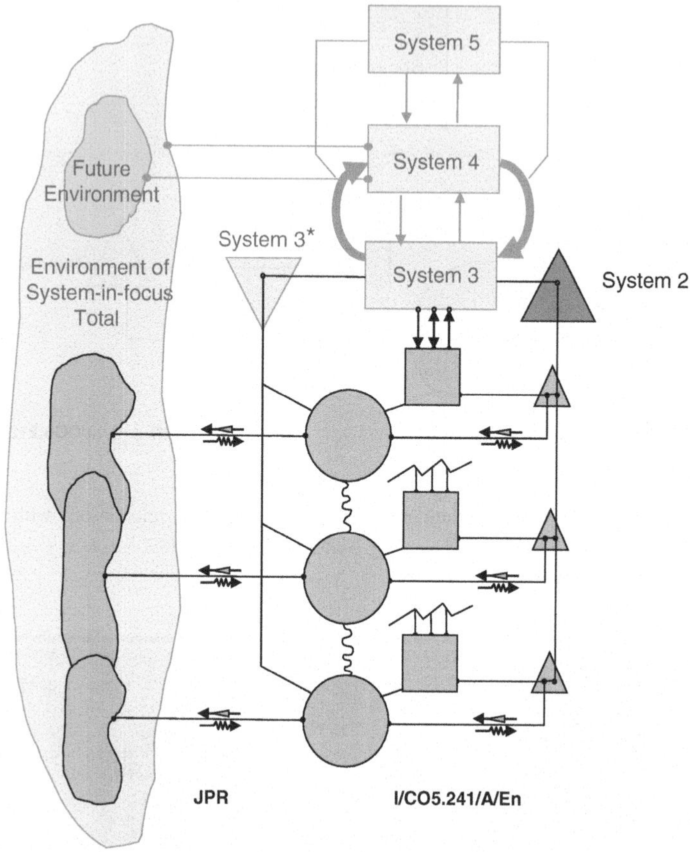

Fig. 1.18 System 2 (Adapted from Beer 1985 [Pérez Ríos 2008a])

products or services). System 2 deals with such issues. Moreover, it is an amplifier of the self-regulating capacity of the units themselves.

Examples of System 2s are: information systems, production planning or tasks programming tools, coordination teams, knowledge bases, accounting procedures, or diverse types of operational norms intended to provide behavioural standards, etc. Typical areas of System 2 activity are, therefore, those associated with personnel policies, accounting policies, the programming of production and operations, and legal requirements, etc. It also incorporates matters related to the organisation's "culture", but more in terms of functioning or behavioural "styles" than of aspects concerning values or identity, since the latter belong, as we will later observe, to System 5.

System 2 mechanisms act on the horizontal axis, in the sense that they do not form part of the vertical line of command (System 3 - System 1). They deal with the transmission of information which is taken from the operational units and, after being suitably filtered, is forwarded by the central regulatory unit to System 3, which has direct authority over System 1 components. System 3 will decide on the necessity of acting or not acting, as a function of the information available.

Consequently, System 2 is directly related to both System 1 and System 3. Similarly, each of System 1's operational units has its own System-2 regulatory component coordinated with the organisation's general regulatory one at the corresponding recursion level (system-in-focus).

Ultimately, System 2 is the principal system responsible for providing System 1's operational units with the appropriate means for maintaining their stability and for ensuring, should this stability be lost due to any internal or external disruption, that steadiness is restored.

Each elementary operational unit comprising System 1 possesses a local System 2 supplying it with information pertinent to the working of the other units; in this way, it has the capacity to coordinate the way they function and interact. All local System 2s are connected to the corporate System 2 (Fig. 1.19), whose task is to feed System 3 (whose function we will consider later on) with information on the operational units and, conversely, to transmit to these units the information required for coordinating their activities.

System 2 is a support for System 3, which is concerned with absorbing vast amounts of variety (complexity) generated as result of the detailed working of the elementary operational units on a daily basis. The idea is to achieve the maximum degree of "automation" for System 1, by designing systems that coordinate and resolve problems which might arise when its elementary units interact and compete for resources.

It is important to consider two points regarding this system. First of all, it should not be regarded as having a routine function. Of course, it needs to develop routines so that oscillations are softened as automatically as possible, but such routines are associated solely with the objective of avoiding fluctuations. The others routines which every organisation creates attenuate variety and play a role in the System 3 – System 1 vertical channel.

The other important question has to do with who should design System 2. Although the function of this system is to aid System 3 so that the set of operations functions harmoniously (Fig. 1.20), System 3 does not have the largest share of

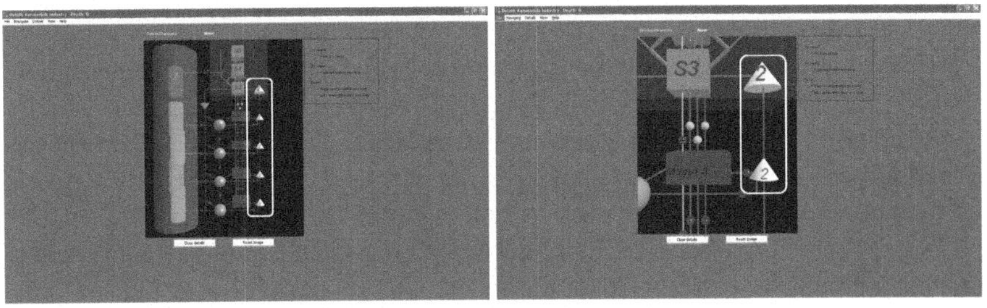

Fig. 1.19 Images of corporate System 2 and local System 2s taken from VSMod® (Pérez Ríos 2008c)

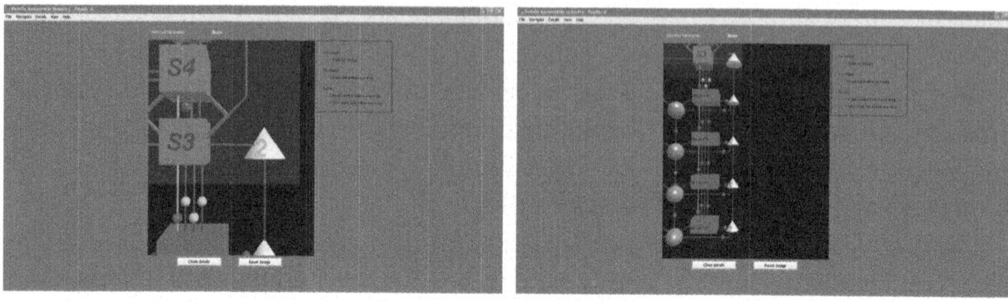

Fig. 1.20 Relationship of System 2 with System 3 and set of Systems 3-2-1. Images taken from VSMod® (Pérez Ríos 2008c)

responsibility for its design. It is the management members of the elementary operational units who together should design the tools, guaranteeing that their behavioural patterns are not in continual collision. Therefore they will do the design work, but of course with the help and experience of System 3. All the same, if we return to the previous recursion level, we see that System 3 contributes assistance and experience, in view of its also forming part of the management of elementary operational units.

1.3.1.3 System 3

This system has the task of managing the set of operational units comprising System 1 (Figs. 1.21 and 1.22). System 3 has to integrate the group, ensure that it functions harmoniously and attempt to exploit possible synergies resulting from the interaction of System 1's operational units. It is responsible for assigning the goals for each of these units (Figs. 1.23 and 1.27), a task it has to accomplish jointly with System 4 and in conformity with System 5. In a moment we will analyse the function of these two systems. Returning, though, to System 3, we note that once such goals have been established, its duty is to share out available resources among the units (Figs. 1.24 and 1.28). In addition, its responsibility extends to determining the accountability mechanisms of the operational units so that it is kept informed about how these are functioning and how far they are complying with their respective goals (Figs. 1.25 and 1.29).

System 3 may be considered the "*Operational Management*" of the organisation. It is the one that is concerned with daily operations. We may summarize its activity by saying that it is concerned with the organisation's "here" and "now". It has to ensure that the operational units (making up System 1) are producing and supplying the market (or its clients/addressees in general) with the products or services that the organisation (and each of its elementary operational units) is supposed to deliver, whilst endeavouring to optimise the use of resources, in other words, achieve the highest possible levels of efficiency and efficacy.

System 3, then, is responsible for optimising the functioning of the whole of System 1 composed of the different operational units. This system has a view of the set as

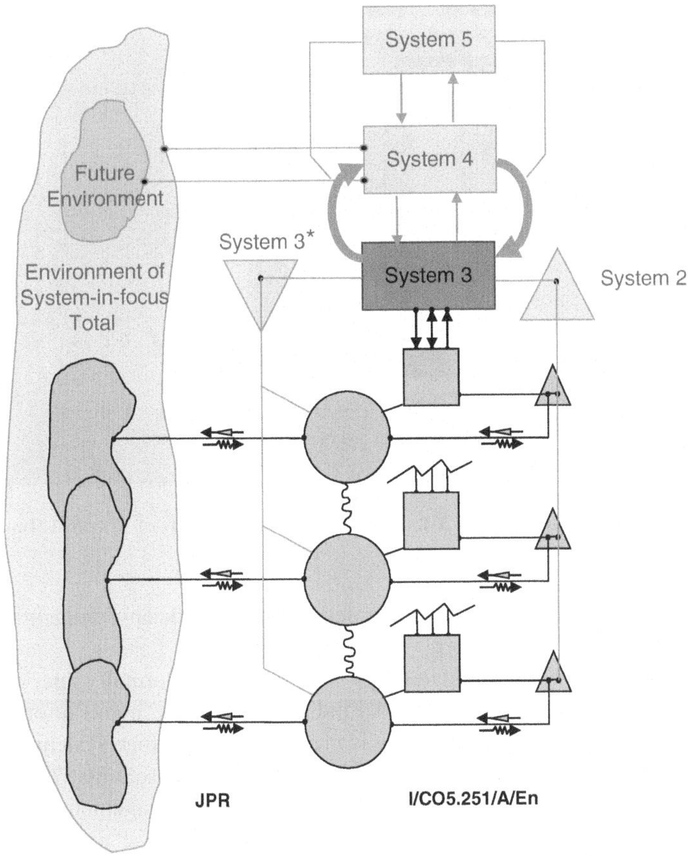

Fig. 1.21 System 3 (Adapted from Beer 1985 [Pérez Ríos 2008a])

a whole which no individual unit possesses, and as such it has the capacity to create synergies within System 1. Summarizing its aim, we will say that it is fundamentally concerned with the organisation's "*here and now*" (Figs. 1.26 and 1.30).

System 3 also has responsibility for attaining the internal stability of the organisation. For this purpose it must employ its support elements, in the design of which it should have played a part, namely, System 2 and System 3* (which we will examine shortly) as well as the lines of communication: negotiation of resources, accountability and vertical transmission of instructions. Of course, apart from the more or less automatic functioning of many of these elements, System 3 should, as the one responsible for the integrity of the set of elementary operational units, ultimately intervene to guarantee the latter's cohesion when this is endangered. But it should always be remembered that direct involvement by the vertical line of authority has to be limited to special circumstances so as not to jeopardise the autonomy of the operational units, which need this autonomy to

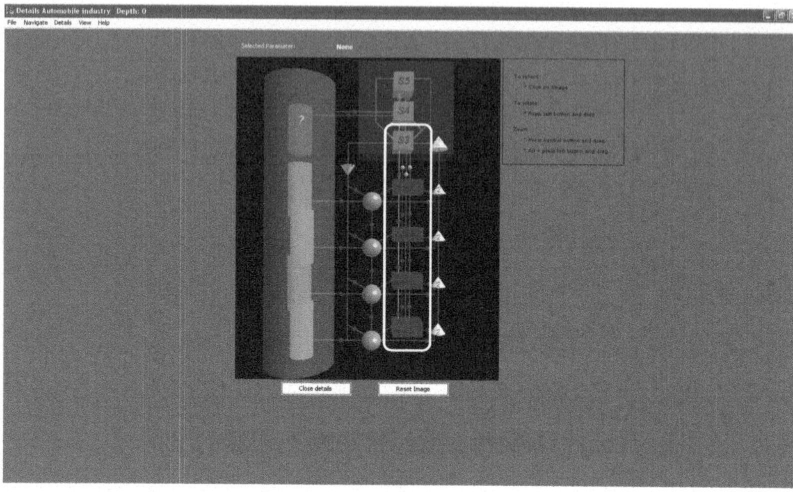

Fig. 1.22 Relation between System 3 and the basic operational units of System 1. Images taken from VSMod® (Pérez Ríos 2008c)

directly absorb most of the variety generated in their specific environments (market, recipients of services).

It is important to bear in mind that System 3 should not normally intervene in the functioning of the elementary units. An indication that the organisation has been well designed and is running smoothly is precisely the fact that System 3 does not need to become directly involved in matters relating to these units. The reason is that their operations should be governed by their own "management" with a high degree of autonomy. We should not forget that each of these units is in itself a complete viable system.

The direct intervention of System 3 should be restricted to transmitting information from the "management" (metasystem) on aspects related to the organisation's aim or purpose, such as setting or modifying goals, or to changes needed in System 1 suggested by System 4 (whose function will be explained shortly) and the negotiation of resources.

The use of direct "authority" as a way of managing is generally an indication of shortcomings in the organisation's design. It is usually attributable to certain of the necessary functions (the ones we are describing) either not existing or not working properly. The vertical line running from System 3 to each of System 1's units may serve to "impose decisions in an authoritarian way", but that is a sign that the organisation is either badly designed or fails to function well. Among reasons for why it should not be employed is System 3's lack of detailed knowledge concerning the large amount of variety (complexity) that exists within each elementary unit. A manager acting in this way would most probably be drastically attenuating the variety of what he aims to "govern", taking decisions based on models related to the problem that lack the requisite variety; this would have the corresponding adverse consequences.

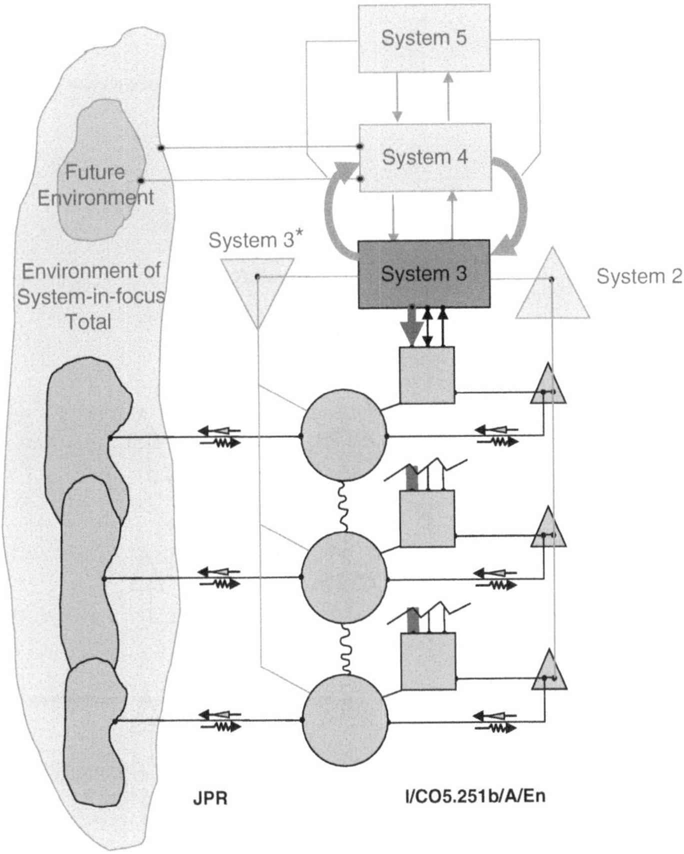

Fig. 1.23 Relation S3–S1 (Instructions)

Another very important aspect associated with System 3 is its relationship with System 4, which we will comment on when we look at this system. For the moment, however, we can say that System 3 should have a fluid, continuous communication with System 4 so as both to transmit to the latter information on the functioning and opportunities/difficulties of modifying System 1, and to receive from System 4 information on the need to modify System 1 in order to adapt to current or foreseen changes in the organisation's environment. We will, then, talk about the System 4-System 3 homeostatic loop, the proper functioning of which is critical for organisations to be viable.

1.3.1.4 System 3*

System 3* is a support system for System 3, its main mission being to obtain information on how System 1 is working, information which cannot be accessed via

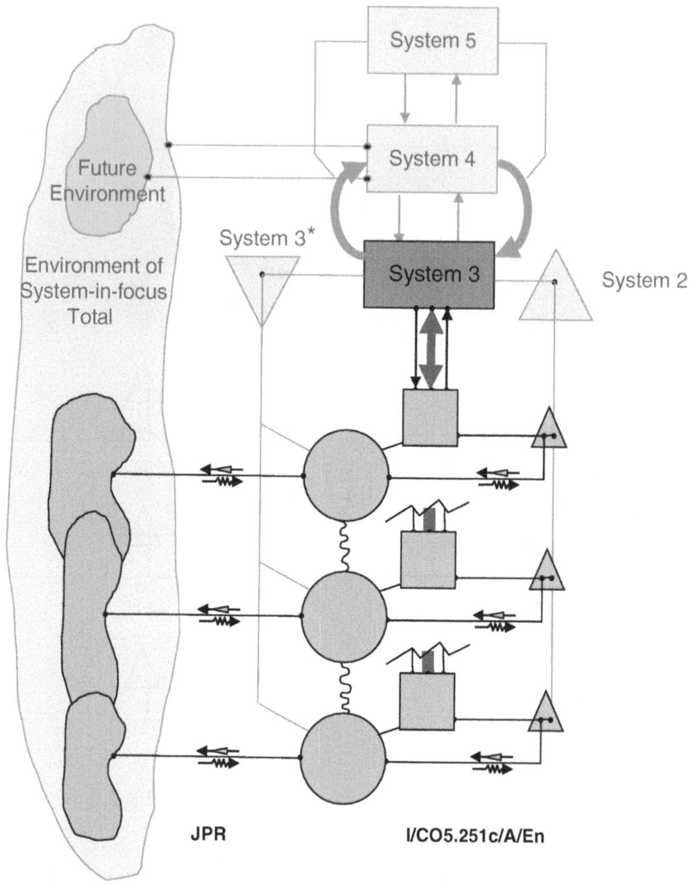

Fig. 1.24 Relation S3–S1 (Negotiation of resources)

the communication channels linking System 1 with System 3 directly, nor via the connection between System 2 and System 3 (Figs. 1.31 and 1.32).

Although information on how System 1 is working should reach System 3 via the normal information channels, System 2 and accountability, there is a chance that part of this is filtered and does not get to System 3. System 3* must be designed so as to resolve this problem.

This system is, like all others which make up the VSM, essential. In this case, the job of System 3* is to complement the information reaching the Metasystem by means of the vertical System 1-System 3 line and via System 2, by bringing additional information. The qualitative difference regarding the information provided by System 3* is that it is not of a "routine" nature and affects the whole of System 1, even if it is picked up in each of the elementary operational units. It supplies information that cannot be supplied either by System 1 or System 2.

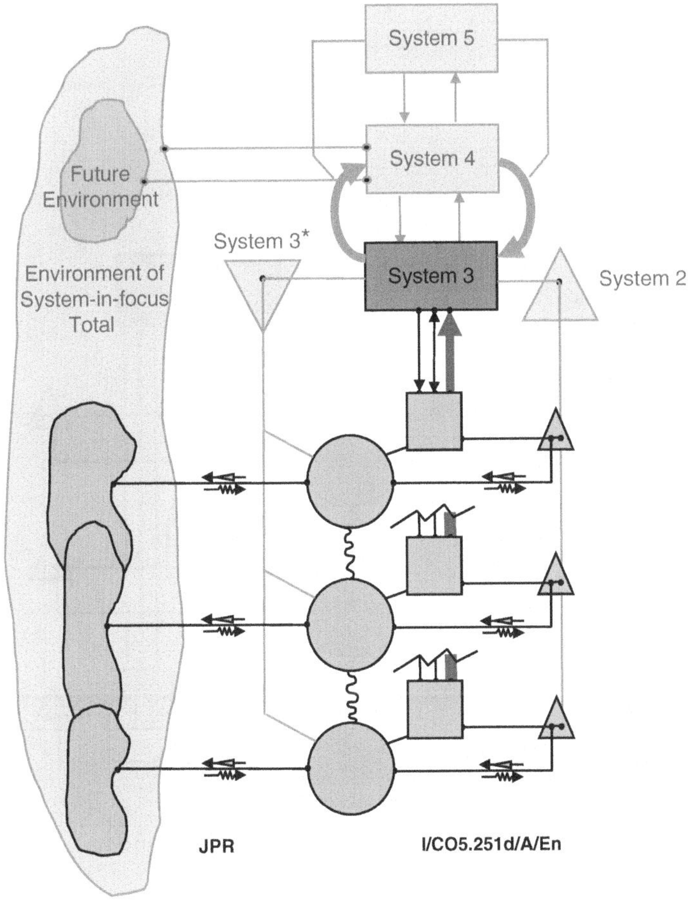

Fig. 1.25 Relation S3–S1 (Accountability)

When we explored System 3, we saw that three information systems converge there. The first, the System 1-System 3 vertical command axis, both (a) transmits information concerning the policies of the organisation and operational instructions to the operational units and (b) receives information on the organisation's internal situation, which includes the algedonic signals that give warning of extreme risk. Secondly, it is the receiver of information filtered by System 2. Both the first and second types of information refer to aspects concerning homeostatic control of the internal ambience, but in the context of more or less pre-established operational routines. However, information is also needed that is not included in these two groups. This must be picked up by System 3*, and represents the third block of information reaching System 3. The latter is not limited merely to transmitting information, for it must also process it. Each operational unit has its auditing mechanisms which generate information relating to synergy for the set of units comprising System 1.

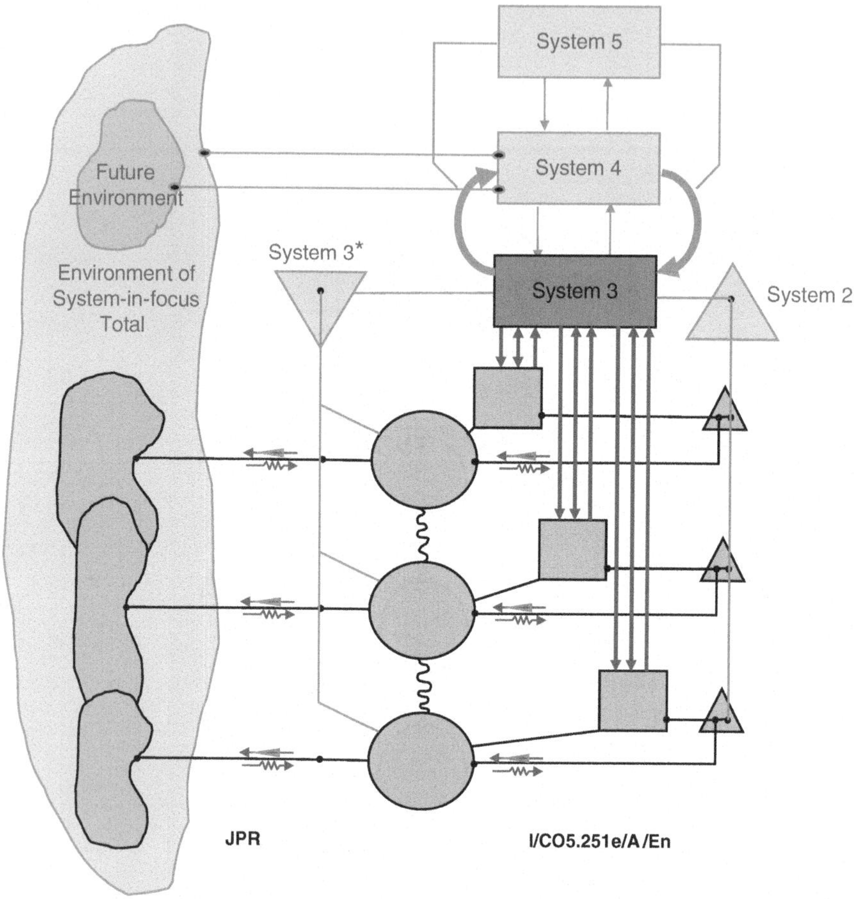

Fig. 1.26 Relation of S3 with each unit of S1

In short, the purpose of System 3* is to ensure that the information between System 1 and System 3 is complete. This is achieved by auditing (e.g., quality audits, opinion surveys, compliance with accounting procedures, etc.), work studies (industrial engineering), operations research, surveys and special studies, etc.

When analysing System 3's degree of development, we must also look at practices such as checks carried out by the operational management in person ("management by walking around") or informal information gathering techniques, apart from the various available auditing procedures to which we have already referred.

System 3* has a great capacity for absorbing variety. If, by way of example, we take the system controlling the behaviour of drivers, we can imagine the effect the existence (known by them) of mobile radar may have on this behaviour. We might use the analogy of a magnet under a sheet of paper lining up the iron filings on top of it. The enormous variety in the orientation of each filing is reduced to only one direction (that of the magnetic field). "Ideally", something similar should occur with the

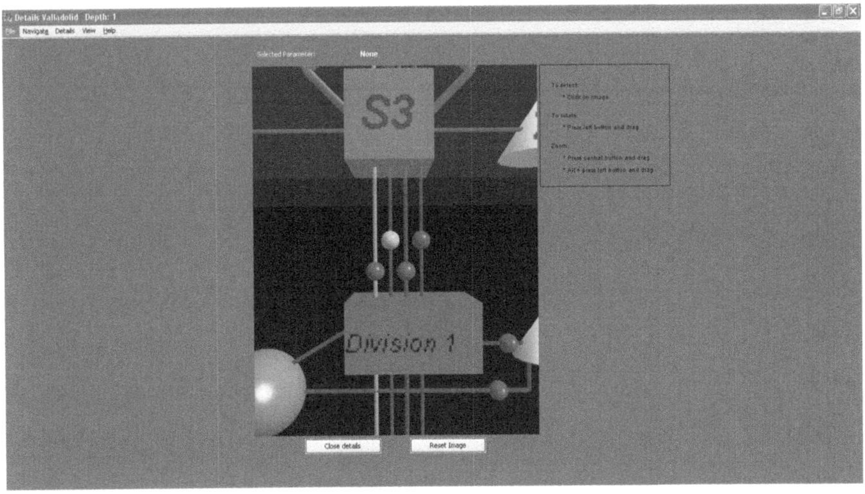

Fig. 1.27 Instructions (VSMod®)

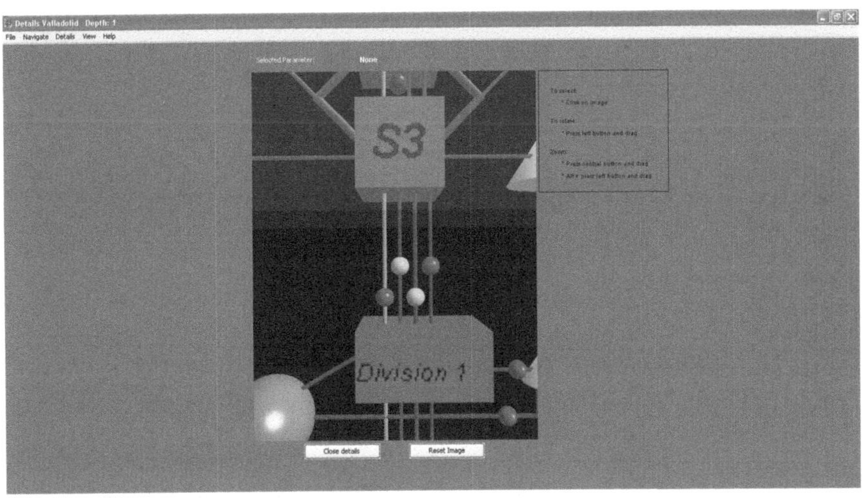

Fig. 1.28 Negotiation of resources (VSMod®)

different types of behaviour of the drivers. Likewise, if sporadic audits take place in an organisation, they will contribute to adjusting the behaviour of its components to the desired type.

1.3.1.5 System 4

Whilst System 3 is concerned mainly with ensuring that the organisation functions today, the principal responsibility of System 4 is connected with the future and

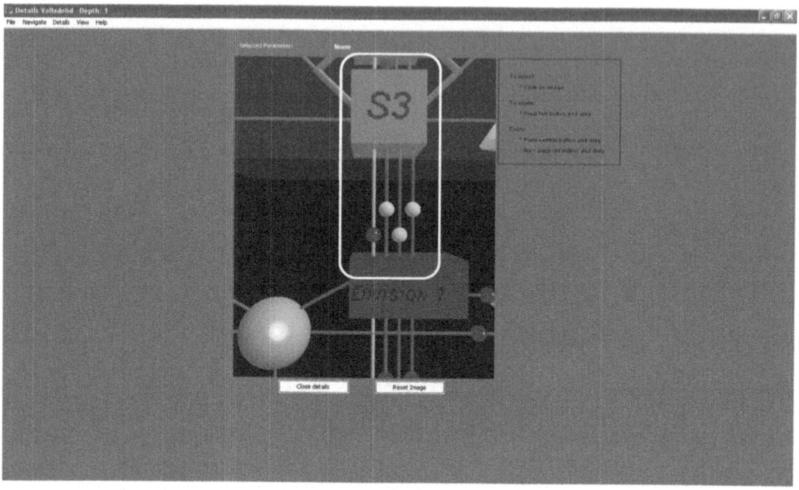

Fig. 1.29 Accountability (VSMod®)

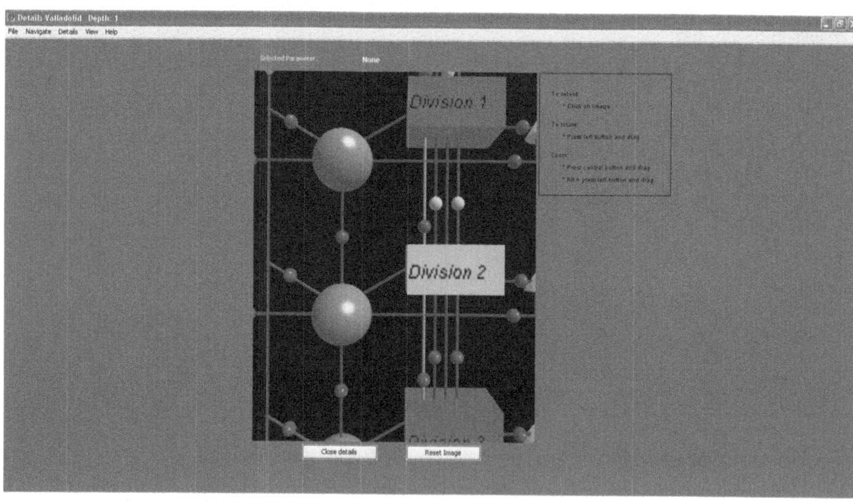

Fig. 1.30 Relation of S3-units of S1 (VSMod®)

(external) environment of the organisation. It represents an essential component of the organisation's adaptation structure (Fig. 1.33). To guarantee that the organisation is always in a position to achieve its goal and maintain its identity despite the changes taking place in the environment (in, for instance, economic, technological, social, political, educational, ecological, commercial or legislative areas), it must be capable of identifying them and carrying out in a timely manner the internal changes necessary for it to remain viable. As Schwaninger (2006, p. 183) argues, "The basis of effective time management is starting earlier, not acting faster". This vigilance and information

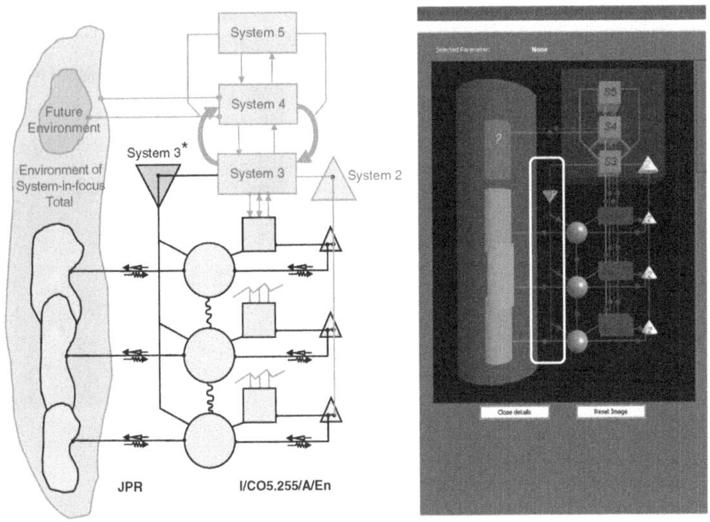

Fig. 1.31 System 3* (Adapted from Beer 1985 and image taken from VSMod® [Pérez Ríos 2008c])

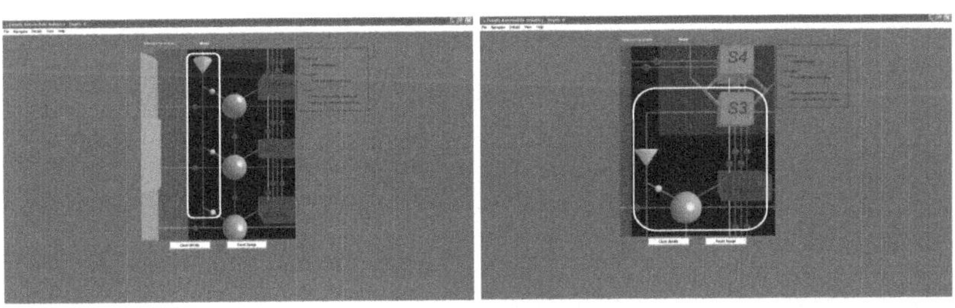

Fig. 1.32 Detail of the relation between S3* and the basic operational units and of S3 with S3* (VSMod®)

transfer together make up the main function of System 4. We may consider the type of *management* it performs is of a *strategic nature*.

In order to do this the organisation must have monitoring (vigilance) systems for both what is currently occurring in the pertinent environment and possible future changes (Fig. 1.34). It is important for this information to be sent to the organisation with the appropriate temporal cadence.

For these functions to be carried out, System 4 must use the right tools for the type of information to be processed. Thus, to assess future-related aspects, it may make use of prospective study tools (e.g., Delphi studies), scenarios, sensitivity analysis and, ideally, construct simulation models. Methodologies such as Systems Dynamics are to be wholeheartedly recommended for this purpose (Schwaninger and Pérez Ríos 2008a).

The construction of models for both the complete system as well as the system-in-focus represents a further element for which System 4 is responsible, and this

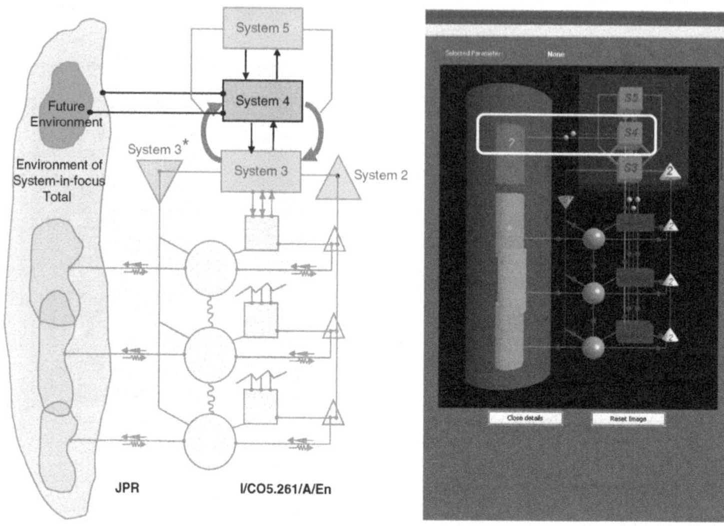

Fig. 1.33 System 4 (Adapted from Beer 1985 and image taken from VSMod® [Pérez Ríos 2008c])

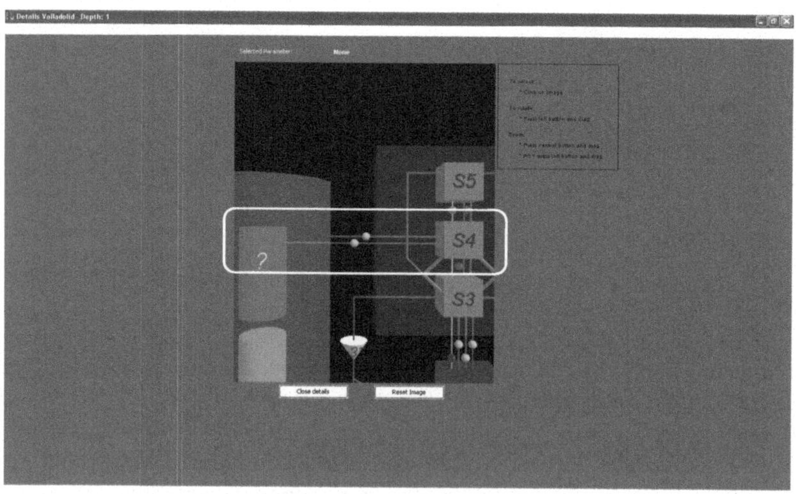

Fig. 1.34 Detail of the relation between S4 and the present and future environment (VSMod®)

entails providing the image of the organisation itself. This image (the visualisation and awareness of it) should be shared with System 3 and confirmed by System 5 (which must guarantee that it corresponds to the image wished for the organisation), as we will see later.

One way to facilitate the functions of System 4 and its communication with System 3 is by constructing what we may call an "operations room", or

Fig. 1.35 Virtual image of the operations room (By courtesy of Malik Management Zentrum St. Gallen). Authorised reproduction

"environments for taking strategic and operational decisions" (Fig. 1.35). This would consist of a decisions environment taking into consideration: the past (by means of data relating to the organisation's history, fundamentally a time path of critical variables); the present (through the availability of real-time data relating to the functioning of the organisation by access to the diverse databases and data sources); and the future (via the information supplied by the prospective studies and, above all, by the results of simulations, permitting an assessment of the different possible effects of alternative decisions regarding the diverse visualised scenarios).

All such information can be articulated in a dynamic scorecard. The difference with the Kaplan and Norton scorecards (1996) lies mainly in the connection of the scorecard, visualising the current results of the selected variables, with the simulation models, which allow an exploration (simulation) of the results of alternative decisions based on this data. The results of these simulations can be visualised in similar scorecards which show, instead of the current values, the values obtained in the simulations.

Ideally, a decisions environment like the one we propose should consist of the following elements:

1. A space where the current results of the organisation's critical variables are displayed graphically and numerically. The use of different colours (e.g., green, amber, red) to show the different areas in which these are to be encountered (indicating a satisfactory result, one that requires vigilance, or an unsatisfactory

one) will facilitate the decision-taking process. This information should be supplied in real time. This information-and-alert system corresponds in part with what Beer calls the Algedonic Channel, which I will comment on at a later stage.
2. A space to provide information associated with the organisation's history (tables or graphs showing the trajectories of significant variables).
3. A space displaying the simulation model on which to test the consequences of the alternative decisions we are faced with over time. The results of these will be shown in a way similar to the scorecard of the organisation or the system-in-focus. A wide variety of simulation tools are available for this task (e.g., Ithink, Vensim, Powersim, etc.).
4. A space offering visualisation of the VSM of the organisation or any of its sub-systems or units. The VSMod® software (Pérez Ríos 2003, 2006b, 2008c) has been designed for purposes including this one. This will allow a quick diagnosis of the organisation's situation and the functions essential for its viability at any desired recursion level.
5. Finally, it is recommended to have a space which can be used to show static or dynamic images (recordings) relating to decision taking, as well as web access via links to interesting information both outside and inside the organisation.

In conclusion, I must add that in order fully to carry out the particular functions of System 4, above all those associated with building the appropriate models and assessing both the strategic and operational repercussions of different configurations and decisions, it is necessary to have the participation of System 3 as well as the approval and cognizance of System 5.

Typical System 4 functions are: research, development and innovation; market research; prospective studies; financial innovations; projects; relations with the environment and strategic planning.

1.3.1.6 System 3–System 4 Homeostat

Now that we are aware of the particular functions of System 3 and 4, it is clear that their interests vary a great deal. The main concern of System 3 is to ensure the present functioning of the organisation ("*here and now*"), whilst that of System 4 is to guarantee steps are taken to continue functioning in the future ("*outside and future*"). Of course, for this to take place System 4 must make sure that System 3 adopts and integrates into the operational units (System 1) those modifications which, according to System 4, will be required in order to ensure future viability. Likewise, as regards informing System 4 about which points are relevant within System 1 and what the restrictions/limitations are, it is System 3 which must intervene and take responsibility for the task. Therefore, interaction between System 3 and 4 is critical for this dynamic link-up between the present and future organisations (Figs. 1.36 and 1.37). Communication between both functions (System 3 and System 4) is normally difficult and conflictive, given the widely differing interests involved.

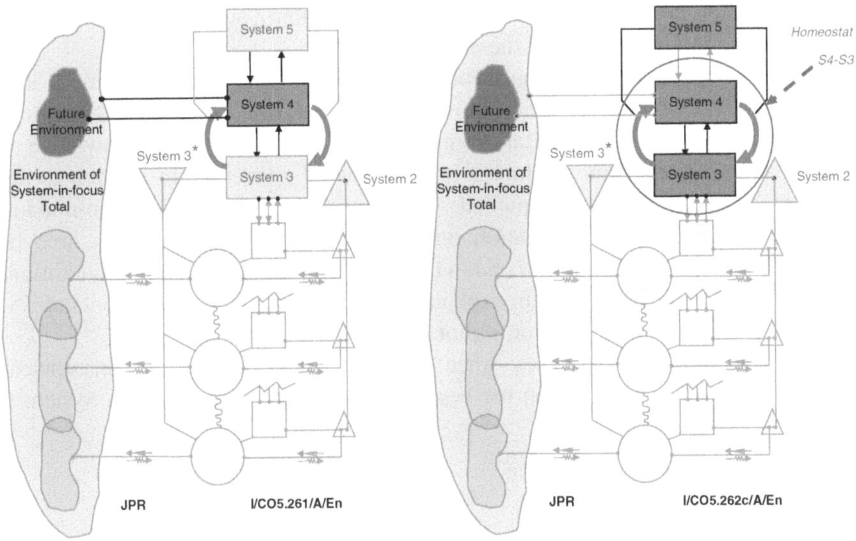

Fig. 1.36 System 4 and System 4–System 3 Homeostat (Adapted from Beer 1985 [Pérez Ríos 2008a])

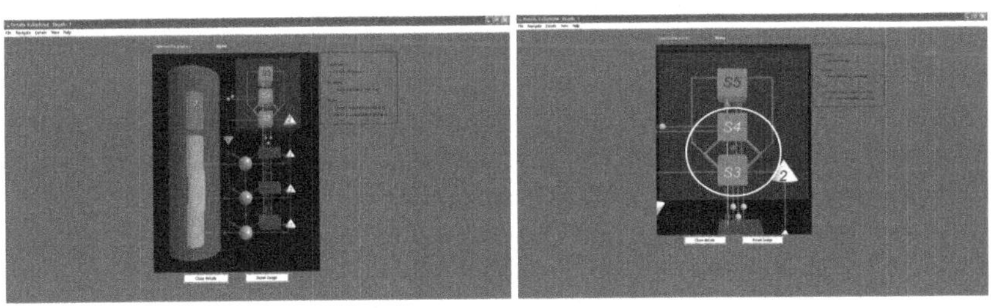

Fig. 1.37 Images of System 4 and of the S4–S3 Homeostat taken from VSMod® (Pérez Ríos 2008c)

Consequently, it is essential to possess the tools to facilitate communication between the two systems. Previously I mentioned several of these, including the use of Systems Dynamics to model the organisation so that both the present and possible future may be visualised in the different models. In this way, the debate will be guided and helped by those models, and not by the somewhat more or less opaque mental models of the different persons involved in it. The work done by Schwaninger et al. (2004), and Schwaninger and Pérez Ríos (2008a) goes into greater detail here. The VSM makes it possible to model the "context" of the problem under study, whilst SD models its "content", representing the variables which come into play, their relations and the resulting behavioural dynamics. Simulation allows an evaluation of the possible effects of the different decisions (interventions) on the problem.

The decision-taking environments (Operations Room), such as those described above, permit the integration of these and other tools.

Regarding the communication difficulty between System 3 and System 4, it is important to mention Beer's latest innovation, called "Team Syntegrity".[2] This tool is specifically designed to facilitate communication, extract as much knowledge as possible from persons and produce a level of shared awareness in relation to the problem being studied unequalled by alternative group decision-making techniques. For further information on Team Syntegrity (TS) and its area of application, see Beer *Beyond Dispute* (1994) and Pérez Ríos (2000). In addition, in Chap. 5 of this present book an explanation is given of the main elements of TS, together with its basic application protocols.

Nevertheless, there are times when what we have described is insufficient for Systems 3 and 4 to agree on the best course of action. That is when System 5 intervenes.

1.3.1.7 System 5

This system constitutes the maximum authority in the organisation, and as such is the only one with the capacity to regulate interaction between System 3 and System 4 (Fig. 1.38). All the variety (problem areas) that these two systems are unable to absorb (resolve) between themselves must be absorbed (resolved) by System 5, the final seal (authority) of the organisation (Fig. 1.39).

System 5's function is to balance the present and future of the organisation, bearing in mind both the internal and external aspects affecting it. It is responsible for establishing the "identity" of the organization, that is to say, defining what it is or what it wants to be and also what "is not or does not want to be" (Schwaninger 2006, p. 151). Such distinctions are also important when it comes to making it clear what the limits of the organisation are, in other words, fixing the boundaries between what forms part of the environment and what represents the organisation. Implicit in this is the establishing of the values, norms and rules of conduct that should prevail and impregnate the organisation at all its recursion levels, namely, its "ethos". These will facilitate the cohesion of the whole set.

Typical responsibilities of System 5 are those determining the vision, mission and strategic goals of the organisation. The type of management it must provide is "*Normative Management*", unlike the "*Strategic Management*" exercised by System 4 (with the contribution of System 3) and the "*Operative Management*" specific to System 3.

Besides keeping an eye on the organisation's stability and internal equilibrium, and its constant adaptation to the requirements of the environment in which it operates in the broad context, System 5 has the task of ensuring that the organisation

[2] Team Syntegrity® is a trade mark registered by Team Syntegrity Internacional Inc. (TSI). Syntegration® is a product line registered by Team Syntegrity International Inc. (TSI).

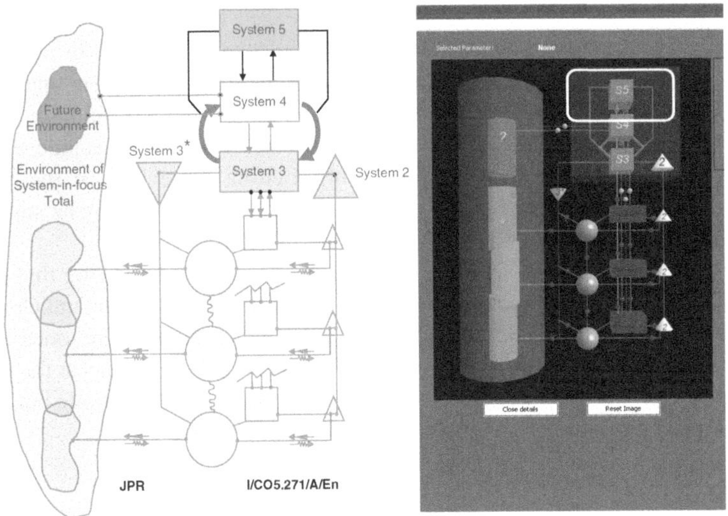

Fig. 1.38 System 5 (Adapted from Beer 1985 and image taken from VSMod® [Pérez Ríos 2008c])

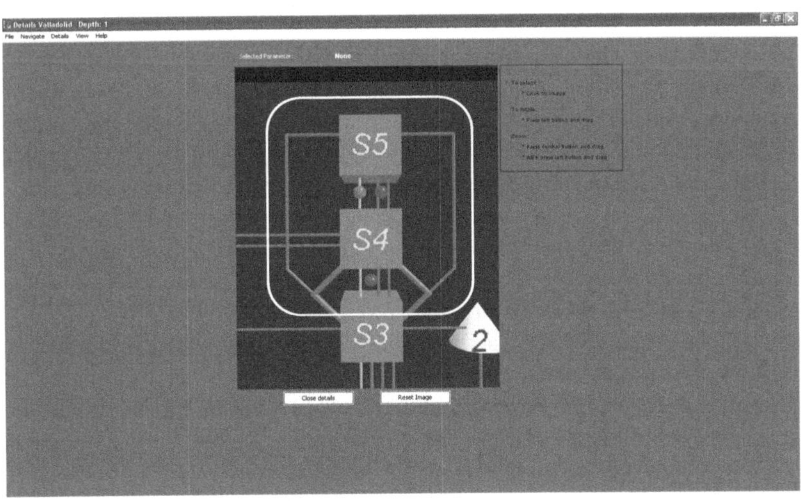

Fig. 1.39 System 5 and the S4–S3 Homeostat. Image taken from VSMod® (Pérez Ríos 2008c)

maintains its identity. However, this concept of identity should be understood in a sense that goes beyond the mere survival of the organisation. Identity in this larger sense signifies the organisation's viability beyond survival (Schwaninger 2006, p. 65). By this we mean that the organisation will be in a position to undergo such radical transformations as changing its sector of activity, which may imply one of the organisation's particular ways of materializing, disappearing only to become another totally different one. The existence of companies aged 100, 200 and even 300 years (In the UK the "Tercentenarians Club" admits as members only those firms that have been around for over 300 years), with what this implies regarding their "materialization" or "instantiation" (Arie de Geus 1997, p. 5), gives us an indication of what we are referring to from the point of view of viability (the capacity to exist independently of changes taking place in the environment). Getting some idea of the changes involved for companies belonging to the "Tercentenarians Club" may be surprising, but it will not be difficult.

Finally, we should complete this description of System 5 by saying that it must contain in one way or another all those involved in the organisation (stakeholders). It is important to include here not only current but also future ones (future generations). A consideration of the impact that our organisation has at the present moment and will have in the future, not only on the social and economic but also on the ecological environment, is unavoidable right now.

1.3.2 Recursive Nature of the VSM

An essential aspect of the VSM is the "recursive" nature of viable systems. By this we mean that every viable system (organisation) contains systems (organisations) that are viable and which in turn form part of systems (organisations) which are likewise viable, and so on and so forth. This characteristic provides the VSM with enormous potential for studying any organisation, whatever it may be, as it will always respond to the same operational principles required by the VSM, regardless of the size, sector, characteristics, geographical area, type of activity, etc.

In Fig. 1.41, we can see the detail corresponding to the next recursion level of the organisation represented in Fig. 1.40. This figure reveals how, inside the ellipses and rectangles representing the elementary operational units (e.g., divisions or projects 1, 2 and 3), there is an exact replica of the general structure of the system-in-focus (rotated 90°). The particularly noteworthy aspect of the recursive conception of viable systems resides in the fact that all of them, no matter what place they occupy in the series of systems, must contain the five systems or functions that determine "viability". For a system to be viable, these five functions must exist recursively at all levels of the organisation. Every unit (system 1) replicates, in structural terms, the whole entity in which it is contained.

This recursive conception is of utmost importance when studying organisations, since it means that "all" systems, whatever their level, must have the particular functions of Systems 1, 2, 3, 4 and 5. An organisation's structural design will be determined by the manner in which it divides the variety of its environment and in which it consequently designs the different recursive levels of its operations in order to deal with it. For organisations of a certain size and complexity, the number of levels and components at each level may result in the VSM study being very dense and complicated. In order to perform this task, among other reasons, the specific software, VSMod®, has been developed, incorporating among other

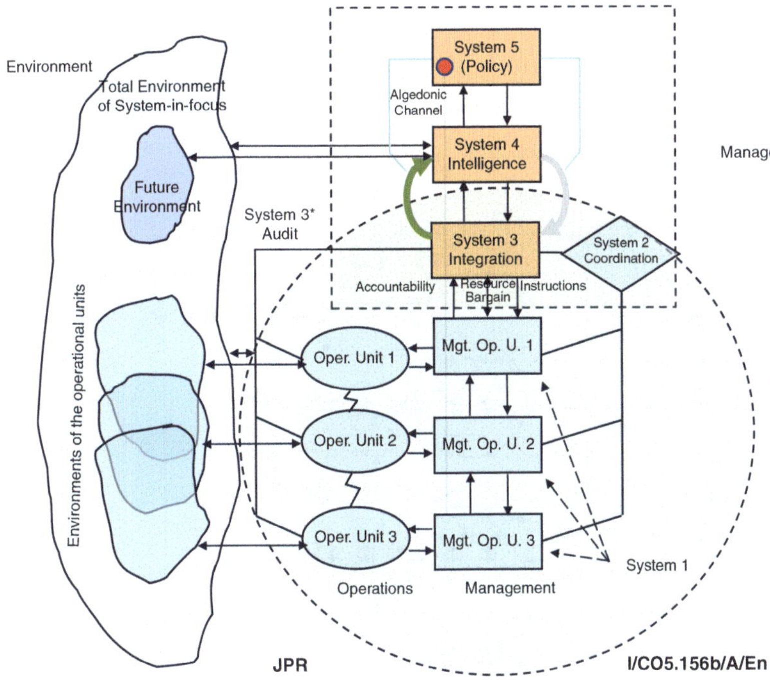

Fig. 1.40 Viable System Model (Adapted from Beer 1985 [Pérez Ríos 2008e])

features that of facilitating the whole process of application of OC and the VSM (Pérez Ríos 2003, 2006b, 2008c).

Figure 1.42 shows a VSMod® screen on which we can appreciate, on the right, the global structure of the criteria and recursion levels of the sample organisation, which in this case is a company in the automobile industry. In Chap. 4 of this book, we will supply a detailed explanation of how an organisation's recursive structure is drawn up, and of how the various navigation maps included in VSMod® can be used to take us through it.

1.3.3 *Information Requirements and Communication Channels*

Having seen both functions that the VSM considers necessary and sufficient for an organisation to be viable, and the model's recursive nature, we will complete this examination of the VSM with reference to another essential aspect affecting the VSM as a whole. This is the diversity of the channels of communication and transmission of information that connect all the functions/systems mentioned with other internal and external elements that play a part in the model and affect the

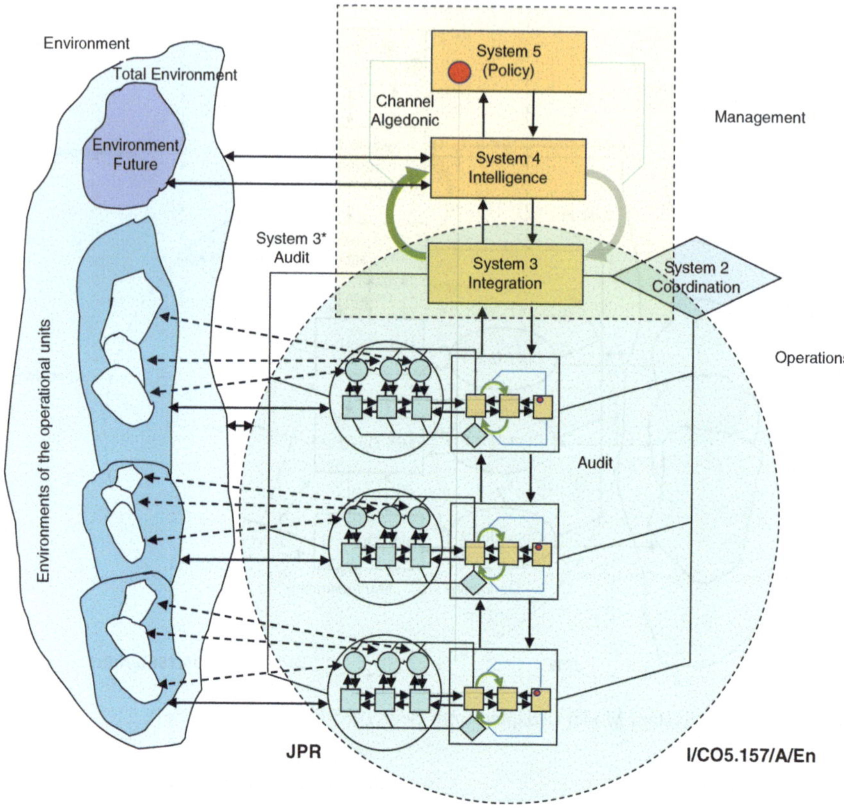

Fig. 1.41 Viable System Model, showing the second recursion level (Adapted from Beer 1985 [Pérez Ríos 2008e])

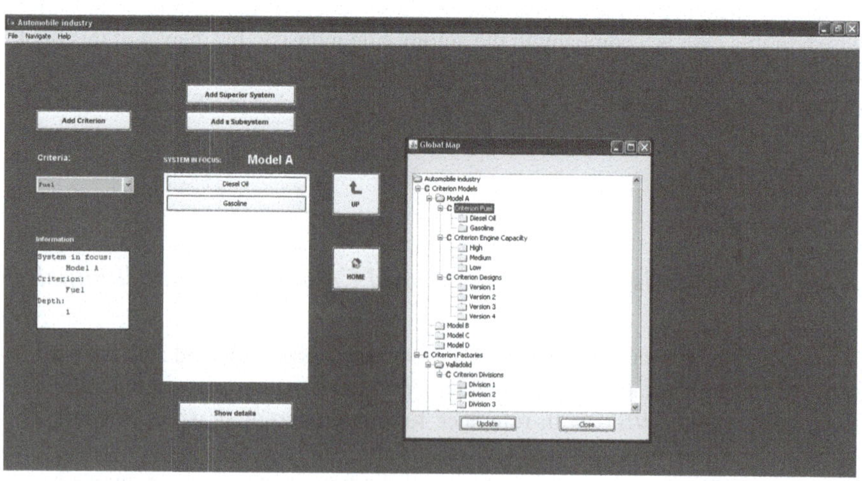

Fig. 1.42 Global map showing the complete recursive structure. Model A (fuel criterion) is selected as the system-in-focus

organisation under study. This side of the application of the VSM is fundamental in terms of designing an organisation's or company's information systems. A deep understanding of the different functions (systems) of an organisation and the communication channels to connect them provides a comprehensive framework for both designing information systems and diagnosing the quality and adequacy of existing ones (Pérez Ríos 2008a).

In the following sections I will refer first of all to the cognitive filters that play a role in the processes of transmission of information among individuals, and which must be borne in mind when designing or evaluating an organisation's information systems. Secondly, I will describe the basic components involved in the communication loops between individuals or organisational units, which will serve as a guideline for assessing whether an organisation's existing channels meet the necessary requirements for communication to be suitably carried out. Finally, I will comment on six of the main general channels which must be present and function appropriately in every organisation in order to ensure viability; their principal function is to absorb all the variety (complexity) faced by the organisation-in-focus.

We should remember here that the "communication" element is an essential part of both the Cybernetics developed and described by N. Wiener in his book "*Cybernetics: or Control and Communication in the Animal and the Machine*" (1948) and, most particularly, Beer´s Organisational Cybernetics.

In social systems, communication normally occurs among people, who, in the case of firms or organisations, need it in order to "decide" and take action. This means that all those elements affecting communication processes among individuals (the sending and receiving of information) should be taken into consideration. Ensuring that the information sent by a person reaches another and gets interpreted in accordance with the former's wishes is not something spontaneous and non-problematic. The reasons for these difficulties, among others which I will refer to later, lie in the different types of filters the information has to pass through before actually reaching the individual (the decider), who must be able to understand the content of the information received, process it and then take a decision (which may be either to act or to generate additional information to reach other decision-takers). Let us take a look at some of the most significant filters.

1.3.3.1 Cognitive Filters

In Fig. 1.43, taken from Morecroft (1988), it can be appreciated how only certain information flows manage to reach the decider nucleus (the decision-making function) and consequently have an influence on the choices and steps taken by the actors (individuals, groups, organisational units) represented by this function. The concentric circles show the organisational and cognitive filters that select and limit the information accessible to the decision-takers.

The first filter represents individuals' cognitive restraints and the notion of "bounded rationality" formulated by Simon (1976, 1981). The persons are limited

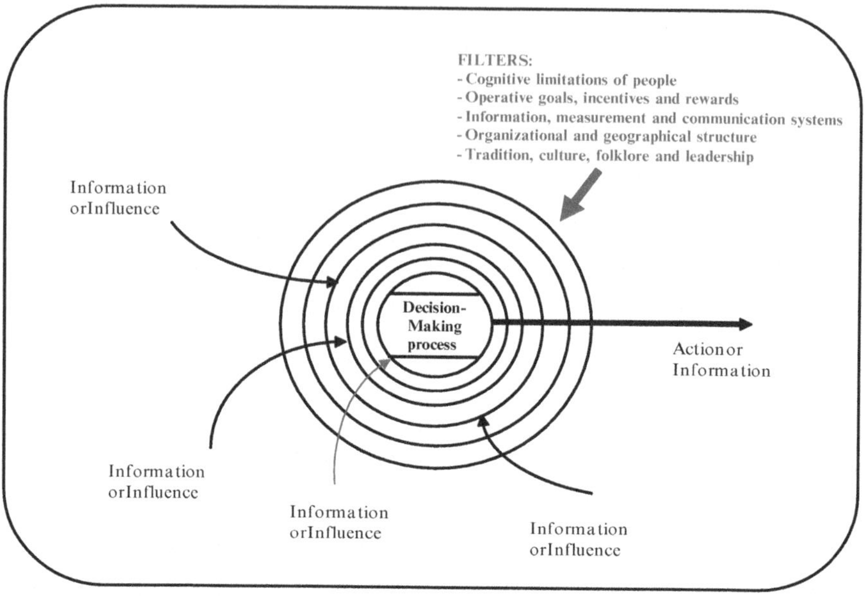

Fig. 1.43 Information filters

as regards the amount of information they are able to process. As a result, they take their decisions on the basis of a few sources of information and in accordance with simple rules ("rule of thumb"). The second represents the influence of operational goals, and of the system of rewards and incentives, on the flow of information. Decisions and actions in companies are conditioned by the goals set and the rewards involved; as a consequence, both must be identified for their influence to be appreciated. The third represents the effect of information, measurement and communication systems. The fourth shows how the organisational and geographical structure affects this flow. Finally, the fifth filter constitutes the influence of factors such as tradition, culture and leadership on the flow of information.

These filters are of use in that they oblige the analyst to give a more thorough description of organisational systems, for two reasons: they require that attention be paid to the sources of information actually used by the decision-takers, and that consideration be given to the common occurrence of shortcomings, bias and error where information is concerned.

In Fig. 1.44, an example is given of connections between decision-takers in which it can be seen how any organisation may be visualised as a network of deciders linked by *information*. Once processed by the decider, this information is then transformed into action, or into further information which will in turn be dealt with by another decider, and so on and so forth.

Having considered the difficulty involving the transmission of information among individuals, and the way in which an organisation is essentially a group of people (deciders) linked by information, we will now focus our attention on the

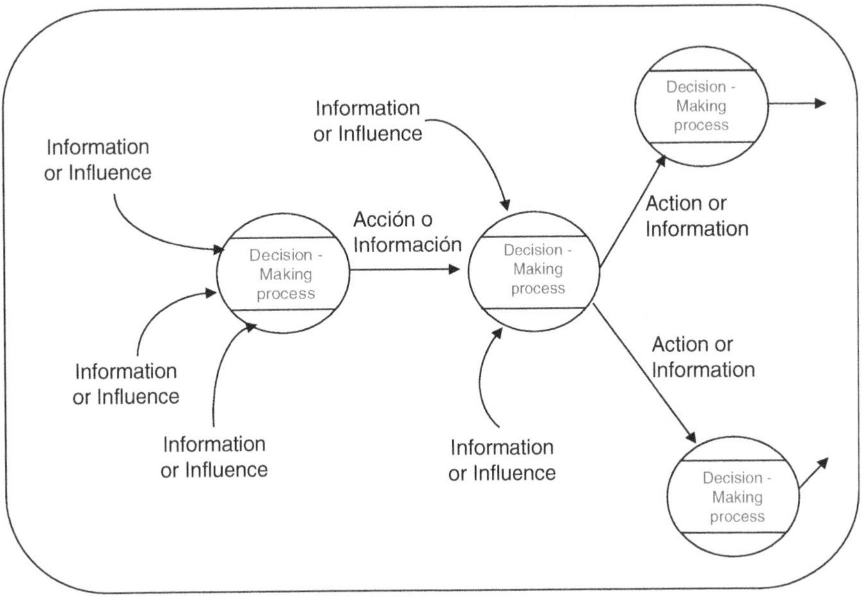

Fig. 1.44 Network of connected deciders in an organisation

design or diagnosis of the channels of communication which connect the diverse functions within the structure of the VSM. In reality, these channels connect those who send information with those to whom it is directed (receivers).

Information is the common element that makes it possible to carry out all the functions deemed necessary and sufficient for an organisation's viability. To a certain extent, information is the equivalent of blood in the human body, insofar as it transports the different nutrients and oxygen for the various organs to function.

1.3.3.2 Information Needs

In Fig. 1.11, which showed a simplified representation of the VSM, we were able to see the main functions (Systems 1, 2, 3, 3*, 4 and 5) and the different environments, as well as several communication channels connecting these elements. Each function needs specific kinds of information (origin, content, frequency, etc.). Let us now take a look at some of the most relevant types of information for each of the systems or functions comprising the VSM.

Beginning with System 1, the information required is related to the functioning of its units of production (elemental operational units). This information will be both internal (the production processes themselves) and external (the specific environment, for example the market).

As regards System 2, here the information needed is concerned with the functioning of the operational units and with current or potential conflicts among them.

System 3 must have information from various sources. First of all, from System 1 it concerns operations, achievement of goals, the necessity of additional resources, etc. From System 4 the information will be associated with the needs for change in System 1 in order to maintain the viability of the business (or the organisation), as well as that relating to instructions or guidelines to be followed. System 3* will provide information on the various audits which have taken place in System 1.

System 4 also needs information from a multiplicity of sources. On the one hand, it will come from the general environment of the organisation (both current and possible future). It must be permanently informed about what is taking place (or might take place) regarding any aspect that may affect it (technological, commercial, political, social, demographic, ecological, etc.). From System 5 it will receive information on targets and goals to be achieved, as well as on the general operational guidelines for the organisation as a whole. System 3 will provide it with information regarding current events within the organisation and the capacity of System 1 to incorporate the changes proposed by System 4. The information processing requirements within System 4 are quite formidable, since it has to process information on the past, present and, above all, the future, converting it into action to be taken by System 3 via System 1.

System 5, responsible as it is for defining the identity of the organisation under study, must possess information enabling it to assess whether the organisation is actually carrying out its aim and whether it is necessary to modify it. In this case, it needs the communication channels which will provide it with the necessary information from all involved (shareholders, workers, clients, suppliers, individuals or groups within the environment that have or may have some kind of relationship with the organisation, etc.). It will also need to be informed about how the organization is running, and about the orientation proposed jointly by Systems 4 and 3. Finally, it must be provided with information critical for the organisation's survival. This kind of information is transmitted via specific channels which are called *algedonic*. The source of the information (emergency warning signals) which they carry is in System 1, but it may reach System 5 if the problem that produces it is not dealt with previously (Systems 3 and 4).

Having seen the functions the VSM establishes as being necessary and sufficient for an organisation's viability, and the information each one needs in order to perform them, and having also considered the model's recursive nature, we will complete this overview with a reference to the communication channels via which the information is transmitted from one function (individuals/deciders) to other.

1.3.3.3 The Channels of Communication

Prior to commenting on some of the main channels of communication and absorption of variety (complexity) which form part of the VSM, I consider it appropriate to describe the components that, generally speaking, any information transmission channel should possess.

The communication channels in the VSM are, as I have said, the elements that connect both the diverse functions specified in the VSM and the organisation with its environment (environments). These channels aim, within the structure of the VSM, to provide a continual balance in the interaction between the two elements which they connect (for instance, the firm with its market, the organisation and its clients, politicians with their electorate, trade union associations with their current and potential members, etc.). This equilibrium (homeostasis) is attained when the information (both in terms of the amount and the content and format) coming from, for instance, the market to the organisation and in turn from the organisation to the market (or from voters to politicians and vice versa, etc.), is appropriate for a dynamic but harmonious relationship between the two, in the sense that it functions in accordance with the wishes of both parties.

Let us have a look at the typical characteristics of a communication channel. Figure 1.45 shows the main components.

In this connection (for example: environment-organisation) there are eight elements: the sender (A), the "transducer" (which converts the information from the sender in order that it is intelligible for the receiver), the channel of communication (which should be capable of transmitting the amount of information per unit of time required, e.g., bandwidth), and once again the "transducer", which de-codifies the information and converts it into the pertinent format for the receiver (B) to interpret it. Then, the other way round (receiver-sender), where roles would now be reversed (sender–receiver), we again find the same four elements.

Therefore, we first of all have sender A, who wants certain information to reach receiver B. For this purpose he sends the corresponding message, M1, containing

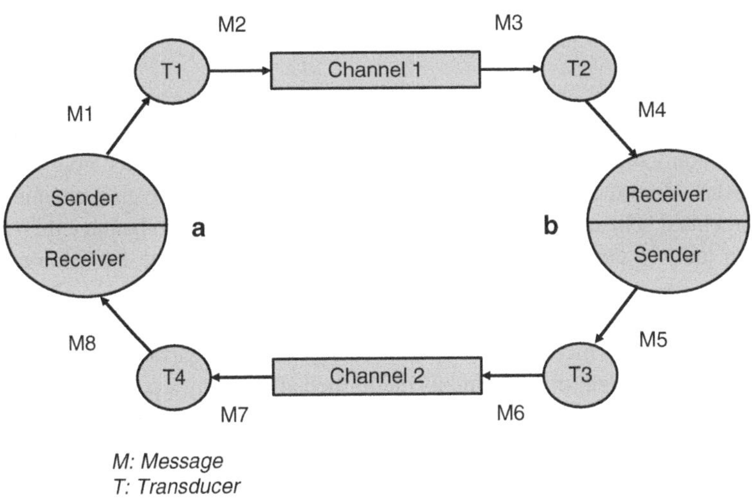

Fig. 1.45 Elements of a communication channel

such information. This must first be codified in order to be sent. This task is performed by the transducer, T1 (a particular case of transducing-converting information from one format to another is a translation involving two languages). Following this, the transduced message, M2, is sent via the channel (Channel 1) so as to reach its destination (Receiver B). What arrives here will be M3, which may differ from M2 depending on the distortion or noise the message picks up on its journey. Subsequently, M3, prior to being interpreted by receiver B, must be duly de-codified and converted into a format that the latter can interpret. This is performed by Transducer T2, as a result of which what eventually reaches receiver B is M4.

Obviously, the purpose of the communication process is to make sure that all the information sent by an emitter (A) reaches receiver B in an intelligible format. In other words, the idea is that M1 = M2 = M3 = M4.

Besides the unidirectional (A → B) route we have just described, good communication requires that receiver B confirms that the information received and interpreted corresponds to what sender A actually intended. For this to be achieved, the communication loop should be closed by means of the response route (B → A), where the roles are inverted, with B now being the sender whilst sender A now becomes the receiver. In this response circuit, the aim is to confirm that M5 = M4 = M6 = M7 = M8. On this route the message must pass once again through the elements similar to those on the way out for its integrity to be corroborated: Transducer T3, Channel 2 and Transducer T4, until message M8 finally reaches the original sender.

The frequent non-existence of this return route, confirming that the information has arrived and has been interpreted according to the intentions of the sender, is the reason for the appearance of many problems in all types of organisations. To these difficulties concerning the sending of information must be added the considerations made previously with regard to cognitive filters; these must be borne in mind both when designing the channels of communication and when supervising their functioning.

If we now direct our attention towards any of the homeostatic connections present in the VSM, in Fig. 1.46 taken from the VSMod® software (Pérez Ríos 2003, 2006b, 2008c, 2008e), we can see the set of elements comprising a Homeostat. Here the eight typical components of a communication channel may be appreciated. The intention behind the homeostatic loops is to balance the variety between the two connected parts or elements (for example, the environment and operations, operations and their management, etc.).

Supposing we want to transmit information from a sender, A, to a receiver, B, in the connection which links them (for instance, the organisation–environment relationship), the eight main elements mentioned above play a part: the sender (A), the "transducer" (which converts the information leaving the sender so that it is intelligible for the receiver), the communication channel (which must be capable of transmitting the amount of information per unit of time required, e.g., bandwidth, etc.) and again the "transducer", de-codifying the information and converting it into the appropriate format for the receiver, B, to be able to interpret it. Meanwhile,

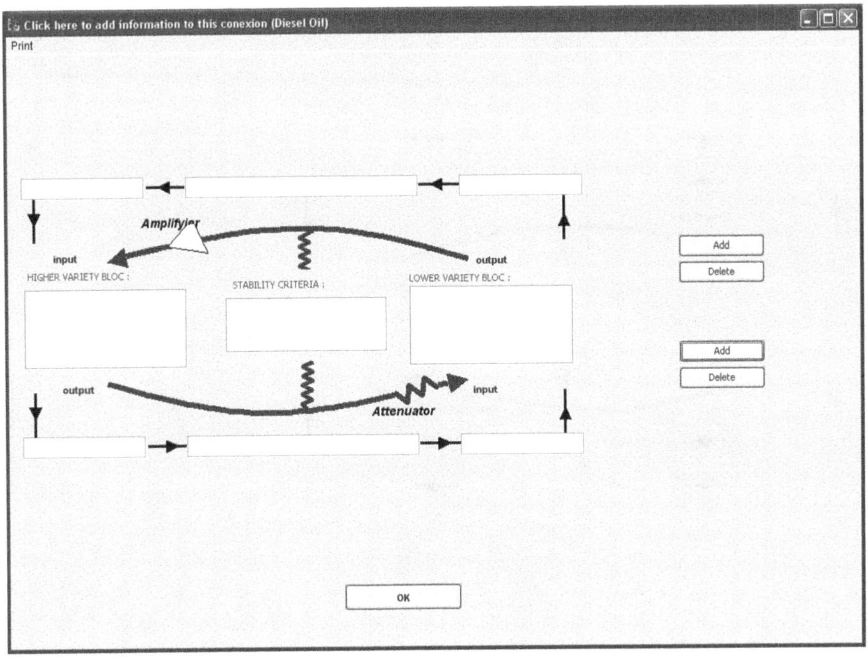

Fig. 1.46 Homeostat (Pérez Ríos 2008c)

on the way back (receiver-sender) the roles would be reversed (sender–receiver) and the same four elements would apply.

Each of these elements must be designed in order that it can perform its function which, in the case of the transducers, is to convert the amount of information per unit of time required from one format to another, and, as regards the communication channels, is to transmit this without any alteration.

Despite our mention in Fig. 1.46 of only one element for each of the eight components, this number may, of course, increase. This occurs, for example, if we employ several channels of communication instead of only one, etc. This is the reason why the VSMod® software (Fig. 1.47) makes it possible to add as many components to each element in the communication channels as required and, in each one, as many information units as needed.

A final aspect to consider in relation to communication channels is that concerning "noise" and the distortion of information. One way to prevent these factors from disrupting the transmission of information is to assign each component excess capacity in order to compensate for this occurrence, whilst another is to employ a certain degree of redundancy when transmitting information (for example, with the use of different channels in order to send the same information).

Knowing, on the one hand, the various communication channels required in any viable organisation and, on the other, identifying each of the eight components which make up a communication relationship between two elements or functions of

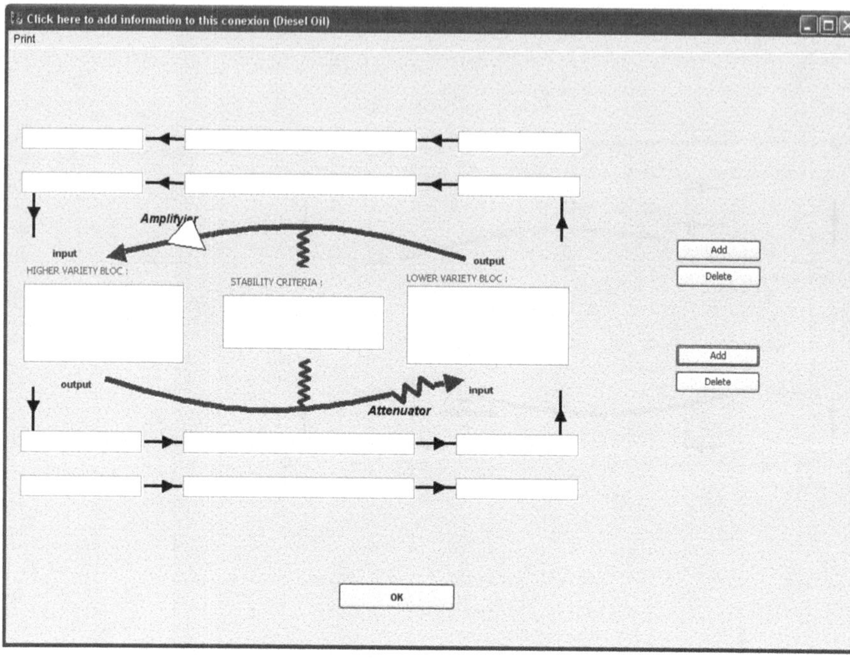

Fig. 1.47 Homeostat including multiple elements (Pérez Ríos 2008c)

the system, is essential when designing any information system to be implemented in an organisation. The diversity of such systems (e.g., Transaction Processing Systems – TPS, Management Information Systems – MIS, Decision Support Systems – DSS, Executive Information Systems – EIS, etc.) already indicate the need to create specific information systems suited to the different "levels" (logical, hierarchical or organisational, etc.) existing in firms and organisations.

In relation to this issue, the VSM offers us a conceptual framework in which any information system can fit, whether it be at the specific recursion level or in the system/function (in the sense defined in the VSM) it aims to serve, etc. We should not forget, however, the role it performs in the organisation as a whole and the relationship it has with other already existing or potential information systems. The VSM provides conceptual guidelines for designing information systems that are based on a deep knowledge of what the organizational levels are and, within each level, which functions are to be assisted, as well as the relationship between these functions and their purpose. In this regard, I believe that the VSM represents a quite sound conceptual basis for information technology professionals, above all those dealing with the design or management of information systems.

In order to complete this study of an organisation's systemic information requirements, I will add that everything we have commented on concerning an organisation in particular should be applied to each and every organisational unit (at the diverse recursion levels) that, taken together, constitute the whole firm (or organisation); in this way, the connection between the various elements of information is guaranteed, as well as the connection between functions at the different existing recursion levels. Figure 1.48 shows certain communication channels corresponding to the system in focus, and, by way of example, indicates the necessary connections between Systems 4 and 5, relating to two recursion levels. Obviously, the amount of connection required will depend on each particular case.

Regarding this aspect, it is interesting to point out how many of the problems (some of them quite serious) which appear in such systems as judicial (and penitentiary), sanitary, environmental, business (e.g., real state, banking sector, etc.) are caused by non-compliance with many of the requisites described previously. In some cases, shortcomings are to be found in the structure (non-existent or badly represented functions), while in others there are no integrated information systems, whilst elsewhere the problem is an insufficient number of communication channels linking functions or, if these channels exist, they miss having some of the basic elements that should be present in every communication channel. In other cases, there is clearly scant use of tools permitting the incorporation of time variables in the corresponding system. Let us consider, taking a health system as an example, the impact of including the *time* variable in the staff design for specialist doctors, and the amount of dynamic complexity entailed (demographic, economic, educational, etc., all of them dynamically inter-related) in order to achieve, over a period of time, a sustainable balance between the medical requirements of the population (at their corresponding ages) and the availability of professionals (trainee doctors, practising doctors, doctors retiring, doctors moving to other geographical regions and, and all these issues in the respective medical specialities, etc.). The examples of systems with similar problems are innumerable. Their inadequate and sometimes highly unsatisfactory way of working is obvious and well-known.

The good news with regard to this systemic dynamic complexity is that nowadays the technology is available to meet it. Methodological tools such as OC, the VSM, Systems Dynamics and many more, together with the accessibility of software to facilitate their application (Vensim®, Ithink®, VSMod®, etc.), make it possible to apply systemic concepts and tools (certain of which are dealt with in this book) which can help to *govern* (in its full cybernetic sense) any of these complex systems in the proper way.

1.3.3.4 Vertical channels for absorbing variety (complexity)

Having analysed the basic components comprising a generic communication channel (sender-receiver-transducers-channels-contents), in the final part of this Sect. 1.1 will comment on the main communication channels that should exist and be dealt with in the design and/or diagnosis of the organisation we intend to be viable. Here it is appropriate for us to concentrate on six fundamental channels. Of course, the number of channels linking functions in the VSM is very large, since every connection between two elements is in fact a channel of communication. Consequently, we will limit our comments to the six essential "vertical" channels, whose function is to jointly absorb all the variety (complexity) facing the system in focus (Beer 1985).

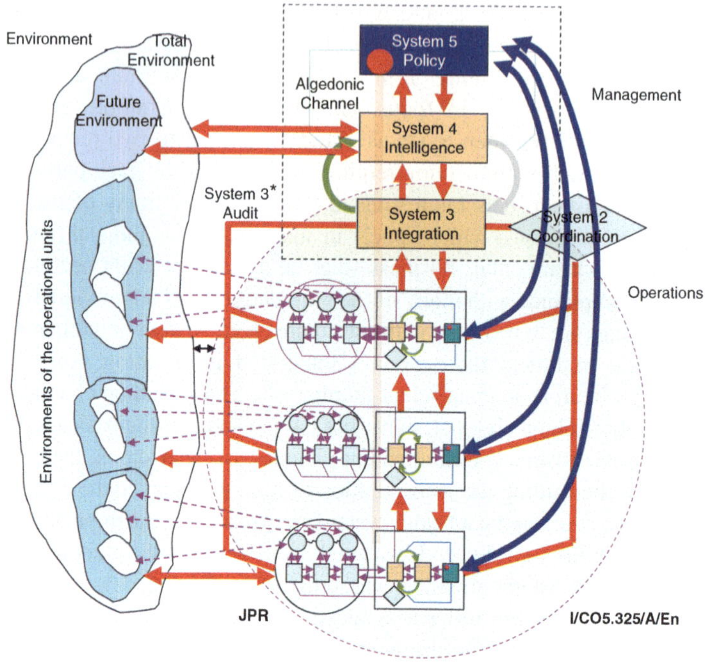

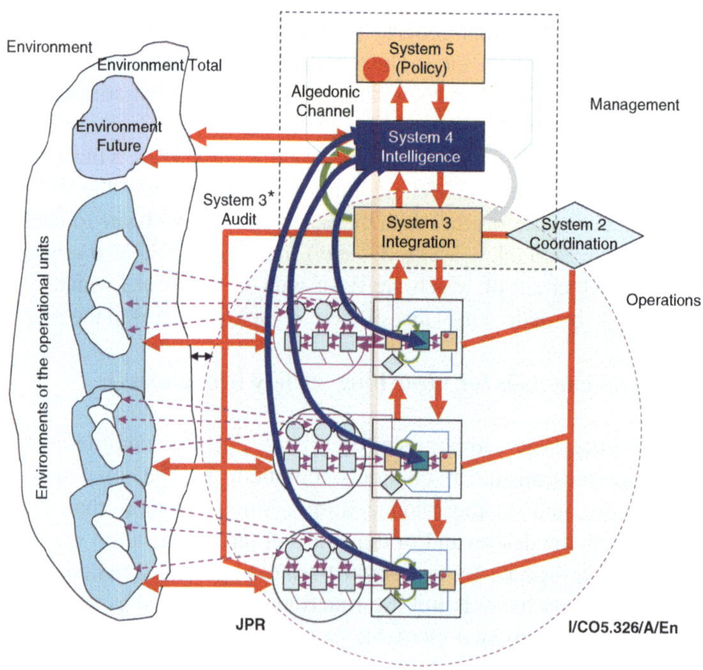

Fig. 1.48 Communication between System 5 and System 4 appertaining to two levels of recursion (Pérez Ríos 2008e)

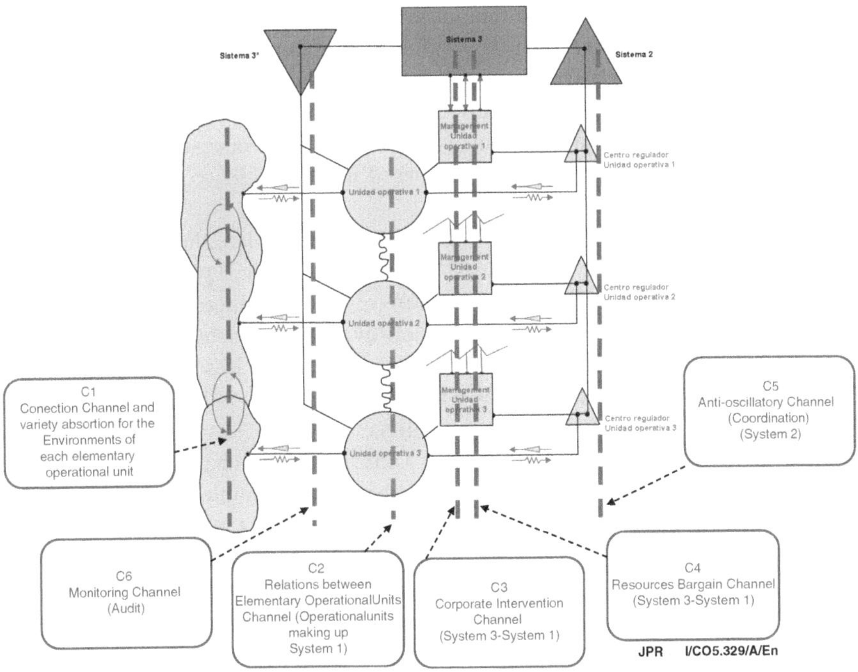

Fig. 1.49 Vertical channels absorbing variety (Beer 1985)

These channels are the following (Fig. 1.49):

- Channel 1 (C1). Channel connecting and absorbing variety between the environments of each elementary operational unit.
- Channel 2 (C2). Channel connecting the various elemental operations (operational units making up System 1).
- Channel 3 (C3). Corporate intervention channel (System 3–System 1).
- Channel 4 (C4). Resources bargaining channel (System 3–System 1).
- Channel 5 (C5). Anti-oscillatory channel (Co-ordination) (System 2).
- Channel 6 (C6). Monitor channel (Auditor).

Another channel that also deserves special consideration is the *Algedonic Channel.*

Among the group of six channels (C1, C2, C3, C4, C5 and C6), C1 and C2 are always to be found in all organisations; they simply exist. Relations between the particular environments of each basic operational unit (C1) will be more or less intense depending on each case, but they are determined. They are relationships in which our capacity to intervene is probably, but not necessarily, non-existent. Despite this, however, we must know of their existence and how they function, assessing what part of the variety within the environment is absorbed as a result of their connections.

As regards Channel 2, something similar occurs. The relations between the operational units are determined, in certain cases, by the production processes themselves, and in others by the relationship between the units deriving from the structure of the system to which they belong (for example: between autonomous communities in a country, between a community's universities, or between divisions of an automobile company, etc.). Our capacity to intervene in these relations may also be limited or non-existent. Nevertheless, it is necessary to know that they exist and to evaluate the variety absorbed in each of these relations via their communication channels.

As for C3 and C4, these channels allow intervention in their design, as they form part of the means by which Corporate Management (System 3) performs its task and defines the management style used. C3, in terms of its intervention through the System 3 command channel, absorbs part of the variety available in System 1 by establishing certain ways in which to act. Channel 4, the "Negotiation of Resources", can also be designed and establishes the means by which negotiation is conducted (the setting of targets, assigning of resources or accountability).

Channel 5 (Anti-oscillatory) is likewise a channel we will have to design for our particular organisation. Its ability to absorb the variety/complexity resulting from the potential conflicts that arise during the interaction of the diverse elementary operational units in System 1 has already been considered.

The last channel to discuss is Channel 6 (the Auditing Channel). Its purpose is to complete the equation which balances the variety absorbed by the six vertical channels against all the variety that must be dealt with in the horizontal dimension of the system-in-focus, in other words, all the complexity the operational units must be capable of handling – that is, the relevant complexity of the specific environments. The variety that must be absorbed by Channel 6 is everything the other five channels have been unable to absorb. In this way, an equal balance between vertical and horizontal complexity is ensured.

This question is likely to be better understood if we position ourselves at the higher level of recursion. Instead of the five systems and, inside System 1, the elementary operational units comprising them together with their corresponding environments and the general environment, we would simply encounter one Environment, the Operations and one Management. The variety, as we know, must be equivalent in the three components. Therefore, the variety in Operations must be equivalent to the variety in Management (Ashby's Law). But if we go down to the next recursion level, this horizontal relationship will become the vertical one we mentioned before.

This property is described in what Beer refers to as the First Axiom of Management, which says that "The sum of horizontal variety disposed by *n* operational elements equals the sum of vertical variety disposed on the six vertical components of corporate cohesion". (See Annex II).

1.3.3.5 Algedonic Channel

Besides the vertical channels we have just examined, there is an additional channel which deserves special consideration: the *algedonic channel*. Taking its name from the words "algos" (pain) and "hedos" (pleasure), this channel in fact refers to the information system that runs parallel to all the vertical channels mentioned so far, whose aim is to transmit alert signals concerning any event or circumstance that could seriously jeopardise the organisation.

This channel has certain special characteristics which will be analysed in more detail in Chap. 2, dealing with the diagnosis and design of organisations. Here I will simply mention the need for it to exist and the capacity it must have to traverse the whole of the VSM's vertical structure, from the initial signal (System 1), through System 3 and, if necessary, System 4, where warning signals from the environment may be given out, until it eventually reaches System 5 with the objective of attracting attention and, should the situation require it, taking measures (Figs. 1.50 and 1.51).

This is a channel which must possess its own filters so as to prevent the passage of all types of signals regardless of the seriousness of the situation causing them to appear. The filters should allow the transfer of only those signals deemed critical for the organisation's survival. In practice, statistical filtering techniques may be employed to detect values of the critical variables appearing outside the range considered acceptable.

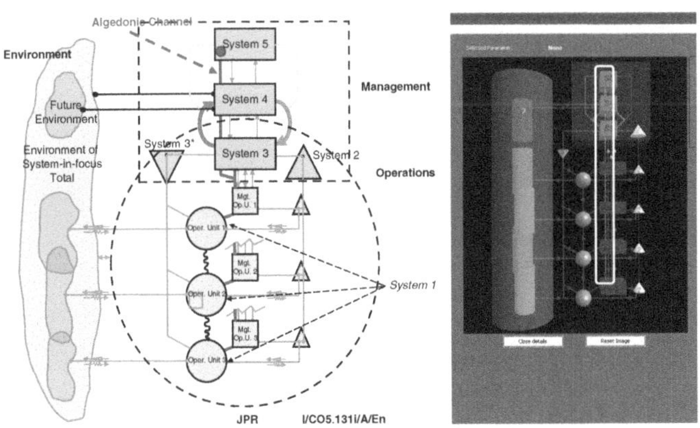

Fig. 1.50 Algedonic channel and image taken from VSMod® (Pérez Ríos 2008c)

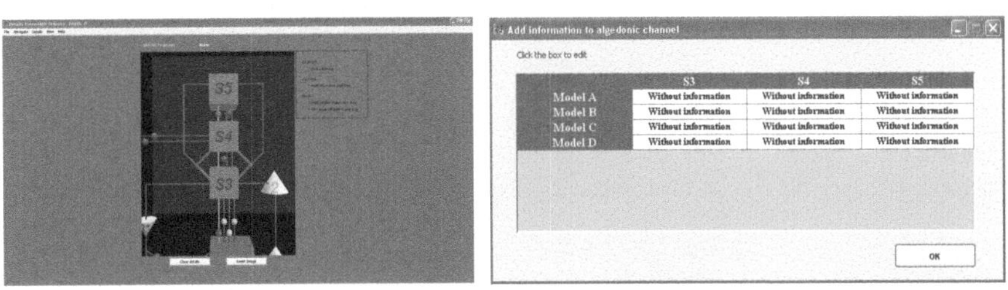

Fig. 1.51 Detail of the algedonic channel and its connection with S5 and the screen harnessing information on all possible algedonic channels in the VSM. Image taken from VSMod® (Pérez Ríos 2008c)

Figure 1.51 shows, on the left side, the algedonic channel going from System 1, through Systems 3 and 4, up to System 5. On the right side of the figure, we can see the information-capturing matrix corresponding to the algedonic channels existing (or to be designed) in the organisation in question. As can be appreciated, the alert signal may originate from any of the elementary operational units in System 1 (the rows of the matrix). In the columns we have Systems 3–5. The element of the matrix is the particular channel which connects a row with a column. Within this matrix element we can introduce as large a number of algedonic channels as we wish.

The reason for incorporating this option in VSMod® is to take into account the fact that the critical problem warned of by the algedonic signal may be resolved either in System 3 or with the help of System 4, or ultimately, if it has not been dealt with earlier, in System 5. In Chap. 4, further information is provided on the role of VSMod® as regards this and other related aspects.

After having looked at several of the essential elements of OC, we will see in Chap. 2 how different components of this methodology can be applied to the design or diagnosis of any type of organisation.

Chapter 2
Diagnosis and Design of Organisations

Now that we have looked at the basic concepts of OC, I will go on to show how these can be applied in both diagnosing an already existing organisation and as a guide when designing a new one. In both cases, the fundamental line of the study is to assess the viability of the organisation or, should this be a new creation, to help it to start out with the right elements for ensuring its viability.

I will divide this study process into four main stages. *Firstly*, we will highlight the organisation's identity and purpose. In this way, we can have a clear idea of what the organisation is (and is not), and what its goal or purpose should (or should not) be.

Secondly, we will analyse how the organisation copes with all the complexity in its environment. In this second stage particularly, we will see how a vertical breakdown of both the environment and the organisation creates a vertical structure of smaller units in the organisation that reduce the complexity each sub-organisation must deal with, facilitating its activity in each case.

The *third* stage will involve an examination of the diverse vertical levels created in the previous stage, to provide us with a detailed introduction to each one. More specifically, at each level we will analyse the components which comprise it (the horizontal dimension), namely: the specific environment of the level chosen, the organisation assigned to the activity corresponding to this environment, the "management" corresponding to this organisation and, finally, a detailed description of the elements which the Viable System Model identifies as being necessary (and sufficient) for ensuring the organisation's viability.

In the *fourth* stage we will review the extent to which the different organisations (and sub-organisations) at the various recursion levels are linked, assessing the coherence among all the elements while mindful of the identity and purpose of the organisation as a whole.

The utility of the VSM for diagnosing and designing organisations goes back to the time it first appeared, when Beer himself used it for this purpose. Various later authors have added to the literature in this context, with contributions of varying importance, always endeavouring to facilitate the application of VSM concepts in practical cases.

J. Pérez Ríos, *Design and Diagnosis for Sustainable Organizations*,
DOI 10.1007/978-3-642-22318-1_2, © Springer-Verlag Berlin Heidelberg 2012

Among the many contributions we can highlight, apart from those by Beer himself (1975, 1979, 1981, 1985), are those made by authors such as Clemson (1984), Espejo and Harnden (1989), Flood and Jackson (1991), Espejo and Schwaninger (1993), Espejo et al. (1996), Yolles (1999), (Schwaninger and Pérez Ríos 2008b) and Jackson (See: Using the VSM for Diagnosis and Design, Jackson 2000, pp. 163–166).

Some developments have been particularly extensive, as is the case of the VIPLAN software created by Espejo et al. (1999), in which Espejo also differentiates the two ways of employing the VSM, either for helping to design an organisation or for its diagnosis (Espejo 2009, Espejo and Reyes 2011, Reyes 2001).

Apart from the authors we have mentioned, many others have contributed to providing guidance on the diffusion and application of OC and the VSM. Various scientific journals have dedicated several special editions to this issue. Among them we can mention: The Double issue "Cybernetics in Focus" by the *International Journal of Applied Systemic Studies* (Guest editors: Pérez Ríos and Schwaninger 2008); the Special Issue on "Action Research in Organisational Cybernetics" by the *Systemic Practice and Action Research* journal (Guest editors: A. Espinosa and A. Leonard 2009) and the most recent Double Issue on "Model-Based Management" by *Kybernetes* (Guest editors: Schwaninger and Pérez Ríos 2010).

2.1 Recognition of Identity

Obviously, the very first step to be taken is to identify the organisation we mean to study/create, in other words, to make explicit its *identity* and *purpose* (Fig. 2.1). The response to the question of exactly what the organisation or system (organisation/company) being studied in fact is may not be a trivial one. Giving a clear answer to this question also implies understanding exactly what the company or organisation is not (Schwaninger 2006, p. 151). Answering these two questions will help us to define what forms part of the organisation and what, on the other hand, belongs to its environment; in this way, we can shed some light on how to separate the organisation

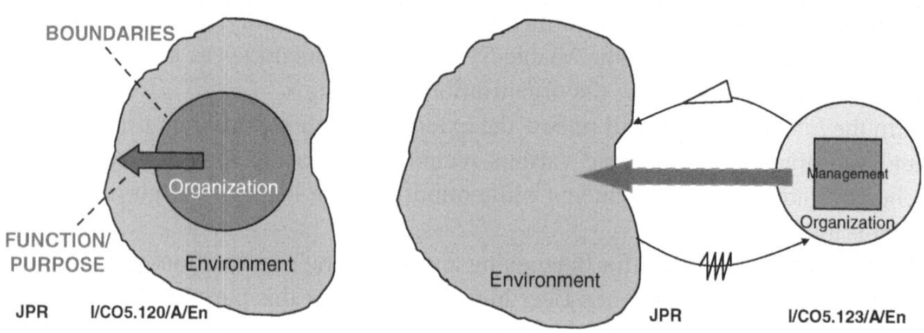

Fig. 2.1 The organisation in its environment. Interaction between the organisation with its management and the environment

from the environment in which it operates. In the area of the firm nowadays, where multiple activities (research, design, production, distribution, etc.) very often are decentralised and spread throughout the world, the question of establishing exactly what constitutes a company – that is, drawing the line between where the company ends and the environment begins – may not always be easy. The same may be said of clearly identifying the firm's purpose. Beer's well-known statement "the purpose of a system is what it does" leads us to diverse opinions on the firm's aim, depending on which observer answers the question. Different observers may attribute different "purposes" to the same firm or organisation. The studies made by Checkland (1981), Checkland and Scholes (1990), Espejo et al. (1999), among others, allow us to go deeper into these aspects.

Understanding as clearly as possible both the purpose of an organisation and its limits is critically important, as these two issues will determine how we design it or, if it already exists, how we diagnose it.

When we examine System 5, we will return to the question of defining the organisation's purpose and identity.

2.1.1 Present and Future Environment

The subsequent second step, once we know the limits of our organisation as well as its purpose, is to identify in greater detail the environment in which it operates. Understanding this environment, its components, the relationships involved, and the role of the organisation therein, will enable us to evaluate the most relevant aspects of this environment in relation to our company/organisation. Among these, we will distinguish between those which have to do with the *present*, namely, current aspects or agents (clients, suppliers, legislation, regulations, competitors, institutions, etc.), and those associated with the *future*. We will lay greater stress here on variables that might have a greater impact on the organisation we are considering (technological changes, new markets, competitors, legislation, regulations, ecological restrictions, etc.). All of this will form part of the whole environment, with the corresponding complexity (variety) the organisation must deal with in order to maintain its independent existence (identity) despite any changes it may face – that is, in order to go on being *viable*.

In relation to this phase, we will mention here certain elements that must be looked at in detail during the diagnosis or design.

1. Firstly, we will identify the fundamental areas to be considered in the environment. These areas will be associated with such aspects as the following:

   - Economic
   - Sociological
   - Political
   - Legislative
   - Institutional

- Markets
- Suppliers
- Competitors
- Technological
- Ecological
- Educational
- Demographic

Obviously, in each particular case the most pertinent areas for the organisation may vary in both number and importance.

2. Secondly, in each of these areas it will be necessary to differentiate between information pertaining to both the present and the future.
3. Thirdly, we will define:

   - The "sensors" we will employ for continuous information-retrieval relating to the previous points.
   - The information sources to be used.
   - The rate at which information should be collected in each case.
   - The communication channels we will use to transmit both present and future information (Fig. 2.2).

Regarding this section on information capture and transmission, we should remember the eight essential components (Fig. 2.3) of any homeostatic loop and communication channel (in the sender-receiver channel: sender, transducer, channel, transducer, receiver, and, the other way round, the same but with the roles of sender and receiver reversed).

Another important point to bear in mind is the way to visualise/present the information. For example, in the case of Systems 3, 4 and 5 (and very often also in the other systems/functions), it is desirable whenever possible to combine numerical with graphic and visual information. A good option, apart from a computer, is to use large electronic and touch screens.

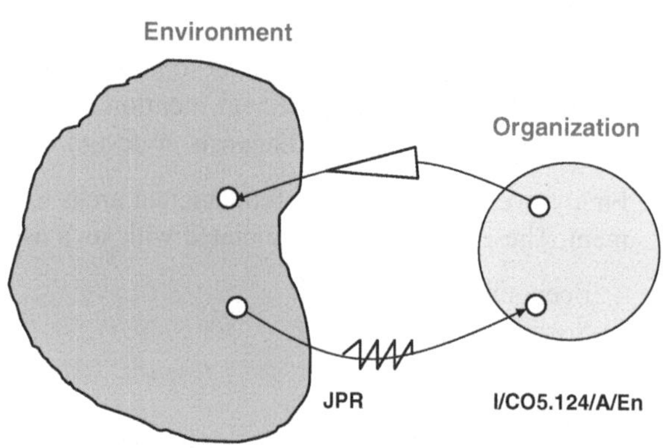

Fig. 2.2 Organisation–Environment communication channels

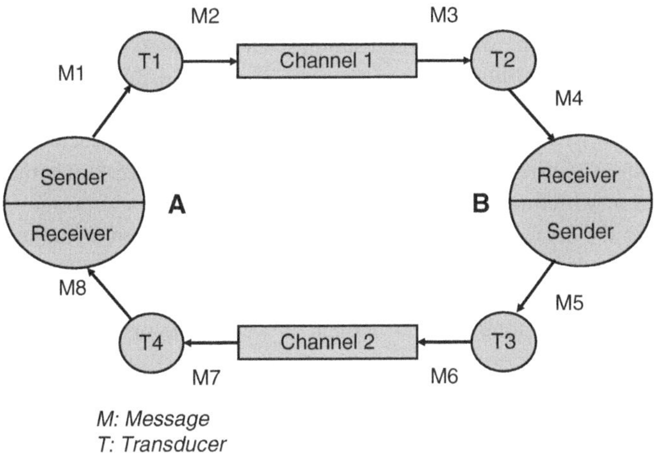

Fig. 2.3 Components of a communication channel

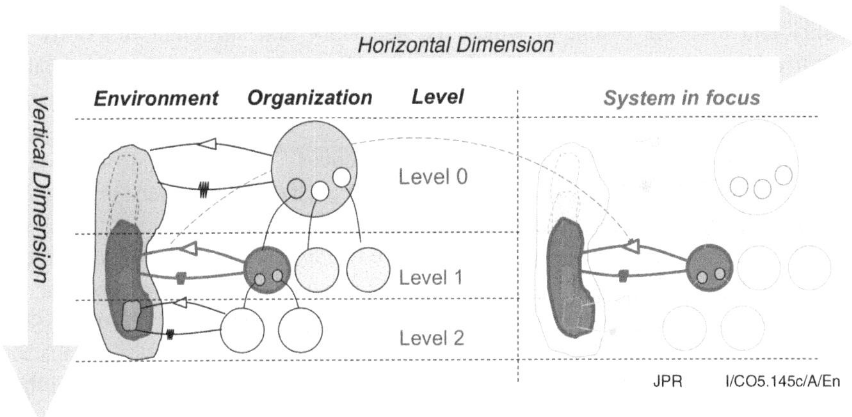

Fig. 2.4 Vertical and horizontal dimension of the system under study

Having identified the organisation, its limits and the environment (present and possible future) in which it operates, as well as having checked all the elements corresponding to the capture, transmission and presentation of information on relevant environmental aspects (*Residual variety*), we can now go on to study the organisation itself, assessing its capacity to achieve its goal or, if we are dealing with a new creation, designing it in such a way that this is ensured.

To assist us in carrying out this task, we will use two spatial dimensions that we will call *vertical* and *horizontal* (Fig. 2.4). In the *vertical dimension* our aim is deal with the amount of complexity facing the organisation in the whole environment, breaking this down into smaller environments inside the first, and these in turn into smaller ones, and so on. The reason behind this division is to design, whilst identifying the different partial environments, the organisations to be entrusted with operating within them. Such organisations will likewise become smaller and smaller, following a similar division process. The aim of this action is to make it easier for each of these organisations and sub-organisations to handle complexity (variety), which will thereby be more approachable. Obviously, each one forms part of a previous organisation, the process continuing until we reach the complete organisation to which they all belong.

Regarding the *horizontal dimension*, this will let us position ourselves at each of the different levels into which we have vertically divided both the environment and the organisation, working with all of them. Once having chosen a specific level, we will identify its corresponding environment as well as the organisation responsible for operating there. The organisation selected for a detailed study at a given moment is called *organisation-in-focus* or also *system-in-focus*. By this we mean that it will be the focus of our attention either for its design or, if that is the case, for diagnosing whether it possesses the necessary and sufficient requisites for its viability. When we study this dimension, we will review the environment, the corresponding organisation, its management and the relationships among them.

Here we will also investigate the inside of the organisation, to take a close look at quality and also the extent to which the necessary and sufficient functions for viability exist. Consequently, we will examine all the components that the Viable System Model indicates as being necessary and which must be functioning properly in the organisation.

In the case of each of these components (Systems 1, 2, 3, 3*, 4, 5, Communication channels, Algedonic channels, components of each of the channels, present and future contents of the environments, or information capturing systems, etc.), we examine three main aspects. First of all, we see if it exists and is represented in the organisation; secondly, once its presence has been confirmed, we look for its quality, that is, the extent to which it has developed in acquiring the necessary elements to perform its function properly; thirdly, with all its necessary means for functioning in place, we observe whether performance in fact happens – in other words, we verify whether it works to achieve its goal (with efficiency, efficacy and effectiveness).

Now let us see how to analyse the organisation by means of both these dimensions, beginning with the *vertical dimension*.

2.2 Vertical Dimension: Criteria and Recursion Levels – Complexity Unfolding

As I mentioned previously, having considered the purpose of the organisation and the environment in which it operates or will operate, we can now deal with the two basic elements which are, the environment and the organisation. Once again, the complexity of the environment is much greater than that which an organisation can

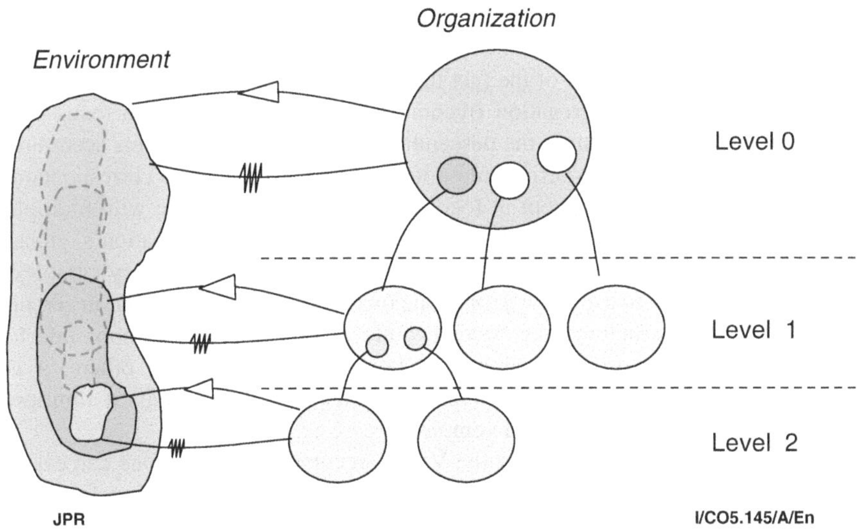

Fig. 2.5 Vertical unfolding of complexity

deploy in order to face all the possible situations that might occur in the environment, even if they are limited to those directly related to the organisation. In the section concerning complexity and variety, it was also seen that one potential mechanism to be used here is the vertical unfolding of complexity. This entails breaking the environment down into smaller ones which are contained in the initial environment; thus, the lesser complexity corresponding to these smaller environments will be the concern of similarly smaller organisations, which in turn form part of the initial organisation (Fig. 2.5).

2.2.1 Criteria and Recursion Levels

To unfold things in this way, we must choose one or more criteria for defining both the partial environments and the organisations they will correspond to when we design the organisation. We will call each level generated in this process of vertical breakdown a *level of recursion*. At each level will be an environment and the organisation which either should or in fact does correspond to it.

It is important to observe here that each organisation appearing during vertical unfolding is a complete viable system. We should not confuse this process with a simple increase in the degree of resolution of the organisation's "image", since such entities are not merely parts of the initial entity, functional or otherwise, but complete viable organisations, with all the characteristics established by the VSM to ensure such viability.

The recursion level which we select for detailed study at a given time is called, as I mentioned in Sect. 1.3, a *system-in-focus* or *organisation-in-focus*. To reiterate what was said there, in view of the fact that there may be several recommendable criteria for vertical disaggregation (recursion criteria), the system-in-focus will occupy an intermediate path in the descending chain of recursion levels according to one or more recursion criteria (unless it is the first or last of its corresponding chain). The image of the system-in-focus as the centre of a sphere with multiple dimensions (recursion criteria) allows us to visualize an organisation's global structure. Of course, in many cases this structure is not necessarily very complex, and it may be enough to use a few or only one recursion criteria. However, in certain organisations this structure may become quite complex, or even impossible to visualise with a two-dimensional image. For this reason, among others, it is particularly convenient to use the VSMod® software, as it permits a limitless inclusion of the required structural complexity.

Figure 2.6 shows an example of the VSM's recursive structure: one can easily see how at level 0 (the convention is to assign the value 0 to the first level) an organisation comprising three elementary operational units (System 1) which appear to their full extent in *recursion level 1*. From these we have chosen the second (situated in the middle) to continue the vertical disaggregation two levels further down. Once again in this example, from the three elementary operational units also contained in this organisation, we select the first to show its full extension at *recursion level 2*. Similarly, from this organisation (which in this example also has three elementary operational units) we select the second of these to show full extension at *recursion level 3*.

In this way, we can observe the four levels of recursion within the organisations we have selected for visualisation. Obviously, we could have done the same with the first and third organisation of recursion level 1, thereby showing the corresponding vertical disaggregation. This has not been done here so as to simplify explanation. Once again, it is easy to appreciate how difficult it is to provide a graphic representation of the whole structure, that is to say, all the organisations to be found at all levels and in accordance with all possible recursion criteria. Hence the need for software like VSMod®, which facilitates visualisation even of the complete structural map (Criteria-Levels-Organisations).

Another example is shown in Fig. 2.7, of an organisation at Level 0 of the disaggregation chain according to Recursion Criterion 2. But at the same height another two organisations can be seen in two vertical disaggregation chains corresponding to Recursion Criteria 1 and 3. In those three organisations we find that (in this example) the first elementary operational unit of the first organisation, the second elementary operational unit of the second organisation and the second elementary operational unit of the third organisation are the same organisation, which is the one fully represented at recursion Level 1. In this example, the disaggregation chain only continues downward (recursion Level 2 and recursion Level 3), following Recursion Criterion 2.

If we went on disaggregating vertically from the organisation shown at recursion Level 1, but still continued the disaggregation chains in accordance with

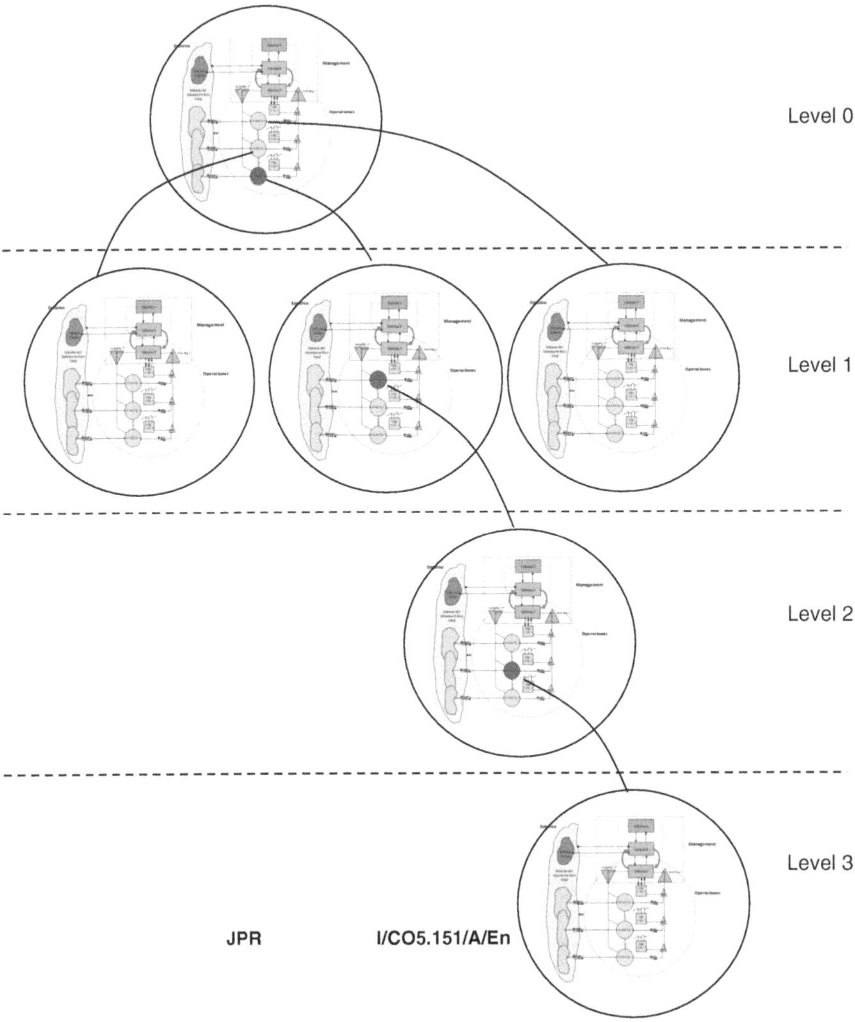

Fig. 2.6 Recursive structure of the Viable System Model (Adapted from Beer 1979)

Recursion Criteria 1 and 3, we would find the organisation located at recursion Level 1 to be the centre where the chains cross. Here the image of course must remain two-dimensional, but were there to be multiple recursion criteria, we could apply a three-dimensional representation. Figure 2.8 shows the system-in-focus or organisation-in-focus we have selected for hypothetical analysis in this case. On the left of the figure we see a three-dimensional representation of the system-in-focus which occupies the central or intersecting space of criteria and recursion levels.

As I have just pointed out, if we select more than one recursion criterion, then we will have several vertical disaggregation routes. But there is also the possibility that, descending in line with a specific criterion and reaching a certain point

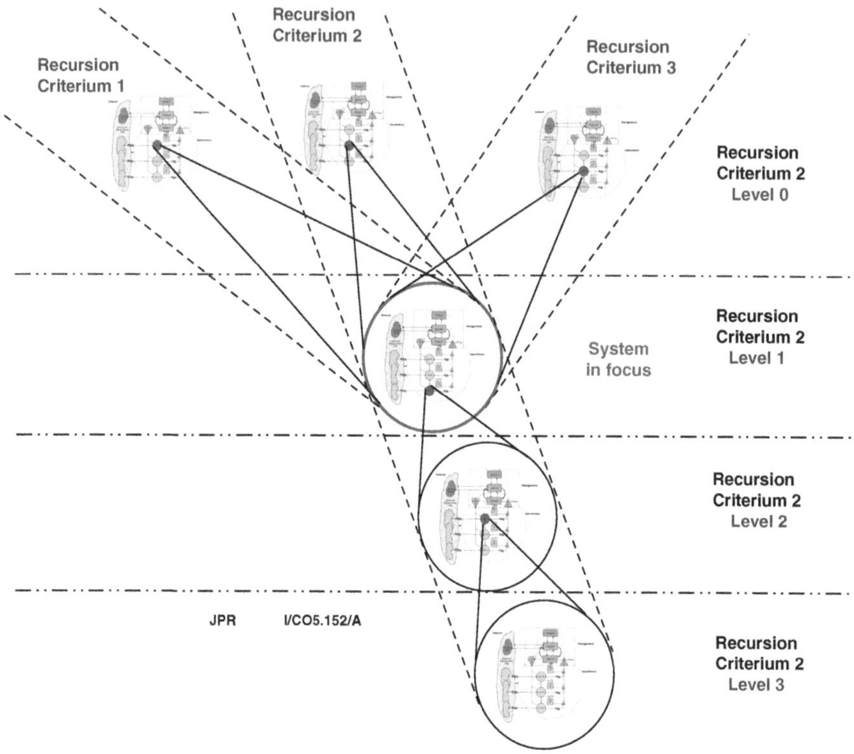

Fig. 2.7 Vertical dimension: Several recursion criteria (Pérez Ríos 2008e)

(a recursion level), we would be interested in using a different criterion to continue unfolding the process of complexity. This would mean that at such a point we change the "dimension" (the new recursion criterion selected) and continue with vertical disaggregation along a different route. This step could be repeated indefinitely at any later stage. It is not difficult to appreciate that, should the organisation be large and the number of criteria substantial, our study will become very complex. Hence our insistence on the suitability of employing specialised software such as VSMod®, which allows us at all times to have access to the global map of the complete system with which we are working, as well as all the information relating to how the vertical breakdown is being generated.[1] The three navigation maps (Global Map, Map 1 and Map 2) incorporated in VSMod® provide such information (Figs. 2.9–2.11).

On the right of Fig. 2.9, we have a representation of the Global Map of a VSM application exemplifying the automotive sector. The purpose of the image is to

[1] In Chap. 4 of this book we give a detailed description of the main characteristics of VSMod® software and of its development since its creation in 2001.

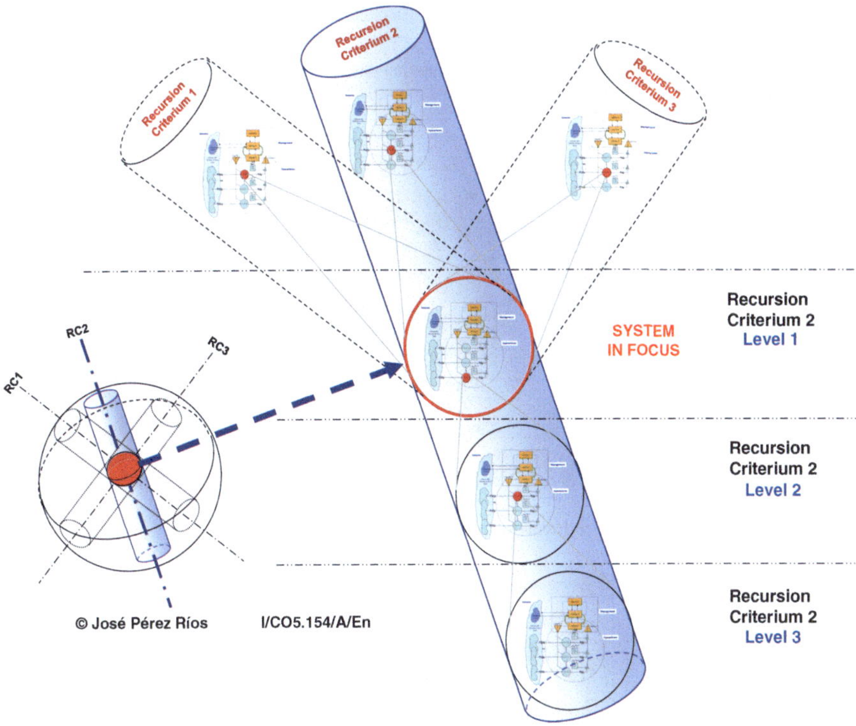

Fig. 2.8 The system-in-focus as the centre of multiple dimensions (criteria and recursion levels) (Pérez Ríos 2008e)

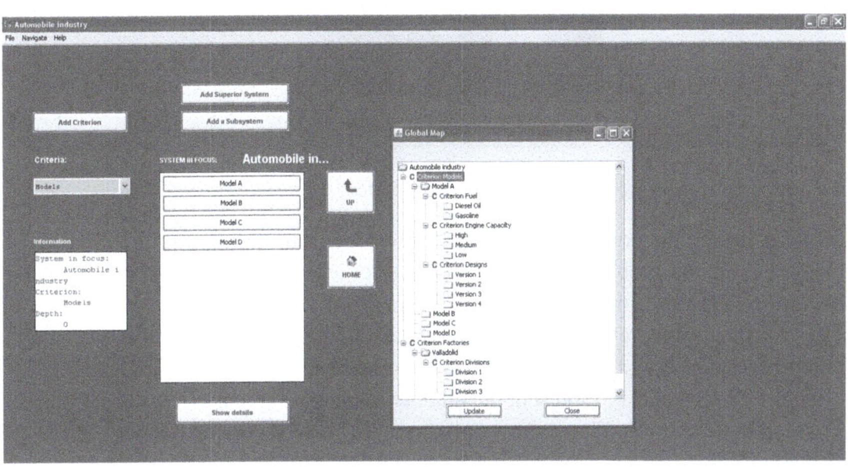

Fig. 2.9 Global map showing the complete structure of a model (VSMod®)

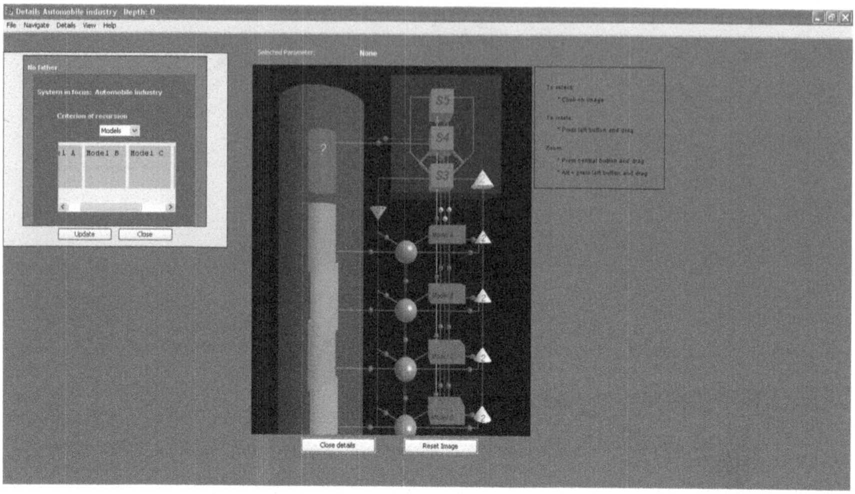

Fig. 2.10 Map 1 showing three levels of recursion (VSMod®)

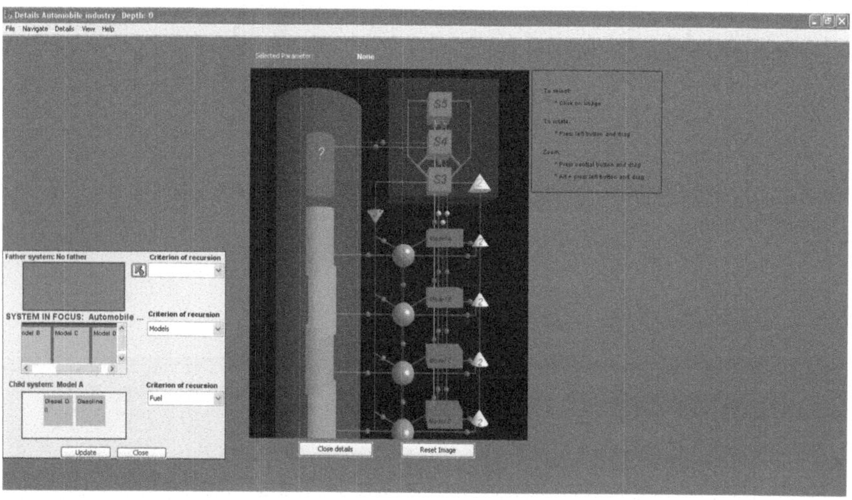

Fig. 2.11 Map 2 showing three recursion levels (VSMod®)

enable us to see the complete structure of the organisation being studied, which in this case is an automobile company. We can see the recursion criteria, the recursion levels for each criterion and the organisations (or systems) at each level of recursion. As the figure reveals, VSMod® makes it possible to visualise the whole structure, regardless of its complexity, in just one image.

Figures 2.10 and 2.11 represent the other two navigation maps (Map 1 and Map 2) provided by VSMod®. These show only three levels of recursion, namely, the level corresponding to the system-in-focus (organisation-in-focus), the one preceding this (parent level) and the following one (child level). The difference between Map

1 and Map 2 lies in the degree of detail for the information included, which is more complete in Map 2, showing as it does all the systems (organisations) at the three levels together with the possible recursion criteria for each.

For many VSM applications, it may be advisable to operate at all times with these three levels visible (Fig. 2.12). In fact, this way of working with the VSM is the one proposed by Beer in his last book relating to this model: *Diagnosing the System for Organizations* (Beer 1985).

Figure 2.13 represents a VSMod® screen shot in which the three navigation maps are seen simultaneously.

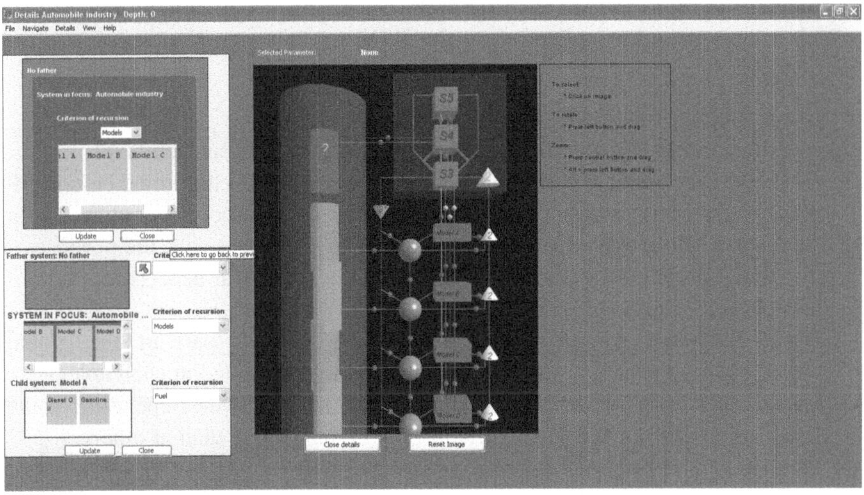

Fig. 2.12 Maps 1 and 2 showing three levels of recursion (VSMod®)

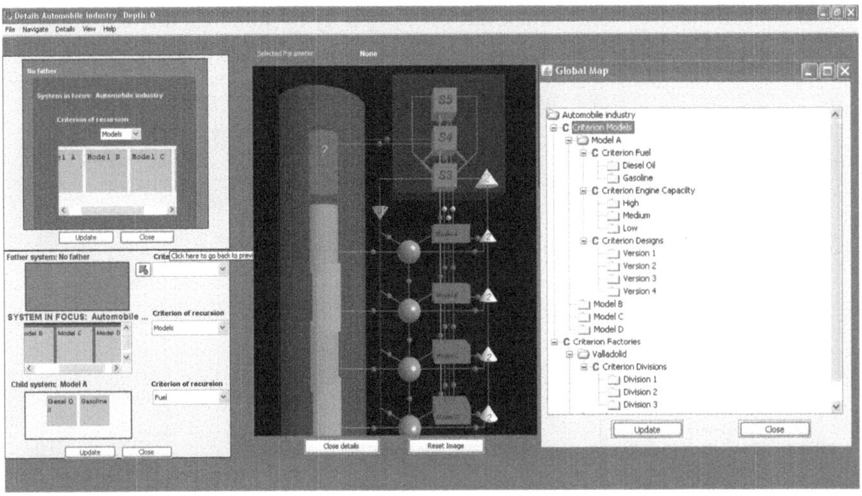

Fig. 2.13 Maps 1 and 2 and Global Map (VSMod®)

2.2.2 Recursion Levels–Critical Factors Matrix

Having performed this vertical breakdown, our next step is to identify the fundamental elements to be taken into account at each level of recursion. In order to achieve this, we select the recursion criterion we wish to use and construct the matrix (Fig. 2.14) which I call the *Recursion Levels-Critical Factors Matrix*, in which the *rows* are formed by the different levels of recursion and the *columns* contain the main relevant points to be considered at each level.

In the following list, I show some of the aspects that must be included frequently as components of the columns in the *Recursion Levels–Critical-Factors Matrix* (which as an aid to the application of the VSM we may regard as an orientative decalogue):

1. Identification of the level (number and description).
2. Identification of the specific environment corresponding to each level.
3. Particularly relevant aspects of the specific environment that must be considered, with an explicit description of the purpose of the specific organisation for each level. Obviously, this description must be congruent with the purpose of the global organisation. However, there may be particular aspects for each of the levels.
4. Identification of the particular organisation that, as part of the global organisation, operates in the specific environment indicated at each level.
5. Identification of all the relevant "stakeholders" in each level. Depending on the level, some may have more significance at certain levels than at others.
6. Identifying the "external agents" whose decisions might have favourable or adverse consequences for our organisation to carry out actions we consider pertinent for meeting the objective of the organisation at each level. In this group, besides individual actors or agents, we will include institutions, firms or organisations in general which have the capacity to influence the organisation.

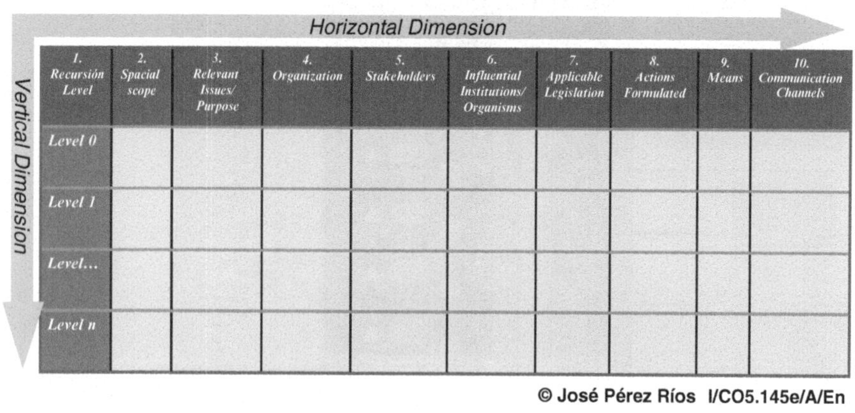

Fig. 2.14 *Recursion Levels–Critical Factors Matrix* (Pérez Ríos 2008e)

7. Individualisation and description of the norms, legislation or regulations, etc. which establish and regulate the activity framework at each level.
8. Describing actions to be undertaken at each level. Here we must specify if we are using the cybernetic study for the design, in which case these actions will be chosen and shaped to achieve the aim of the organisation, or if our intention is to diagnose the organisation, in which case we would evaluate the on-going actions and their adequacy for the outcome of the organizational diagnosis.
9. The description of the action must go hand in hand with all the necessary components for it to be successful (what, who, how, when, where, with what means, at what cost, with what requirements/specifications, etc.).
10. Description of the main communication channels to be utilised to connect with the environment. In this context, we should remember that it is necessary: (a) to clearly identify the content of the information to be transmitted (b) the means by which this is to be done (c) to check that the communication channels exist, and (d) to make sure that each one has the essential elements required by all such channels to perform their functions properly.

We should not forget that each of these elements must be designed so that it can perform its function, and that, in the case of transducers, this means converting the amount of information required per time unit from one format to another, whereas for communication channels it is a question of transmitting information without loss of integrity.

Similarly, we should bear in mind that as regards communication channels there may be "noise" and distortion of information. As I mentioned above, one way to prevent an alteration in the transmission process is to provide each of the components with more than enough capacity to compensate for this, and another is to have a certain degree of redundancy when transmitting data (for instance, by using different channels to send the same information).

Finally, and in relation to the *Recursion Levels-Critical Factors Matrix*, I should point out that the one given in Fig. 2.14 is obviously two-dimensional. In the rows as shown, we can appreciate the levels of recursion for a single recursion criterion (not shown in the figure), whilst the columns refer to a single organisation at each level. Nevertheless, in a real, more complex case, we may come across situations which are much more difficult to represent:

(a) One of these would be the case where there is more than one organisation at one or several recursion levels. In that case, the matrix would have a "depth" for these levels that would correspond with as many layers (matrices) as organisations or sub-systems existing at the level in question. The problem of two-dimensional representation could be resolved by introducing sub-elements within the level, with several embedded organisations.
(b) Another case would be the one in which we employ diverse recursion criteria. Here the solution would be to construct a different matrix for each recursion criterion. A more complicated variant would start from a vertical disaggregation in accordance with a recursion criterion RC1 and allow us to find several levels, one of which is interesting for us to continue this disaggregation process, but

now using another recursion criterion RC2; other recursion levels would then appear in this second dimension or recursion criterion. Needless to say, a two-dimensional graphic representation becomes complicated in such a situation.

I mention these cases in order to show the necessity of using the right tools for dealing with the complexity we wish to represent, in this case the *Recursion Levels-Critical Factors Matrix*. Once again, the VSMod® software (in its 1.4 version) accomplishes this aim. It has been developed to make it easy to visualise the matrix structure on the computer screen without any restriction. Changing the recursion criterion, or visualising organisations belonging to a specific recursion level, is done by simply clicking with the mouse on either one on the screen itself, which allows the matrix we wish to visualise and feed with fresh information to appear.

2.2.3 Structural Pathologies

Apart from allowing us to identify the pertinent environmental levels associated with our organisation and its operational scope, which we can visualise in the previous matrix by means of the rows, vertical unfolding can also be useful for diagnosing "holes", that is to say, the level at which the organisation taking responsibility for dealing with the corresponding complexity and problem areas either does not exist or, if it exists, is insufficiently embodied.

In Chap. 3 of this book, entitled "Pathologies of Organizations", we describe some of the typical pathologies related to the vertical unfolding of complexity. The three groups of *pathologies* that normally affect organisations are: *Structural, Functional* and those concerning *Information*. Structural pathologies are those in which at certain levels organisations do not exist, and are directly related to the vertical unfolding we are looking at here. Pathologies identified as structural are:

1. Non-existence of vertical unfolding
2. Lack of recursion levels (first level)
3. Lack of recursion levels (middle levels) and
4. Entangled vertical unfolding. Various interrelated memberships

By way of example, let us now look at the third of these *Lack of recursion levels (middle levels)*:

This particular pathology occurs when areas of relevant environment for the organisation in question meet up with no corresponding organisational element exists. Consequently, the problems in that area of the environment are not dealt with in a specific or focussed way by the organisation. Such matters are addressed rather inadequately by organisations from either the next or previous recursion level or, as is more likely, simply go unaddressed, remaining unresolved (Fig. 2.15).

A typical example of this pathology may be encountered in supra-municipal transport systems, or in problems associated with the provision of services such as the water supply or waste disposal, etc. Such services usually extend beyond

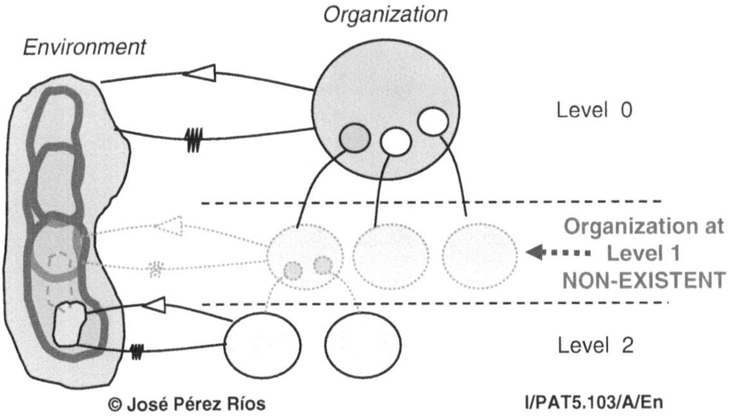

Fig. 2.15 Pathology P1.3. Lack of recursion levels (middle levels) (Pérez Ríos 2008b)

municipal boundaries. Dealing properly with these supra-municipal necessities requires the setting-up of organisations corresponding to those recursion levels. However, these organisations do not usually exist, and if they are created they tend to be made up of mere groupings of nearby municipalities. However, the issue to deal with may implicitly require that we consider a different spatial and institutional framework. Current issues relating to metropolitan areas, or to rivers that cross a large number of provinces, towns and other administrative and even national boundaries, are examples of this problem area.

An instance of the benefit of creating organisations at these intermediate stages, as well as a consideration of problems on territorial scales different from the municipal and lower levels or from provincial levels, may be seen in the work done by Pérez Ríos and Martínez concerning the application of these concepts to spatial treatment in a supra-municipal university context (Pérez Ríos and Martínez 2007). Figure 2.16 highlights the levels of recursion identified in this study and the images corresponding to the graphic representations of the VSM in two and three dimensions by means of the VSMod® software (Pérez Ríos 2003, 2006b, 2008c and 2008e). We should mention that the recursion criterion used, and shown in the image, is one of space (this is a town planning project in a university context).

In addition, in Fig. 2.17 we are shown an example of the *Recursion Levels-Critical Factors Matrix* used in the afore-mentioned study by Pérez Ríos and Martinez. We can observe both the different rows (levels of recursion identified in the study as pertinent) and their corresponding description, as well as the columns with the factors for which relevant information has been obtained. Similarly, in the matrix elements we can appreciate the type of data deemed necessary throughout the study. As this is an on-going project, the diverse matrix components will undergo enrichment in line with its development.

This study reveals the enormous capacity of the VSM for diagnosing the main problems (and also opportunities) at each recursion level, by means of the vertical disaggregation process I have just commented on and with the aid of the *Recursion*

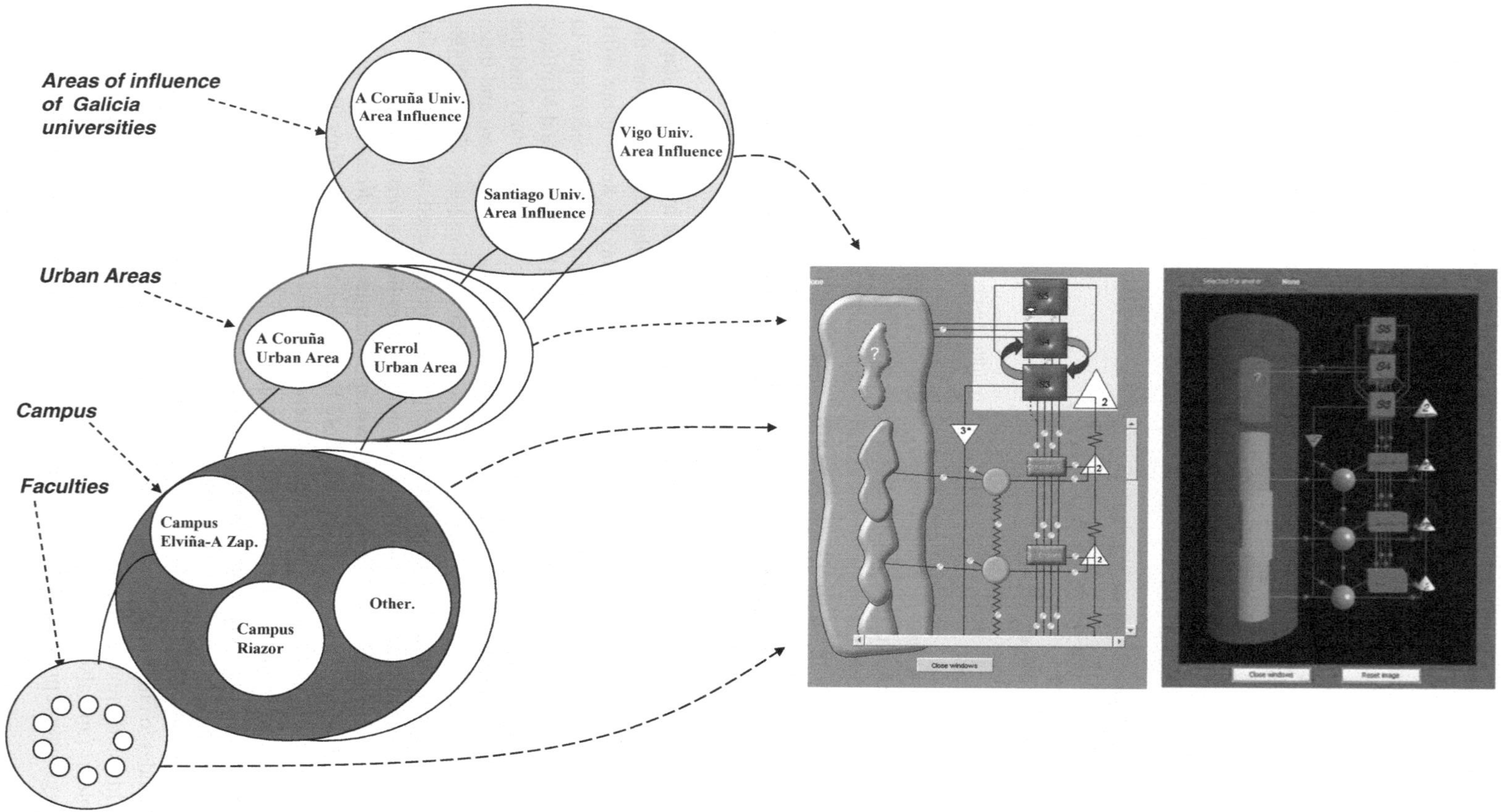

Fig. 2.16 Levels of recursión in the UDC and image of the VSM in two and three dimensions taken from the VSMod® software (Pérez Ríos 2008c)

1. Recursion Level	2. Spacial Scope	3. Relevant Issues/ Purpose	4. Organization	5. Stakeholders	6. Influencial Institutions Organisms	7. Applicable Legislation	8. Actions Formulated	9. Means	10. Communication Channels
0	Galicia. Territorial Scale 1	-Social Function of the universities. -Relationship with the urban policy.			-Xunta de Galicia. -Consellerías: Education, Territorial Policy, Housing, Environment and sustained development. -Unversities: A Coruña.; Santiago de Compostela; Vigo.	1. Act 10/1995 on Town and Land Planning of Galicia. 2. Ground/Building Act of Galicia (December 2002). 3. Act 11/1989 on Galicia University System Planning. 4. University Act 6/2001 5. UDC standing Rule.	-Contribution of the UDC to the Town-Planning Guidelines in Galicia (in progress) -URB 16. (Campus Elviña) University Residential Area		
1	Urban Region A Coruña Ferrol Territorial Scale 2.	-Accessibility. -Range (number of potential students) -Visibility of the UDC in the cities, small towns and villages. -Economic and social development of the urban region. -Connection with the business network.			-RENFE.(Spain's Railway System) -Cities: ACoruña Ferrol and all the rest in the Urban Region. -UDC. -Xunta de Galicia. (Commuting)		-URB 1. Territorial Accessibility: shire Public Transport Suburban Trains, and coach network. -URB 12. Parking Lots -Parking Lots at Railway Stations. -URB 13. Bus, Train Station Campus Elviña. -URB 15. Research Area. Creation of new enterprises.		
2	a) Urban A Coruña. b) Urban Ferrol.	-Accessibility. -Integration University/city -Cohesion university/city. -Structuring of public equipments and urban services with the university.			-Cities of A Coruña. -UDC. -City of Ferrol.	Urban Master plan of A Coruña (1995). Urban Master plan ofFerrol.	-URB 2. Enlargement of Urban Coaches network. -URB 17. Bicycle lane pedestrian Path from the city centre to the campus.		
3	a) Campus A Coruña	-Adaptation to the European Union directives on Universities degrees. -Urban attraction -Urban and architectonic referent (model of sustained development).			-UDC -City of A Coruña.	-Urban Plan for ElviñaA Zapateira Campus (1991) and its modification in 2002. -Environment Plan.	-URB 11. Campus Center -URB 10. Area 30.Elviña Campus coach. -URB 8. Redesign of Zapateira Square. -URB 9. Scientific-Technological Park. Botanical Park. -URB 16. University Residential Area (Campus Elviña).		
4	Single Buildings.	-Functionality. -Comfort and Environment Managing. -Optimizing spaces.			-UDC -Institution Board		Actions at each particular centre.		

Fig. 2.17 Recursion levels-critical factors matrix (Pérez Ríos and Martínez Suárez 2007)

Levels-Critical Factors Matrix, Above all, it shows how useful the VSM is for identifying the need to create organisations that cover the relevant areas, in this case spatial ones, for the main organisation (in this case a Spanish public university and its geographical area of influence). Application of the VSM made it possible in this case to identify 17 specific actions related to urban planning issues. Several of these had an impact not only on that dimension but also on other aspects related to questions such as the purpose of the university (e.g., attracting more students, providing more services for the community), the transformation (sociological and demographic) of a part of the city where this university is located, the modification of various systems of transport (bus, inter-municipal railway and a bicycle lane), the increase of supply in student accommodations, the likely impact on a reduction in the price of rented flats by increasing their supply as an indirect consequence of some of those actions, and the transformation of the university into a reference point for sustainable development. These are only a few of the examples of the wide-ranging effects this study has brought about (and is continuing to bring about at the time of writing this book).

It is appropriate to emphasise that thus far, within the process of applying the VSM, we have employed only the phase of vertical disaggregation of complexity. No reference has yet been made to the implications of a study with the VSM in its horizontal dimension, that is to say, the one associated with each and every one of the existing organisations in the structure in question (with their diverse internal components).

2.3 Horizontal Dimension: Choosing the System-in-Focus: The Complete System and Its Functions

In the previous section, we saw how to go about absorbing variety (complexity) in the environment by breaking it down in a *vertical dimension*, allowing us to identify, in line with the selected recursion criteria, the pertinent levels of recursion for each, as well as existing organisations or, in the case of designing a new organisation, those to be recommended at each level. We have also seen that each level corresponds to a row of the *Recursion Levels-Critical Factors Matrix*, in whose columns we find the factors or aspects that are essential for studying the organisation.

After creating or diagnosing the general structure of our particular system (organisation), and having identified the different relevant levels of recursion, we can now proceed to analyze each organisation involved in the various environments. As previously stated, we will call the one selected for this detailed study the *organisation-in-focus* or *system-in-focus*.

This *horizontal dimension*, which now centres attention on the components in the matrix row corresponding to *Level/Organisation-in-focus*, is the one that allows us to continue absorbing the environment's variety (complexity), albeit restricted now to just one part, namely that of the *Level/Organisation-in-focus* chosen. Essentially in this dimension, we will analyse the following three elements: the specific environment of the organisation-in-focus, the organisation-in-focus and its management. In Fig. 2.18 we can see on the left an outline of the environment with the embedded organisation and, in turn, the latter's management forming part of it. In the centre of the figure the same features are shown but now the organisation together with its management are separated from the environment in which it operates; in this way we can better visualise the channels attenuating and amplifying variety, which permit the organisation to approach the particular variety

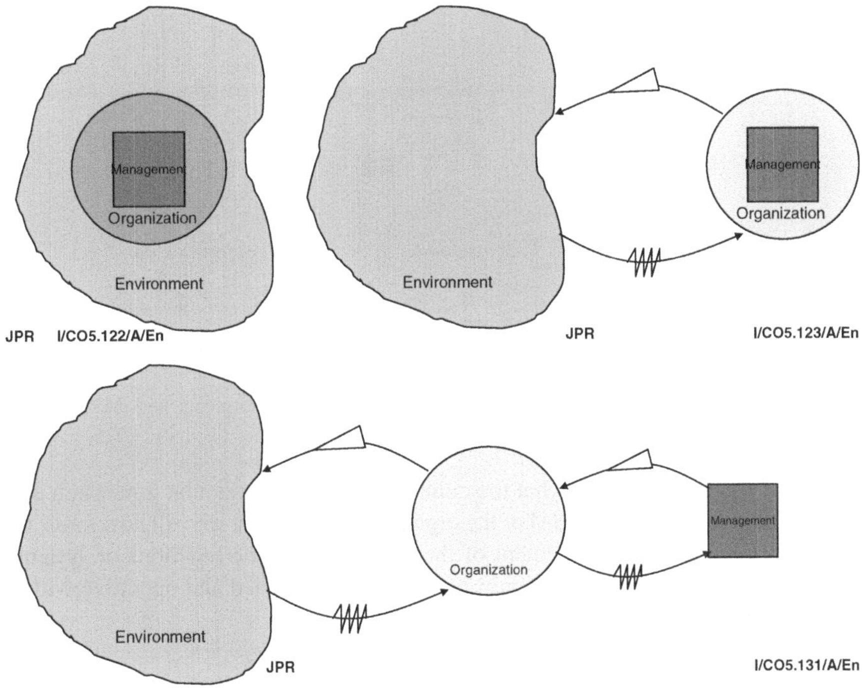

Fig. 2.18 Horizontal dimension (Environment-Organisation-Management)

of the environment in accordance with the afore-mentioned Ashby's Law. On the right side of the figure we now separate management from the organisation which it directs in order, once again, to reveal the attenuating and amplifying channels that will enable management to deal with this complexity.

Now that we have identified the three essential components corresponding to the recursion level selected and, within this, the organisation-in-focus, the next step will be to study the latter's structure. In this way, we will be able to assess the actual presence and development of the five previously mentioned systems or functions deemed necessary and sufficient according to the VSM, as well as the network of communication channels feeding them.

On the right side of Fig. 2.19, we can observe the content of each of the three essential components (environment, organisation/operations and management, also referred to as environment, system and meta-system). The whole of the VSM can be viewed, with all the vital functions or systems (System 1, 2, 3, 3*, 4, 5), the present Environment, the future Environment and the Channels of communication. One may appreciate how, inside the circle representing the operations/system, there are three components which in turn have their own operations and management. They are the elementary operational units making up System 1. There are three in the example shown, but obviously there may be any number. Each would be the organisation-in-focus if we were to go down to the following level of recursion.

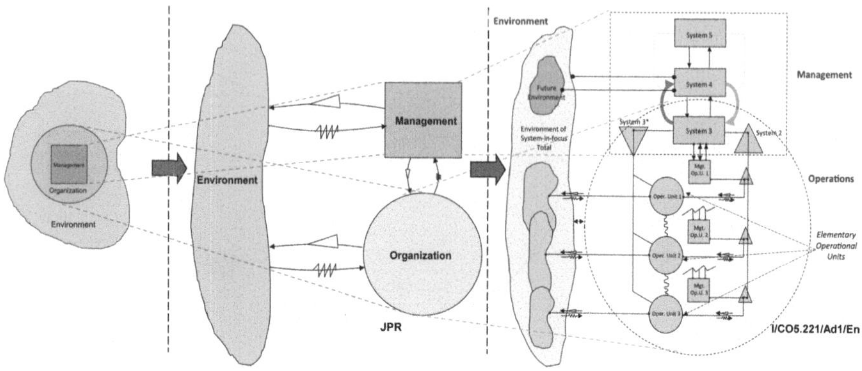

Fig. 2.19 Horizontal dimension (Environment-Organisation-Management) and MSV of the system-in-focus (Pérez Ríos 2008a)

Having understood, then, what the components of the horizontal dimension are, and how they lead us to the VSM of the organisation-in-focus, we will now move on to consider each particular element of the VSM, that is, the functions or systems which according to the model should be suitably represented and operative within the organisation.

Centering our attention on our *organisation/system-in-focus*, the sequence of analysis will be as follows:

- We will start by reviewing each of the systems or functions separately, with special emphasis on System 1, in view of its containing the diverse operational units that will, as explained above, embody the following systems-in-focus as we descend to the subsequent level of recursion.
- Following an individual study of each component, we will complete our diagnosis with a look at the vertical connections of the organisation-in-focus.

  A consideration of the functions/systems of our system-in-focus (Fig. 2.20) will be based on the following outline:
- First of all, we will analyse the *Management meta-system* (*System 5, System 4 and System 3*) and its relationship to the environment of the system-in-focus.
- Next, we will deal with the *set of operations* (*System*) of our *System-in-focus*, comprising *Systems 1, 2* and *3*, together with the special *System 3**.

The reason for inverting the study sequence, which would normally focus on analysing System 1 first of all, and then the rest in numerical order, resides in the fact that when designing an organisation it makes no sense to delve into the operational units if the nature and purpose of our organisation (system-in-focus) are unknown to us. The systems approach described at the beginning of this book clarified the sequence of steps for the study of any system: firstly, identifying the system in which the system-in-focus is subsumed; secondly, recognising the aim/purpose of our system-in-focus within the containing system; and, finally, looking at the particulars of either the design or diagnosis of the organisation analysed.

Let us begin, then, with a review of the Management Meta-system.

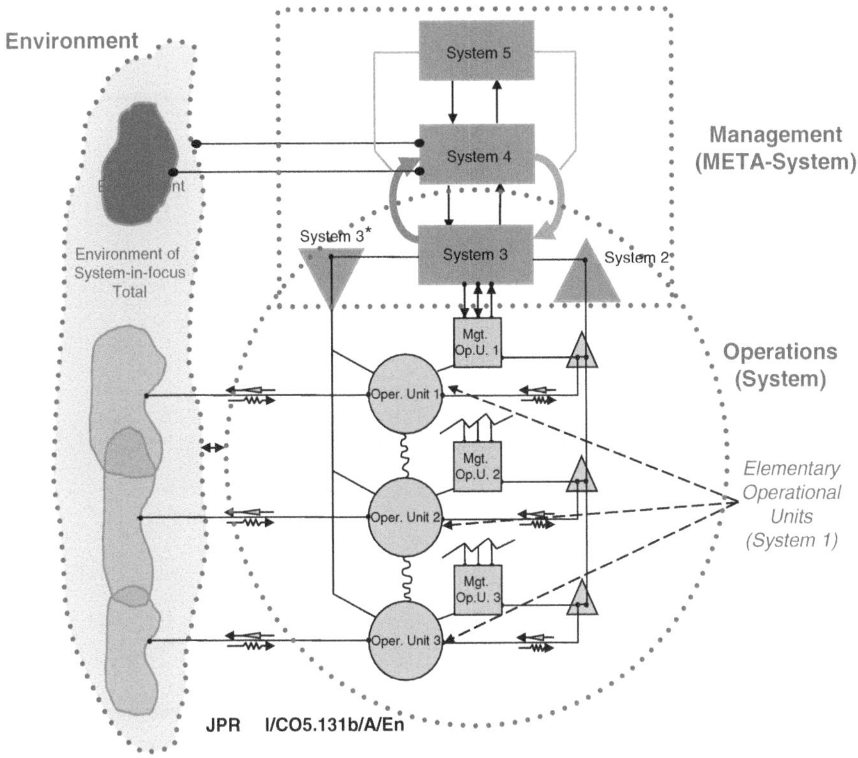

Fig. 2.20 The system-in-focus (Environment-System/Operations-Meta-system/Management) (Pérez Ríos 2008e)

2.3.1 Management Metasystem (System 5, System 4 and System 3)

In all systems or functions that make up the VSM, we can consider two basic groups of questions. The first aims to determine the very *existence and constitution of the system*, in other words, to discover whether it exists and, if it does, to assess its embodiment in terms of its capacity to carry out the required function. The second group of questions tries to analyse, wherever pertinent, the system's *relations with the other systems and the environment*. In this context, there are also two main dimensions in which this relationship is encountered: one may be regarded as horizontal (above all with the environment or, in the case of Systems 3 and 1 with System 2) and the other vertical, referring to links between the different systems or functions.

2.3.1.1 System 5

In Sect. 3 of Chap. 1, I explained the characteristics and goal of this system and its role as the "closure" of the organisation (Fig. 2.21). Consequently, when it comes to

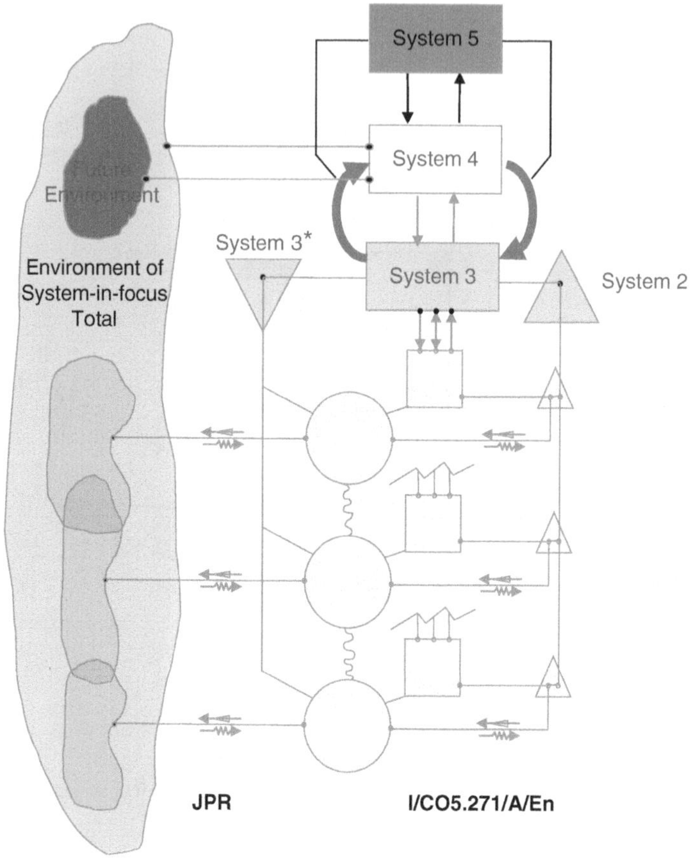

Fig. 2.21 System 5 (Pérez Ríos 2008e)

"diagnosing" both its presence and degree of development, we should take into consideration the most relevant questions regarding these aspects.

Not attempting to be exhaustive here, I will mention a few examples of questions that can be posed concerning various essential points:

In Relation to the Existence of System 5 Elements

- Is there a formal declaration (explicit or written) regarding the organisation's inspirational vision?
- Is there a (written) formal declaration on the mission of the organisation?
- Are there documents recording the actual translation of this mission into strategic targets and objectives for the organisation?

In Relation to the Quality of System 5 Elements

- Does the list of strategic goals and objectives cover all fundamental aspects of the organisation? As an example of these in the case of companies, we may mention those identified by Drucker: clients and target market; geographical area; issues relating to survival, growth and profitability; philosophy of the firm; and desired public image (Drucker 1954).

In Relation to the Existence of Organisms/People with a Role in System 5

- What are both the personal and collective organisms with a function related to some of the previous points?
- Examples of organisms which have (or should have) particular System 5 functions are: a company's Board of Directors; a university Social Council; the Economic and Social Council in an Autonomous Community; the management team of a firm or organisation.

In Relation to the Working and Efficacy of Organisms with System-5 Functions

- Is there consensus in each of these organisms regarding what the organisation is or intends to be (that is to say, its identity)?
- Are there adequate procedures for transmitting the information generated in System 5 to the rest of the organisation?

In relation to the communication channels

- Which existing communication channels allow System 5 to be informed of events in the organisation concerning matters relating specifically to this system, and which ones transmit the precise information to the rest of the organisation regarding the Vision, Mission, Goals, Identity, etc.?
- Are there proper "sensors" to receive the information via the algedonic channel?
- Does the algedonic channel connect the appropriate points, and are its eight typical components of a communication channel suitably developed?

A second group of questions in relation to System 5 refers to the government of interactions between Systems 4 and 3, that is, the System 4-System 3 Homeostat (Fig. 2.22). As previously mentioned, System 5 is responsible for achieving an equilibrium between the present functioning of the organisation and its preparation for the future; these are functions fundamentally typical of System 3 and System 4, respectively. Therefore, other points to take into account are listed below.

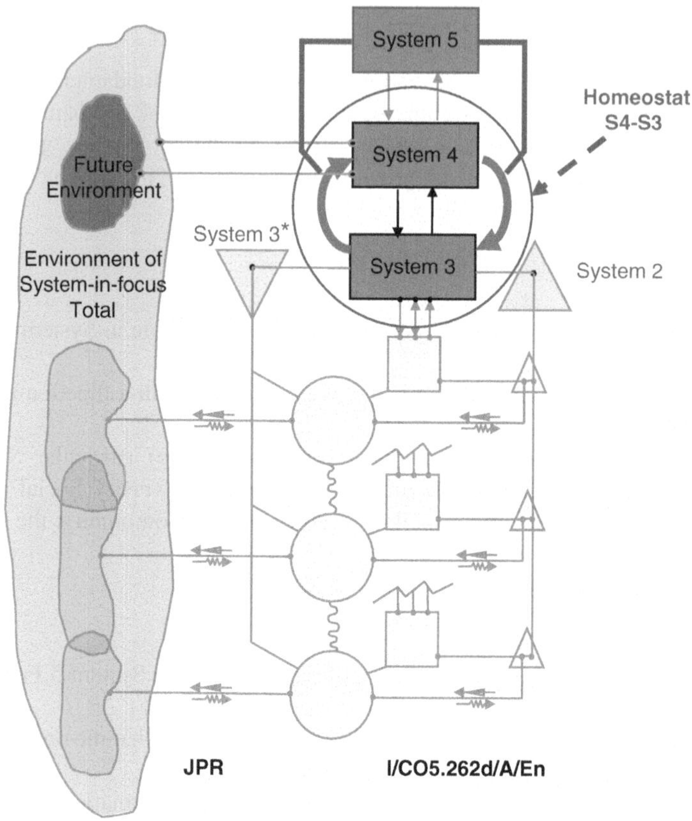

Fig. 2.22 System 5 and System 4-System 3 Homeostat (Pérez Ríos 2008e)

In Relation to Managing the System 4–System 3 Homeostat

- Have procedures been drawn up (temporal cadence, adequate space, topics to consider) to facilitate interaction between representatives of System 5 and the essential components of Systems 4 and 3?
- Are there procedures or elements that warn System 5 of the need to intervene in order to resolve the issues that Systems 3 and 4 in combination are unable to resolve?
- Is there something similar to the "Operations room or decision environment", described in Sect. 3 of Chap. 1, to assist the components of the Meta-system (Systems 3-4-5) in studying the given problematic situations (Fig. 2.23)?

Finally, a further set of questions concerning System 5 should be addressed toward assessing the extent to which the entire organisation shares the same vision and identity, etc. For this purpose, it is necessary to explore how such aspects are

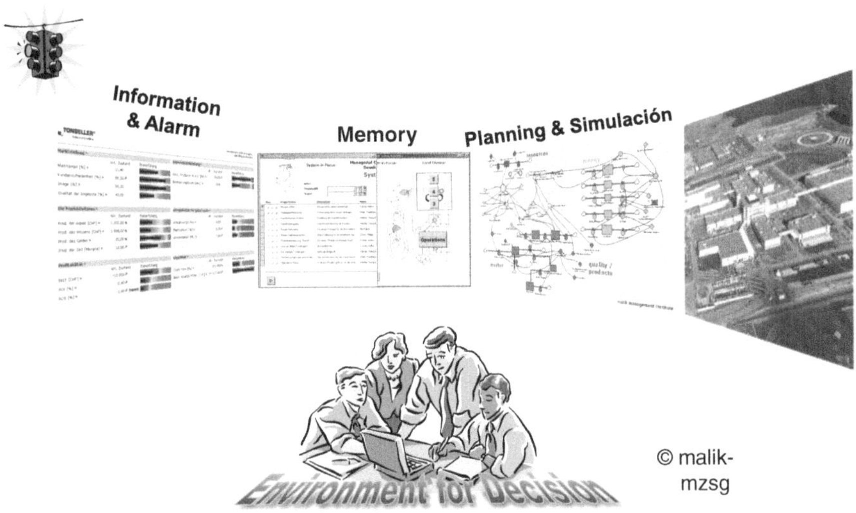

Fig. 2.23 Elements of an "Operations Room". Courtesy of Malik Management Zentrum St. Gallen. Authorised reproduction

perceived both inside the organisation-in-focus and on the preceding and subsequent levels of recursion (Fig. 2.24).

Coherence in the Perception of Identity Among Different Recursion Levels

- Is the identity assumed in System 5 shared and understood by System-1 components?
- Is the identity assumed in System 5 of the system-in-focus coherent with that of the preceding recursion level?
- Do formal or informal procedures exist for communicating and sharing identity between System 5 of the system-in-focus and that of the previous level or levels of recursion?

Now that we have an idea of the organisation's identity, and have also ascertained the types of diverse elements necessary for System 5 to perform its function, let us take a look at System 4.

2.3.1.2 System 4

In Sect. 3 of Chap. 1, I described the main functions of System 4, so it is now appropriate to make an evaluation, on the one hand, of *the existence and composition* of this function in the organisation we are scrutinising,, and, on the other, of the *quality of its performance*, and finally to investigate the quality of the

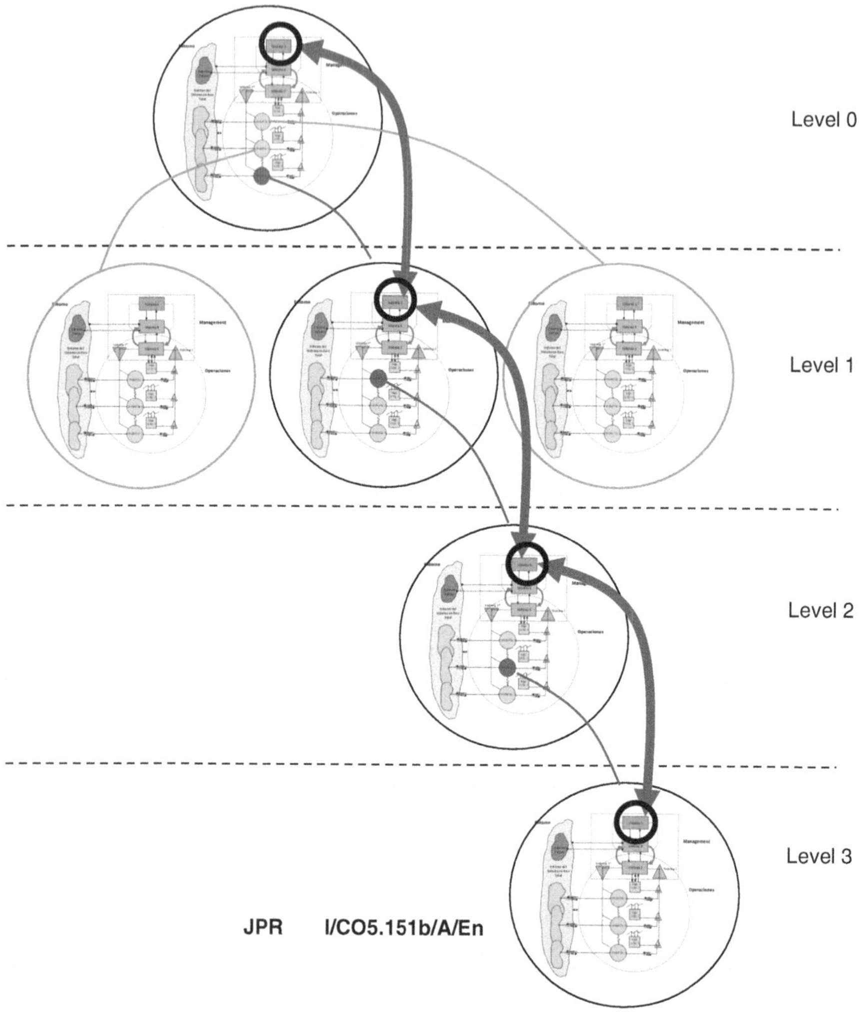

Fig. 2.24 Connexions between Systems 5 of different recursion levels (Pérez Ríos 2008e)

connection between System-4 elements and the remaining systems or functions of the complete system in our particular organisation (Fig. 2.25). Some of the questions that should be raised, or points that should be made explicit, are now outlined.

Concerning the Existence and Quality of System 4

- A description of the management, individuals or organs (Departments, Sections, Units, etc.) whose activity is associated with the purpose of System 4.

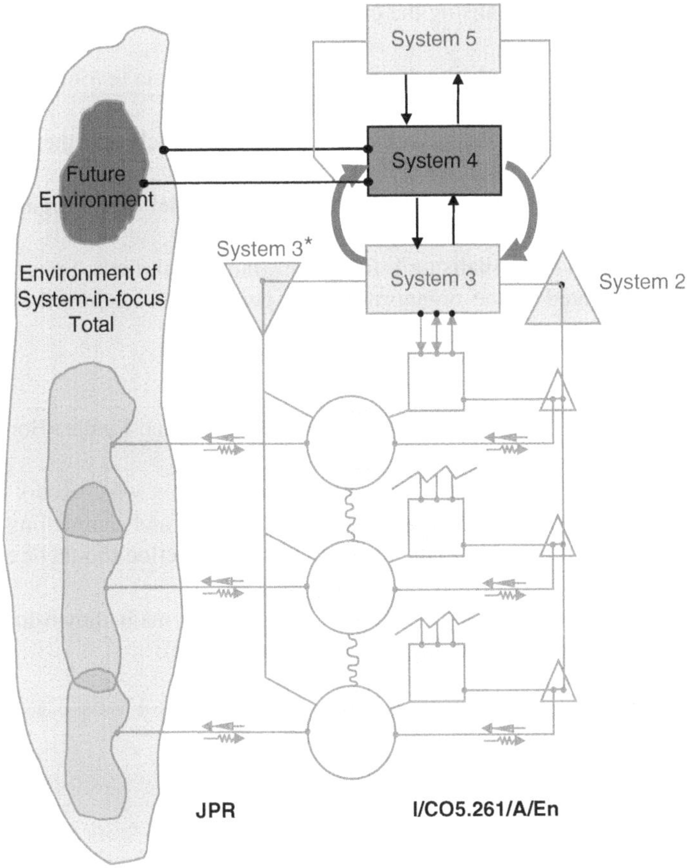

Fig. 2.25 System 4 (Pérez Ríos 2008e)

- An explicit description of the activities that each of the former undertakes, and which are related to the purpose of System 4.
- A description of the means employed by the organisation to help the System-4-related activities to the above-mentioned managers, individuals or organs. In this context, it should be ascertained whether, among other things:

  (a) Simulation models exist (e.g., System Dynamic Models, or Simulation Models in general based on other methodologies).
  (b) Tools are used for carrying out prospective studies (e.g., Delphi Method).
  (c) Methods are employed to explore alternative decisions based on scenarios.
  (d) Other methodologies, methods or techniques different from the former are employed. If this is the case, they should be described.
  (e) There is something similar to the "Operations room" or "Decision-taking environment" previously referred to, the principal components of which are:

1. Element for visualising the current results of the critical variables, fed in real time;
2. Element for visualising the organisation's past data (evolution over time of the relevant variables);
3. Screens for visualising both the simulation models and their results, to provide information for decision making;
4. Screens for visualising the Viable System Model of the organisation in question and its various recursion levels;
5. Element/s for visualising information (numerical, texts, images, videos, etc.) related to the organisation and pertinent to feeding the decision-taking process.

"Horizontal" Relations: System 4: Environment (Present and Future) Homeostats

Given that the fundamental role of System 4 is monitoring what occurs or might occur in the environment, capturing pertinent information and channelling (including "transduction") this to within the organisation, this function should be explicitly dealt with.

In Sect. 3 of Chap. 1, it was seen that some of the main dimensions in the environment to be taken into account were (among others):

Commercial
Social
Demographic
Technological
Political
Legal
Economic
Ecological
Educational

In this review section, when considering the "horizontal" axis we must take into consideration the development of:

(a) The "sensors" installed or available in the environment. In this context, we must evaluate, on the one hand, the type of sensor employed or to be employed and, on the other, where these are located and to which dimension they correspond.
(b) The "transducers" that will convert the information captured into an intelligible language for the various elements in the organisation.
(c) The "channels for communication" currently used or which will be used to transmit this, with consideration given to both their "capacity" (e.g., Bandwidth) and their temporal cadence.
(d) The "recipients" of this information (persons, sections, groups, etc.) and
(e) The manner in which this information is or will be shown (e.g., by means of graphs, numerical data, texts, videos, etc.) and the support (written format

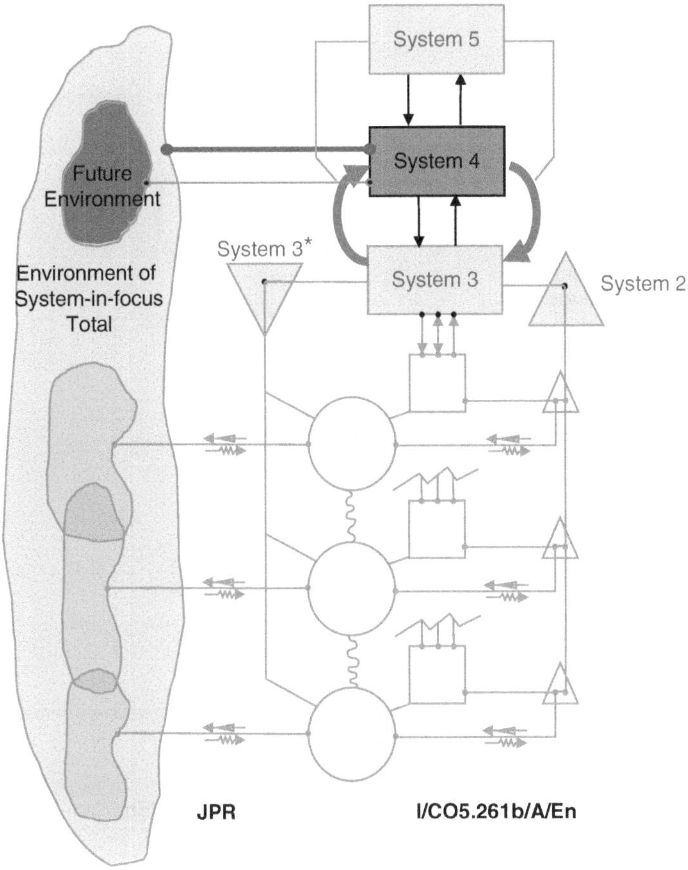

Fig. 2.26 System 4 – Present Environment (Pérez Ríos 2008e)

or via personal computer screens or large-format screens in decision-taking rooms, etc.).

These fundamental aspects should be assessed in the two critical homeostats, the "System 4-Present Environment Homeostat" (Fig. 2.26) and the "System 4-Future Environment Homeostat" (Fig. 2.27).

Here are some examples of questions to be considered in each one.

System 4-Present Environment Homeostat

– Description of the "sensors" available in the environment for capturing information concerning elements of the present environment related to our organisation. By way of example, if the latter is a company, such elements may be associated with dimensions such as:

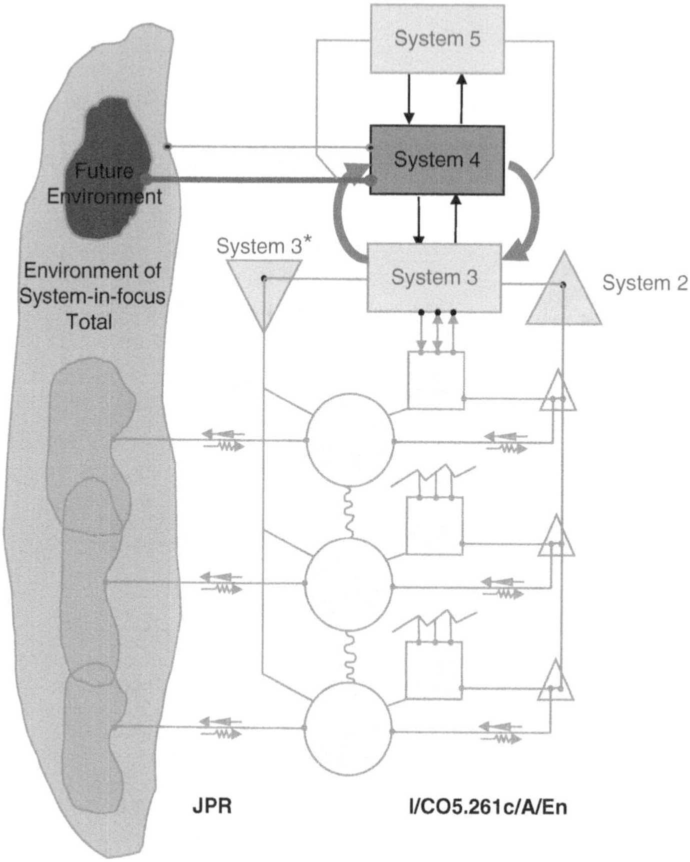

Fig. 2.27 System 4-Future environment (Pérez Ríos 2008e)

- Presence and behaviour of our competitors
- Emerging markets
- New technologies
- Legal changes
- Impact of globalisation
- Modifications in the sector (mergers, takeovers, etc.)
- Impact of current regulations relating to environmental issues
- etc.

– Characteristics of the communication channels and of all their components.
– "Recipients" of the information and how it is presented.

System 4-Future Environment Homeostat

Besides looking into the environment's foreseeable trajectory in each of these fundamental dimensions, we must also evaluate the effect such changes may have on our organisation; as a result, we should undertake, among other actions:

- A review of our vision
- A review of our mission
- A review of our objectives
- A review of our business model
- The chances of profitable growth
- An evaluation of the new challenges for our organisation (for example, for a company these may be: future potential competitors, technological changes, changes in market behaviour and other previously-mentioned environmental dimensions).
- The necessity and chances of transforming our organisation (market, products, structure, etc.)
- The necessity and chances of expanding internationally
- etc.

Functioning and Communication

Following this evaluation of the degree to which System 4 is present in our organisation, what it comprises, the means at its disposal, its functions, its dealings with the (present and future) environment, and the actual development of the two homeostats connecting this system with the environment, it is now appropriate to consider how it is linked with the other systems/functions of the organisation under study. In particular, we should analyse its connection with System 3 and System 5, as well as with the other organisations belonging to different levels of recursion in our system as a whole, assessing the quality with which these relationships work.

Relations with System 3: System 3–System 4 Homeostat

I said before that the main role of System 3 is to manage the organisation's "here and now", that is, the daily situation of the elements that make up System 1, with the help of System 2 and System 3*. The organisation's viability depends on its adapting to the changes and needs determined by the evolution of the environment. Detecting and conveying these to the interior of the organisation is the mission of System 4. Therefore, we should make sure that there exist, on the one hand, communication channels between System 4 and System 3 (with all the components required for them to work properly) and, on the other, the means to facilitate dialogue between these two systems so that both of them are in a position to transmit necessary information to the other system. In the case of System 3, such information will be concerned with restrictions and specific timing constraints within System 1 for the appropriate (non-destructive) adaptation to take place. As for System 4, this will be data on the changes considered necessary to be implemented by System 1 if the organisation is to remain viable. This interaction between System 4 and System 3 is accounted for by the System 4-System 3

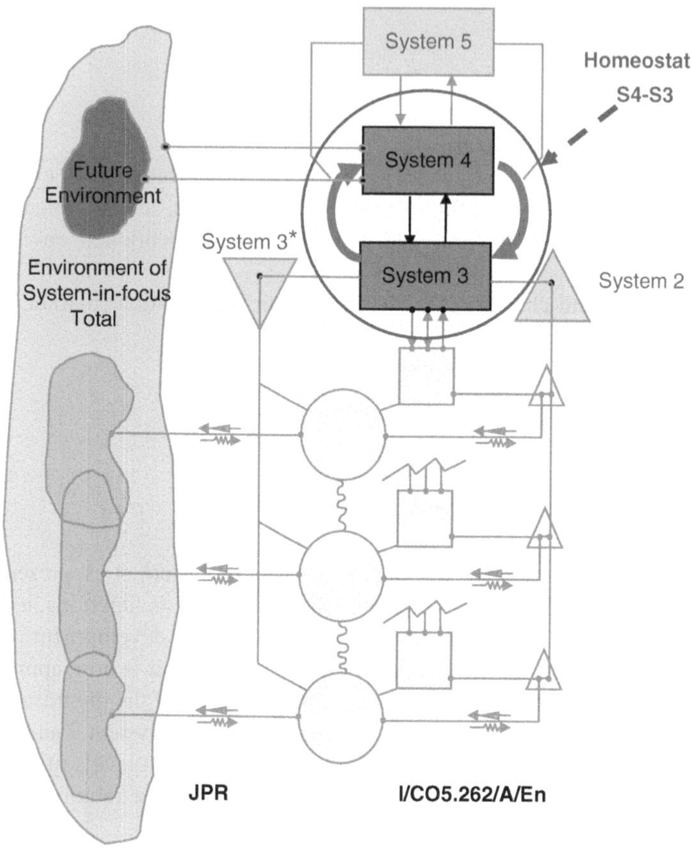

Fig. 2.28 System 4–System 3 Homeostat (Pérez Ríos 2008e)

Homeostat; its proper functioning is critical for an organisation's viability since, as we saw before, this unit is its adaptation organ (Fig. 2.28).

As a consequence, the questions or aspects which must be carefully considered are those such as:

- Describing the formal channels of communication between System 4 and System 3. Reviewing in each of them the eight typical elements of the homeostat (components, transducers, channels), temporal cadence, etc.
- Responding to the same question, but now in terms of the informal communication channels (meetings called, etc.).
- Describing the available resources for facilitating "conversation" between representatives of System 3 and System 4. In this context, one should check for the existence of the types of aids referred to in Sect. 3 of Chap. 1, such as:
- Methodological and functional: Simulation Models, scenarios, prospective studies, software tools for specific purposes (Interdelphi, Col-KCap, etc.).

– Related to physical support: visualisation panels, large-format computer screens, networked computers, etc.

Concerning this question, the availability of an "Operations Room" or a "Decision-taking environment" such as the one mentioned previously is fundamental for facilitating "conversations" between Systems 3 and 4.

In cases where the complexity and size of the problem requires it, the use of group decision techniques (Brainstorming, Nominal Group Technique, etc.) is to be recommended, or, if possible, Team Syntegrity. Chap. 5 of this book explains the fundamental nature and basic application protocols of Team Syntegrity.

Relations with System 5

In the description of System 5′s characteristics, an indication was given of some of its needs for communicating with the rest of the organisation. Consequently, we should simply verify:

– The existence of both formal and informal communication channels between System 4 and System 5.
– The nature and composition of these channels. Once again, we should make sure that all the typical components of a communication channel are present, properly developed and working.
– In the line of communication between System 5 and System 4, we must check above all:
  • Its existence (the variety of lines of communication, formats, frequency, etc.).
  • The content of the information transmitted (aspects regarding the Vision, Mission, Goals, Instructions and commands regarding actions to take, etc.).
– In the line of communication extending from System 4 to System 5, we should check:
  • Its existence (variety of lines of communication, formats, frequency, etc.).
  • The content of the information transmitted (issues relating to adapting the organisation to present and future needs; questions concerning the Vision, Mission and Goals, etc.).
  • The existence of the algedonic channel warning of serious risks for the organisation´s survival.
  • The make-up of the algedonic channel: connecting elements (where the "sensors" are installed and how information within System 5 is visualised, who receives it, how it is shown), transducers, and channel characteristics (capacity).

Finally, I must add that the link between the System 3–System 4 homeostat and System 5 was dealt with when we analysed System 5.

Relation Between Systems 4 in the Different Recursion Levels

Given that System 4 has to be continually examining the possibilities of change and evaluating them with the aid of various tools such as Simulation Models, etc., and with the contribution of System 3, it is clear that assessments of both the diverse strategic as well as general options should be coherent between the different organisations situated at the different recursion levels in the global organisation (Fig. 2.29).

Certain tools like Systems Dynamics allow us to build models with varying degrees of aggregation; therefore, it is possible to make that the outputs of more

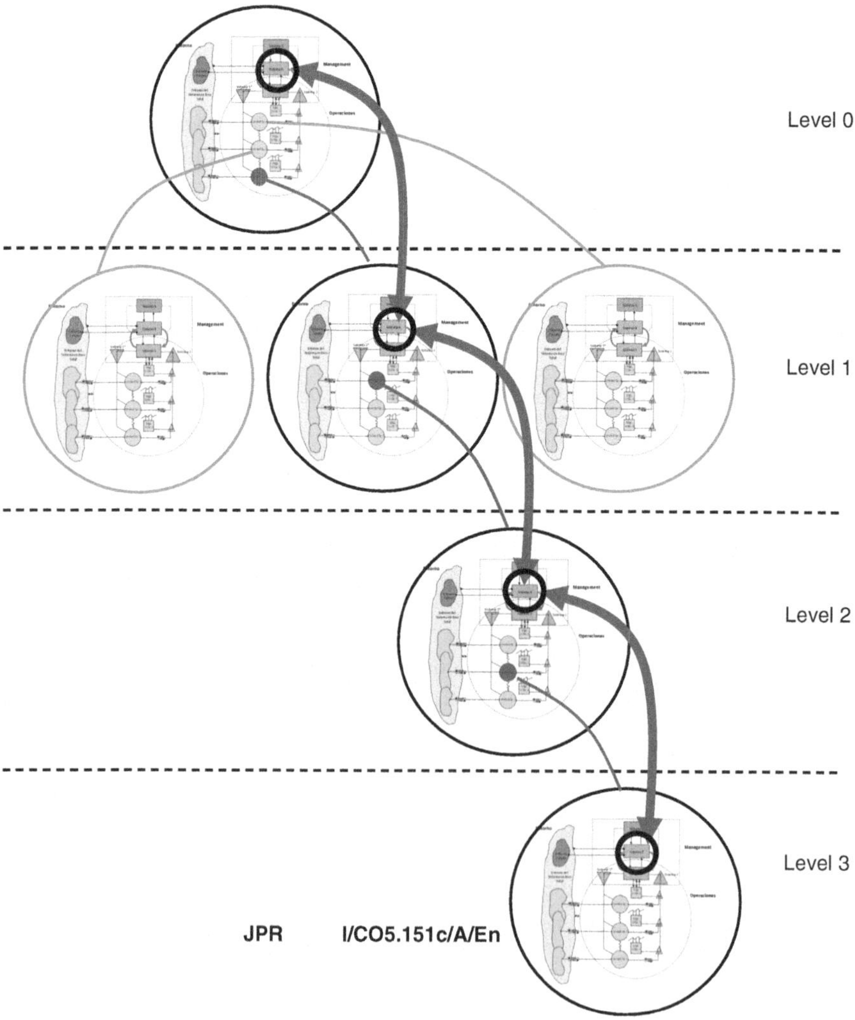

Fig. 2.29 Connections between Systems 4 for different recursion levels (Pérez Ríos 2008e)

detailed models be the inputs of more aggregated models, with the result that the consistence and coherence between the different models can always be verified.

This check is especially necessary in the VSM, as all strategic planning processes are linked via the model's recursive nature. Each organisation is part of another at the previous recursion level, and so on and so forth. Thus, we should make sure that this coherence really exists.

As regards this point, we should ask such questions as:

- Do the models employed in System 4 permit the inclusion of different levels of aggregation which make it possible to connect aspects of the organisation that correspond to various recursion levels?
- Are there any formal or informal procedures for checking the coherence of the procedures for strategic planning, simulation, exploration of scenarios, etc., among the diverse levels of recursion?
- Are there any communication channels between the different Systems 4 at different recursion levels?

Having examined the components of the organisation-in-focus's Meta-system (Management), referred to as System 5, System 4 and the System 4-System 3 Homeostat, our next step is concentrate on the operations of the organisation or System. To recapitulate, this comprises System 3, System 3*, System 2 and System 1, with all their corresponding communication links. Also, we have seen that System 3 has a dual role, insofar as it belongs to both the System and the Meta-system (together with System 4 and System 5), a point to which I will return at a later stage.

2.3.2 *System (Organisation/Operations: System 3, System 3*, System 2, System 1)*

2.3.2.1 System 3

System 3 (Fig. 2.30) is the third component (alongside System 4 and System 5) of the organisation-in-focus's "meta-system", which is equivalent to the "Management" of the set of operations in the system-in-focus made up of System 3, System 2 and System 1, in addition to System 3*. As we can see, System 3 is present in both components, that is, in the Meta-system and the System (or set of operations), which gives it a peculiar position. This has been studied by authors such as Yolles (personal communication, 2007), who in order to explain this dual role differentiate between System 3a and System 3b, depending on the type of activity in which System 3 is involved.

The basic function of this system is, as I have already pointed out, to manage the current functions of the organisation in order for it to continuously supply the environment with what its responsibility designates it to provide (goods, services, etc.). This function is generally referred to (when drastically simplifying Beer's

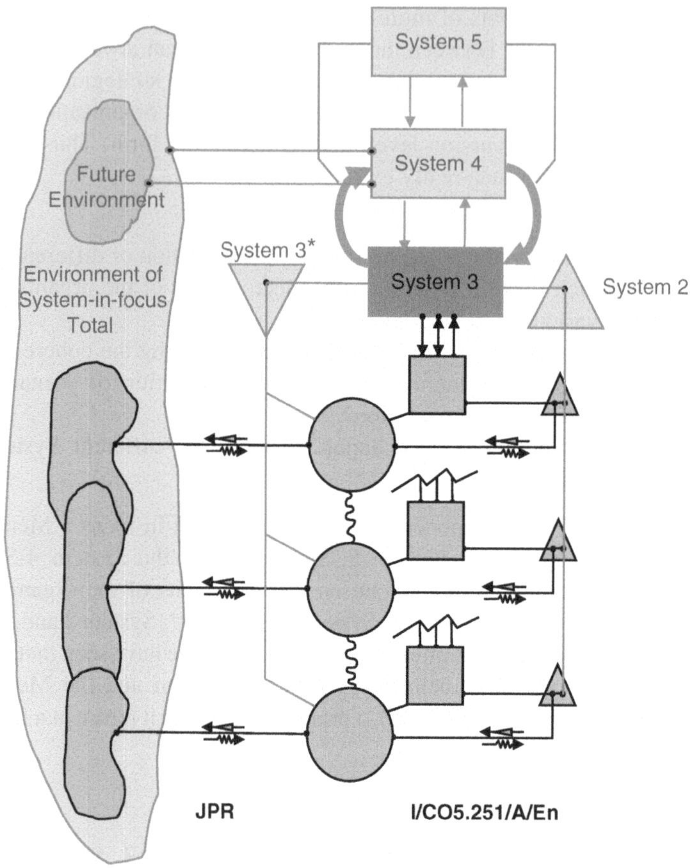

Fig. 2.30 System 3 (Pérez Ríos 2008e)

intentionally broad term, implicit in System 3) as that of "Management and integration" or also "Implementation and integration".

However, another function of this system is to continually transform System 1 so that, without putting its normal operations in danger of collapsing, it can incorporate the incremental modifications or even radical changes proposed by System 4 and agreed to by System 5 as necessary for viability (beyond survival). In this case, System 3 acts as a transmitter of downward information.

A further function of System 3 is to inform System 4 about the real "chances" of transformation in System 1, including information picked up by the elementary operational units that constitute the latter in their respective environments; such information may concern both the present and future environment, but at their most reduced level. In fact, when capturing this type of information, we could regard it as more typical of System 4, which strictly speaking is the case, since by descending to the following recursion level where the new system-in-focus would be one of those elementary operational units, we would be looking at functions corresponding to

System 4. These connections between recursion levels are somewhat intellectually complex, but this is perfectly manageable once the VSM as a whole has been mastered. Now System 3 acts as a conveyor of upward information.

Returning to the role of System 3 as an integrator of System 1 components and the latter's link with the Meta-system, it is appropriate to recall the three essential kinds of activities it performs in relation to System 1 and its components:

(a) *Setting goals* for each of the units comprising System 1, as well as conveying information from the "Meta-system" regarding the translation to this level of the "Vision", "Mission", "specific Goals" and "Ethos"; in other words, the way the organisation should behave, its character and how it is hoped that it should be seen or perceived both externally and internally (Fig. 2.31).

(b) *Negotiating resources*. In order to make it possible to meet its objectives and deal with the other issues mentioned, each elementary operational unit in System 1 must be supplied with the resources required for it to function.

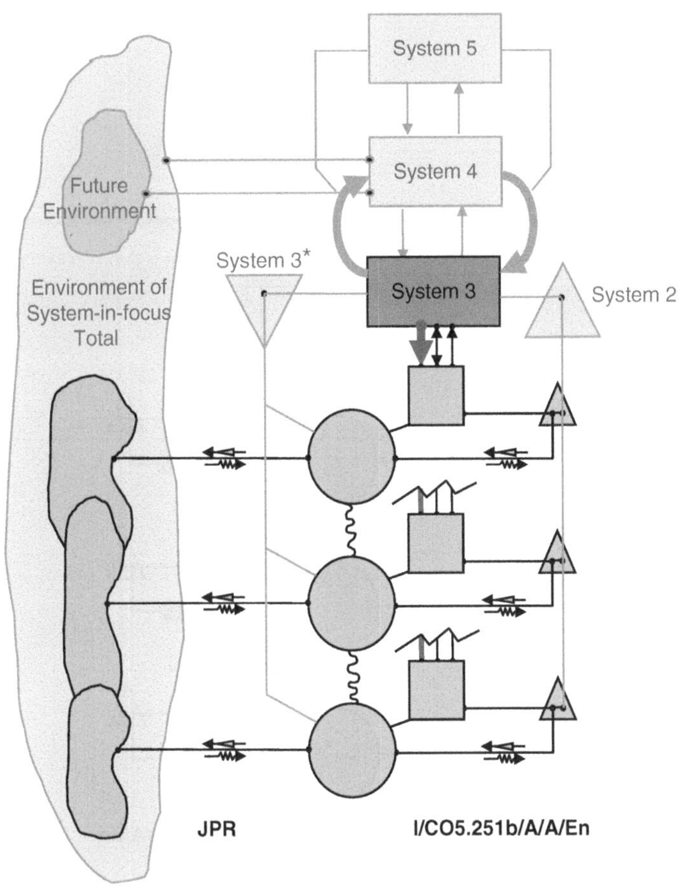

Fig. 2.31 System 3 (Transmission of instructions) (Pérez Ríos 2008e)

This process of "negotiation of resources" is handled jointly by the "Management" of each of the elementary operational units making up System 1 and System 3 (manager responsible). Together they will reach an agreement on the available resources, bearing in mind that the only system which possesses a global vision of the whole of System 1 and the needs of each of its elementary units is System 3 (Fig. 2.32).

The assigning of resources to each unit must be accompanied by a commitment from the latter to meet the specified objectives. In this context, I consider that techniques like "Management by objectives" may be helpful.

(c) Finally, once the objectives have been set and the corresponding resources allotted, the *Accountability* procedure should be established. The "Management" of each elementary operational unit in System 1 should keep System 3

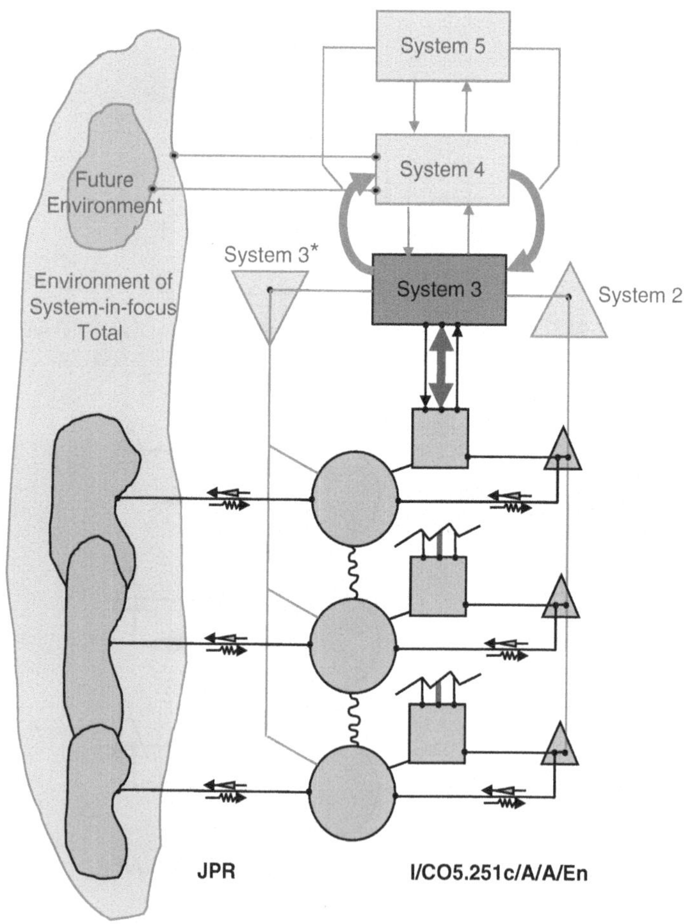

Fig. 2.32 System 3 (Negotiation of resources) (Pérez Ríos 2008e)

informed as to how far objectives are met within their unit. In addition, they should tell this System about any risk or aspect which may seriously affect compliance (Fig. 2.33).

Now that we have "identified" the main functions of System 3, we will go on, as we did when examining System 1, to evaluate, on the one hand, *the existence and composition* of the System-3 function in the organisation under study, and also to inspect the *quality of its performance*, considering finally the quality of the *connection* between System 3′s elements and the other systems or functions of the complete system of the organisation in question. Below are some of the questions to be asked or points to be made explicit.

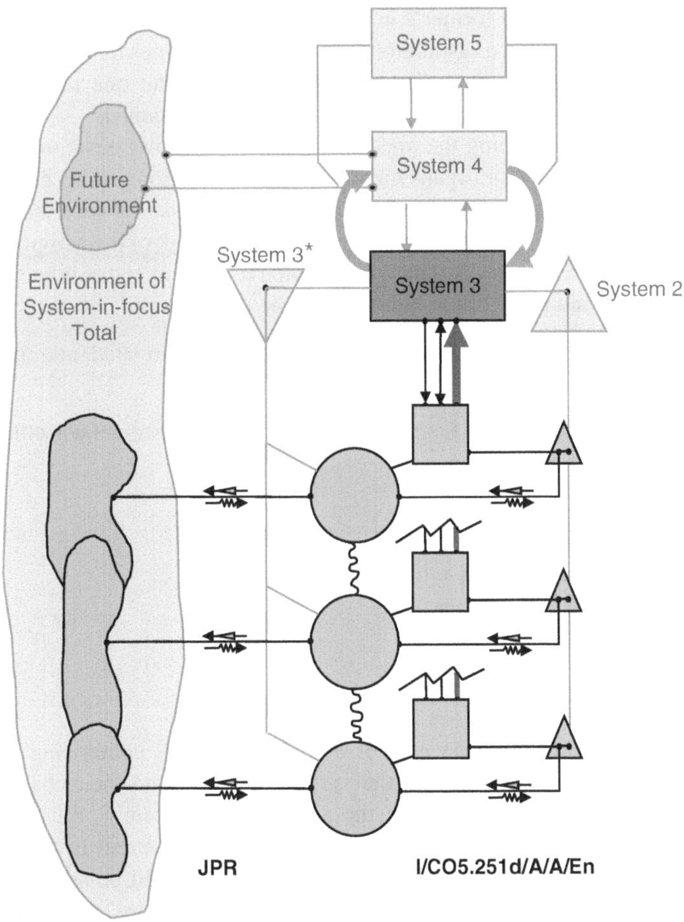

Fig. 2.33 System 3 (Accountability) (Pérez Ríos 2008e)

Existence and Composition

System 3 is normally one of the five VSM systems that is practically always quite well represented, which is logical when we consider that, if it did not exist, the organisation-in-focus's operations unit would be formed by a set of components (its elementary operational units) that would attempt to achieve their aims individually, paying no attention to the effect of their actions on the rest. Chaos and "every man for himself" would predominate. Obviously, such a situation cannot be sustained for very long.

Consequently, the first set of questions should relate to questions concerning aspects such as:

– Identifying and describing the managers, individuals or organs (Departments, Sections, Units, etc.) whose activity is associated with the integrating aim of System 3.
– Describing each of the former's activities relating to the purpose of System 3. It is important to make a distinction between the two types of System-3 activity previously referred to, analysing, on the one hand, the one more related to System 4 and, on the other, the one more related to System 1.
– Identifying and describing the means employed by the organisation to help the managers, individuals or organs mentioned previously to perform their System-3-related tasks. Once again, a distinction should be made between the two kinds of System-3 activity, with a study made, on the one hand, of the activity nearer to System 4 and, on the other, of that more related to System 1; this is because some of the tools or aid elements to be used may be different.

The following examples may be cited as System-3-related activities for a company:

– First of all, as management functions characteristic of System 3 we will list those relating to the areas of:

  • Marketing and Sales
  • Human Resources
  • Productivity and Quality
  • Production and Operations
  • Engineering
  • Accounting
  • Budgeting

– Secondly, System 3 has the task of defining the units comprising System 1 (the complete operations unit of the system-in-focus) and their characteristics (Fig. 2.34). Here, System 3, with the approval of System 5, must define the components of System 1, the limits of each and the resources to be employed. At the same time, the purpose or aim of each unit should be specified, which concrete objectives underpin this aim, what resources are involved (human, financial, technological, physical, etc.) and, finally, what indicators are to be

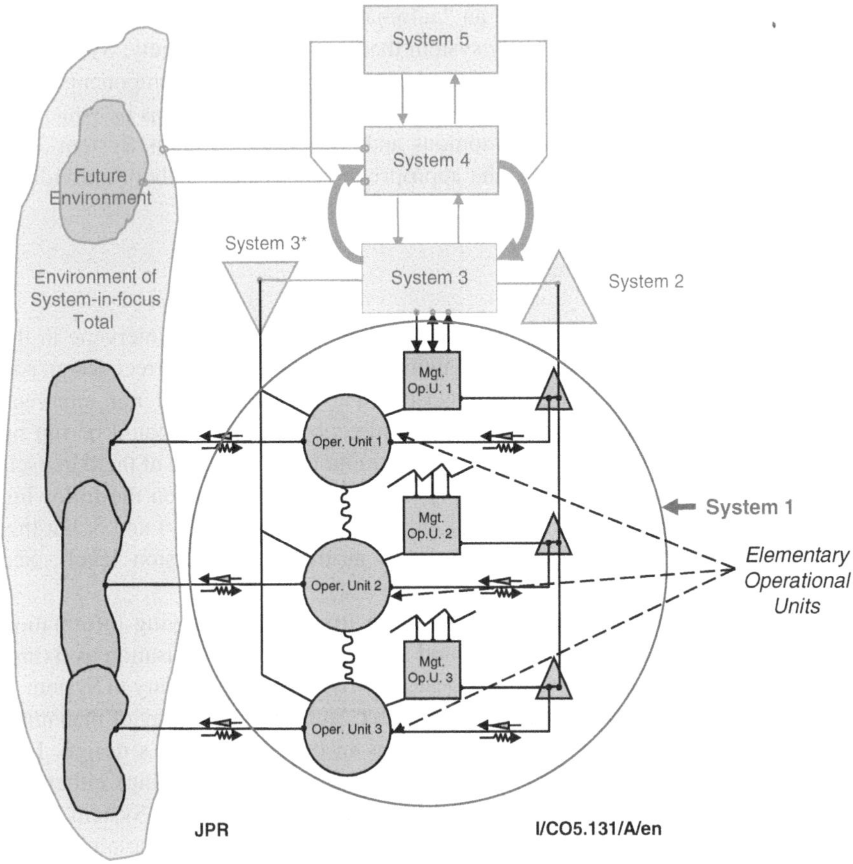

Fig. 2.34 System 1 (Pérez Ríos 2008e)

used in order to measure the extent to which each elementary unit meets these objectives. It is important to decide on indicators which are coherent with each area deemed critical for the organisation (see System 5).

– Thirdly, System 3 has to integrate the different elementary units that go to make up System 1. It must ensure that the various units work in harmony so that they perform their tasks in a coordinated and stable manner. For this to be achieved, System 3 also has the support of System 2 and System 3*, which we will examine later in greater detail.
– A further activity of System 3 is that of designing the components to include in System 2. It should not be forgotten that the aim of this system is to facilitate coordination among the elementary units, so that ideally these can work harmoniously and without any conflict. In order for this to occur, it is vital that System 3 supply all the information on both the whole of System 1 and on each of its units (goals, resources, etc.), to enable the construction of the coordination

mechanisms that make possible an "automatic" functioning without the necessity of direct control by the only system that could do this, namely, System 3.
- At the same time, System 3 must intervene in designing the components to be included in System 3*. Just as System 2 helps to create the means by which the elementary units work in a harmonious and coordinated fashion, System 3* is responsible for contributing to the appropriate "behaviour" by both individuals as well as units or their parts.

Quality of System 3 Performance

It is important to remember that this system should not normally intervene in the workings of the elementary operational units. An indicator of the correct design and functioning of the organisation is precisely that System 3 need not intervene directly in matters concerning these units. This is because they should be run by their own "management" with a high level of autonomy, since each of them in itself is a complete viable system (if we apply the "zoom" and focus on the following recursion level, we will once again be looking at Systems 1, 2, 3, 4 and 5, but this time belonging to the new system-in-focus at the next recursion level). See Figs. 1.40 and 1.41.

Direct involvement by System 3 should be limited to conveying information from the "meta-system" on aspects related to the aim of the organisation as fixing/modifying objectives, or to changes suggested by System 4 as necessary in System 1, and to the negotiation of resources. Using direct "authority" as a way of managing is, generally speaking, a sign of shortcomings in the organisation's design. It is usually due to certain necessary functions (those we are describing) either not existing or not working properly. Use of the vertical line between System 3 and each of the units in System 1 to "impose decisions by authoritarian means" indicates that the organisation has been badly designed or is not working as it should. Among the reasons against employing this measure is System 3′s lack of detailed knowledge concerning the variety (complexity) within each of the elementary units. A manager acting in this way would most likely be drastically attenuating the variety of what he is endeavouring to "govern", by taking decisions based on models of the problem without the requisite variety, with the corresponding harmful consequences. The impact on both the general performance of the unit affected and on the motivation and self-esteem of the managers concerned may be a very negative one.

The next point to consider when diagnosing the adequacy of System 3, or to bear in mind when designing a new organisation or system, is the relationship between that system and all the others. Let us have a look.

The Relationship Between the Elements in System 3 and the Other Components of the Operations Set (System)

We will now, therefore, review the content of the relations between System 3 and the three remaining components of the operations set (or system), namely,

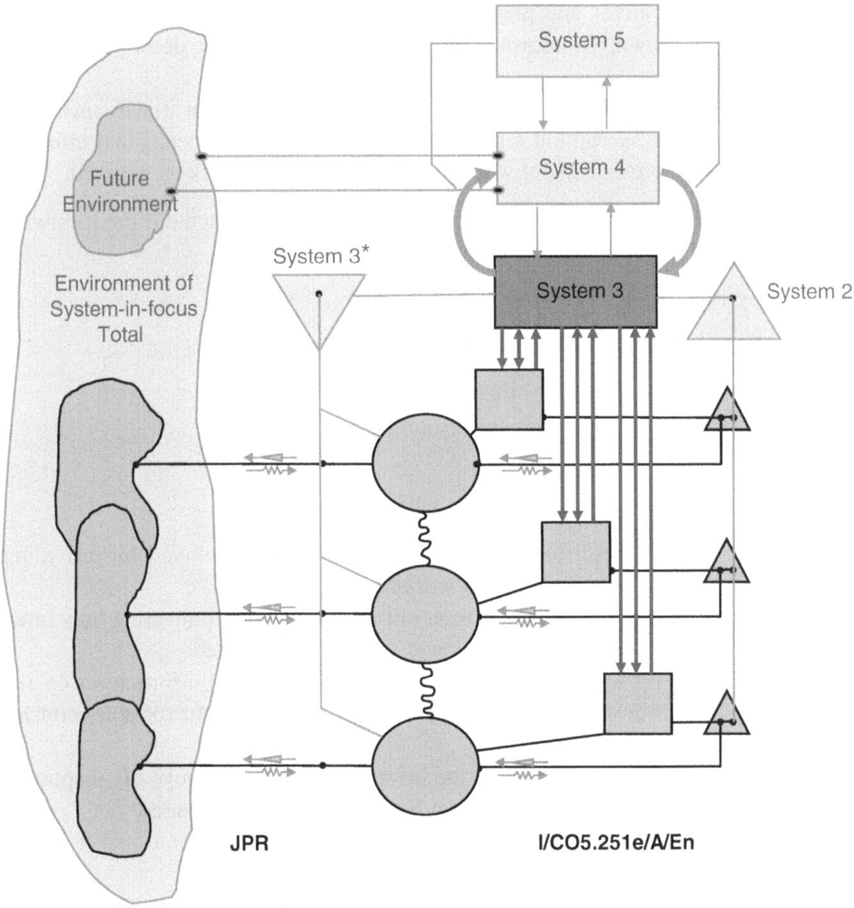

Fig. 2.35 Relationship of S3 with each unit in S1 (Pérez Ríos 2008e)

System 1, System 2 and System 3*. We will begin by commenting on the relations, in this case vertical, between System 3 and operational units in System 1 (Fig. 2.35).

Vertical Relations with the Operational Units in System 1

The questions to be answered in connection with this set of relations concern aspects such as the following:

- Regarding the managerial style, that is, the manner in which System 3 relates to those responsible for the elementary operational units, there should be a response to questions like:

- How the objectives and planning are set out. Specification of the approach used (Top-Down, Bottom-up, Interactive, etc.). Explicit description of the management style.
- Indicate if use is made of "Management by Objectives" or its variants.
- Mention if an "exception report" system is used, which means that information is only requested/sent when something does not work as planned.

– Relating to issues handled in the *Resources bargaining* indicate if the following are included:

  - Objectives
  - Means to achieve them
  - Deadlines
  - Rewards for each or all of them
  - Periodicity of negotiation over resources
  - etc.

– A description of how *Accountability* will be handled.

  - Identifying and describing the information systems employed for providing information on how each unit is working.
  - Specifying whether this is real-time information. If not, indicating how often information is emitted for the diverse variables controlled.
  - Indicating whether warning signals are used to supply information on the seriousness of deviations from the objectives highlighted in variables considered critical.
  - Evaluating the extent to which the information to be conveyed (exceptional reports) is suitably selected, so that System 3 is not overloaded.
  - Indicating whether Score Boards suited to the specific operational units are used.

– Describing the method and means employed for transmitting the pertinent *information* in accordance with the System 3-System 1 vertical line.

  - Indicating whether formal procedures are used for sending the information to the "Management" of the operational units. If so, specifying which type.
  - Explaining whether information is given to individuals or to groups.
  - Describing whether information is provided on a fixed regular basis or "depending on the necessity".
  - Specifying the technological resources employed (E-mail, Intranets, etc.).
  - If the means are informal, explaining what they are, and how and when they are used.

Horizontal Relations with System 2 and System 3*

Having examined some of the questions to be considered in the relationship between System 3 and System 1, let us now review certain features of the relations System 3 has with System 2 and System 3*.

Relationship with System 2

I said before that System 2 is a system supporting System 3 (Fig. 2.36), with the task of absorbing large amounts of variety (complexity) generated in System 1 as a consequence of the daily workings of the elementary operational units. A sound organisational design is one which, striving for the maximum degree of operational "automation" for these units, establishes systems for coordinating and resolving problems resulting from interactions among the operational units of System 1 and their competition for the available resources.

Given that the aim is make it easier for System 3 to integrate System 1 components, the former must intervene or at least participate in the design of these systems or coordination tools.

Therefore, responses must be given to questions such as:

- The extent to which System 3 is involved in identifying and proposing System-2 coordination systems.

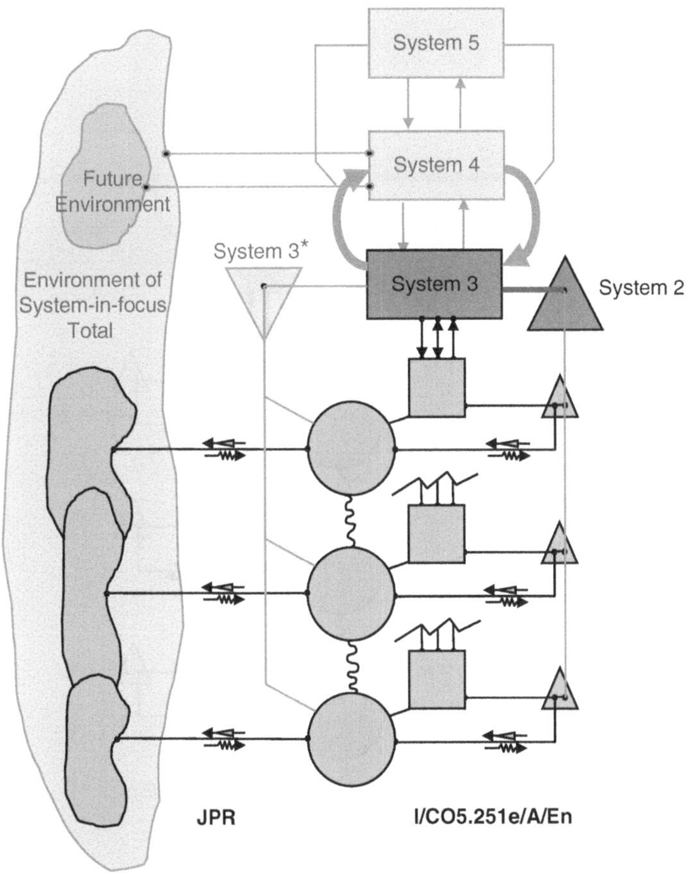

Fig. 2.36 System 3 (Relations with System 2) (Pérez Ríos 2008e)

- Procedures and channels by which information concerning conflicts among the elementary operational units is supplied to System 3.

It is clear that whenever we are referring to the transmission of information we should not forget the essential elements involved therein (sender-receiver elements, transducers and channels of communication).

Relationship with System 3*

With the functions and necessity of this system having been described already in Sect. 3 of Chap. 1, I will limit myself here to recalling the need to verify that the information provided by this channel for use in System 3 is, in the first place, pertinent and, secondly, that it successfully reaches this system (Fig. 2.37).

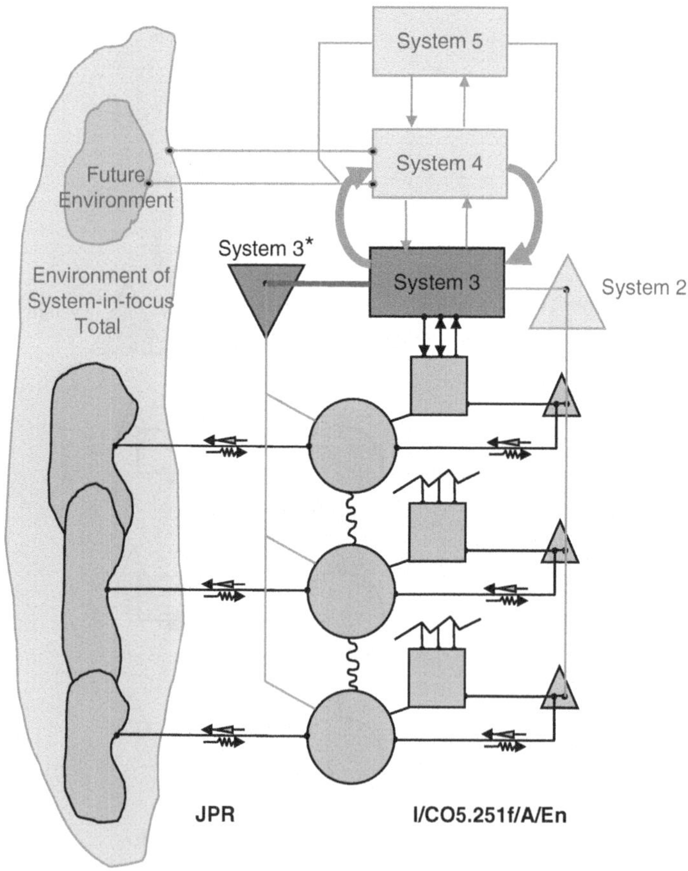

Fig. 2.37 System 3 (Relation with System 3*) (Pérez Ríos 2008e)

We must, therefore, respond to questions concerning:

- The number and description of "existing channels capturing information".
- The issues they attempt to assess.
- How we can be assured that the information captured is complete and arrives with the required temporal cadence for being useful to System 3.

Algedonic Channel

As was seen in Sect. 3 of Chap. 1 when we reviewed the various communication/information channels, the algedonic channel (see Fig. 1.50) has certain special features. This channel's sensors should be positioned at points critical for the organisation. It is a vertical channel transmitting alert signals which, originating in the elementary operational units when one of the variables deemed critical surpasses the alarm threshold, go vertically towards System 5. Of course, they first of all reach System 3, which should deal with the problem; if, however, this does not occur and the alarm is still activated, the message will go through all the systems until arriving at System 5 of the organisation-in-focus. That system, then, will be activated in this exceptional situation, and will , intervene in response to the emergency warning from System 1.

These algedonic channels should be designed specifically for each organisation. In each case it is necessary to define:

- Which variables are to be monitored.
- The nature of the "sensors" at the point where the problem may occur.
- The characteristics of the transducers.
- The design of the communication channel (capacity of the channel).
- The nature of the "activators", that is, the "warnings" at the signal's destination point/s.
- Where the "warnings" (signals by light, sound, images, voice, etc.) should be located.
- The individuals to whom these signals should be directed.

In the section we will see later covering the vertical dimension of System 1, algedonic channels will be described in greater detail.

2.3.2.2 System 3*

In addition to what was said earlier concerning this system (Fig. 2.38) and its relation with System 3, as well as to the description given elsewhere (Sect. 3 of Chap. 1), it is now appropriate to consider the existence of this system/function, its connection with the elementary operational units and the way it works. Among the questions to be dealt with are ones such as:

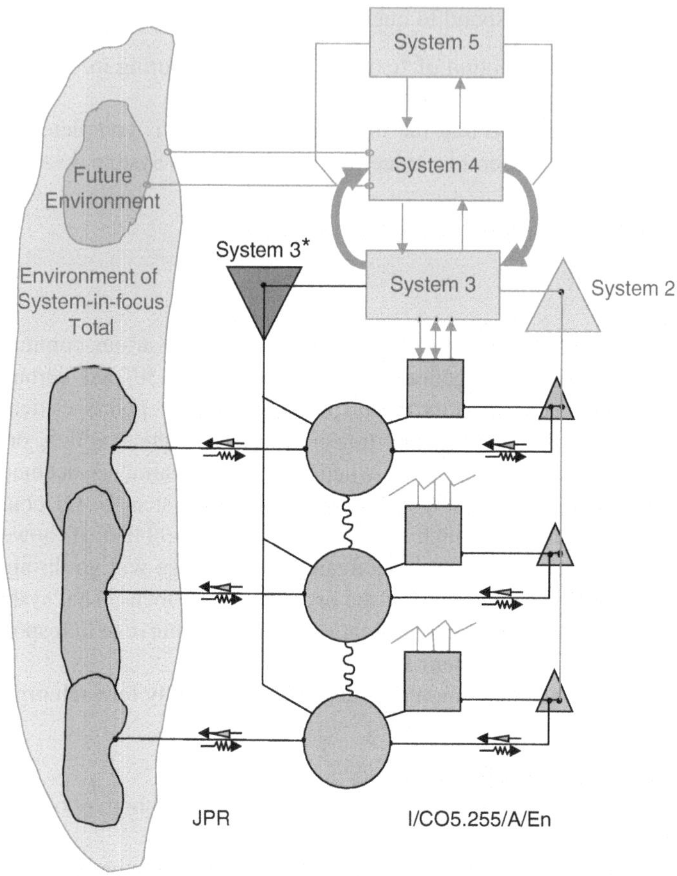

Fig. 2.38 System 3* (Pérez Ríos 2008e)

- Identifying the channels designed for complying with the particular functions of this system (for example, auditing various aspects of the functioning of the operational units, such as quality, integrity, working atmosphere, etc.).
- Describing each of the issues monitored and for which information is captured.
- Explaining the manner in which they obtain information within System-1 operational units.
- Indicating the periodicity of the sampling or capturing of information.
- Showing how information is transmitted to System 3. Regarding this point, we must once again assess the kind of components that are typical of communication/information channels (elements to connect, type of information to transmit, transducers and channels).

As I pointed out when studying System 3, the data provided by System 3* (Fig. 2.39) will be analysed and, should actions be required, these will be directly conveyed by System 3 to System 1 via the vertical information transmission line, in

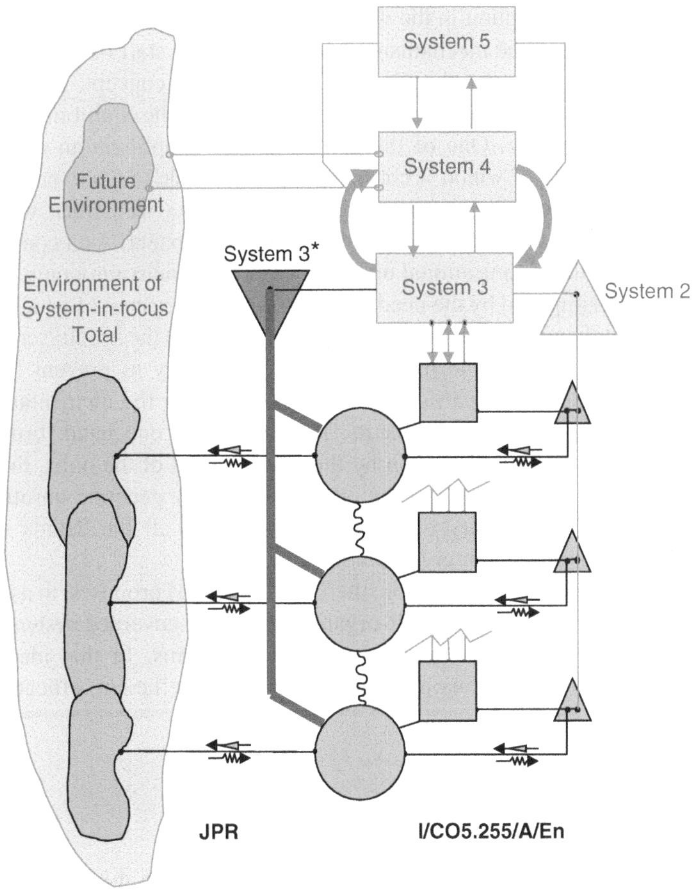

Fig. 2.39 System 3* (Auditing channel) (Pérez Ríos 2008e)

this case in the form of instructions, orders or the type of action the specific situation demands. All the same, intervention by System 3 will not necessarily take place via the above-mentioned vertical channel. In certain situations an analysis of the information generated by System 3* may give rise to the design of a new coordination element (System 2) for tackling the problem detected, and as a result direct involvement via authoritarian means will not be necessary. We must remember once again that the use of this channel is, except in extraordinary circumstances, a sign of failure, in the sense that the organisation is not working as it should. If the organisation is well designed, according to the bases set down in the VSM, the very workings of the various systems/functions and the appropriate transmission of information by the many channels linking all the systems/functions and the organisation with the environment will make it unnecessary for System 3 to intervene via the authoritarian pathway.

This characteristic, implicit in the whole design of the VSM, has, among others, a justification related to the mechanisms I described at the start of this book when, in covering the framework of the "Variety Engineering" concept, I said that the so-called attenuators and amplifiers were necessary to attain the equilibrium in variety required by Ashby's Law. One of the most powerful amplifiers an organisation possesses is the people of which it consists. If it is possible to get everyone to put all their effort into ensuring that the organisation works well, then we will be amplifying the capacity of its managers to an enormous extent. As a consequence, it is important that the organisational units are given maximum autonomy, allowing for the restrictions imposed by the need for cohesion of the system of which they are part, in order that they make use of all their potential to face the specific complexity affecting each one. This is the reason why we should try to prevent the direct intervention of System 3 in particular matters concerning the elementary operational units. If such intervention occurs, it will, on the one hand, bring about a restriction in the capacity for action by the management of the units, limiting at least in part such capacity, and, on the other, most likely generate unsatisfactory results, given the impossibility of System 3′s knowing all the details (variety/complexity) within the elementary operational units.

As a means of general amplification, therefore, the VSM proposes, to as large an extent as possible, the creation of self-organised and self-governed systems within a succession of self-organised and self-governed systems. In this idea resides one of the keys of its enormous potential for achieving efficient, efficacious and effective organisations.

2.3.2.3 System 2

The rationale of this system (Fig. 2.40) having already been discussed, it is now advisable to assess the degree to which it manifests, together with its functioning and relation with the other systems.

- In relation to its existence, that is to say, the quality of its representation in the organisation-in-focus, some of the aspects to analyse are:
  - A description of all the functions, tools, procedures, etc., whose function is related with coordinating, reducing chaos and increasing order in the organisation, in its System 1.
  - A description of the communication channels connecting System 2 and System 3. I have already mentioned that System 2 must filter the information generated in System 1 (within each of its elementary operational units), and convey to System 3 those aspects referring to situations of instability which the self-control mechanisms provided by System 2 are unable to resolve; in this case, direct intervention by System 3 is required.
  - An identification of the communication channels that exist between the "corporate" System 2 (by which is meant the one serving the system-in-focus's System 3) and the System 2s of the elementary operational units.

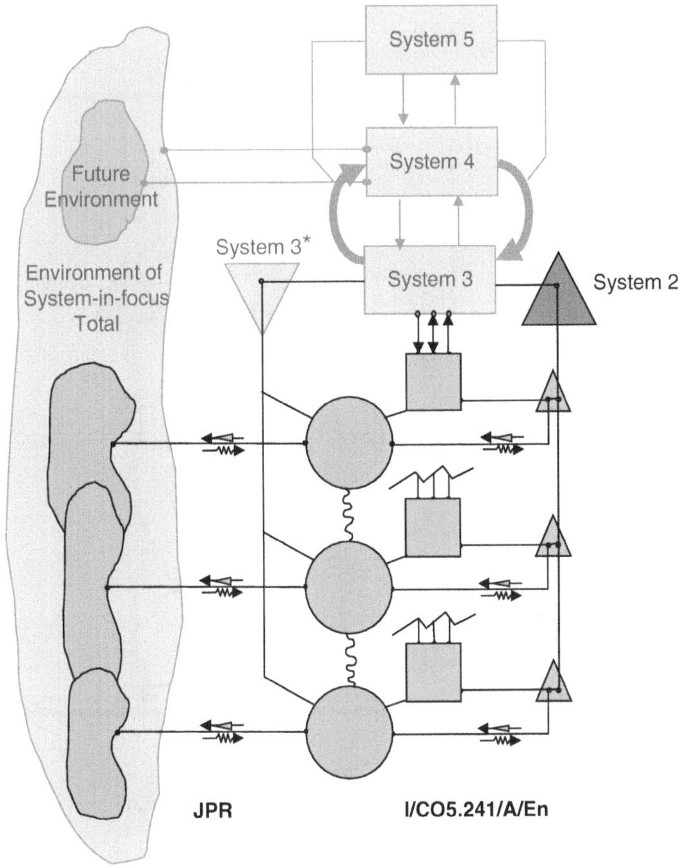

Fig. 2.40 System 2 (Pérez Ríos 2008e)

The "corporate" System 2 (Fig. 2.41) must act as a collector of the information transmitted by the local System 2s corresponding to each of the operational units constituting System 1, which provide information on unresolved conflicts affecting the different units.

In addition, the "corporate" System 2 is responsible for sending to the local System 2s of the elementary operational units the relevant information coming out of System 3 (new working norms, new programming, changes in style, new accounting and legislative regulations, etc.).

This dual channel of vertical communication linking the "corporate" System 2 with the System 2s of each elementary unit must also be well designed and monitored. Therefore, we must again check typical elements (elements to connect, type of information to transmit, transducers and characteristics of the channels).

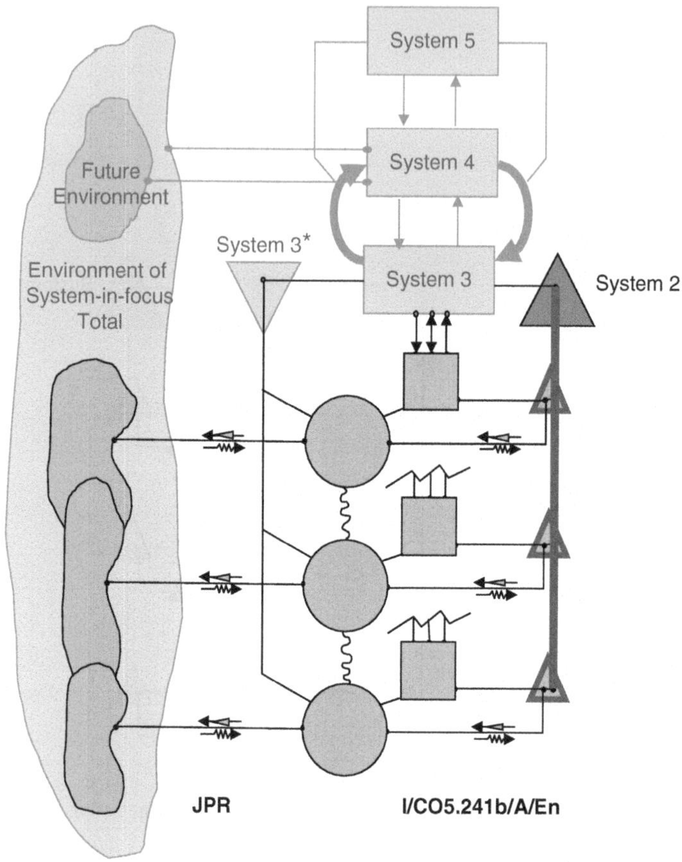

Fig. 2.41 System 2 (Coordinating channel) (Pérez Ríos 2008e)

- A final consideration concerns those who play a role in designing the procedures or tools, etc., pertinent to System 2. It is appropriate that this should obviously be done by the representatives of System 3, as only they have a global vision of the set of units comprising System 1. However, those representing the local System 2s belonging to each of these units, together with their local management representatives, should also intervene.
- This multiple participation is necessary to ensure coherence of procedures and other coordination tools employed among the organisation's diverse levels of recursion.

Consequently, questions relating to the following aspects have to be considered:

- Identifying the persons belonging to System 3 who play a part in designing System-2 elements.
- The same question referring to the management of the elementary units.

- Further questions looking more deeply into whether meetings are held to do this work and, if so, who is involved, how these meetings are called, where, when and what are the means and information used, etc.

2.3.3 System 1: The Operations Units

After this analysis of all the systems (Systems 2, 3, 3*, 4 and 5) whose aim it is to contribute to System 1′s doing what it is supposed to do in line with the purpose of the organisation, we must now check to see that System 1 (Fig. 2.42) has everything it needs in order to perform its function.

System 1 can be made up of several elementary operational units which, for example, in the case of a firm may consist of different product lines, or in

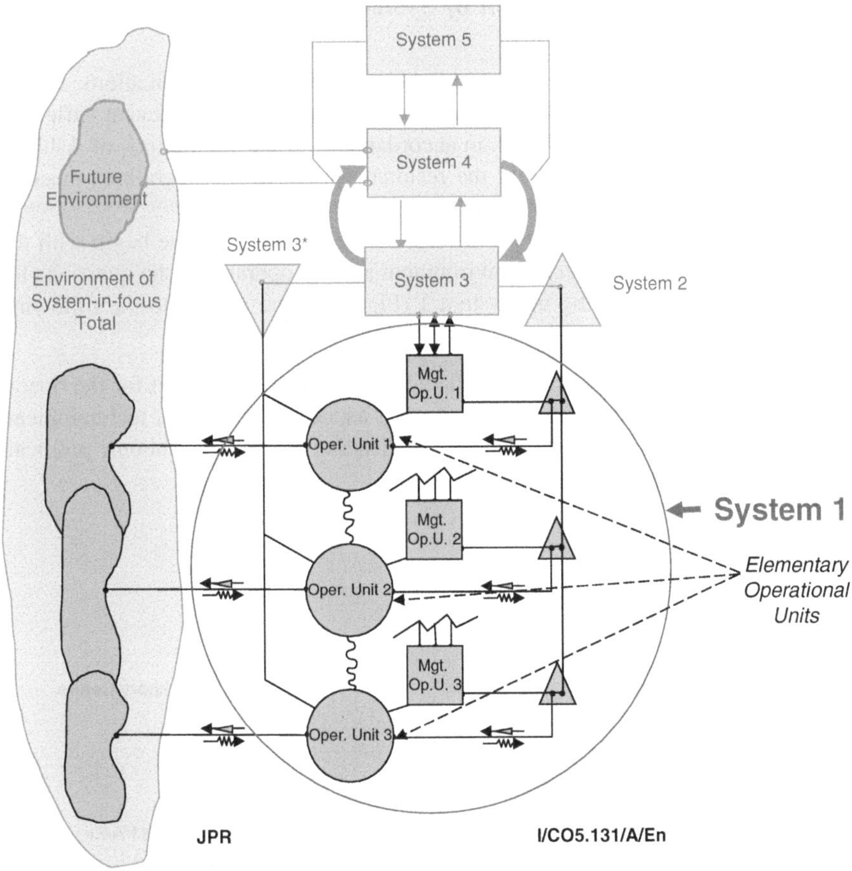

Fig. 2.42 System 1 (Pérez Ríos 2008e)

a university of the different faculties, or in a health system of the various health areas, or in a country of the distinct autonomous communities, etc. From the structural point of view of the VSM, the components of each unit are always the same and consist of: (a) the specific environment, (b) the operational unit in the strict sense (the operations), (c) the management of the operational unit and (d) the specific System 2 of each operational unit. These four elements are connected by information channels so that information flows continuously, guaranteeing a dynamic balance between all the components (see Beer's *First and Second Principles of Organisation*, Appendix II); the ultimate aim is to make sure that the operational unit provides the environment with the goods or services that constitute its reason for existing, and that all of these units provide the goods or services of the organisation-in-focus.

2.3.4 Horizontal Dimension of System 1

These four elements or components, with their connecting communications, constitute the set of relations in System 1′s horizontal dimension. The relevant variety in the environment must be absorbed, in accordance with the stipulations of Ashby's Law, by operations, and similarly the residual variety of the operations must be dealt with by their management.

The questions to be raised are to a certain extent familiar. If we begin with the relationship between the specific environment and the operations, the questions for each operations unit making up System 1 (Fig. 2.43) are related to the following elements:

- Identifying the aspects in the environment thought to be relevant for the operational unit. A detailed description of each aspect (commercial, technological, competition, economic, demographic, legislative, ecological, labour, political, educational, etc.).

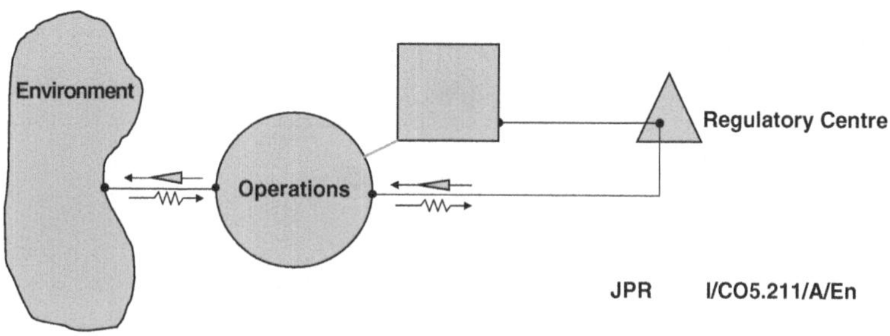

Fig. 2.43 Basic operations unit making up System 1

- Identifying the sensors at our disposal for capturing information associated with such aspects (what kind, where, how often information is captured, how it is transmitted, etc.).
- Describing the transducers converting this information into the proper format for being sent via the communication channels to those in operations who receive it.
- Characteristics of the communication channels (types, capacity, etc.).

We would ask similar questions to assess the quality of the communication channels from operations to the environment. Here we try to ascertain who is addressed by the information sent from operations. Again, we will need to check the characteristics of the transducers (for both operations/sender and environment/receiver) in addition to the channels employed.

In order to clarify these ideas, let us look at an example based on firms in the press sector. In this case, we would need to examine, in the elements of the channel between the target public and the newspaper publishers: (a) the position of the sensors, in order to receive information on how satisfied readers are with a particular paper; (b) the way in which information is captured and the format in which it is to be sent; (c) the channel to be used for transmission (e.g., via Internet or conventional mail, or by telephone, etc.); (d) the method for converting and presenting the information when reaching the newspaper, so that it can be consulted by those who are going to analyse and use it. In the opposite direction, that is, the channels between the newspaper and the readers (and supposing, say, that our aim is to enlarge our audience), we would have: (a) the format in which the message will be sent; (b) the channel to be used for maximum amplification (one such amplification channel employing current technologies of Web 2.0 would be to recommend to users/readers that they pass the message among themselves).

Obviously, in each particular case it will be necessary to consider the specific elements involved, but the structural components are always the same.

The next set of relations to explore has the task of connecting Operations with their corresponding Management. To achieve this, the latter has the assistance of its specific System 2. Once more, the particular questions to be raised refer to the existence of the communication channels needed for the information sought by Management in carrying out their task of running operations. That information needs to arrive correctly. Again we will examine: the type of information to be captured, the points where it is obtained, the frequency, the means of transmission, the transducers, the types of channel used and the format in which the Management of the unit receive it. In the opposite direction, we will need to explore how Management transmit both information and decisions to the action points within the operations they direct. Once again we will need to determine the convenience and design of the amplifiers required to increase management's capacity for influence.

Finally, and in relation to the interaction between the Management and Operations of an elementary operational unit, we must bear in mind many of the aspects referred to when we studied the relationship between System 3 and System 1, since this is the same as the relationship between the Management and

Operations of an elementary operational unit when we go to the next recursion level, in other words, when our organisation-in-focus (system-in-focus) is one of the elementary operational units of the current organisation-in-focus.

2.3.5 Vertical Dimension of System 1

Having studied the *horizontal* relations of the elementary operational units' components, that is, their relation with the environment and the interconnection between management, the operations it directs and the use of System 2 as support for managing the unit, we must now turn our attention to those connections with the rest of the system-in-focus in which the operations units play a role. These are:

(a) Relationship between the elementary operational units themselves.
(b) Relationship between the "Managements" of each elementary operational unit.
(c) Relationship between each "Management" of an elementary unit and System 3 (Fig. 2.44).
(d) Relationship between the System 2s of the different operational units and "Corporate" System 2 (directly connected to System 3).
(e) Relationship of each operational unit with System 3*.
(f) Relations between the specific environments of the elementary operational units.
(g) Algedonic channel.

All the relationships I have just mentioned refer to *vertical* channels of communication and absorption of variety (complexity) which, taken together, must be capable of absorbing all the variety that, in the horizontal dimension, must be faced by the elementary operational units so as to fulfil their aim of providing the

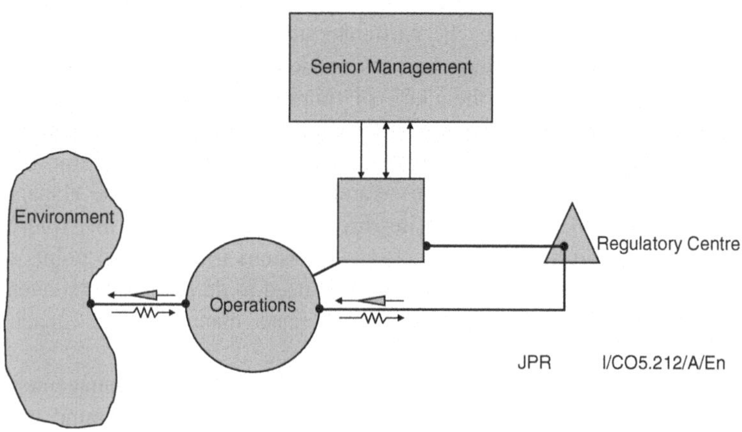

Fig. 2.44 Elementary operational unit of System 1 and relation with System 3 (Corporate or "Senior" management)

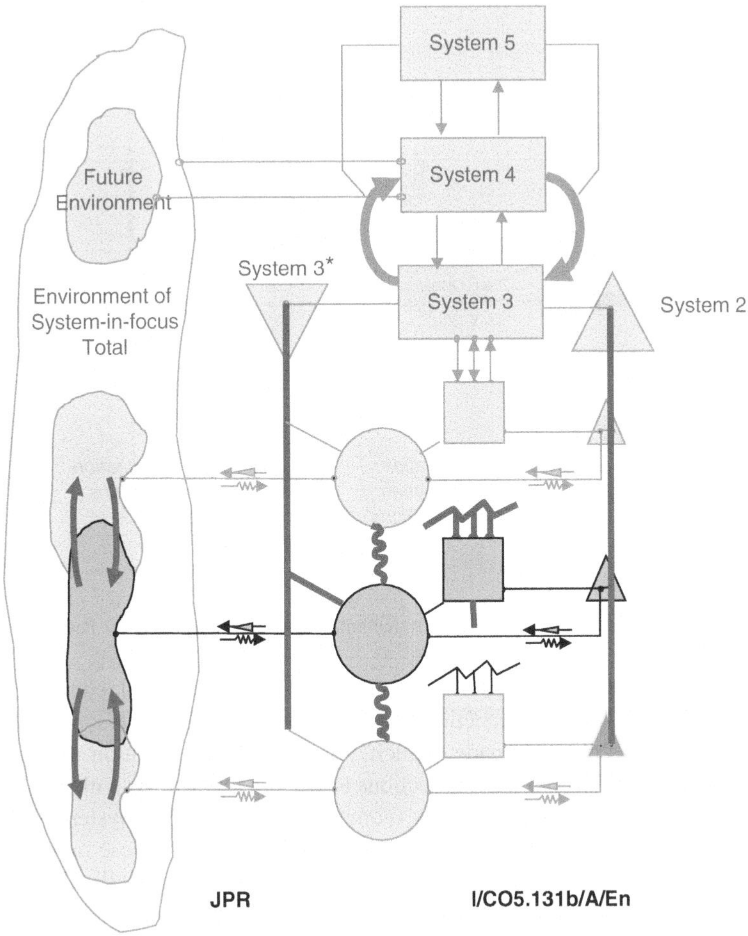

Fig. 2.45 Vertical dimension of System 1 (in the VSM set) (Pérez Ríos 2008e)

environment with their products or services (Figs. 2.45 and 2.46). Ideally, all variety is equalised at this crossing (see Beer's *First Axiom of Management* in Appendix II).

2.3.5.1 Relation Between the Elementary Operational Units Themselves

Beginning with the operational units, these may be related to a greater or lesser extent, either because they form parts of supply chains, in which the products leaving one unit then enter others (inputs), or because they deal with partial aspects of particular services, etc. (Fig. 2.47).

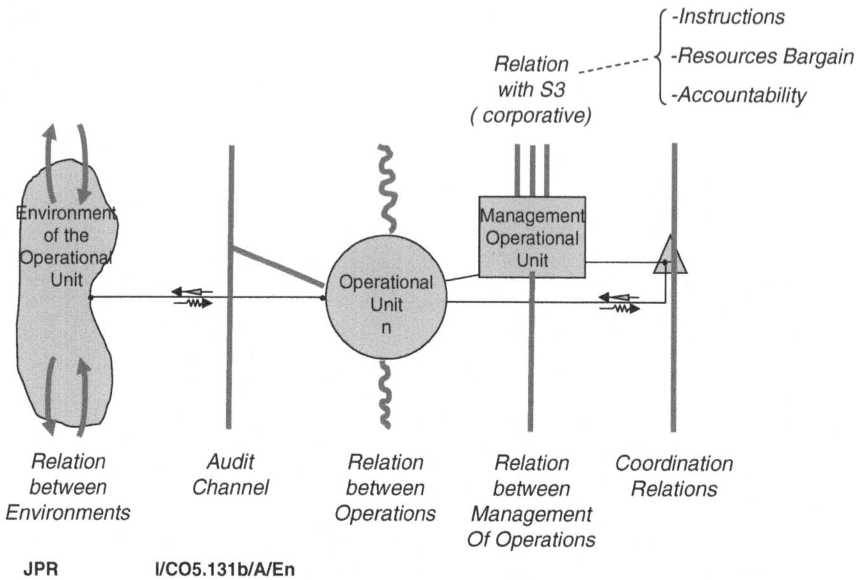

Fig. 2.46 Vertical dimension of a System 1 elementary operational unit (Pérez Ríos 2008e)

It is appropriate in this case to study the precise detail of such relations. Consequently, the type of connection that might exist (physical, personal, informative, financial, etc.) must be made explicit. Again, the ideal situation would be for incidences resulting from these connections to resolve themselves within the actual relation rather than conveying variety (complexity) to the Meta-system. Conflicts between the diverse operational units not resolved directly by these must be dealt with by System 2s. Finally, those which have not been addressed will, after passing through all these filters, reach System 3, which will then have to intervene and finish with the problem.

As we know, calling for System 3 to act must always be an exception. A smooth-running organisation should be able to resolve the endless number of problems that occur in its operational units within the framework of System 1.

The questions we should ask ourselves regarding this section for the organisation under study relate to:

- Whether there are relations between the operational units.
- A detailed description of each one of these relations.
- The communication channels between the operational units.
- The characteristics of these channels (a review of the eight typical components and the type of information circulating).
- The frequency (whether there is a permanent continual connection, or whether it is at fixed intervals, or sporadic and ad hoc).
- The linked individuals/organs belonging to the units.
- Etc.

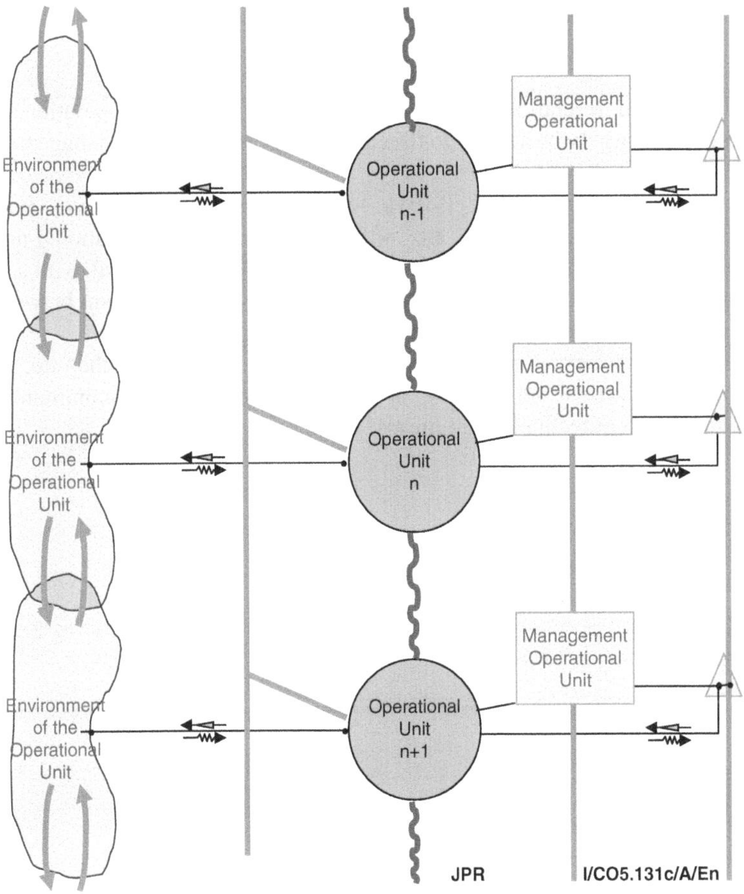

Fig. 2.47 Relations between elementary operations (System 1) (Pérez Ríos 2008e)

Here it must be observed that there may be multiple connections among the basic operational units and, as a result, a two-dimensional graphic representation would not serve. What is more, the content of these relations may be of quite diverse characteristics. Therefore, we once again stress the usefulness of possessing software like VSMod®, as it allows us to visualise the complete matrix of interrelations among all the elementary operational units regardless of their number, as well as to introduce in each relationship between units all the information required regardless of format. It permits the introduction, apart from texts, images or videos, simulation models representing either production or operations processes. In Chap. 4, which shows the characteristics of VSMod®, such possibilities are examined in greater detail.

2.3.5.2 Relation Between the "Management" of Each Elementary Operational Unit

What I dealt with in relation to the links between the elementary operational units themselves can largely be applied to the connections between the "Management" of each of them (Fig. 2.48).

In the previous paragraph, I have referred only to connections between individuals or units and sections, etc., within the production (operations) units of the diverse units, which permit the latter, directly linked, to deal with aspects pertinent to this relationship. I am now going to focus on the relation between the "Managements" of each unit.

This involves ascertaining whether such relations exist and, if they do, seeing how they are carried out (formal or informal meetings, tele-communication employing different technological means, etc.).

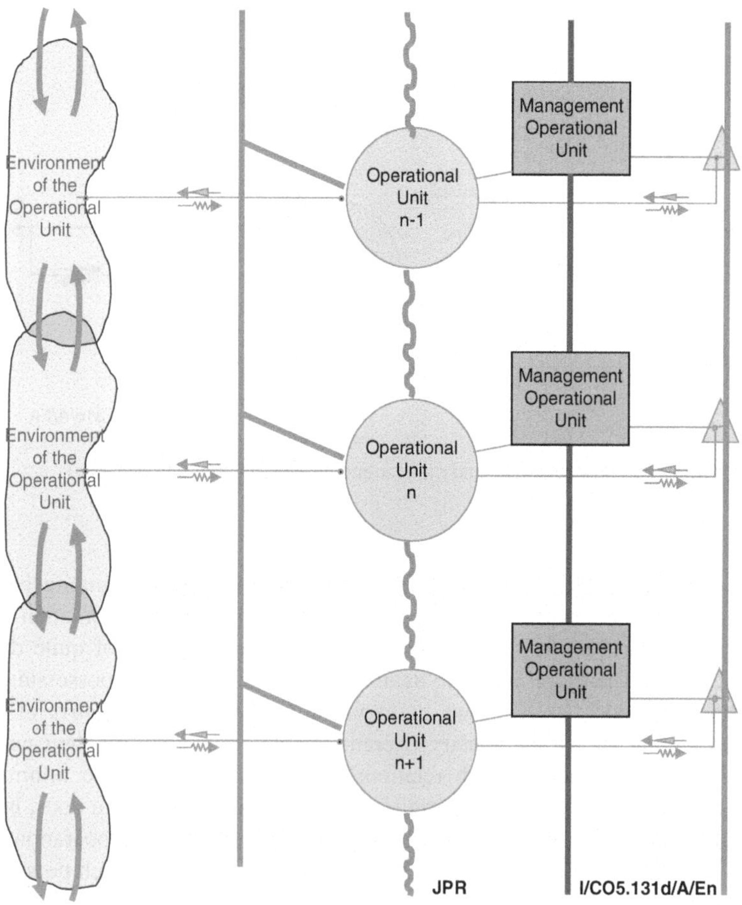

Fig. 2.48 Relations between the "managements" of the elementary operations (System 1) (Pérez Ríos 2008e)

We again undertake a thorough exploration of each communication channel and check the following: what information is transmitted, which parties are connected, how the information is "transduced" at the points of both emission and reception, the capacity of the channel or frequency, etc.

2.3.5.3 Relation Between Each Elementary Unit "Management" and System 3

This relation was observed from the point of view of System 3 when we analysed that system. The kind of relations and their content are the ones described there although here, they are studied from the viewpoint of the "Management" of the elementary units (Fig. 2.49).

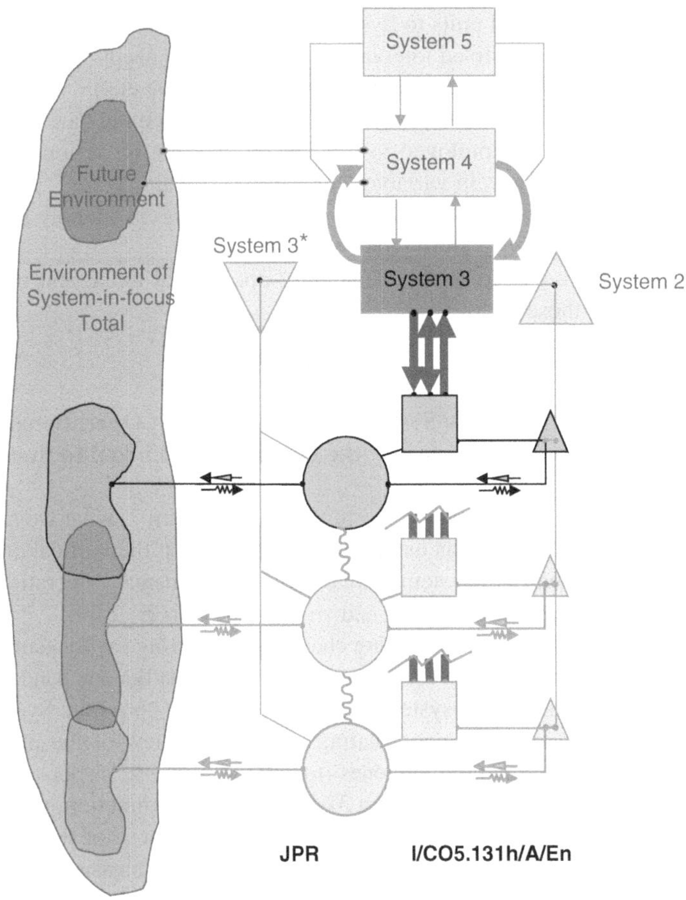

Fig. 2.49 Relations between the "Managements" of elementary operations (System 1) and System 3 (Pérez Ríos 2008e)

Now, depending on the management style ("Top-Down", "Bottom-Up", Interactive, Management by Goals, etc.), we examine how the System 3 on which each unit "Management" depends is informed or consulted.

Apart from the aspect corresponding to the process of *Negotiating resources* (goals, means of achieving them, deadlines, rewards associated with each or all of these, or how often resources are negotiated), we should make an in-depth analysis of how *Accountability* is done (the information systems used to give information on how each unit is progressing, as well as the frequency with which information is transmitted, including details of whether this is continuous in real time, discontinuous at fixed intervals, sporadic (ad hoc), or only when requested, etc.).

In addition, we should specify the method and means by which the relevant *information* is transmitted through the vertical Elementary Operational Unit-System 3 line, checking, among other things:

- If formal procedures are used for channeling the information from the "Management" of the operational units to System 3. If so, which ones.
- If information is sent at fixed intervals or "according to needs".
- What technological tools are employed (Email, Intranets, etc.).
- If methods are informal, specifying which, how and when they are used.
- If warning signals are employed to provide information on serious deviations from the assigned targets in variables considered critical.
- If the type of information to be sent (exception reports) is suitably selected in order to prevent System 3 from overloading.
- If Score Boards are used in the elementary operational units, and if they are connected with those of System 3.

2.3.5.4 Relation Between the System 2s of the Different Operational Units with "Corporate" System 2 (the One Directly Linked to System 3)

As I have previously commented on the functions of System 2, what we should do now when considering diagnosis or design is to ensure that the vertical communication relations between the System 2s that serve the elementary operational units and corporate System 2 actually exist and work properly (Fig. 2.50).

It is via the ascending and descending channels connecting the System 2s of the elementary operational units and corporate System 2 that, on the one hand, information circulates from the former systems to the latter, giving corporate System 2 the opportunity either to adapt its coordinating elements in view of the information received or to consider creating new ones (together with those responsible for the elementary operational units and System 3). In a downward direction, we will have the flow of information between corporate System 2 and those of the elementary units, informing them of the new "programs" or of the new measures designed to harmonise activities, etc.

Consequently, the questions we should review are concerned with verifying whether:

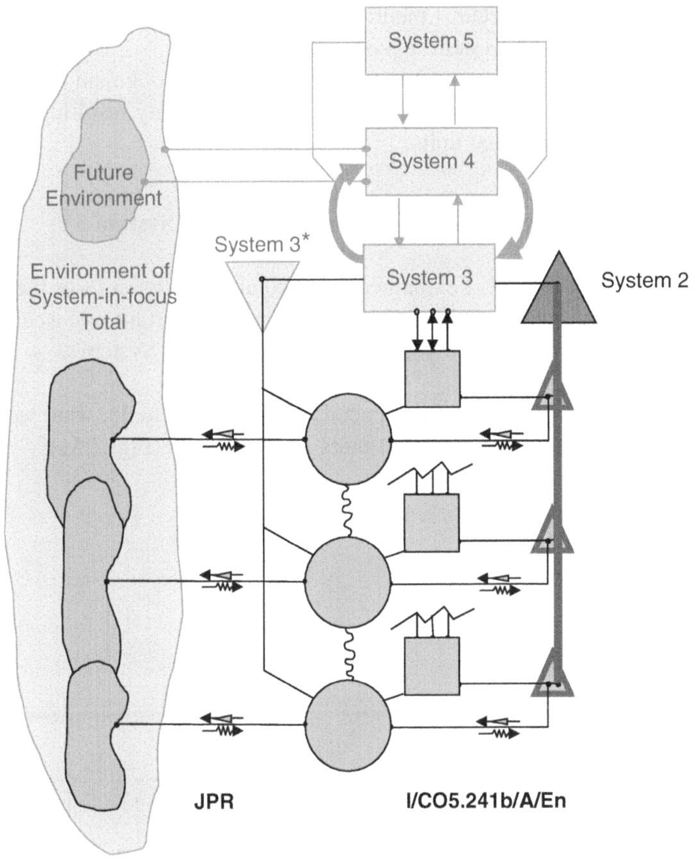

Fig. 2.50 Relations between the System 2s of elementary operations (System 1) and corporate System 2 (Pérez Ríos 2008e)

- There are both ascending and descending channels linking corporate System 2 with the System 2s of each individual operational unit.
- The representatives of each elementary operational unit play a part in designing System 2, in collaboration with corporate System 2 and with the assistance of System 3.
- The communication channels meet the conditions demanded for complying with their function as information transmitters (identification of the information to be transmitted, elements to be linked, transducers at the point of emission and reception, capacity of the channels and temporal cadence).

It is fitting to remember at this juncture the particular characteristic of these channels from the point of view of their routine nature. We should bear in mind that the routines they deal with are exclusively associated with coordination among the elementary operational units, that is to say, they help to soften any behavioural oscillations which might occur. I mentioned previously that other routines must be dealt with on the vertical System 3–System 1 axis.

This distinction is important, given the difficulty of recognising the nature of System 2 and its enormous capacity for absorbing the variety resulting from interrelations between operational units.

2.3.5.5 Relation Between each Operational Unit and System 3*

In the section on System 3*, I explained the special characteristics of the information that this system must supply to System 3, and its important role as a generator of information which neither System 2 nor the vertical System 3 – System 1 channels provide.

Bearing in mind the function and special nature of System 3*, what we must do for each of the elementary operational units is to ascertain (Fig. 2.51):

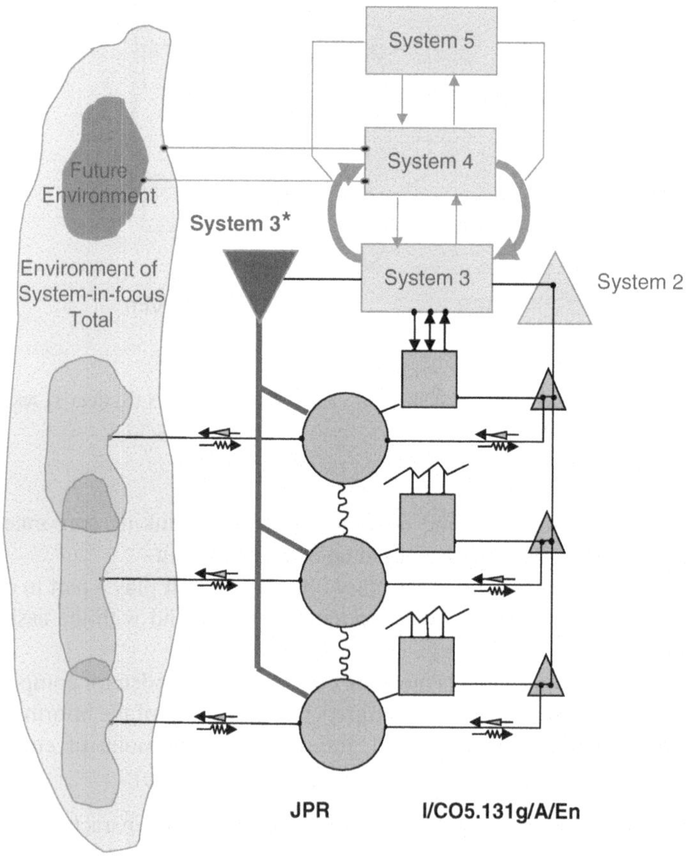

Fig. 2.51 Auditing channel that links System 3* and elementary operations (System 1) (Pérez Ríos 2008e)

- The existence of procedures specifically created for capturing information of this type, for instance, audits. These may relate to finance, accounting, opinion surveys, staff motivation, quality, industrial engineering studies, etc.
- The procedures used to capture the information (their quality).
- The means by which communication is made to members of the operational units, about both the need to carry out these activities and the ways they are put into practice,.
- The characteristics of the channels via which the information is transmitted (what information, where and how it is captured, transducers, the capacity of the transmission channels, who the recipients are, how the information is presented to them, etc.).

2.3.5.6 Relations Between the Specific Environments of the Elementary Operational Units

One aspect which may appear to be outside the organisation being studied concerns the relations which might exist between the elements of the environment that are in some way associated with it. Such relations may arise spontaneously, or they may be occasioned to a certain extent by the organisation itself. Acknowledging the existence of these is crucial as, on the one hand, they can act as enormous absorbers of variety (complexity), which consequently does not need to be absorbed by the organisation, and, on the other, they may produce an effect on the diverse organisational units in System 1 or even among operational units of different levels of recursion. Let us clarify these aspects with some examples.

An example of the first case, in which variety is absorbed, would be the design of a customer assistance policy by firms providing maintenance services for a commercial brand of a particular organisation (for instance, computer equipment), or services for the sale of cars directly to the customer by car dealers. These activities absorb a great deal of variety, saving the organisation a particular task; in the case, for example, of car dealers, this involves the whole process of making a sale, such as dealing with the various visits made by a potential buyer, demonstrations or test drives, etc.

Examples of the second inter-relationship, in which knock-on effects are produced, may be the impact resulting from the sale of a particular product which replaces another from the same company. Here, an operational unit carries out its activity in its environment (market), but in doing so it enters the environment (market) of another operational unit. A study of the behaviour of these two markets is essential for the whole organisation, so that it can adequately evaluate its product and commercial policies.

Once again, in order to diagnose or design our organisation, we must ask ourselves (Fig. 2.52) these questions:

- What are the relevant environments for our organisational unit?
- Which other environments are they are related to?

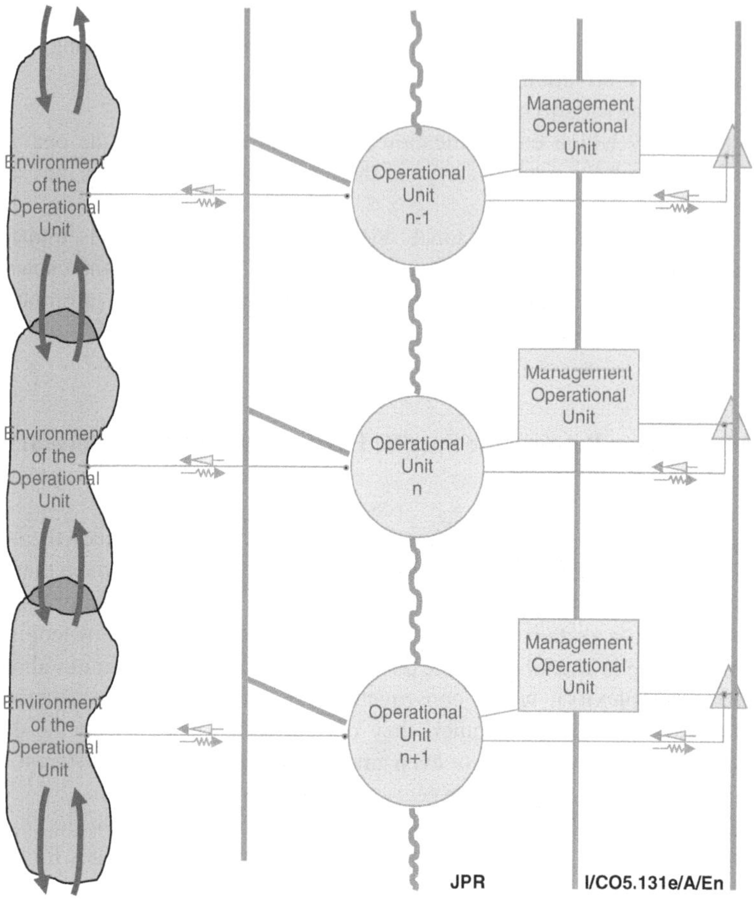

Fig. 2.52 Relations between the environments of the elementary operational units (System 1) (Pérez Ríos 2008e)

- How do these environments interact?
- What information circulates in this relationship?
- To which other environment should we have our specific environment related?
- What type of activity or relation should we try to activate?

2.3.5.7 Algedonic Channel

Within this block of vertical System 1 relations, I will mention the *algedonic channel* (let us recall that it takes its name from the combination of the words *algos*/pain and *hedos*/pleasure), as it is inside this system, and because its constituent operational units are the sources for some of the signals that, potentially joined to others arising in the environment, will, if they get past the activation thresholds, reach System 5 and cause it to act.

This information system runs parallel to all the vertical channels we have looked at so far. Its function is to transmit alert signals regarding any event or circumstance that might seriously endanger the organisation.

This channel must have its corresponding filters, to prevent the flow of any and all kinds of signal, regardless of the seriousness of the situation generating it. The filters must exclusively permit only those signals deemed critical for the organisation's survival. In practice, statistical filtering techniques may be employed to detect values of the critical variables which appear outside the acceptable trajectory.

Given the importance of this channel (Fig. 2.53), we should ascertain:

- First of all, whether it exists. Obviously, there may be multiple channels, with each corresponding to any particular aspect considered vital for the organisation.
- The variables to be monitored.

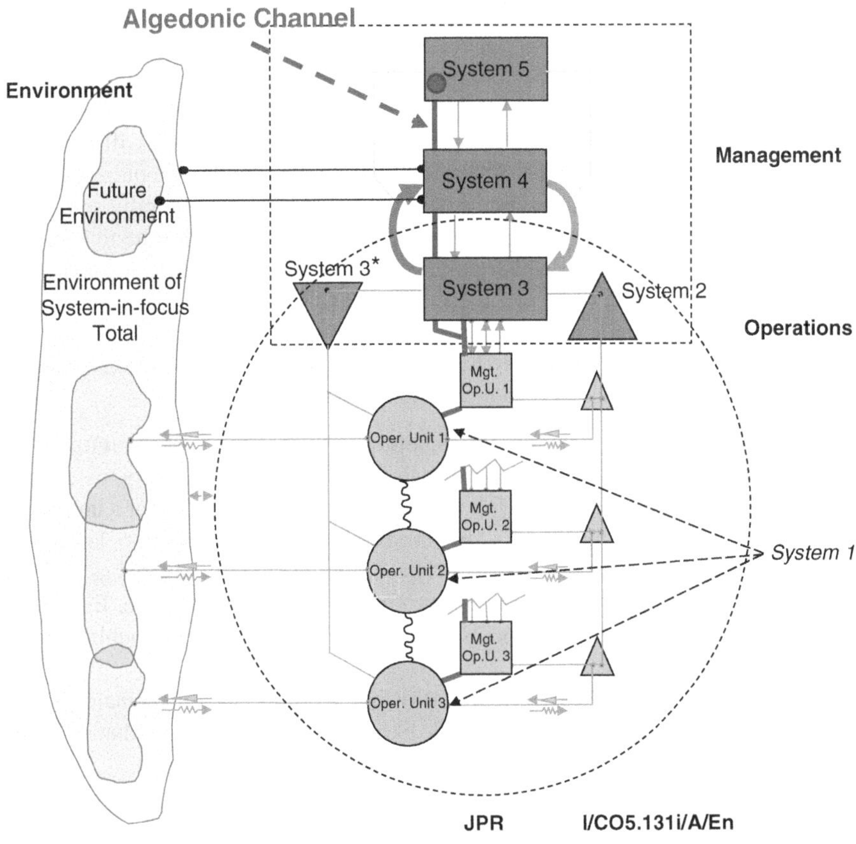

Fig. 2.53 Algedonic channel (Pérez Ríos 2008e)

- The location of the sensors.
- The activation thresholds, that is, the value at which the alarm signal is transmitted. Here it may be convenient to establish several alert levels depending on the progressive gravity of the situation.
- That activation must take place at the exact moment the diverse thresholds are exceeded.
- The channels via which warning information is to be sent.
- The characteristics of these channels (elements connected, transducers to be used, capacity of the channels for the amount of data per time unit, etc.).
- The existence of means for filtering information in order to avoid the circulation of irrelevant information and its unduly reaching the higher levels of the organisation.
- The elements receiving the alert information. We should specify which signal receivers in Systems 3, 4 and 5 are pertinent.
- In System 4, we must additionally have reception points for signals from the environment that are also related to critical information for the organisation's survival.
- This information combined with that coming up from System 1 and emitted by System 3 (after considering a possible resolution of the alerted problem within its scope of activity) will be elaborated and sent off to System 5 if thought to be critical.
- If System 5 considers that the gravity of the situation is such that it will apply the measures previously prepared albeit de-activated until actually required. These action plans cannot be improvised (they must not be) since, generally speaking, once an emergency situation has occurred, there is not enough time to analyse, model the problem, evaluate alternatives, choose the right ones, decide on action and finally act. By the time all these steps have been taken, the damage will undoubtedly have been done.
- The solution to this dilemma is to have drawn up beforehand the various plans of action for the different foreseeable emergency scenarios.

As regards this point, the cases in Spain (not to mention other countries) of the ship "Prestige" (the image of the decision-takers acting erratically, as clearly demonstrated by the ship's route, with the devastating consequences for a large part of the Galician coast and others), or catastrophic fires detected too late, etc., represent a painful indicator of the lack of suitable algedonic channels as well as of appropriate action repertoires (action protocols) for cases like these. Examples of reasonably well designed protocols are to be encountered in the public health sector (risk of epidemics, etc.).

The best intentions, however praiseworthy they might be, are unfortunately quite ineffective in vital emergency situations like those that algedonic channels are designed to detect.

A further reflection leads us back to System 4 and the Operations Room we mentioned when discussing this system. The existence of already constructed models (although, of course, subject to modification and updating) which permit an immediate simulation of the effects of an exogenous event on our organisation and environment, and which allow us to evaluate in a very short time the "foreseeable" results of diverse measures to deal with this event, are to be wholly recommended in all organisations. It stands to reason that they are even more necessary when the risk of possible damage is greater as a result of their absence.

2.4 Coherence Among the Different Recursion Levels

So far in the first stage, we have defined or clarified the identity and purpose of the organisation under study. Then, in the second stage, we have identified the recursion levels with their respective environments and organisations pertinent for our organisation (to be diagnosed or designed) to deal with the complexity of the environment in the vertical dimension of unfolding complexity. We have also, in the third stage of the study, revised each of the components of the VSM corresponding to all the organisations belonging to the global one with which we are concerned. The final step, therefore, is to check on (or, if we are designing a new organisation, to ensure) the coherence and structural unity among all the different organisations, at their diverse levels of recursion and in accordance with the corresponding recursion criteria.

The idea, for instance, is to make sure that the identity and purpose of the organisation proposed at level 0 are shared by all sub-organisations at all levels, although obviously adapted in each case to the particular circumstances of each (products, services, markets, etc.)

Consequently, when it comes to verifying coherence among the organisation's different System 5s (at their different recursion levels), we should assess aspects such as the following (Fig. 2.54):

- Is the identity attributed to the organisation as a whole at recursion level zero assumed and understood by all organisations corresponding to the various levels of recursion?
- Do formal or informal procedures exist for communicating and sharing identity among all the organisation's System 5s?

Just as it is essential that the identity and aims of the organisation are shared by all its components, something similar occurs with orientation to the future and the adaptation of the organisation to necessary or recommended changes (Fig. 2.55). I have already said that the purpose of System 4 is to take responsibility for the outside and for the future of the organisation so as to transmit this information and, in conjunction with System 3 and with the approval of System 5, modify (adapt) System 1; in this way, the latter can remain viable over time regardless of the changes taking place in the environment.

This process of evaluating the scenarios, the impacts of the various strategic options and the implications of the different changes in System 1, must be carried out in all the organisations at all levels of recursion. Again, it is necessary to ascertain that the modifications being considered and planned at a specific recursion

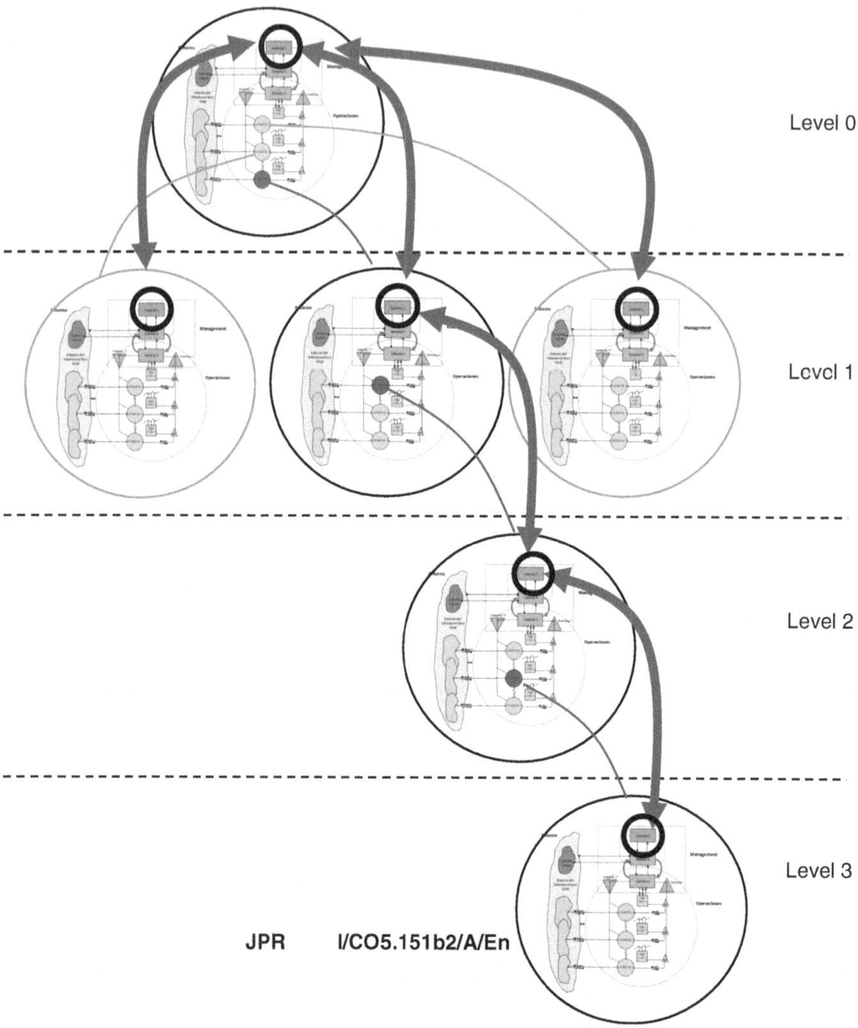

Fig. 2.54 Coherence among the System 5s of different levels of recursion (Pérez Ríos 2008e)

level are compatible with those being attempted at other levels. As a result, checking that this is actually the case, organisation by organisation, is an absolute necessity.

The corresponding questions, therefore, will relate to reviewing the:

- Existence of formal or informal procedures for verifying coherence among the various activities (strategic planning) undertaken in the different organisations at the diverse levels of recursion.
- Identification of the tools available for putting into practice this evaluation (for example, simulation software allowing one to work with various degrees or

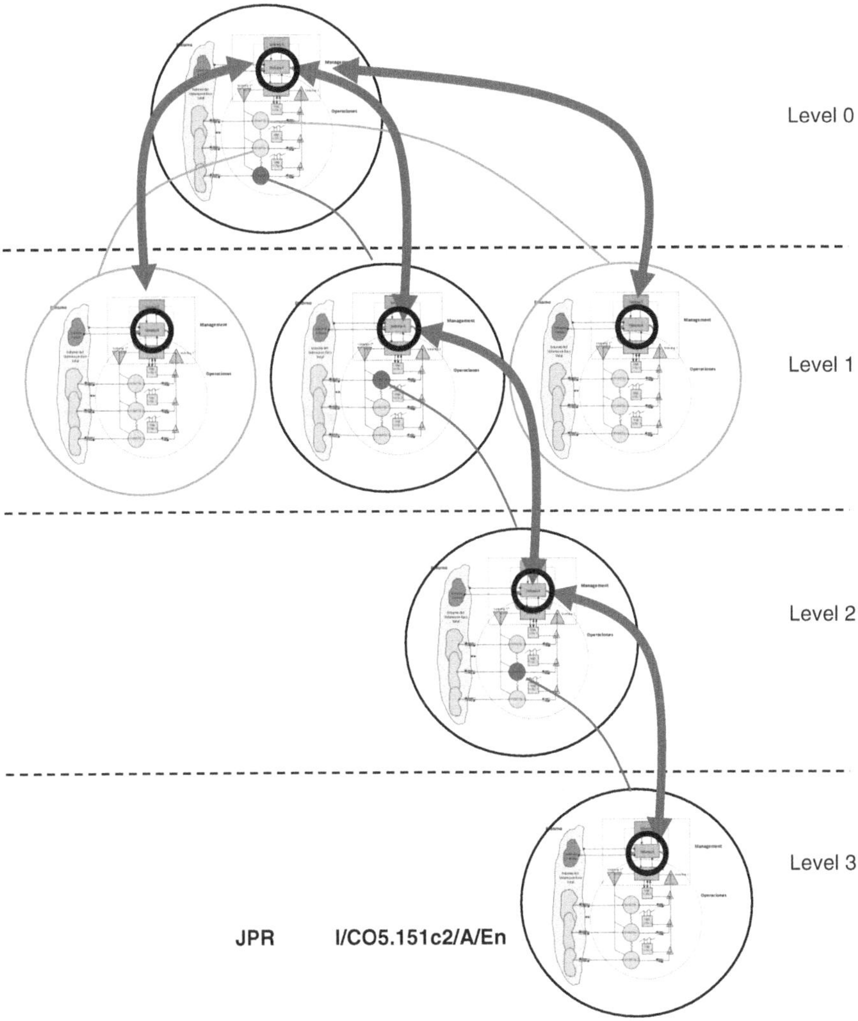

Fig. 2.55 Coherence between the System 4s of different recursion levels (Pérez Ríos 2008e)

levels of detail, and embedding models so that coherence and consistency are to a large extent assured).

- Verification of the existence of communication channels among the different System 4s located at different recursion levels.

Everything we have said in relation to System 4 is likewise applicable to the System 4 – System 3 homeostat. Clearly, this point refers to issues involving a great deal of variety and extension, and these will have to be identified and dealt with in each particular case. The aim of this section is simply to draw attention to the need

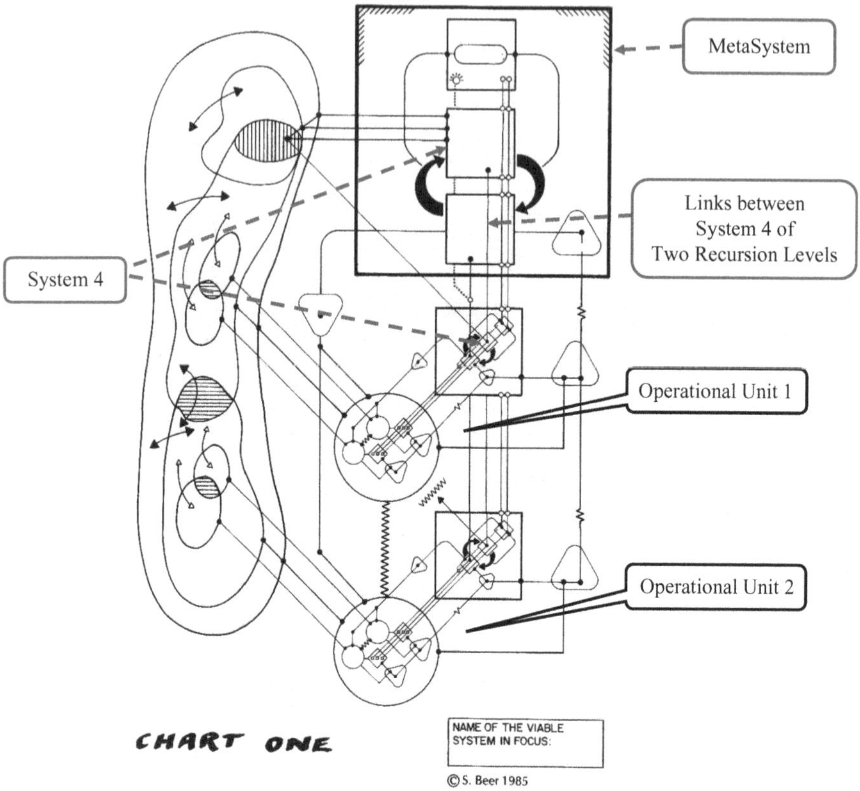

Fig. 2.56 Connections between the different systems or functions situated at different levels of recursion (Based on Beer 1985) (Pérez Ríos 2008e)

to guarantee coherence among the various activities across all the organisation's diverse levels.

Figure 2.56 offers a complete representation of the VSM provided by Beer (1985). With it, we can appreciate the connections among the various systems or functions situated at different levels of recursion. One of these is illustrated in the figure, in particular the link between System 4 of the Elementary Operational Unit 1 and System 4 of the organisation-in-focus. It can also be seen how the environment corresponding to System 4 of the elementary operational unit is contained within the environment corresponding to the system-in-focus's System 4.

A detailed examination of all the elements and relations contained in this figure gives us an idea, on the one hand, of the great complexity of the model but, on the other, of its "relative" simplicity, as a result of the same elements being repeated at the different levels of recursion.

In any case, what I want to highlight in this section is the deeply systemic nature of the VSM, that is, how each organisational unit (system) belongs to another which encompasses it, and that this in turn forms part of an even bigger one, and so on and so forth, making up a single organisation.

The need for the functions and aspects involving organisations at their various levels of recursion to be linked and coherent by now should be more apparent, granted, of course, that we are talking about the same global organisation or system.

Chapter 3
Pathologies of Organisations

Having considered in Chap. 1 certain basic cybernetic principles and the main elements of the VSM, and in Chap. 2 the way in which they can be applied in diagnosing or designing organisations, I will now turn to some of the pathologies which most commonly occur in organisations or companies (see Pérez Ríos 2008b). As we know from medical practice, detecting a pathology is essential when it comes to prescribing the treatment required for the diagnosed deficiency.

In the case of organisations, a knowledge of all the most frequent pathologies, the individual characteristics of each one and the indications for dealing with them is in itself very useful for the managers responsible, as it enables them, on the one hand, to identify the problem rapidly and, on the other, to decide on how it might be dealt with. One class of diagnostic examples found in other areas of Systems Thinking employs common structures called "archetypes" (Senge 1990), which facilitate conversation among the managers involved to speed up the process of identifying the particular problem. In the case of OC, there are also studies with a similar aim (Beer 1989; Schwaninger 2005; Espejo 2008; Hetzler 2008).

In order to list the diverse potential pathologies, I will use a conceptual outline similar to the one in Chap. 2 concerning the diagnosis and design of organisations. First of all, we will see pathologies related to what we can consider a vertical dimension, that is to say, those concerning the organisation's structural design in relation to the general environment and the various environments which it contains. I will call those encompassed here *Structural Pathologies*. Next, we will look at those related to the adequacy of organizations (at all recursion levels) to the prescription made by the VSM about functional subsystems and their relationships. I call these *Functional Pathologies*. Finally, the third group subsumes *information systems and communication channels pathologies*.

J. Pérez Ríos, *Design and Diagnosis for Sustainable Organizations*,
DOI 10.1007/978-3-642-22318-1_3,

3.1 Structural Pathologies

The pathologies included in this group are related to an inadequate treatment of the total complexity faced by an organization. The organization and its relevant environmental size may indicate a division of the environment into sub-environments, and the same with the organization. This vertical unfolding of complexity enables it to comply with Ashby's law, each sub-organization having to deal with less complexity (variety). Dividing up the environment into smaller environments and assigning these to the corresponding organisations means that the latter are faced with less complexity. The pathologies normally showing up in this context are concerned with either the absence of this process of division (when in fact it is necessary), the absence of organisations corresponding to some particular level (environment), or confused organisational memberships (multiple-dependence relationships).

The pathologies identified in this group are: (1) Non-existence of vertical unfolding, (2) Lack of recursion levels (first level), (3) Lack of recursion levels (middle levels) and (4) Entangled vertical unfolding with various interrelated level memberships. Let us now have a look at these in detail.

3.1.1 Non-Existence of Vertical Unfolding

The inexistence of vertical division that is needed gives rise to excessively large organisations in which the scope of activity to be undertaken is disproportionate. The lack of adequate vertical unfolding renders it difficult or even impossible for a single large organization to deal with the total variety which it faces (Fig. 3.1).

The result of this pathology is a dysfunction of the organisation in terms of appropriate care given to either customers or recipients of its goods or services.

Recommendations in such cases relate to identifying the proper sub-environments so as to create the sub-organisations to deal with each one. In this way the complexity (variety) to be dealt with is less; this complexity also becomes more conducive to absorption by each of the organisations fulfilling the requirements of the Law of Requisite Variety (Ashby).

3.1.2 Lack of Recursion Levels (First Level)

A second structural pathology also associated with the vertical division process of the environment and the organisation occurs when this process, although it exists at various levels of the organisation, begins, however, only at a second level. The consequence is that there is no corresponding organisation at the first level whose function would address the complexity of the entire environment which lies beyond the scope of the different sub-organisations.

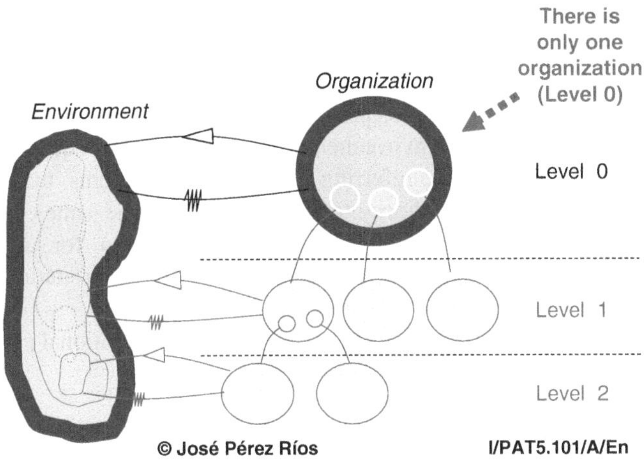

Fig. 3.1 Pathology P1.1. Non-existence of vertical unfolding (Pérez Ríos 2008b)

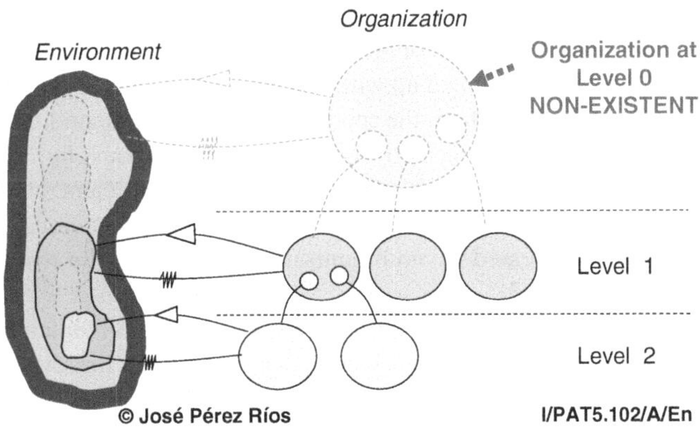

Fig. 3.2 Pathology P1.2. Lack of recursion levels (first level) (Pérez Ríos 2008b)

This problem is indicated when parts of the environment are found to lie beyond the reach of the organisation, belonging to areas in which the latter cannot intervene (Fig. 3.2).

Typical examples of this pathology are ecological problems which transcend individual countries. Even if different countries have the proper legislation for their own territory, they may be incapable of dealing with unsuitable activity beyond national boundaries. Supranational legislative attempts to cover these inclusive regions are examples of higher-level intervention. But in certain cases, such organisational levels do not exist or are incomplete. The result is that undesired actions in these "shadow" regions are left unaddressed.

Another instance is to be found in judicial systems, in which both the national and certain supra-national jurisdictions do in fact participate. A problem arises, however, when the superior-level system does not include all countries. This makes it possible for criminals to evade judicial action within those regions outside the scope of comprehensive and integrated jurisdiction.

The cause of these "unassailable" problems at that particular level is a particular absence: organisations whose environment would involve the required wholeness do not yet exist. In the example referring to ecological problems, there should be international bodies with the authority to act at that level. The same can be said of judicial systems. International judicial courts should exist for all countries, eliminating "shadow" regions that are inaccessible to either national judicial systems or partially enabled international ones.

The creation of these organisations means, from the organisational point of view, completing the corresponding level of recursion.

3.1.3 Lack of Recursion Levels (Middle Levels)

Another common structural pathology is the absence of intermediate organisational levels. This occurs whenever areas of the relevant environment for the organisation we are considering are not matched up with corresponding units of organisation. As a result of that absence of structure, the specific problems corresponding to this area of the environment are not tackled with the needed focus by any specific organisation. Rather, they are dealt with in a clearly insufficient way either by organisations at the next recursion level or by those from the previous level; more commonly, they are addressed by no organisation at all, with the result that they remain unresolved (Fig. 3.3).

A typical example of this pathology can be found in supra-municipal transport systems. Many municipal corporations have transport services for residents in their particular municipal area. But in a large number of towns today, many people who carry out their daily activity there live in nearby towns or even in ones that are far

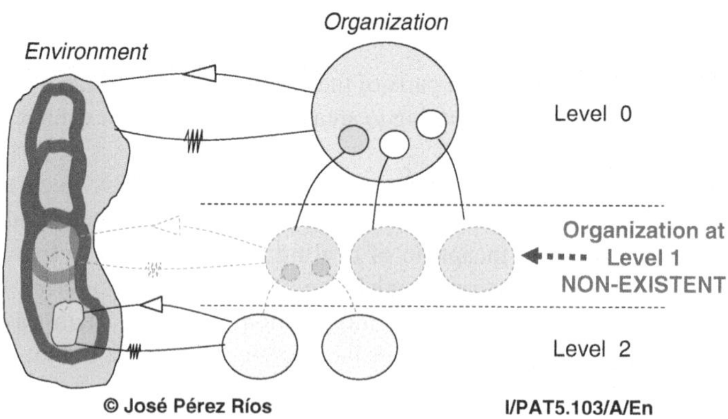

Fig. 3.3 Pathology P1.3. Lack of recursion levels (middle levels) (Pérez Ríos 2008b)

away. Consequently, as an alternative to their own car, they need to use public transport. For this option, transport services should consider the spread of the population beyond the main towns, so that lines and timetables are designed on the basis of residents in other areas. Similar situation of course may affect other types of services such as water supplies, waste disposal, etc.

The appropriate attention to these necessities in supra-municipal environments depends on the creation of organisations corresponding to such recursion levels. Obviously, the organisations in question may be permanent or temporary in accordance with the need to design the pertinent service systems, but at all events they should be made so as to deal with the complexity (variety) of those particular areas of the environment.

The current debate, for example, in many Spanish towns about the creation of "Metropolitan Areas" is one such issue. Nevertheless, the point we are making here is that it is not simply a question of joining together a few municipalities in order to form metropolitan areas, but of setting up organisations to deal with the spatial integrals typical of the particular problems to be tackled. The mere fact of adjacency among bordering municipalities does not necessarily define the issue. The municipalities to be incorporated, alongside other kinds of institutions, will be determined by the necessities relating to the problem.

An example of the benefit resulting from setting up organisations at these intermediate levels, as well as how to deal with problems at territorial scales other than those of the city and province, can be found in the study by Perez Ríos and Martinez on the application of these concepts to spatial concerns in a supra-municipal university environment (Pérez Ríos and Martínez 2007).

3.1.4 Entangled Vertical Unfolding. Various Interrelated Memberships

This pathology is encountered in the case of organisations which while having relations with others – in the sense that they contain them or are contained by them or correspond to various ways of unfolding complexity according to different criteria – do not have the appropriate communication channels among those organisations with common membership relations, or where the necessary representation of the different organisations in the organs requiring it does not exist.

In the current globalised economy, the occurrence of multiple memberships in organisations and crossed membership relations at different levels may be relatively common.

These multiple relations may bring about identity conflicts if the various organisations connected by mutual membership relations have different identities or "raisons d´être" (possible conflicts among them regarding the organisational "raison d´être", ethos, mission, values, etc.) as represented in their corresponding System 5s.

3.2 Functional Pathologies (VSM)

Having analysed certain pathologies associated with vertical partitioning of complexity and the manner in which this is distributed throughout different organisations at different recursion levels, we will now examine some of the common pathologies relating to each of the organisations that compose the total organization, which I call *Functional Pathologies*. The aim is to see whether the essential functions (systems) necessary for the organisation's viability exist and work adequately.

With a view to facilitating our study of these pathologies, we will list the ones that appear in each of the five systems (functions) of the VSM (Systems 5, 4, 3, 3*, Homeostat 4–3, System 2 and System 1), concluding with some that affect the organisation as a whole.

3.2.1 Pathologies Related with System 5. Identity Not Defined or Ill Defined. "I Don't Know Who I am"

3.2.1.1 Ill-Defined Identity

An initial and serious pathology may show up when, as a result of poor design or functioning of System 5, a clear idea within the organization about its identity is not present (Fig. 3.4). This may be summed up in the sentence, "I don't know who I am". The symptoms of this deficiency are failures among members of the organisation to agree on the organization's purpose, or even ignorance of what it should be. In a company, this problem may be reflected in the absence of a clear specification of the products it should produce or the services it should provide, or in doubts concerning the markets to be targeted. In the case, for instance, of non-profit organisations, such doubts may relate to the organisation's mission, the image it wishes to portray, or how it wants its beneficiaries in the environment to perceive it.

We can find examples of this System 5 deficiency in firms which have launched products that did not correspond to the image the public had of the company, or that were not even representative of the product line with which a particular brand of the company was associated.

Of course, this does not mean that firms should not incorporate novelties in their portfolio of products and services. The point is that this should be done without in any way forgetting the image desired for the company. If that image is to be changed, the revision should be managed coherently. Unless this occurs, confusion will arise both in the environment (market) as well as within the company itself. When we looked at the function of System 5, importance was given to its role as generator and transmitter of the organisation's image internally (its vision, mission, values, goals, ethos), so that the actions of all the people and organisational units are aligned according to that conception of the organisation.

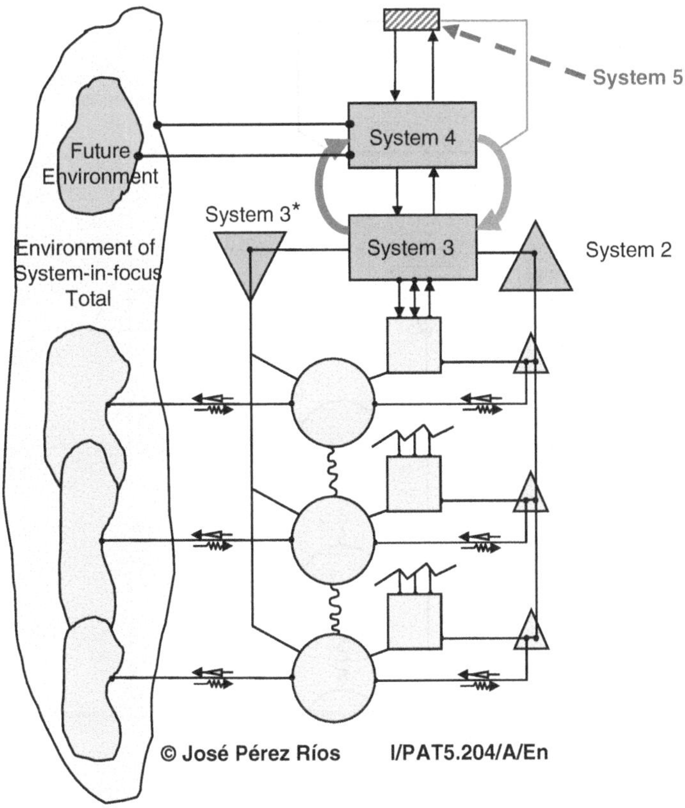

Fig. 3.4 Pathology P2.1. Ill-defined identity (Pérez Ríos 2008b)

3.2.1.2 Institutional Schizophrenia

Another variant of this pathology occurs when two or more different conceptions of the same organisation coexist (Schwaninger 2005). This would represent a "schizophrenia" (derived from the Greek *skhizein*-to divide and *phren*-intelligence) in the organisation itself, with different views pulling it in different directions (Fig. 3.5).

The way to avoid these dysfunctional configurations or performances is by an appropriate design for System 5, equipping it with all the necessary elements (organs, information channels, representation of different stakeholders, etc.) for it to be able to function so as to specify in a clear way the mission, goals and, in general, the ethos of the organisation, as well as to transmit this throughout the whole of the organisation and ensure that it has been fully understood.

It is a good idea to check on how the organisation is perceived both in the environment (markets, those receiving services, etc.) and within the organisation itself, in order to monitor how its image evolves. Such information obtained by System 4 should be continuously sent to System 5, with a view to considering

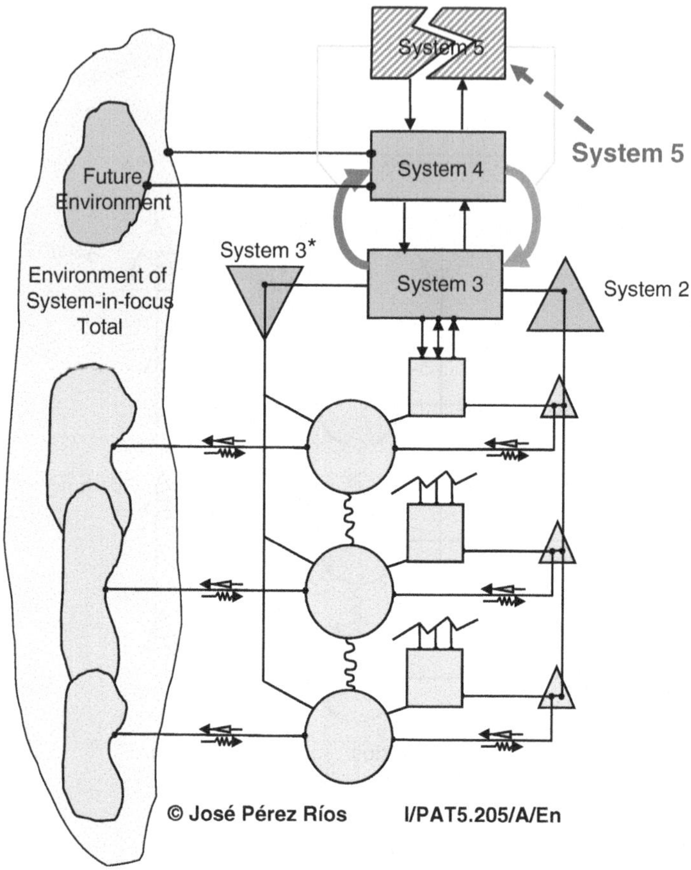

Fig. 3.5 Pathology P2.2. Institutional schizophrenia (Pérez Ríos 2008b)

whether it is appropriate to reinforce or re-direct the image portrayed, or, if need be, to change it.

3.2.1.3 System 5 Collapses into System 3 (Non-Existing Metasystem)

A further possible pathology relating to System 5 is engendered when it intervenes directly in System 3. This may occur when System 4 is either very weak or does not exist.

Here there is a direct relation between System 3 and System 5, which now intervenes in System 3's own affairs (managing the organisation's "here and now"), causing two adverse effects. One is the limiting of System 3's capacity of action (autonomy), with the further hindrance that System 5 lacks the wealth of information (variety) to which the other has access (via direct channels with the elements of

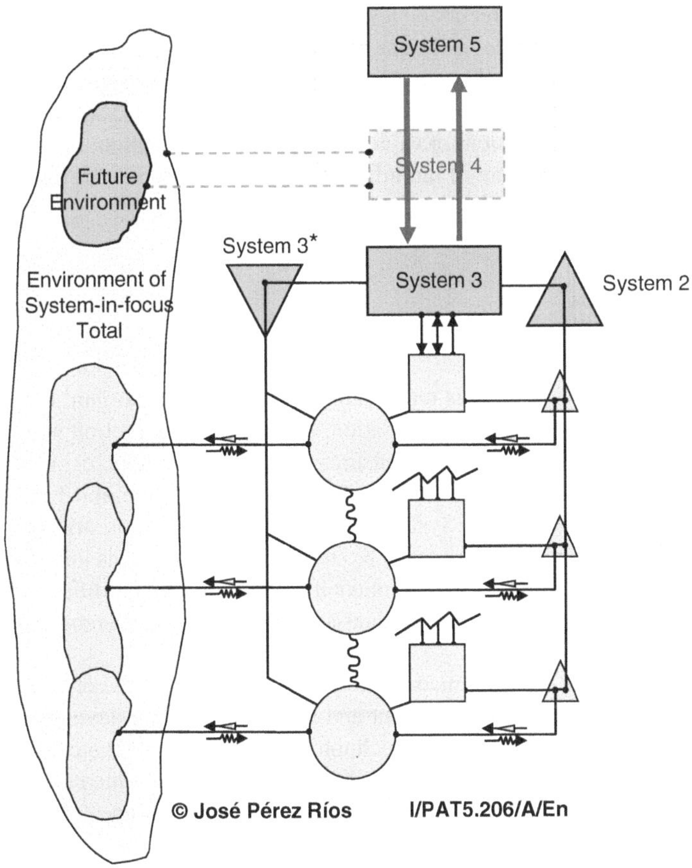

Fig. 3.6 Pathology P2.3. System 5 collapses into System 3 (Pérez Ríos 2008b)

System 1 and via Systems 2 and 3*); as a result, its intervention from a position of "authority" may harm the functioning of System 1. A second adverse effect is the weakening of System 5's own function which, together with the absence or weakness of System 4, might cause the organisation to be without an integral Meta-system (5-4-3). The related functions of keeping an eye on the "outside and the future" and also of defining identity, establishing the corporate ethos, mission, values, goals, etc., are seriously impaired and, as a consequence, the organisation's viability. The prognosis is the possible disappearance of the organisation, at least as an independent entity (Fig. 3.6).

3.2.1.4 Inadequate Representation Vis-à-Vis Higher Levels

A further potential pathology of System 5 results from its inability to represent the whole of the organisation that presides (the system-in-focus) over higher systems to which it belongs (previous recursion levels). This produces a disconnection between organisations pertaining to different recursion levels within the same global organisation, a disjuncture that can disrupt overall functioning due to incoherence among the different organisations at the various levels (see Sect. 2.4, Chap. 2). In this case, the chain of transmission for values, mission, etc., throughout these levels may be interrupted, or the content of the information transmitted may be distorted.

3.2.2 Pathologies Related with System 4

We said before that System 4 is responsible, as its adaptation organ, for observing the "outside and future" of the organisation. Its continual interaction with System 3 (System 4–System 3 Homeostat) ensures that the novelties of incorporation required by the organisation are transmitted in adequate time and form for their possible implementation into System 1. Likewise, restrictions arising from the constitution of System 1 are relayed by System 3 to System 4. This joint functioning (System 4-System 3 Homeostat) will make it possible for the modifications needed in System 1 to take place on a continual and gradual basis, thereby ensuring the organisation's viability.

If System 4 either operates inadequately or does not exist, the organisation will lack information relating to the current and foreseeable future development of the environment (markets, competitors, technologies, evolution of the company itself, etc.), consequently jeopardising its viability. Let us now examine certain frequent pathologies associated with an inadequate functioning or design of System 4.

3.2.2.1 "Headless Chicken"

Examples of a dysfunction in System 4 are failures to modify, when appropriate, the products or services offered by the organisation, excessive time taken to change or adapt the latter to market needs, the weak introduction of new products, or introducing the wrong type of product. In general terms, the signs of deficiency in System 4 are associated with the difficulty or inability of the organisation to modify its lines of products or services or the image of the company which they imply. The chances are, should System 4 still not exist, that sooner or later the organisation will disappear, at least as an independent entity (Fig. 3.7).

The comparison with a chicken whose head is suddenly cut off but which continues to run around for a short while, may indicate what can happen to organisations that either have no System 4 or have a badly functioning one. They go on operating until the time arrives when they can no longer provide the goods or services requested by their customers or beneficiaries.

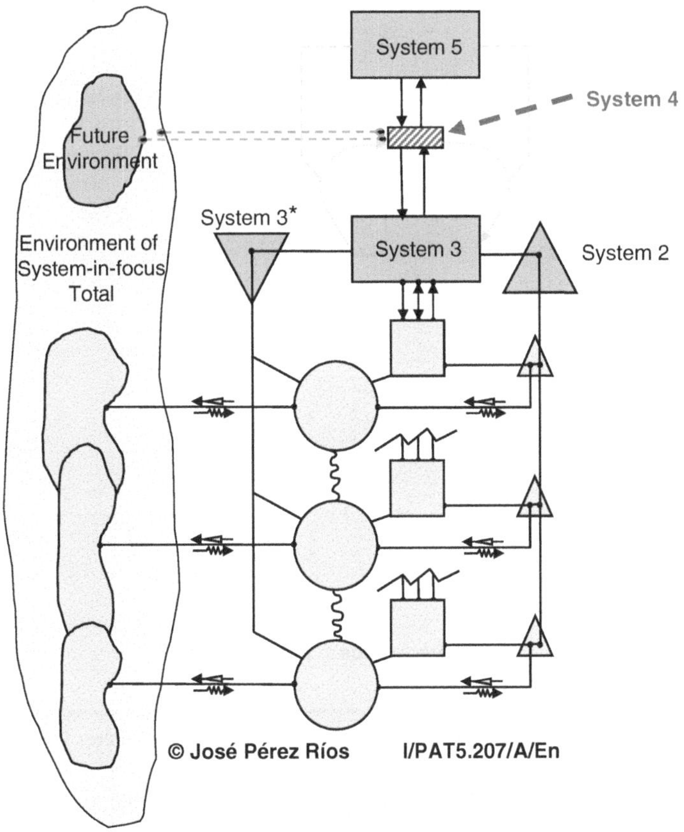

Fig. 3.7 Pathology P2.5. "Headless chicken" (Pérez Ríos 2008b)

3.2.2.2 Dissociation Between System 4 and System 3

Another common pathology related with System 4 is caused by a poor connection with System 3. That factor ensures that the System 3-System 4 Homeostat will fail to function, with the consequences I will now relate. It may be that the organisation is, in fact, correctly examining the current and future development of the environment and obtaining information on whether it is advisable to incorporate new products, services, technologies, etc. In addition, perhaps System 3 is keeping good control of the elements of System 1, and supplying the market with the required products and services. However, this momentarily felicitous situation will cease to hold after a time, as the changes which take place in System 1 (and its particular environments) will not be relayed properly to Systems 4 and 5, nor will the innovations detected by System 4 as suitable for incorporation into the organisation be assimilated by System 3 and subsequently implemented in the elements of System 1. The result of such dissociation is the inability of the organisation to adapt to changes, both from outside and from within the organisation

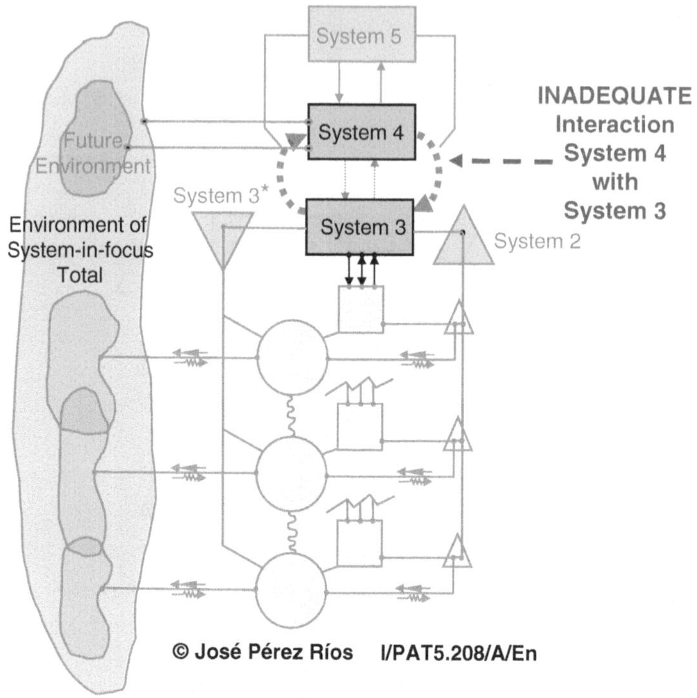

Fig. 3.8 Pathology P2.6. Dissociation between System 4 and System 3 (Pérez Ríos 2008b)

itself. Internal changes must also be processed by System 4 so that, together with data from outside, they provide a synthesis enabling the direction of future work (Fig. 3.8).

We can find a symptom of this dissociation in those cases where System 4 perceives System 3 as being "short-sighted", or failing to see anything beyond the immediate, or in cases where System 3 perceives System 4 as being unrealistic, and unaware of the restrictions imposed by the organisation's daily operation (the "here and now").

The likely result of this dissociation and lack of communication between System 4 and System 3 is that the organisation will be unable to adapt to external and internal changes, with the consequent endangering of its viability.

The means of avoiding such problems is analysed in detail in this book in Sect. 1.3 of Chap. 1 and Sect. 2.3 of Chap. 2. There a description is given of the requirements for the successful design and functioning of the System 4-System 3 homeostat.

3.2.3 Pathologies Associated with System 3

System 3 and System 1 are normally possessed by all organisations, as they make it possible for the products and services that are supposed to be provided to reach the market or the particular environment. Nevertheless, the fact that they exist does not guarantee that they will perform well.

I mentioned above the kinds of problems engendered by a lack of communication between System 3 and System 4, and the corresponding effect on the activity of the System 4-System 3 homeostat, ranging from a dysfunction to its failing to work altogether. Everything described there is also applicable to System 3.

We can here look specifically at the pathologies caused by a dysfunction of System 3, regarding its task of integrating the elements in System 1.

3.2.3.1 Inadequate Management Style

A direct relationship between System 3 and the elements in System 1 takes place, as was stated previously, through three main channels which are instrumental in: "Resource bargain", "Accountability" and "Relaying of instructions". Besides, one of the requirements for the viability and smooth functioning of System 1 elements is that they have sufficient autonomy to deal individually with the complexity (variety) of their specific environments (markets, beneficiaries).

Excessive direct intervention by System 3 in matters relating to operational units (a too-authoritarian style of management), apart from overloading the vertical line of command, limits the capacity to act (autonomy) on the part of their "management". If we add to this System 3's inability to directly absorb on its own the horizontal variety which the various operational units (elements of System 1) have to handle (for which they themselves should have the capacity to respond), the result will be a dysfunction of System 1 (Fig. 3.9).

Symptoms of this condition are such commonly heard complaints, among those responsible for System 3, as: "I can't do everything by myself . . ." or "If I don't do it, it won't get done . . .", or, to make matters even worse, allegations that those responsible for the operational units are inadequate: "My subordinates are useless . . .". Another indicator of the possible appearance of this pathology is encountered in organisations in which the managerial style of the individual or individuals responsible for System 3 is perceived by the managers of the operational units to be too authoritarian.

System 3 ought to enable the whole of System 1 to operate smoothly simply by means of the channels and support elements (System 2, System 3* and the communication channels) that must exist; if these function properly, then it is practically unnecessary for System 3 to intervene directly (in matters of daily operation). A very intense intervention by System 3, accompanied by interference in the activity of System 1 elements, is indicative of the organisation's (Systems 3-2-1) poor design or incompetence on the part of those managing System 3.

The principal function of a good System 3 is to design just the right components (System 3*, System 2 and the channels of communication with each System-1 component) for the organisation which it must run (integrate) to operate almost autonomously. Its intervention should be restricted to dealing with the exceptions that those in charge of the different elements in System 1 are incapable of handling,

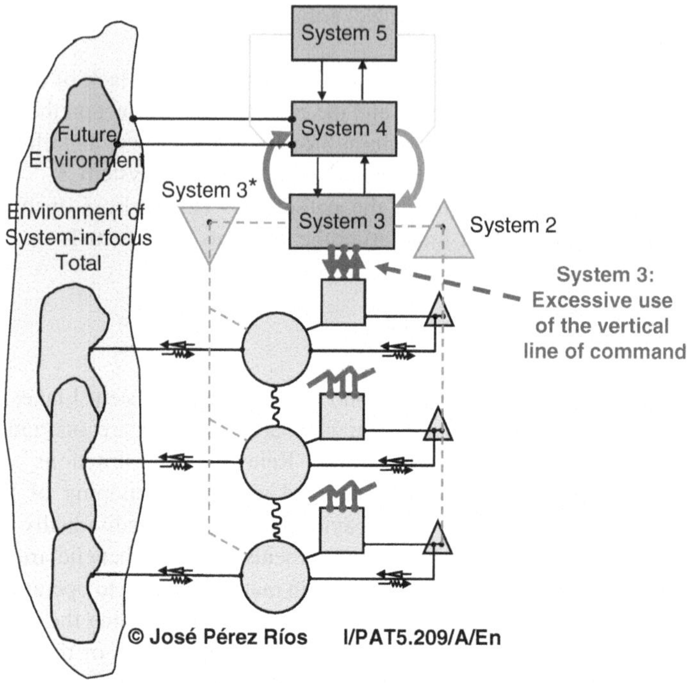

Fig. 3.9 Pathology P2.7. Inadequate management style (Pérez Ríos 2008b)

as well as any unforeseen situations in both the environment and inside the organisation on which decision-making is beyond the remit of these managers.

3.2.3.2 Schizophrenic System 3

Given the characteristics of System 3 and its relationship with System 4, it is worth pointing out its particularity: the fact that it belongs to both the *System* (Operational unit) and the *Metasystem* (Management of the operational unit). This means that its functions derive from both of these inclusions. When it operates as part of the *Metasystem* (Management), it must channel to System 4 data relating to incidents, restrictions, etc., typical of System 1, and to the latter information from Systems 4 and 5 on modification requirements within System 1, together with instructions, regulations, etc., from both of them. When it acts as part of the *System* (Operational unit), it must deal with the working of the organisation it directs and integrates, with the support of Systems 2 and 3*. The type of aspects to be dealt with in either one case or the other may differ at any given time.

One possible problem is that these two functions – the simultaneous inclusions described above – are poorly related and integrated within System 3 itself. This would cause it to behave "schizophrenically". If both these aspects are not

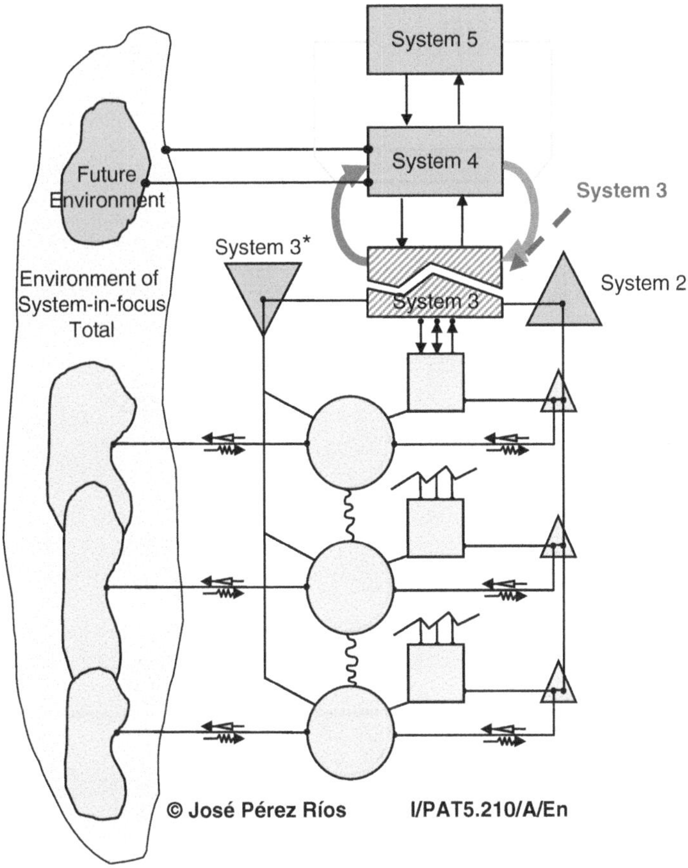

Fig. 3.10 Pathology P2.8. Schizophrenic System 3 (Pérez Ríos 2008b)

integrated harmoniously, the functioning of System 3 will be affected by problematic internal tension (Fig. 3.10).

3.2.3.3 Weak Connection Between System 3 and System 1

When there is a weak relationship between System 3 and the elements making up System 1, that is, when power lies in the operational units (for example, the divisions in a company), the result is that System 1 as a whole does not operate smoothly. In this case, due to the lack of an integrating system (System 3) to provide guidelines, assign resources and make sure (Accountability) that the units operate appropriately, the only way to co-ordinate the elemental operational units is by way of corporate System 2. But this system lacks authority over the elements in System 1 which, should it attempt to impose co-ordination, will be perceived by them as a bureaucratic burden and will, as a result, be unwelcome (Fig. 3.11).

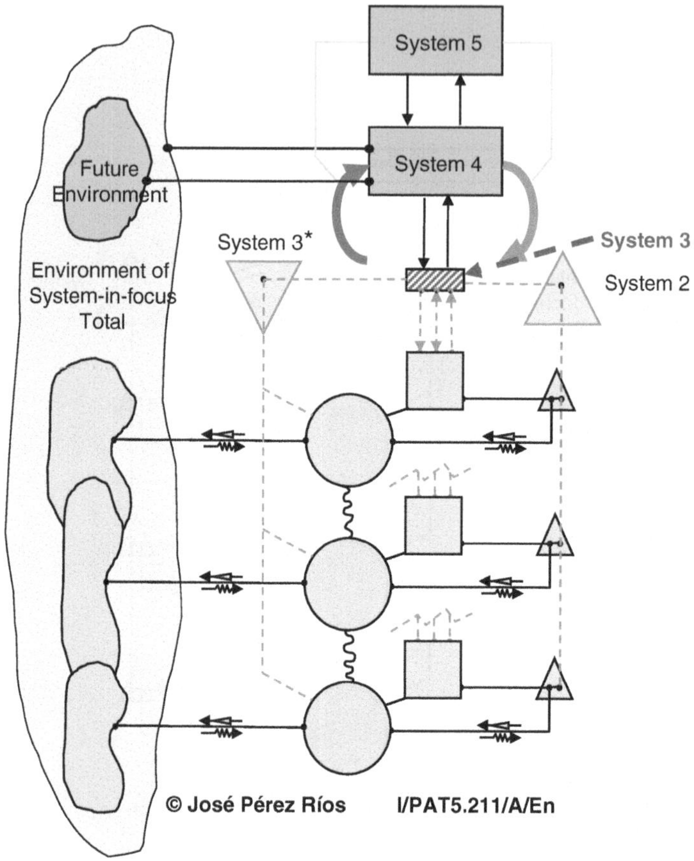

Fig. 3.11 Pathology P2.9. Weak connection between System 3 and System 1 (Pérez Ríos 2008b)

The consequence of this pathology is that the units making up System 1 will work anarchically. They may opt for the "each man for himself" tactic in the face of difficulties deriving from either market developments, conflicts regarding the jurisdiction or areas of influence of the various elemental operational units.

3.2.3.4 The Hypertrophy of System 3

A further common pathology associated with System 3 is its bloating or hypertrophy, accompanied by an insufficient development of both System 2 and System 3*. The problems engendered here are partly similar to those resulting from a too-authoritarian managerial style, as mentioned above, but exacerbated by a lack of assistance from both System 2 and System 3*. Both these systems play a crucial role in absorbing the complexity deriving both from the functioning of each of the System-1 elements and from their interaction. It is too much to expect all such complexity to be absorbed exclusively by System 3. If that absorption should be attempted by greatly developing System 3, so that it intervenes directly in the affairs of the base units, that step will result in the managers of these units feeling discouraged, alongside the cost and probable inefficient functioning stemming from this solution (Fig. 3.12).

One of the essential principles of OC is to endeavour to make systems (organisations) self-regulating; for this purpose, one key is to locate the point of decision as close as possible to where the corresponding need for decision occurs. Consequently, the corresponding operational units should have sufficient capacity both to decide and to act; in other words, they should be allowed the necessary

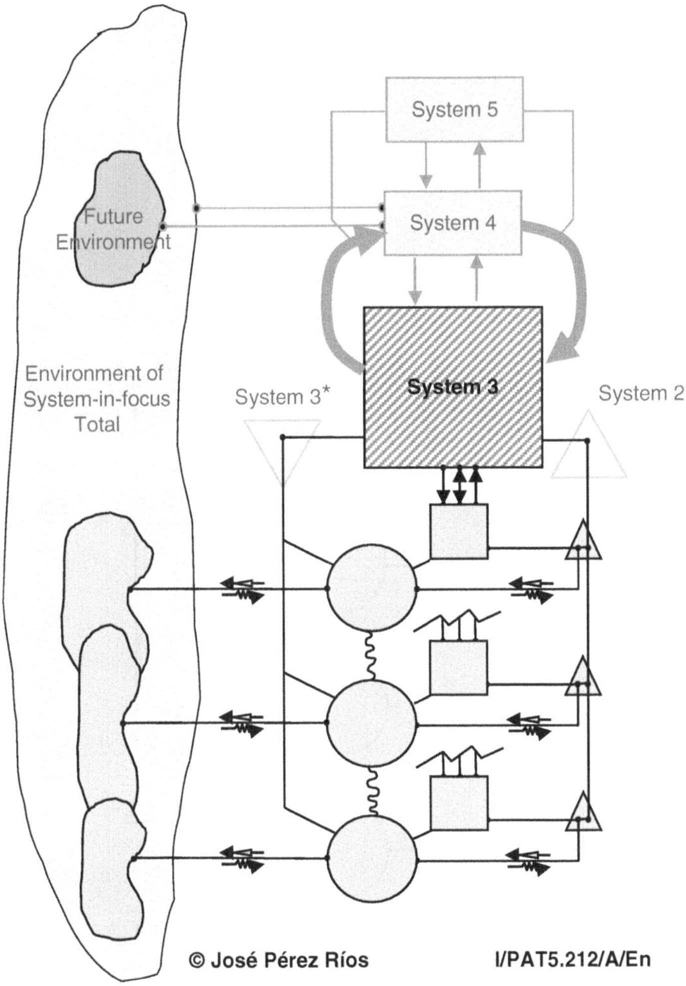

Fig. 3.12 Pathology P2.10. Hypertrophy of System 3 (Pérez Ríos 2008b)

degree of autonomy, limited only by cohesion requirements for the organization as a whole. A hypertrophy of System 3 runs contrary to this option.

3.2.4 Pathologies Associated with System 3*

3.2.4.1 Lack or Insufficient Development of System 3*

The pathology most frequently associated with this system is that resulting from either its absence or its failure to function adequately (Fig. 3.13). The aim of System 3*, as a support body for System 3, is to absorb enormous amounts of variety by mechanisms like accounting, financial, maintenance or quality audits, industrial engineering studies (in production systems), opinion surveys, etc. System 3*, besides complementing data reaching System 3, either via System 2 or directly

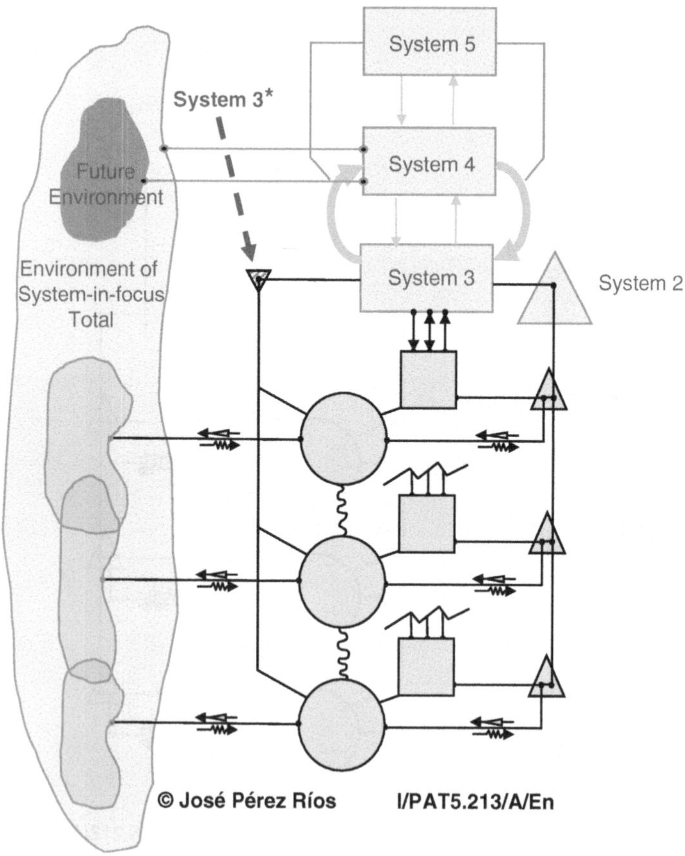

Fig. 3.13 Pathology P2.11. A poor System 3* (Pérez Ríos 2008b)

from System-1 components, contributes to the behavioural alignment of the members of the operational units. Particular examples, such as speed controls for motorists by means of mobile radar, or various surveys regarding the quality of certain services, demonstrate how useful they are.

The results of the absence of System 3* in an organisation are evident. Proliferation of inappropriate activities may appear, practices which are not aligned with the different processes and operational norms of the organisation, or even unethical behaviour (relations with suppliers, workers, customers, etc). The same can be said in the case where certain elements corresponding to System 3* exist but which are not applied or do not function properly. Examples would include surveys held on the extent to which certain levels of documentation tasks are complied with (such as medical case histories), but which are either announced beforehand, or permit those responsible for them to include "false" or "invented" information once they have been warned of their imminence.

The necessary precautions to take before such actions should not be confused with, for instance, the intention of carrying out sampling or audits on a secret basis and without previously informing the operational units. Obviously, these units should be told that audits are going to take place, and should be informed about what is going to be measured. The reason for such interventions is to improve the functioning of System 1 by detecting faults and subsequently correcting them (via System 3) by the action of System 1. The aim is to complement the information sent from Systems 1 and 2 to System 3.

An equivalent of these System-3* interventions may be medical "check-ups" carried out on people after a certain age. The goal is not "intervention for the sake of it" but rather one of prevention, warning in advance of possible health problems which, due to their being detected in the early stages, may help to resolve them or even prevent them from appearing.

3.2.5 Pathologies Associated with System 2

System 2 is responsible for contributing to the harmonious behaviour of the elemental units in System 1. Let us have a look at some pathologies typical of its poor design or functioning.

3.2.5.1 Disjointed Behaviour Within System 1 (Each to His Own)

One sign of the dysfunction of System 2 (corporate and also specific for each of the individual operational units) is the existence of problems resulting from interactions among the elemental operational units constituting System 1 (Fig. 3.14). The following are indicators of this pathology: a lack of collaboration among the operational units, no solidarity in competition for common resources, coordination problems among its activities, or the lack of a continuous process flow, when linked, from certain units to others. In general, signs that System 2 either does

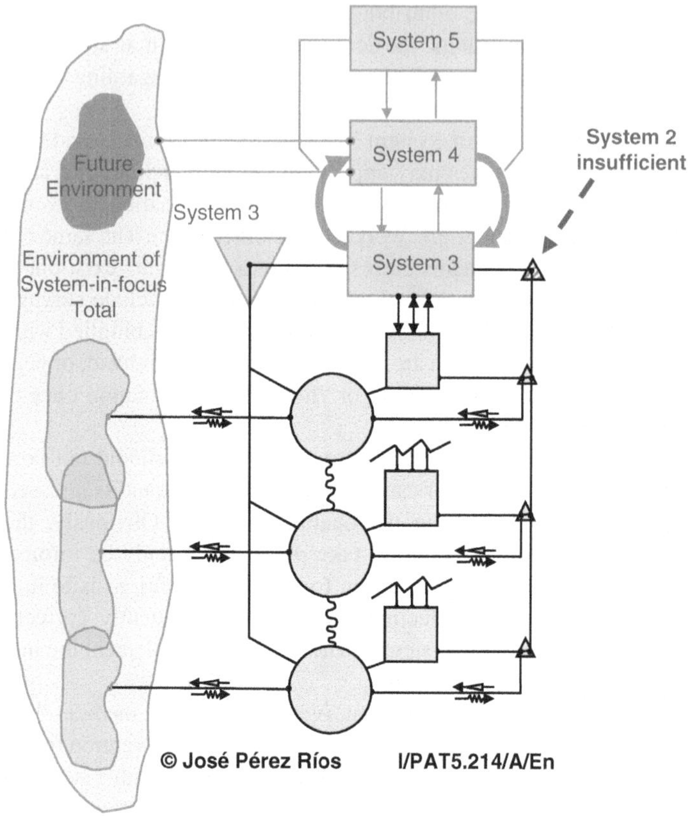

Fig. 3.14 Pathology P2.12. Disjointed behaviour within System 1 (Pérez Ríos 2008b).

not exist or fails to work properly occur when the operational units behave somewhat anarchically, and when this can be dealt with solely by the direct intervention of System 3 (which more than once I have signalled as a potential indication that the organisation is badly designed or suffers from a dysfunction).

To resolve this problem, it is necessary for System 2 to have a good design at both the corporate level (providing information about the different operational units directly to System 3 as well as to System 2) and at the levels serving the different operational units. When we analysed this system, I indicated that those who should act on designing the coordination of elements to be employed by System 2 for the smooth functioning of System 1's various operational units, are mainly the managers of these units, with the support of System 3.

3.2.5.2 Authoritarian System 2 (Authoritarian Bureaucrats)

Another problem occasionally observed in association with System 2 is that it is perceived by the management of the operational units as an authoritarian group attempting to impose certain working methods. In this case, System 2 will be unable to carry out its task successfully, as its purpose is to contribute to a better relationship among the operational units, providing them with means of coordination rather than orders. System 2's image as being authoritarian detracts from its real nature (since only System 3 has authority over System 1), and may result in non-compliance with the actions which the processes designed by this system recommend. The example of traffic regulations for motorists (as an instance of System 2) helps us understand that such regulations are not orders but measures that facilitate and improve the safety of traffic flow on roads and motorways. Broadly speaking, these norms are welcomed by the general public, who regard them as contributing to their safety and not as orders they must obey (Fig. 3.15).

The way to avoid any such perception, as we have remarked, is through the joint participation of the operational units and System 3 in the design of Systems 2 (both corporate and for each operational unit).

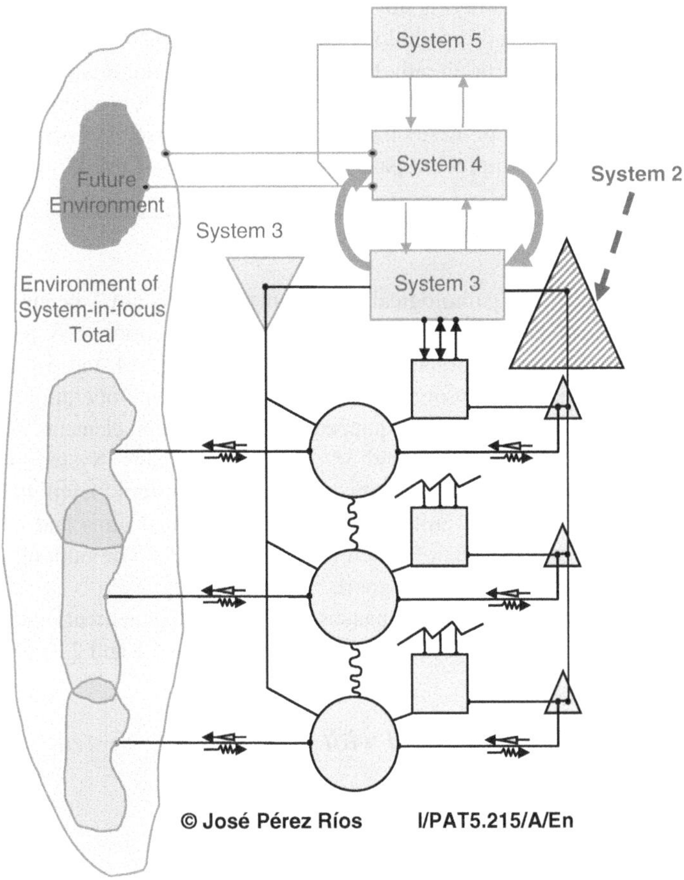

Fig. 3.15 Pathology P2.13. Authoritarian System 2 (Pérez Ríos 2008b)

3.2.6 *Pathologies Associated with System 1*

3.2.6.1 Autopoietic "Beasts"

Regarding potential pathologies related to System 1, these are mainly concerned with unsuitable activity by the elemental operational units. An example would be when one System-1 unit, or all of them, become "*Autopoietic Beasts*", to use the term given by Werner Schuhmann (1997) to describe organisations for which individual goals are their only reason for being, regardless of any consideration transcending their interests.

System 1's operational units belong to higher units (the complete System 1 itself as well as the whole of the organisation in focus), and consequently their activities should be viewed within the framework of the larger whole. An example from biology is cancer, which is caused by cells that grow and spread throughout the organism in which they are contained, pursuing their own growth and expansion, and, in so doing, finally destroying this host organism and consequently themselves.

In the case of System 1, this pathology manifests itself when one of the elemental operational units acquires or already has disproportionate domination over all the other units which, in combination with it, constitute System 1, producing a negative effect on the development of these other units. This, of course, will occur if System 3 lacks sufficient power to prevent pathological behaviour of this kind (Fig. 3.16).

3.2.6.2 Dominance of System 1. Weak Metasystem

A further instance of the pathological development of System 1 occurs when its overall presence, power and domination over the other functions or systems necessary for the viability of the organisation (Systems 2, 3, 3*, 4 and 5) is absolute (Fig. 3.17). This represents an organisation dominated by the operational units of System 1, which, to a large extent unequipped with coordination elements (System 2), integrating components (System 3 and 3*), adaptation organs (System 4 and 3–4 Homeostat), and those indicating identity, mission, etc. (System 5), will behave like a combination of operational units seeking their individual aims and competing among themselves on the basis of "each man for himself". The outlook from the viability standpoint is obviously not good.

The appropriate treatment for the causes of the pathologies mentioned depends on the design of all the VSM functions described in Chaps. 1 and 2 of this book.

3.2.7 *Pathologies Associated with the Complete System*

3.2.7.1 Organisational Autopoietic "Beasts"

Apart from pathologies directly related to the different systems (functions) of the VSM, there are other more general types connected with dysfunctions that affect the whole organisation.

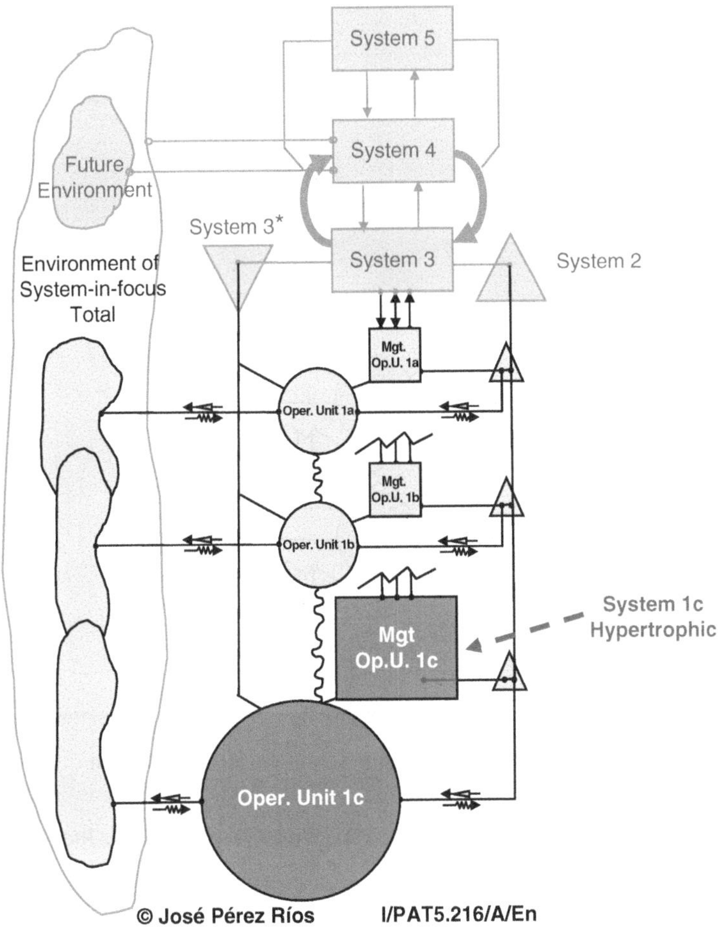

Fig. 3.16 Pathology P2.14. System 1, Autopoietic "Beasts" (Pérez Ríos 2008b)

One pathology is characterized by the appearance of hypertrophies, or aberrant autonomous behaviours within the complete system (the organisation). I am referring here to those functions that aimed at helping System 1 to work better (that means providing the environment with the goods or services the organisation has decided to supply). Because these are functions "at the service of" System 1, these functions may become obsessed with achieving their own goals relating to growth and power, regardless of whether or not they contribute to facilitating the task of System 1. Such a pathology also may appear in Systems 2, 3* and 4. Examples can be found in administrative departments that make procedures, conventions, etc. – originally created as part of System 2 to help the tasks of System 1–their "reason for being" and supposedly, as a result of a change of focus, that of those they should serve. Exaggerated bureaucracy may be included in this group. Exaggerated bureaucracy may be included in this group. Departments or bodies characterised

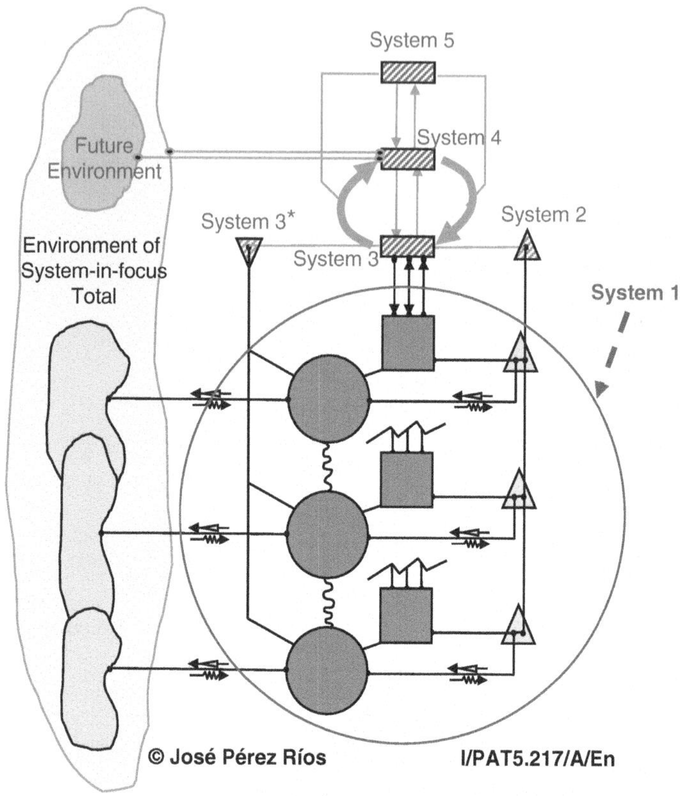

Fig. 3.17 Pathology P2.15. Dominance of System1. Weak metasystem (Pérez Ríos 2008b)

by such behaviour correspond, genuinely, to those entities Schuhmann called "autopoietic beasts" (Schuhmann 1997).

However, besides the more or less obvious case of short-sighted bureaucratic hypertrophy, other occasionally more serious examples exist. One of the most notorious is that of entire organisations which are created to comply with a specific function in society or a company, but which, with the passing of time, eventually take as their main aim their own existence as an organization rather than furnishing the service for which they were devised.

As for intra-organizational examples, we can find manifestations of these pathologies in service departments which place their own existence and preservation of power-sharing before their attention to the people, departments, etc., in the company or organisation they are supposed to serve.

Pathological behaviour of this type, whether within organisations or by whole companies, gives rise in the short term to a dysfunction of the organisation in its area of influence as well as affecting the motivation of those involved; in the long term, however, should the damage be widespread and persistent, it may lead to the destruction of the organization that contains those who act in this way, and consequently of themselves.

3.2.7.2 Lack of Metasystem

Another pathology referring to the entire organisation stems from the absence or weakness of the Metasystem, which, we must remember, comprises Systems 3, System 4 and System 5. This may happen in organisations where, as a consequence of growth, more (or exclusive) attention has been given to developing System-1 elements; initial success with certain products or services has led the organisation to focus on supplying the market with the required goods or services, while paying little attention to developing its management system (Metasystem), or the functions of System 3, 4 and 5. Regarding System 3, I have already mentioned its double role as part of the System (Operations) and the Metasystem (Management). When this pathology arises, System 3 may have developed to a certain extent, but only in terms of activity related to managing and integrating System-1elements and not to interacting with System 4. This interaction of Systems 3 and System 4 is essential for guaranteeing the organisation's adaptation and consequently its viability (Fig. 3.18).

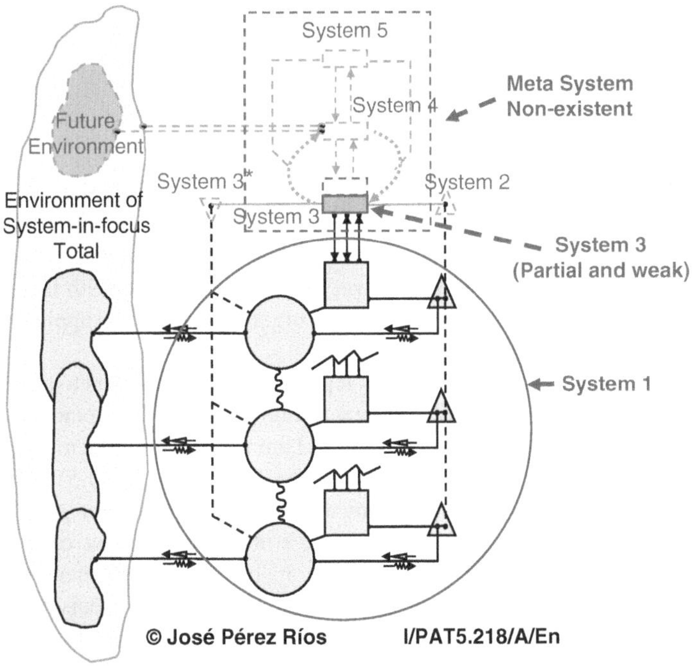

Fig. 3.18 Pathology P2.17. Lack of metasystem (Pérez Ríos 2008b)

The prognosis for organisations suffering from this pathology is also clear. Should this structure be maintained and the required functions (Systems 3, System 4 and System 5) not be developed, the organisation will cease to be viable.

One variant of such pathology occurs when certain activities associated with the particular functions of these systems, although they take place, are not sufficient clarified. They are applied in a somewhat diffuse way by some managers, with no clear identification as to their corresponding functions, or how they are related or how they are to be performed. Despite their possible attenuation, the effects are similar to those of the previous case.

3.3 Pathologies Associated with Information Systems and Communication Channels

In Sect. 1.3 of Chap. 1, I commented on the role of communication channels within the VSM as elements connecting all the functions/subsystems of the organisation, and the persons who compose it, as well as the organisation with the different parts of the environment. Furthermore, mention was made of the requirements needing to be met by a channel, if it is to suitably fulfill its function as a transmitter of information. Therefore, what I intend to do in this section is to point out certain possible pathologies associated with the existence and constitution of communication channels and, in wider terms, to the information systems.

3.3.1 Lack of Information Systems

The first pathology to be mentioned is related to the absence of information systems or (if there is something that can supposedly be assimilated to them, such as certain computer applications for helping with very specific decisions) with their inability to provide the infrastructure needed for the organisation to be supplied with the essential information for each of its parts.

Information is the element that makes it possible decision-takers to be connected and for the various functions of the organisation to be put into practice. When I speak of the absence of Information Systems, I am referring to systems of a general nature that link the different functions (Systems 1, 2, 3, 3*, 4 and 5). It is evident that if they do not exist, the other systems will operate more or less in isolation. Of course, any system needs, in order to work, a minimum amount of information concerning the other parts of the organisation, but if this information is either incomplete, inappropriate in some cases or late in others, then decisions taken on the basis of such information are unlikely to be well conceived. An organisation with this quality of information will find it difficult to achieve its purposes in a long-lasting and stable way.

Despite this need for adequacy, I should point out that information systems do not necessarily consist of sophisticated informatics tools (even if these may be desirable). What is important is not so much the technological tool employed to capture, transmit and show the information, as the fact that systems actually exist to carry out such tasks and that the decision-takers have the information when they need it.

Designing information systems for the entire organisation implies a thorough familiarity with it. In particular, it implies precise knowledge of the various functions, their relationships with one another and with the environments, as well as the necessary characteristics which the communication channels should possess in each case. For this reason we believe that an understanding of the VSM offers an essential conceptual framework for orienting the design of information systems in any organisation.

3.3.2 Fragmentation of Information Systems

Another series of problems and dysfunctions in an organisation may be the result of information systems that exist and are useful for specific activities within the organisation but which operate in a context of insularity. They possess all the elements for capturing, storing and processing data and information, but act like closed systems from the point of view of the information generated. The problems that might result from there being multiple computer applications or software packages functioning in isolation, touch on the following aspects: the possible inconsistency of the data handled in different functions, lack of knowledge concerning its availability and redundancy when acquiring it, with the corresponding increase in staff and financial costs; in general, there is the difficulty of integrating the information and having it circulate regularly throughout the multiple channels that feed the functions necessary for the viability of the organisation as the global system it is. Optimising the parts in a system under no circumstances guarantees the optimisation of the whole system. Therefore, information must circulate continually and uninterruptedly throughout the entire organisation. Only that condition makes it possible to take decisions that affect the whole in a suitably informed way.

The fragmenting of information systems, their manifestation as information islands, or the non-existence of infrastructure to link them up in a continuous and uninterrupted manner, will mean that the organisation is without a fundamental element for its proper functioning. The consequences will be, among others, lack of coordination, inconsistencies, certain functions remaining oblivious to what is going on in others, and a general increase in costs. Moreover, such consequences are likely to be accompanied by an inadequate long-term supply, to the market or specific environment, of the organisation's goods or services, leading eventually to its failure.

3.3.3 Lack of Key Communication Channels

Besides structures designed to distribute information among the essential functions of the VSM, there should also be an "infrastructure", that is, the channels of communication connecting all those components that share information, which should have the capacity necessary to "transport" the amount of information required in each case.

Regarding this, the pathology I would like to deal with now is the one caused by an insufficient network of communication channels. If certain functions which should be linked by information are not, because either the channel responsible for linking does not exist or, if it does exist, fails to comply with any of the requirements to which every communication channel should adhere if it is to carry out its proper function, then the network is incomplete. (Every communication channel must ensure that all the information emitted from a source reaches the receiver in a format which the latter finds intelligible and in the right time for it to be useful, and also subsequently ensure that the sender receives the information saying that the message has arrived and has been understood by the receiver.) The result of such inadequacies in the system are functions that fail to perform their tasks appropriately, due to a lack of information or because it is partial, unintelligible or delayed, and consequently useless. Statements such as "Nobody tells me anything" or "I have to get to know in other ways", among others, indicate a poor communication network.

The prognosis for an organisation with these deficiencies is inefficient behaviour as well as a proliferation of conflicts between those attempting to do the work that corresponds to their different functions.

3.3.4 Lack of or Insufficient Algedonic Channels

The inexistence (or insufficient presence) of *algedonic channels* is a particularly serious situation. As I remarked earlier, these are essentially concerned with transmitting information about any incident arising in System 1 (or also appearing in the environment and captured by System 4) that may have an important (and even vital) impact on the organisation's viability. Its design and proper functioning are critical for, if need be, warning System 5 about the appearance of real threats to the organisation's survival, and prompting that system to intervene.

The prognosis for an organisation with deficiencies associated with either a poor design of the *algedonic channels*, or their dysfunction or, in particular, the absence of those requisites, is, if the problem is not detected in time and is sufficiently serious, that the organisation is likely to disappear

3.3.5 Communication Channels Which Are Incomplete or of Inadequate Capacity

A further deficiency related tp the communication network is the specific design of the channels. If these lack certain of the elements I have described as essential for a communication channel to do what it should do, the two functions that are supposedly connected are not completely connected in fact. The absence of transducers or their inadequacy, or the limited capacity of the channels to transmit the requisite amount of information per unit of time, will mean that, although the channel supposedly exists, it fails to perform its function of having the information arrive properly. The same thing will occur if the design and choice of the "sensors" at the points of emission, or the way in which the information is shown to the receivers, are inadequate.

Statements like "No-one can understand this information", "No-one can read this", "The information I'm sent is incomplete", "The information I receive is useless because it's not the kind I need", "The way in which I receive the information is no good", "When I receive the information it's too late", "I didn't know the information hadn't arrived", "The receiver hasn't understood the message", or "It isn't what I meant", etc., are indicators of communication-channel deficiencies.

The consequences for the organisation of deficiencies like these are similar to the ones described previously concerning the lack of communication channels.

3.4 Final Thoughts on the Design and Diagnosis of Organisations by Means of the VSM

Applying Beer's VSM to both the design and diagnosis of organisations makes it possible, on the one hand, to guarantee that they will be equipped with the necessary and sufficient elements required to ensure their viability and, on the other, to identify which elements are not embodied as they should be, whether they function poorly, or whether, despite having the necessary structural components for smooth operation at least initially, there is a dysfunction on account of deficiencies associated with the information systems and communication channels.

In this chapter we have identified some of the most common pathologies in organisations, classified in three main groups and each corresponding to one of the essential dimensions of OC application. The first group includes those I refer to as *Structural Pathologies;* in the second are the ones I consider to be *Functional Pathologies;* and in the third group we find *Pathologies associated with information systems and communication channels.*

The availability of this taxonomy of pathologies may, besides providing certain keys for identifying and subsequently correcting commonly occurring problems in organisations, also be particularly useful for helping managers to apply the VSM in organisations. One of the reasons highlighted by various researchers as possibly accounting for the relatively slow process of adoption and application of OC in companies and organisations in general, is, as I have already indicated, the difficulty experienced in understanding and applying it. The availability of new technological tools such as VSMod® software (Pérez Ríos 2003, 2006b, 2008c) combined with the introduction of application guidelines may, I believe, be useful in terms of both understanding the OC/VSM methodology and applying it. In Chap. 4, in fact, we take a look at the VSMod® software. Following a brief description of the genesis of this software, I will set forth its main functionalities.

Chapter 4
The Software for Applying the VSM: VSMod®

4.1 Introduction

In the last decades, a great change in information and communication technologies has taken place, particularly following the advent and proliferation of the Internet. These changes have to a large extent transformed the way in which firms operate and compete. They have generated new business opportunities as well as giving rise to improvements in productivity. Some of the schools belonging to the field of Systems Thinking have benefited from these new tools whilst others have not, at least to a sufficient degree. We believe this to be the case with the Organisational Cybernetics of S. Beer (Pérez Ríos 2006b).

Over more than a decade we have been developing, within the Systems Thinking Group at the University of Valladolid, software tools aimed at facilitating the application of diverse systems methodologies. and among these Organisational Cybernetics in particular. More specifically, in this area we have created software tools that enable us to apply the Viable System Model to the diagnosis and design of organisations, and also to organise different phases of the decision process termed Team Syntegrity, whose essential elements we will take up in Chap. 5. Already, as part of a research project financed by the Spanish Ministry of Science and Innovation (Ref.: CSO2010-15745), the creation of a software meta-tool is quite well developed nowadays, allowing the incorporation of a range of systemic methodologies which in turn can be used. In the next paragraphs I will focus attention solely on the basic elements of VSMod® software (Pérez Ríos 2003, 2006b, 2008c, 2008e).[1] This software has been developed in order to make it easier to study complex problems with the help of the Viable System Model described in Chaps. 1, 2 and 3.

The number and variety of VSM applications for both diagnosing and designing organisations have grown considerably since this model was created (Espejo and Harnden 1989, and Schwaninger and Pérez Ríos 2008b). The possibility afforded

[1] VSMod® is made available at the following address: www.vsmod.org

J. Pérez Ríos, *Design and Diagnosis for Sustainable Organizations*,
DOI 10.1007/978-3-642-22318-1_4,

by the VSM for analysing a problem from various points of view by selecting different criteria and levels of recursion, as I pointed out in Sect. 1.3 of Chap. 1 and 2.2 of Chap. 2, is a very powerful and important characteristic of the model. Its capacity for travelling vertically through several dimensions allows it to identify the recursion levels that reflect the means whereby an organisation can best attempt to deal with the complexity of the environment in which it operates. However, this analytical potential also implies an increase in the model's complexity. If we employ different criteria and recursion levels, the number of elements to be taken into consideration grows very rapidly. For each level of recursion there should likewise be identification of the complete set of systems/functions (Systems 1, 2, 3, 3*, 4 and 5), communication channels (including the algedonic channel), transducers, environments, relations between the environments, relations between the elements of System 1, as well as all the information components pertinent to each of these. As a consequence, the task of identifying each component and the registering of corresponding information is inherently rather complex, and is compounded by the difficulty of maintaining control of the place we are at any given time of the study.

One of the reasons for creating VSMod® was precisely that of facilitating such a task. Others are associated with the incorporation in VSMod® of an introductory guide to using the VSM, which gives advice concerning the main aspects characterising the model as well as on how to use it for both designing and diagnosing organisations. The inclusion of examples relating to some of the most common pathologies may, I believe, also help to make the application of the VSM more accessible.

4.2 A Brief History of VSMod®

The origins of VSMod® go back to October 2001, when the first prototype of VSMod® was presented to S. Beer and A. Leonard on the occasion of Professor Beer's visit to the University of Valladolid to receive from it the title of Dr. Honoris Causa (when, as I have already mentioned, I had the honour to serve as his laudator (Pérez Ríos 2001)).

In July 2003, in Crete (Greece), the first version VSMod® 1.0 was introduced (Pérez Ríos 2003), at the *47th Annual Conference of the ISSS*. This version was designed to work with only one computer and in a local context.

In June 2005, in Maribor (Slovenia), at the *WOSC 13th International Congress of Cybernetics and Systems and the 6th International Conference of Sociocybernetics*,[2] the VSMod® 1.1 version (Pérez Ríos 2006a and 2006b) was presented. This is the first version designed for being used via Internet. It was possible to access the software via Internet at all times and to upload it on the user's computer, the only requirement being connection availability to the software

[2] An indicator of the welcome given the new software was the granting by the *WOSC* Congress organisation of the *Kybernetes Research Award for Highly Commended Paper* for the paper in which it was presented (Pérez Ríos 2006a).

website. Once activated, users could create as many studies or projects as they wished. When the particular work had been done, this version made it possible to keep the information generated in the user's computer, both for storing and for future use should there be a later need to continue with the work.

In May 2006, in Liverpool (U.K.), at the *Fourth Metaphorum Conference,* the VSMod® 1.2 version was presented. This is the perfected version of the 1.1 in which, besides improvements in strengthening the application, several new modules had been added concerning how to deal with relations among the environments, relations among System-1 elements, the explicit incorporation of the algedonic channel, and the possibility of providing a graphic representation of System-1 elements with their relative sizes corresponding to specific comparison parameters chosen by the user.

In March 2007, in St. Gallen (Switzerland), on the occasion of the *The Fifth Metaphorum Conference*, the VSMod® 1.3 version was introduced (Pérez Ríos 2007b). This is the first version of VSMod® to exist in three dimensions. It provides the user with greater clarity in visualising relations between the different function and communication channels within the VSM, as well as showing the whole system-in-focus in a single image, regardless of the number of elements comprising System 1. A zoom function makes it possible to have the image recede or bring it closer, and also to rotate or shift the complete image, with the result that visualisation of the model is enhanced.

In May 2007, in Athens (Greece), during the *3rd National and International Conference of the Hellenic Society for Systemic Studies* we introduced an improved version of VSMod® 1.3, particularly in terms of the menus and screen design (Pérez Ríos 2007c). At this conference the *Hellenic Society for Systemic Studies (HSSS)* gave the author of this book, José Pérez Ríos, the *Honorary HSSS Award* as a *Distinguished Scientist* for his contribution to the development of software applicable in the field of Organisational Cybernetics.

Nowadays, developmental work on the VSMod® is aimed at including, in addition to functional improvements associated with structural design and methodological guidelines, the possibility of creating collaborative VSM models via the Internet. This version (the prototype of which is now available) will allow various researchers or VSM users to engage in synchronous or asynchronous teleworking with the same viable model.

Prior to a more detailed examination of how the VSMod® works, let us survey some of its most relevant characteristics.

4.3 Main Characteristics of VSMod® (v.1.3)

The current version of VSMod® (v.1.3) permits the following activities:

- Creating a new study or modifying an existing one.
- Selecting as many recursion criteria as the researcher or user needs.

- Including within each recursion criterion whichever levels of recursion are deemed appropriate. When a particular level has been selected, we can once again determine the criteria according to which we are going to identify additional levels. These recursion criteria may be either previously created or new ones.
- Using a global navigation map showing the structure of the study (recursion criteria, levels of recursion and all the sub-systems of the VSM study), whilst allowing us to move around and change our system-in-focus by simply clicking on its name with the computer mouse. The sub-system thus selected will then become the new system-in-focus.
- Using two extra navigation maps. These show the system-in-focus, the previous recursion level and the following one. We can go backwards or forwards by simply clicking on either level on the map.
- Once we have positioned ourselves on the chosen system-in-focus, we can add as many sub-systems (System-1 elements) as we wish.
- Visualising the complete detailed map of the VSM corresponding to the system-in-focus.
- The map (graphic representation) of the VSM contains all the information entered by the researcher or user in all the components, namely: Systems 1, 2, 3, 3*, 4 and 5; all of the homeostatic loops, all relations among elements; all the transducers, amplifiers and variety attenuators corresponding to each homeostatic loop; all the environments; all relations (in their many possible combinations) among environments, all relations (in their many possible combinations) among System-1 elements (sub-systems) and in the environments (both at the present time and regarding future potential scenarios).
- The user of VSMod® can add information to the model in any format (text, audio, video, graphics, simulation models, links to web pages, etc.) and in every one of the VSM components.
- Adding information in the algedonic channels. VSMod® allows the inclusion of all the algedonic channels considered appropriate.
- Including as many relevant parameters for describing System-1 elements (sub-systems) as are deemed necessary.
- Re-drawing the elements (sub-systems or elementary operational units) of System 1 in accordance with the parameter selected, so as to reflect the relative size of certain elements compared with others within this system.
- Entering information in any of the possible relations among System-1 elementary operational units. This information may be as complete as the user wishes (blueprints, drawings, videos describing processes, simulation models, etc.).
- Entering information in any of the possible relations among environments (System-in-focus and its sub-systems).

All the above-mentioned functions relating to the addition or visualisation of information may be carried out at each of the recursion levels identified for the model. This is facilitated to a large extent by using the Navigation Maps, whose detailed functioning I will examine later.

Having surveyed the main characteristics of VSMod®, let us have a closer look at how it works.

4.4 Description of VSMod®

To illustrate how to use VSMod®, by way of example we will consider a VSM project (currently under development for the University of A Coruña) on urban design in a university context (Pérez Ríos and Martínez Suárez 2007). We will start by showing how a VSM study is created and how its general structure is defined. Following this, we will see how the three navigation maps included in the software can be used in order to facilitate shifting from one of the diverse recursion levels (and criteria) to another. Then we will describe the general VSM map (a graphic representation of all its components), and also how to enter information in each one. We will finish our tour of VSMod® with an illustration of how the VSM can be combined with other methodologies or tools by means of VSMod®, with special emphasis on Systems Dynamics.

4.4.1 Creation of a New Study

VSMod® is available in various formats depending on the type of use, for instance: (1) individual use by accessing and downloading it via Internet from the web address where it can be found (www.vsmod.org), (2) individual use by permanent installation in the user's computer and (3) collaborative use. We will now take a look at its use in the first case (individual user who downloads the software from the web address at which it can be accessed). Its operation in the case of permanent installation is practically identical. When used cooperatively it requires a more detailed explanation, although the means by which the VSM and VSMod® are applied are very similar.

The first step is to register as a user of the application in order to obtain the password required for accessing the software. With this password, it is possible to download the software and create as many VSM studies as the user wishes, as well as modifying those already created. Having given the study or project a name, one can start to work with it. The first thing to do is select the language in which one wishes to work. Currently VSMod® is available not only in Spanish and English but also in Russian and Greek. When we have chosen the language the general screen will appear (Fig. 4.1a, b), on which we can open the project we are working on (or create a new one). Following this operation, the main screen of the application will appear (Fig. 4.2a, b). Here we can specify the general structure of the VSM study. Let us see how to do it.

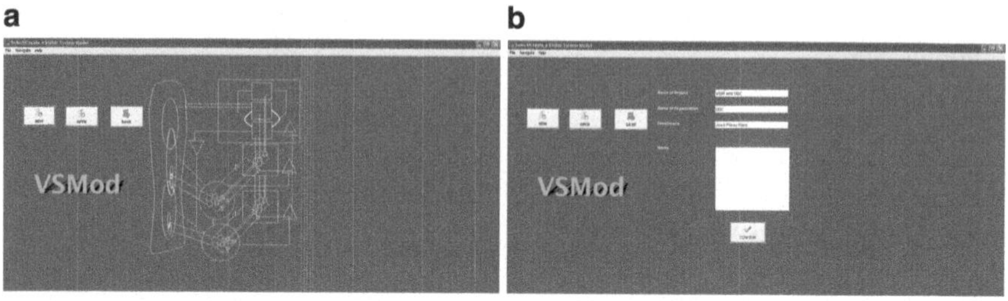

Fig. 4.1 Initial screen (**a**) General. (**b**) Creation of a new project

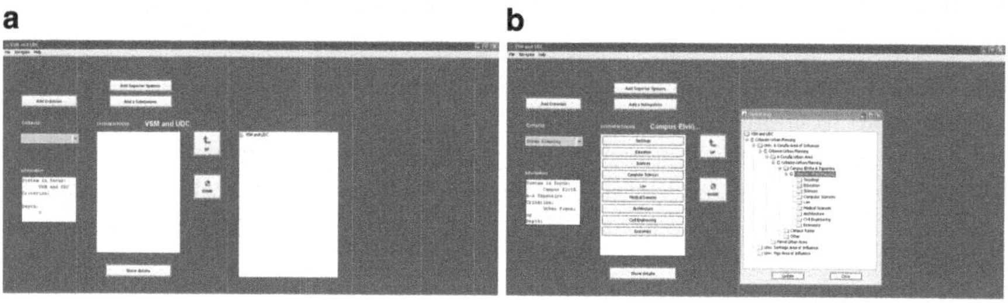

Fig. 4.2 Main screen (**a**) before beginning to create the structure and (**b**) after creating the structure

4.4.2 Creation of the General Structure

We start to build the structure of a VSM study by selecting the criteria we will use for identifying the recursion levels. We can add as many recursion criteria as wished. Once we have selected a particular level of recursion, we can begin to name and add the sub-systems that make up this level. We should remember that these sub-systems are the elements that comprise the system-in-focus where we are situated. This is identified by the corresponding criterion and level of recursion.

Now that we have defined and incorporated the desired elements (sub-systems) at a specific recursion level, we can move down to the next level simply by using the mouse to click on the name of the sub-system selected. Then this sub-system will become our new system-in-focus. Once there, we can again repeat the same process as when we started, that is, choose a new recursion criterion (or employ one of those already included in the model) and, once it is selected, name and add, as we like, the new elements (sub-systems) of System 1, of the system-in-focus. The new sub-systems will appear on the screen as we create and add them.

At any moment we can move down through all the recursion levels simply by clicking on the name of the sub-system we desire. Likewise, we can move to the previous recursion levels by clicking on the arrow provided. An option which is also possible at all times is to go directly to the first recursion level, whichever level we are at, by using the "Home" button.

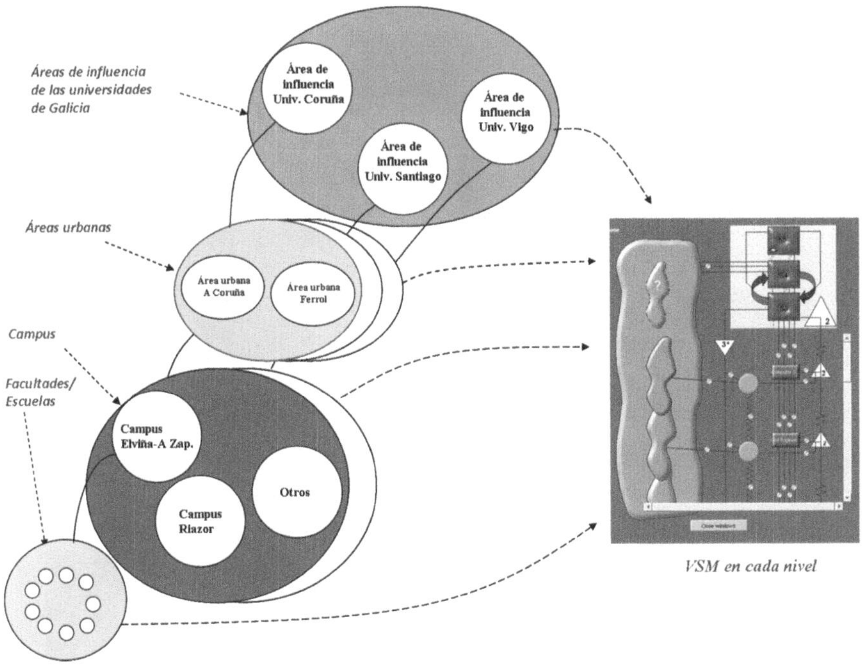

Fig. 4.3 Structure of the VSM for the UDC (example with a single recursion criterion: urban planning)

Taking the example of the "University of A Coruña" (UDC) in Fig. 4.3, we can see part of its structure. The four levels of recursion deemed relevant according to the "spatial" (geographical or urban) criterion may be appreciated.

In the first level we can see the complete public university system for the autonomous community of Galicia, represented by three universities (University of A Coruña, University of Santiago de Compostela and University of Vigo) with their respective geographical areas of influence (Fig. 4.4). If we select "Area of influence of University of A Coruña", we will see at the next recursion level "Urban area of A Coruña" and "Urban area of Ferrol" (Fig. 4.5). If then we select "Urban area of A Coruña", we will be at the following level with three sub-systems corresponding to the various UDC campuses in that city: "Elviña-A Zapateira", "Oza" and "Others" (Fig. 4.6). Once again, if we select the sub-system "Campus Elviña-A Zapateira", we will move to the subsequent level of recursion corresponding to the faculties and technical schools on that campus (Fig. 4.7). The following level would be made up of each of these faculties or schools.

The process we have followed for determining recursion levels, that is, the process of complexity unfolding, leads us to the following recursion levels:

- R-0. The Autonomous Community of Galicia.
- R-1. The urban region A Coruña-Ferrol (Direct area of influence of the University of A Coruña).

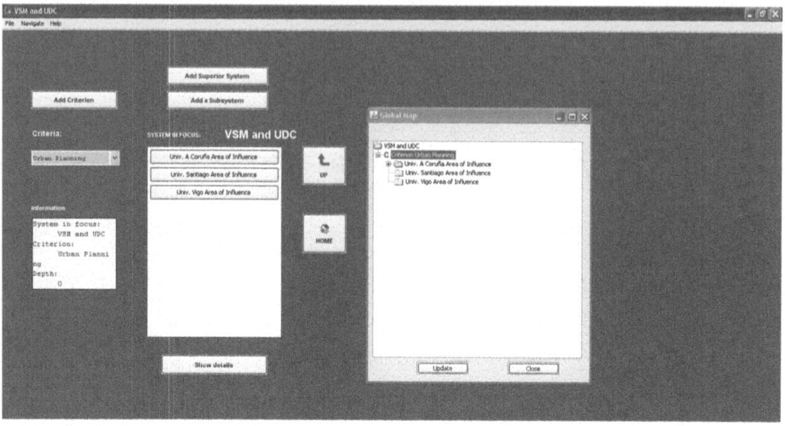

Fig. 4.4 Recursion level: Galicia university system

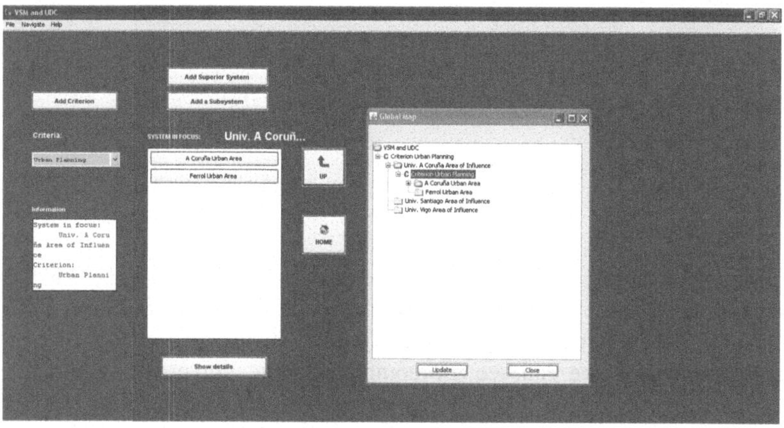

Fig. 4.5 Recursion level: area of influence of the UDC

- R-2. The urban area of A Coruña and that of Ferrol.
- R-3. The campus of A Coruña and that of Ferrol.
- R-4. The Centres, Buildings and other installations of the UDC.

The recursion criterion employed is "spatial" (related with "urban planning"), but we could have used other criteria for unfolding complexity, such as "academic", "administrative", etc.

The more recursion levels and sub-systems we add, the more difficult it will be to establish our position within the structure of the model. In order to solve this problem VSMod® includes, as I mentioned previously, three navigation maps: Global Map, Map 1 and Map 2. Let us now have a look at how we can use these maps to navigate through the system's structure.

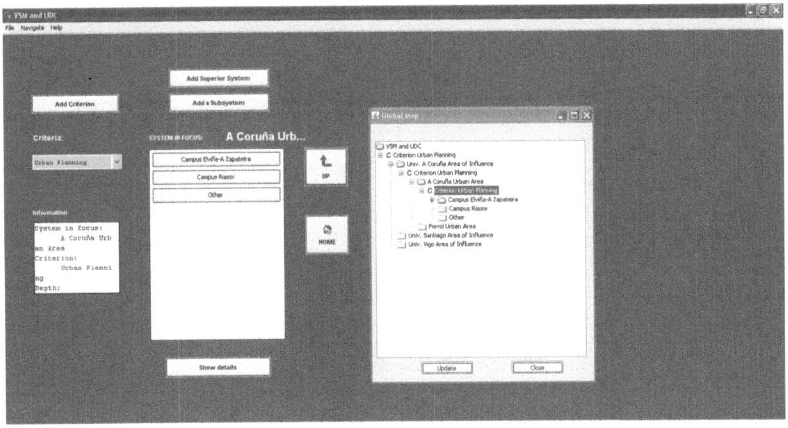

Fig. 4.6 Recursion level: Urban area A Coruna

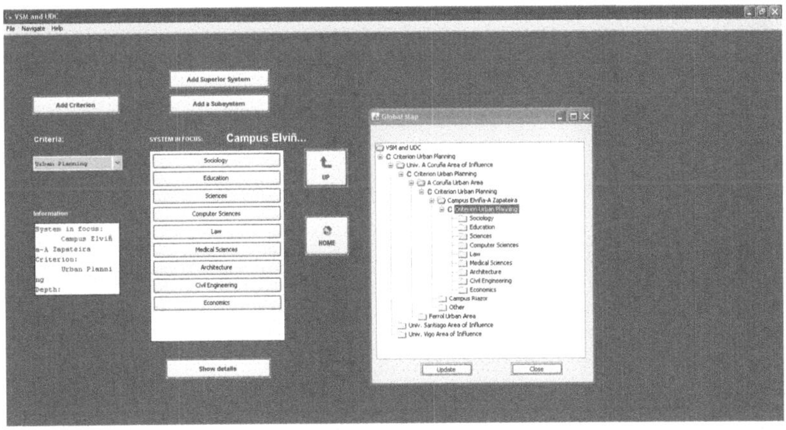

Fig. 4.7 Recursion level: Campus Elviña-A Zapateira

4.4.3 Navigating Through the Structure

The most complete navigation map included in VSMod® is what we call the Global Map (Fig. 4.8). This map is visible at all times (if we want it to be) whilst we create the recursive structure of the model, allowing us in this way to see its development as we build it up, as can be appreciated on the right side of the images in Fig. 4.9. It is also present and visible when we stop at a particular recursion level and work with the VSM graphic representation of the chosen system-in-focus (Fig. 4.10). The user decides whether to have it visible or leave it hidden.

This map shows the entire structure of the VSM, enabling us to navigate through it either up or down, or to go directly to a particular position in the structure (corresponding to a recursion criterion and specific recursion level) and select it

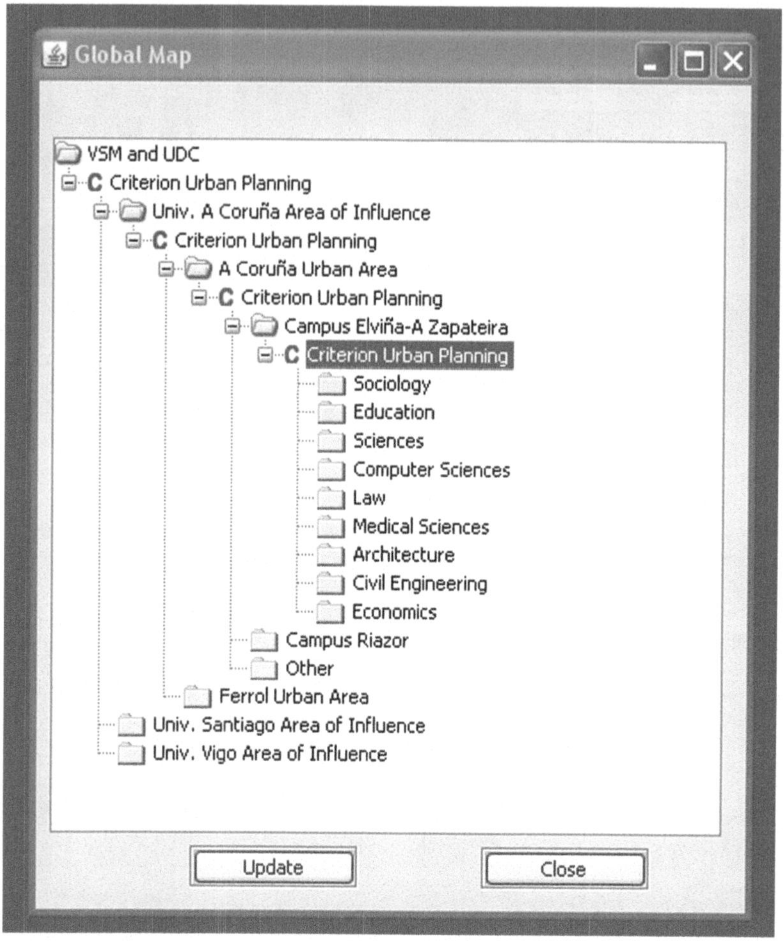

Fig. 4.8 Global Map, showing recursion criteria (C) and recursion levels

as the system-in-focus. Once this has been selected, we can visualise the graphic representation of the pertinent VSM. We can change the system-in-focus simply by clicking with the mouse inside the Global Map.

Besides this navigation tool, VSMod® also includes two additional maps called Map 1 and Map 2.

In Map 1 (see the top left section of Fig. 4.11) three levels of recursion are always shown simultaneously. It illustrates the system-in-focus as well as the previous and subsequent recursion levels. If we click on the part of the map corresponding to the previous recursion level, it will take us there. In this case, we will now still see three levels, but at one recursion level higher up. The same thing occurs if, instead of clicking on the area of the previous level, we do it on any of the sub-systems for the following recursion level: the application will take us there, and on the screen we will once again see three recursion levels, but one level lower down.

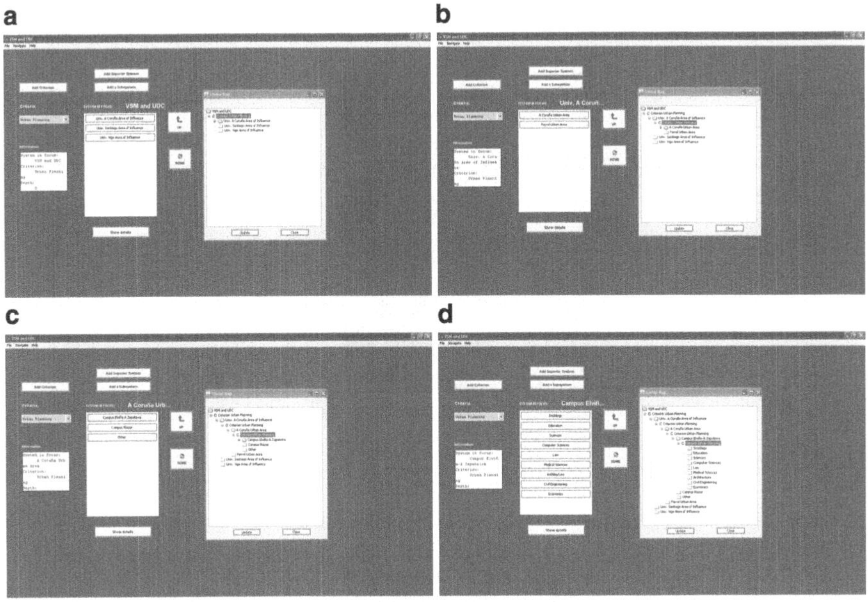

Fig. 4.9 Evolution of the Global Map during the creation of the recursive structure

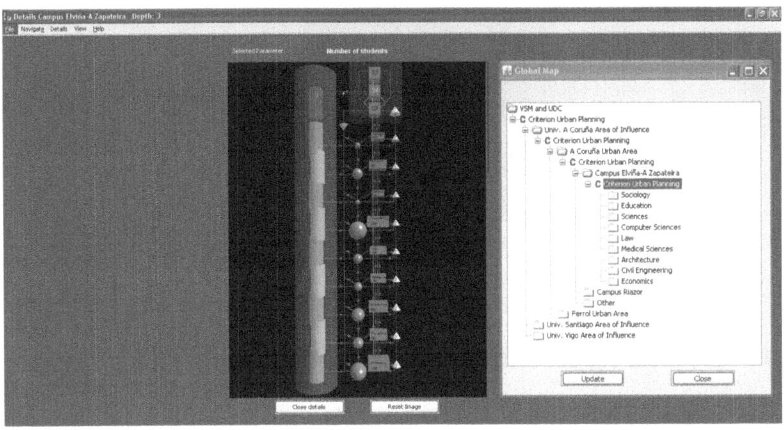

Fig. 4.10 Global Map and VSM

Map 2 (see the bottom left section of Fig. 4.12) has a similar function, but provides more detailed information. It likewise shows three recursion levels simultaneously, but in addition it includes all the sub-systems within each of them. We can access any of these simply by clicking on the name of the sub-system we wish to examine. The application will position us there, and that will be the new system-in-focus.

In Fig. 4.13, Map 1 and Map 2 can be seen together, and in Fig. 4.14 the three maps are shown: Global Map, Map 1 and Map 2.

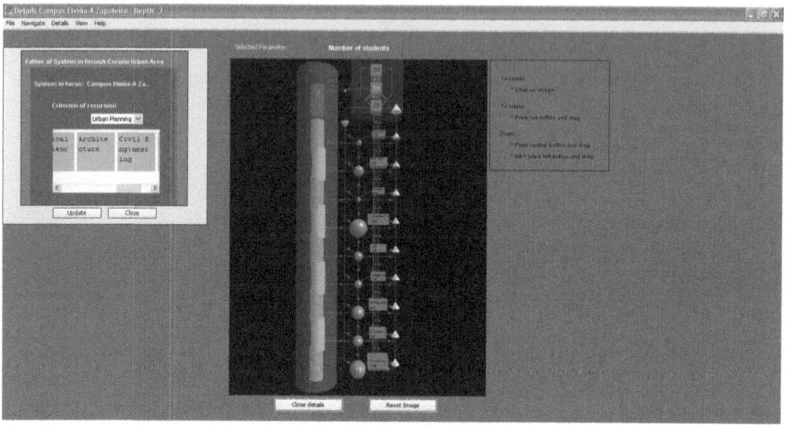

Fig. 4.11 Map 1

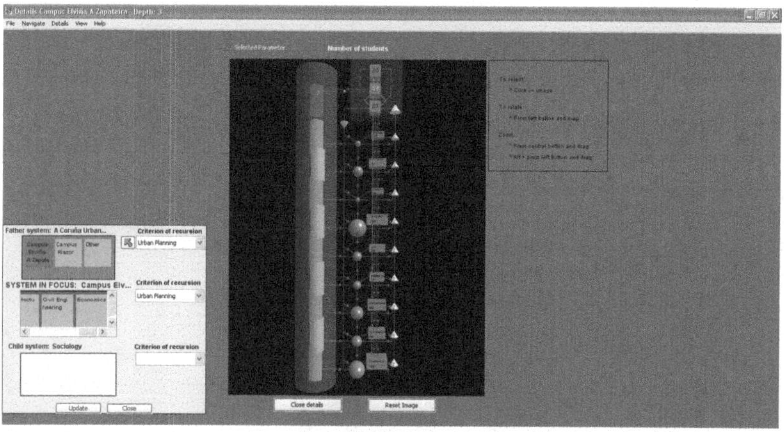

Fig. 4.12 Map 2

4.4.4 Graphic Representation of the VSM

Having decided on the system-in-focus with which we want to work, we can then go on to visualise the complete VSM map of this system. To do this, we click on the option "Show details" on the bottom part of the main screen (Fig. 4.15). A graphic representation (Fig. 4.16) of the system-in-focus will thereby appear. On this screen all elements are "active" in the sense that we can enter information in all of them.

Now we will explain how to enter information in each of the elements on the VSM map: System 1, System 2, System 3, System 3*, System 4, System 5, Homeostats, Communication channels, Environments, Relations among environments, relations among System 1 elements and algedonic channels. An interesting point to highlight is the modification in colour intensity an element undergoes when information is

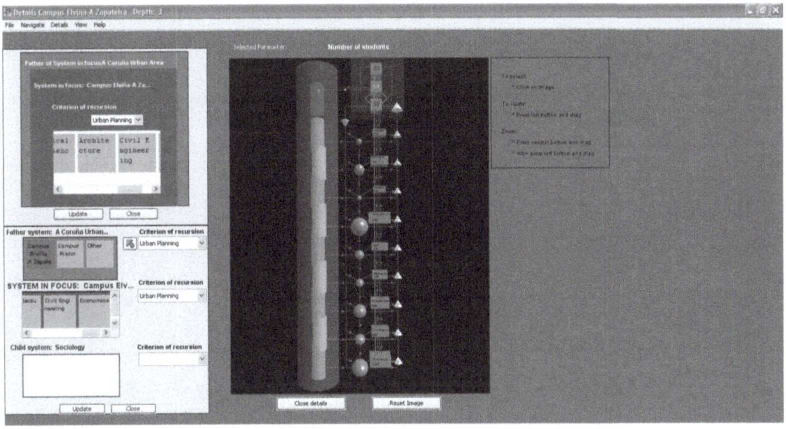

Fig. 4.13 Map 1 and Map 2

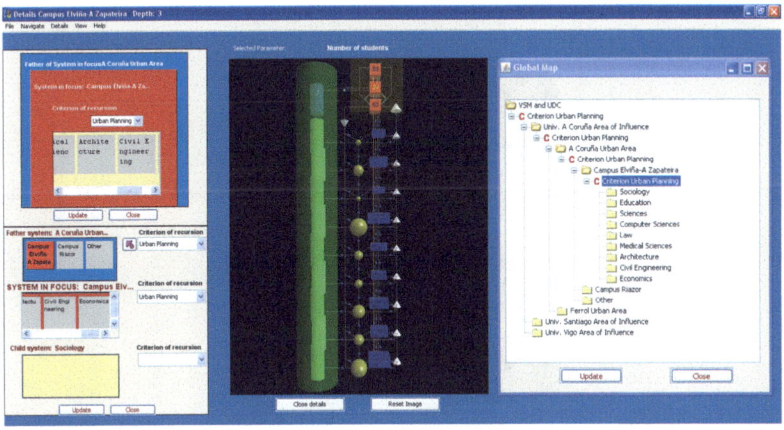

Fig. 4.14 Map 1, Map 2 and Global Map

entered. This has been included in VSMod® to inform the user about which VSM elements contain some information and those that for the moment do not.

4.4.4.1 System 1: Entering Information

In order to enter information in System 1 (Fig. 4.17), we simply click on the System-1 element we wish to work on, and a screen capturing information similar to that shown in Fig. 4.18 will appear.

We can add as many text fields as we wish, and within each we can also add, simply by clicking, all the files in whatever format (text, audio, video, image, etc.) that we consider appropriate (Fig. 4.19). The inclusion of a file is represented by the presence of a "paperclip" over the text field accessed (Fig. 4.20).

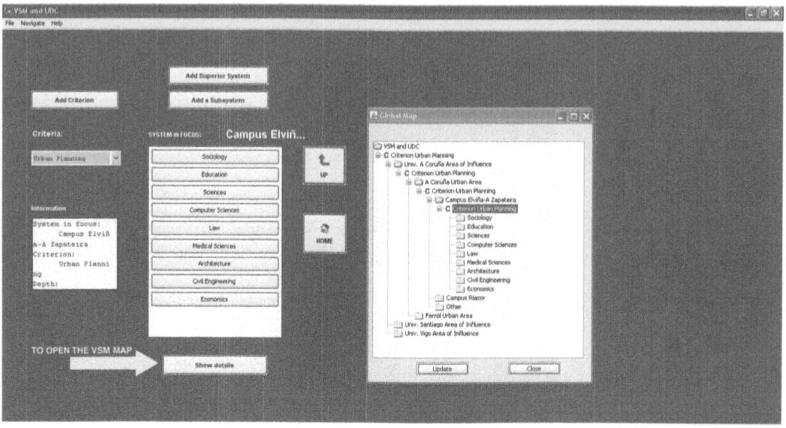

Fig. 4.15 Selecting visualisation of system-in-focus

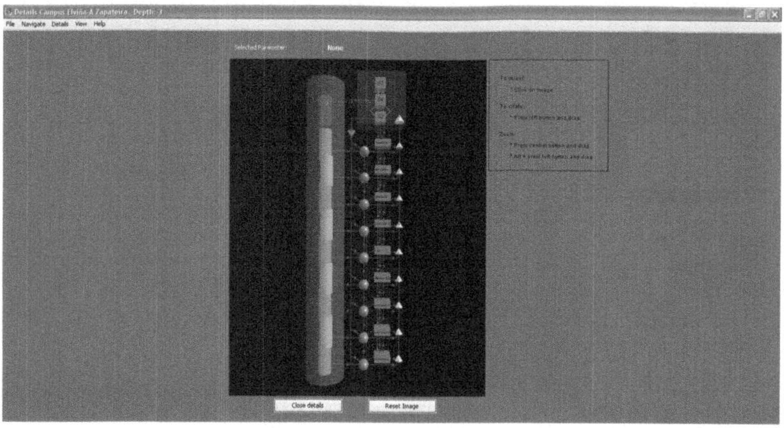

Fig. 4.16 VSM of system-in-focus

4.4.4.2 System 2 and 3*: Entering Information

To enter information in System 2 we click on "System 2" on the VSM map, thereby obtaining a screen like the one shown on the right side of Fig. 4.21. Here we can add whatever System 2 components we require, and can enter in each of them all the information (in whatever format) we deem necessary. Whenever we add an element of information (file), a "paperclip" will appear associated with the System-2 component to which we have linked this information. The number of "paperclips" indicates the number of files added. All this information is incorporated by means of a screen like that in Fig. 4.22. The right-hand side permits information entries in System 2, and the left-hand side in System 3*.

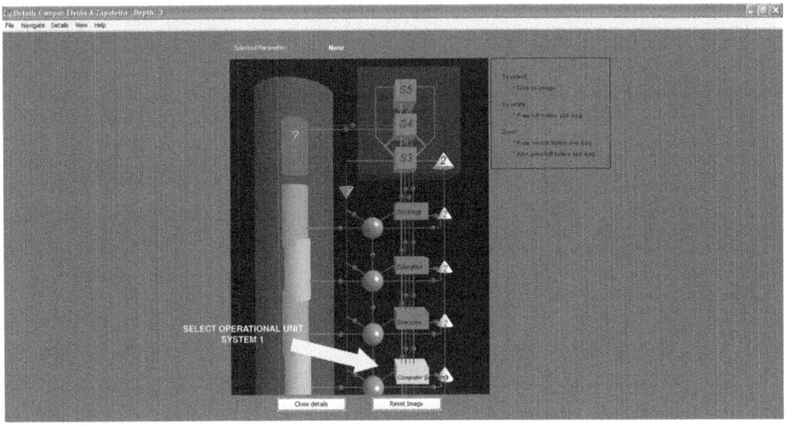

Fig. 4.17 Selecting System 1 element

Fig. 4.18 Screen capturing information

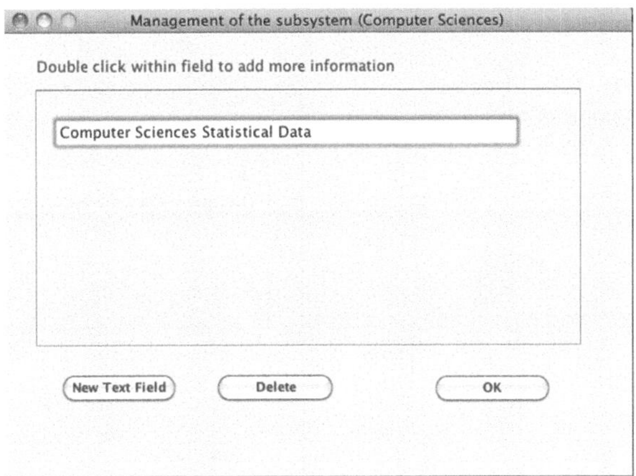

As regards entering components or information relating to each of these in System 3*, the procedure is similar to that we have just described for System 2 (Fig. 4.23).

4.4.4.3 Systems 3, 4 and 5: Entering Information

Entering information in the other three systems (Systems 3, 4 and 5) is done in a way similar to that which I have just explained for Systems 1, 2 and 3*. If on the VSM map we click on System 4, another information-capturing screen will appear like the one given in Fig. 4.18. Here we can add as many information components as we wish, and can attach to each all the files (in whatever format) we need (Fig. 4.19).

A very important point concerning the possibility of entering information inside System 4 in the VSM, is that we can include simulation models, and especially

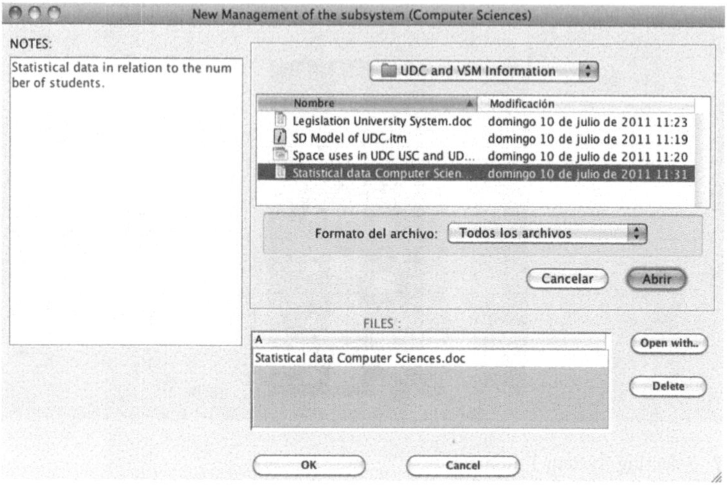

Fig. 4.19 Screen for adding files

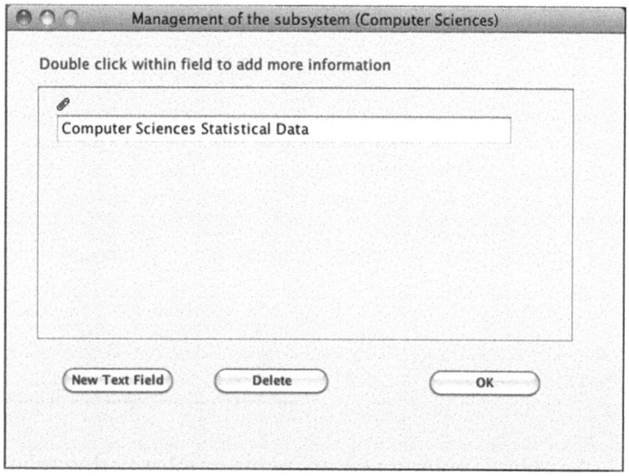

Fig. 4.20 Visualising number of files

System Dynamics simulation models. This capacity is of considerable significance, as it allows us to combine, both simply and naturally, two extremely complementary methodological fields, namely Organisational Cybernetics and Systems Dynamics (Schwaninger and Pérez Ríos 2008a).

Regarding the procedure for entering information in both System 3 and System 5, it is similar to that described for System 4.

4.4.4.4 Homeostats: Entering Information

In the same way we entered information in Systems 1–5, we can also do in each one of the homeostats contained in the VSM. If, for instance, we select the loop linking

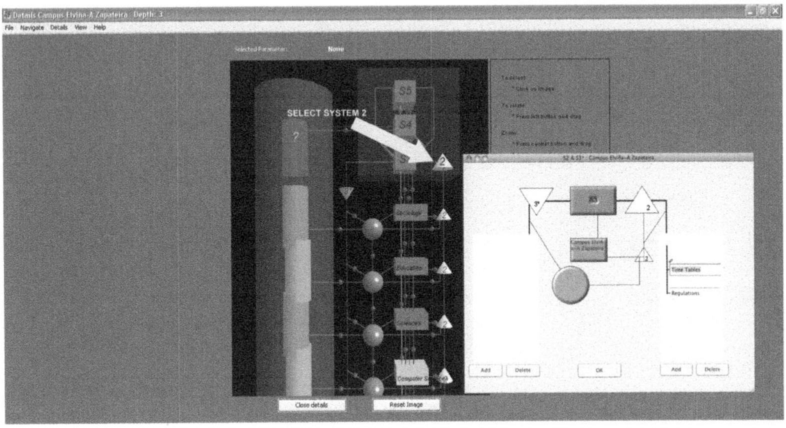

Fig. 4.21 Information – capturing screen (System 2 and System 3*)

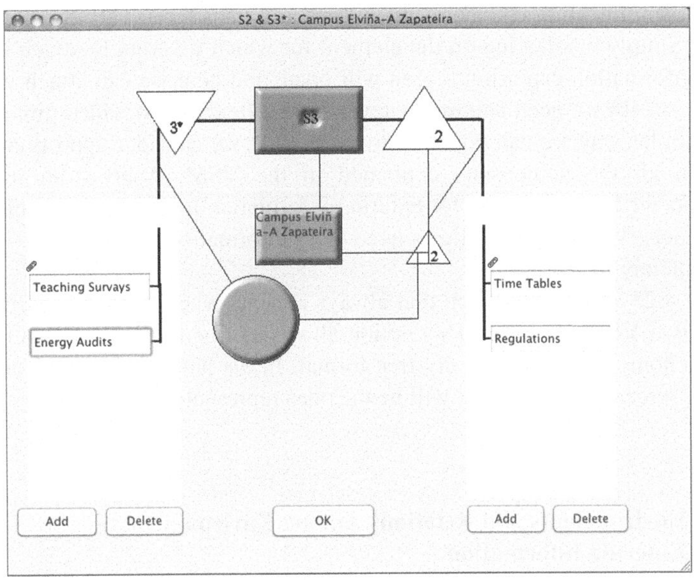

Fig. 4.22 Information-capturing screen (System 2)

System 4 with the Future-Environment of the system-in-focus and click on it, a new screen will appear like the one shown in Fig. 4.24a. On this we can appreciate the distinct components of the homeostatic loop: the two blocks connected via the corresponding channels, the amplification channel (which connects the block with lower variety with the one with higher), the attenuation channel (linking the block with higher variety to the one with lower) and all the corresponding transducers. If necessary, it is possible to add as many amplification and attenuation channels (with their transducers) as are deemed necessary. We can import into each of these

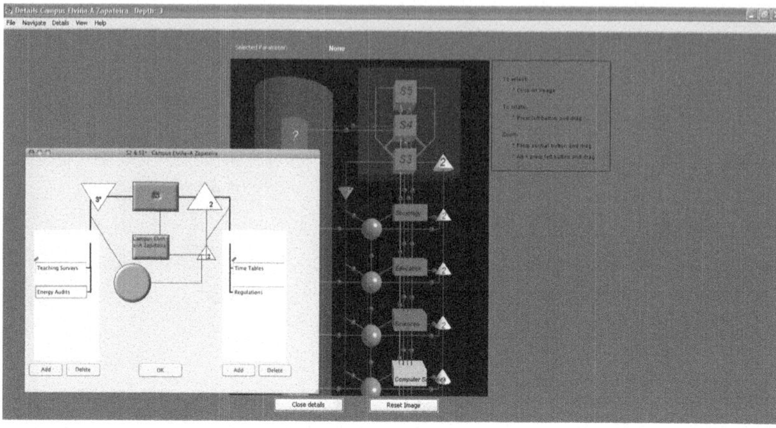

Fig. 4.23 Information-capturing screen (System 3*)

elements (amplification channels, attenuators and transducers) all the information we wish. Simply by clicking on the element for which we want to attach information, an information-capturing screen will open, and here we can attach whatever files (Fig. 4.24b) we need and in whatever format (text, audio, video, image, etc.).

In a similar way we can continue to enter what we consider appropriate information in all the homeostats contained in the VSM. Apart from using the homeostats we have just seen, for entering information in the diverse communication channels, VSMod® also allows us to enter information in each of the relations in a completely free format.

Figure 4.25 shows the option that always appears whenever we click on a link between two VSM elements. This option allows us to enter information by using either the homeostat or the totally free format. In the latter case, the information-capturing screens which appear will be the ones represented in Figs. 4.18 and 4.19.

4.4.4.5 Environments and Relations Among Environments: Entering Information

In order to enter information in the different environments, whether in the "future" environment or in those corresponding to the diverse elements making up System 1, we simply click on the one we want. Information-capturing screens will then open similar to those we have seen in the previous sections.

An interesting option worthy of more attention is the possibility of entering information in each of the potential relations among the different environments (Fig. 4.26). Obviously, we will limit ourselves to selecting the relations we believe to be pertinent to the VSM study we are undertaking.

Figure 4.27 reveals the drop-down menu that permits us to select the option of entering information in "Relations among environments".

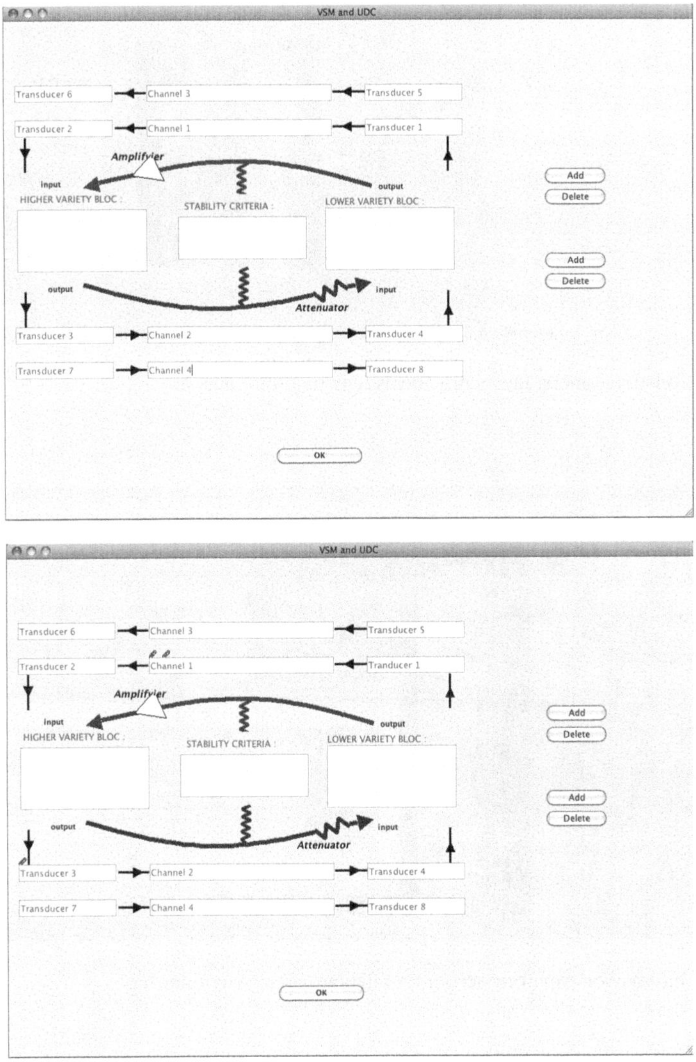

Fig. 4.24 (**a**) Capturing information in the Homeostatic loops. (**b**) Information annexes in the components of the loops

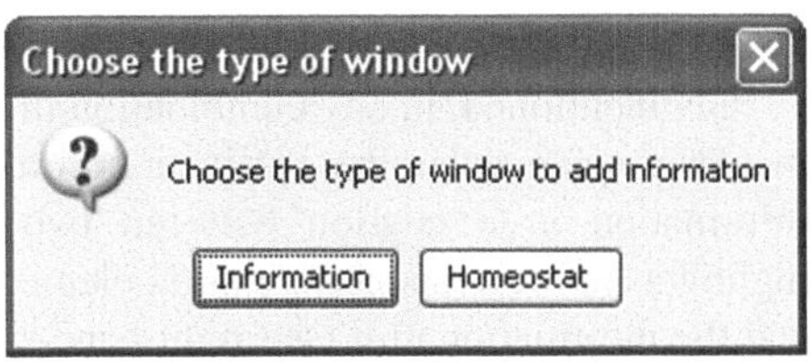

Fig. 4.25 Selecting format for entering information

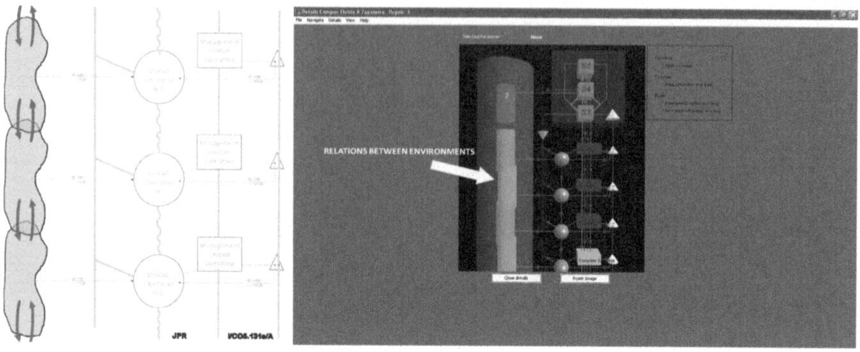

Fig. 4.26 Relations among the environments (entering information)

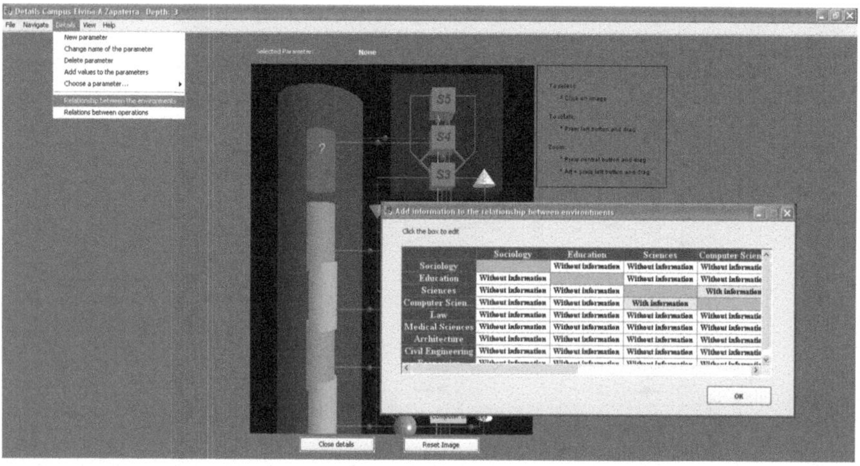

Fig. 4.27 Information-capturing screen for relations among environments

These interactions are handled by means of a matrix that shows us all possible relations. In the connection between environments where we consider it a good idea to enter information, we need only click on the corresponding matrix element, and then enter the information via the information-capturing screen similar to the one described above.

In Fig. 4.28 we can see the matrix of relations among environments. As I have already mentioned, in any combination of relations represented by elements in the matrix we can enter the pertinent information in each. Once we have entered information in a relation between two environments in particular, VSMod® highlights the corresponding matrix element to indicate the existence of the relation and the information in it (see right-hand side of Fig. 4.28).

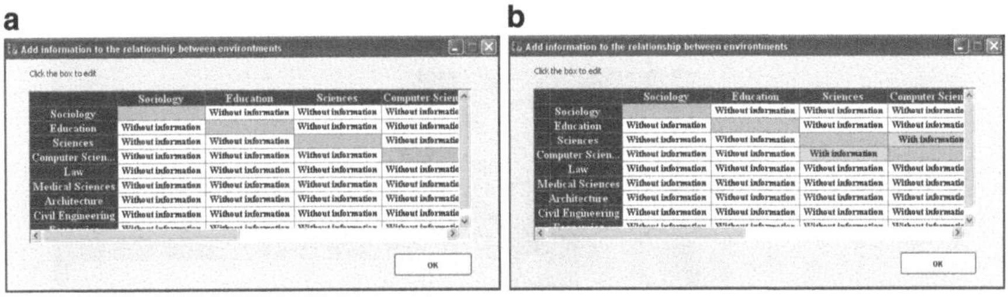

Fig. 4.28 Matrix of relations among environments (without and with information)

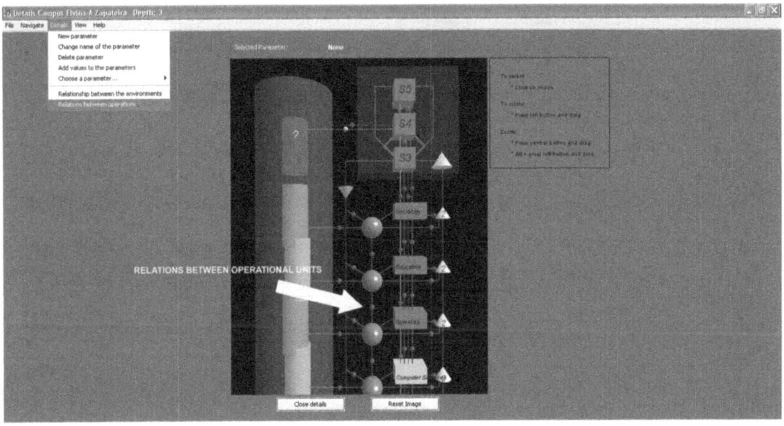

Fig. 4.29 Relations among elemental operational units (components of System 1)

4.4.4.6 Relations Between System-1 Elements: Entering Information

The way in which we handled relations among the different system-in-focus environments is similar to the one we use in order to deal with relations among the different elements (elementary operational units or sub-systems) that constitute System 1.

In Fig. 4.29 we see the drop-down menu that allows us to choose the option for entering information in “Relations among Processes”. A matrix showing all the potential relations among these elements makes it possible to introduce information on the relationship between the couple of System-1 components selected (Fig. 4.30). It is important to remember that the kind of information introduced can be as varied as we wish. For example, in the case of System 1, it may be appropriate to provide quite exhaustive descriptions of operational processes. This can be done with drawings, plant lay-outs, videos showing the processes, photographs or anything else giving information concerning the interaction of System-1 elements, including simulation models (Fig. 4.31).

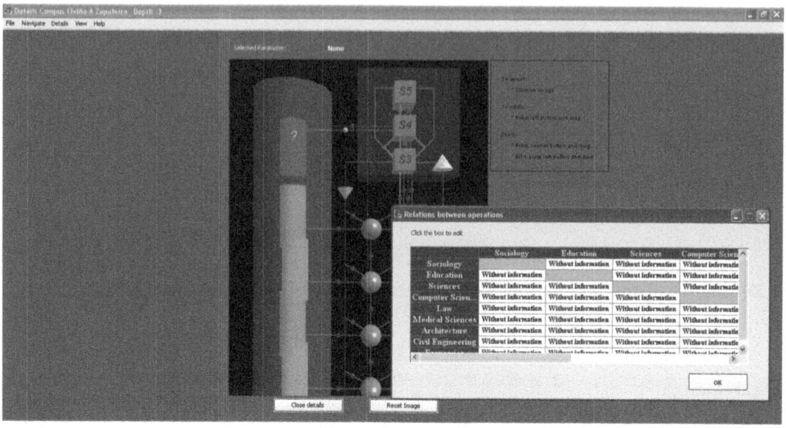

Fig. 4.30 Information-capturing screen for relations between operational units

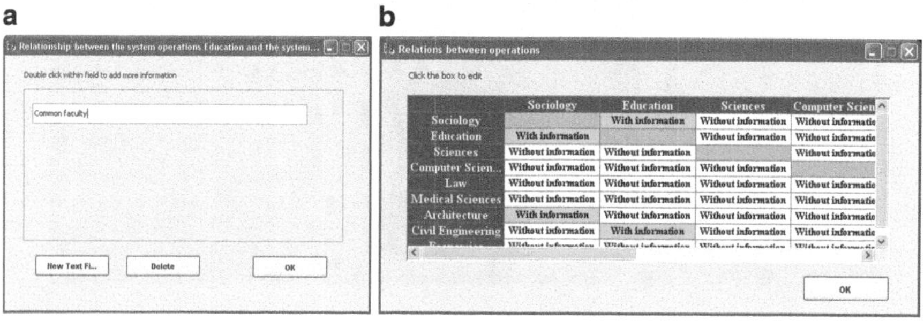

Fig. 4.31 Visualising information in relations between operational units (example)

4.4.4.7 Algedonic Channel: Entering Information

The purpose of this channel, of vital importance for the system's viability, is to alert System 5 of any circumstance which might endanger the survival of the system as a whole. Information must be transmitted very quickly from System 1, where the problem arises, until it reaches System 5. The characteristics of this special channel, together with its design and purposes, can be entered in the VSM by means of the corresponding information-capturing screens. This is possible by simply clicking on the algedonic channel on the VSM map and entering the information and attachments we require (Fig. 4.32). The warning signal may also be activated as a consequence of information detected by System 4 in the environment, which, in conjunction with information from System 1, will warn System 5 of the need to intervene. VSMod® permits the entering of information in the various possible communication combinations involving the diverse elementary units that constitute System 1.

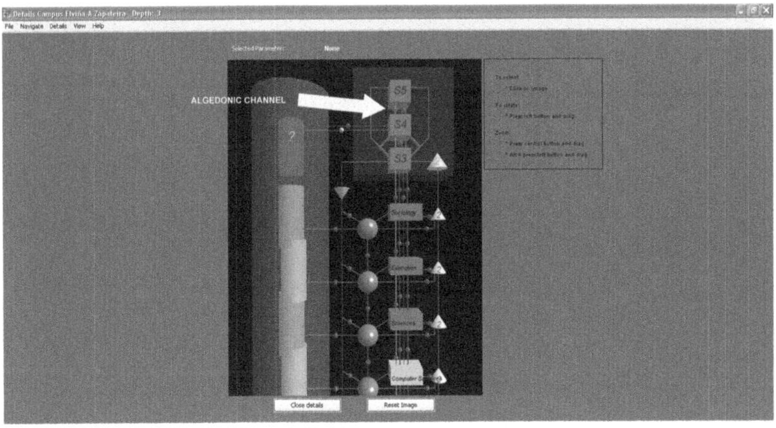

Fig. 4.32 Selecting the algedonic channel

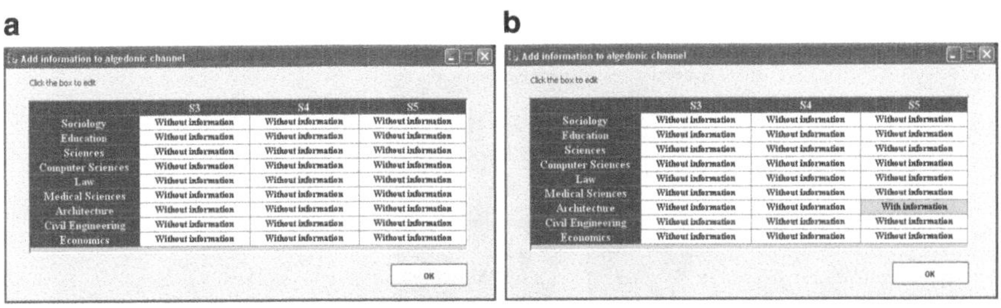

Fig. 4.33 Algedonic channels (without and with information)

The use of a matrix (Fig. 4.33) – in whose rows we have the different elementary operational units of System 1, and whose columns show System 3, System 4 and System 5 – allows us to make use of the different communication and alert options from System 1 to the Meta-system (System 3, System 4 and System 5). To enter information, we simply need to select the matrix element corresponding to a particular communication and warning channel. The information-capturing screens we have already seen on several occasions will then appear.

As in general for all VSMod® elements, once information has been entered, the colour changes, becoming lighter as a sign that it contains information. In the image (Fig. 4.34) enlarged by the zoom provided by VSMod® the algedonic channel selection button can be seen to be lighter, indicating that information has been entered.

4.4.4.8 Representation of System 1

The last function I am going to describe in this overview of VSMod® concerns the possibility of representing System-1 elements in such a way that their relative sizes

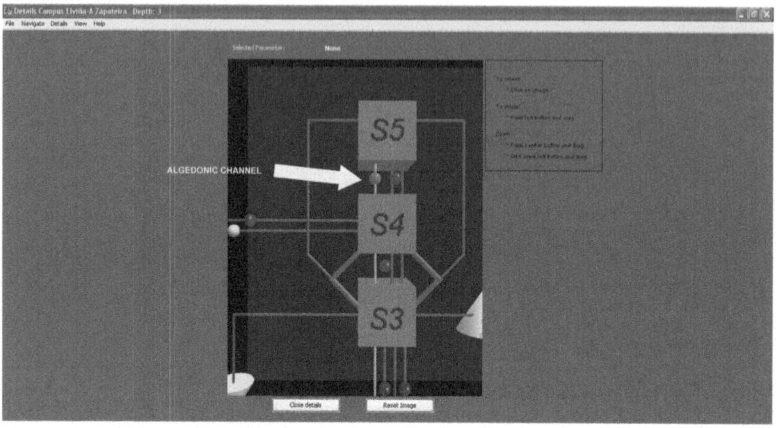

Fig. 4.34 Enlarged image of the algedonic channel, indicating that it contains information

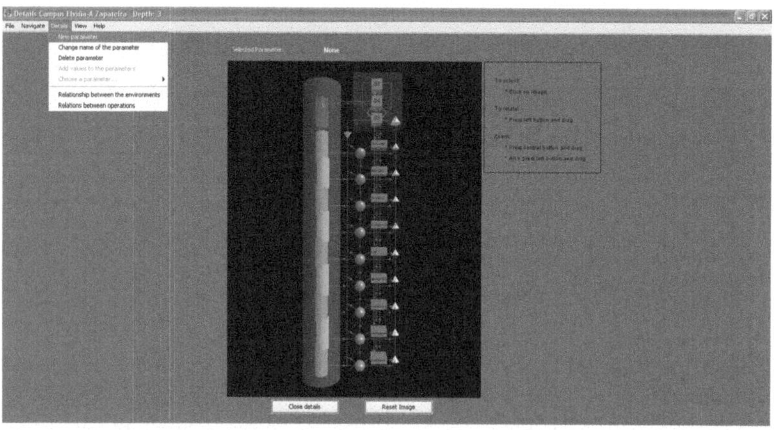

Fig. 4.35 Adding a new parameter

are reflected. This allows a visualisation of the relative importance of System-1 components (of the system-in-focus selected) in accordance with a specific parameter chosen to make this comparison. The first thing to be done is enter the parameters we deem relevant for these elements (e.g., we can use revenue by sales for the different divisions of a firm, the number of students matriculated in the different faculties of a university, the number of inhabitants in different towns in a province, etc.). We do this by selecting the option "New parameters" on the drop-down menu (Fig. 4.35).

Once the parameters have been entered, we will give them the corresponding values which later will be employed in their representation on a relative scale. For this we will use the option "Adding values to the parameters" (Fig. 4.36). Finally, to show these System-1 elements with their relative sizes, we will select the option

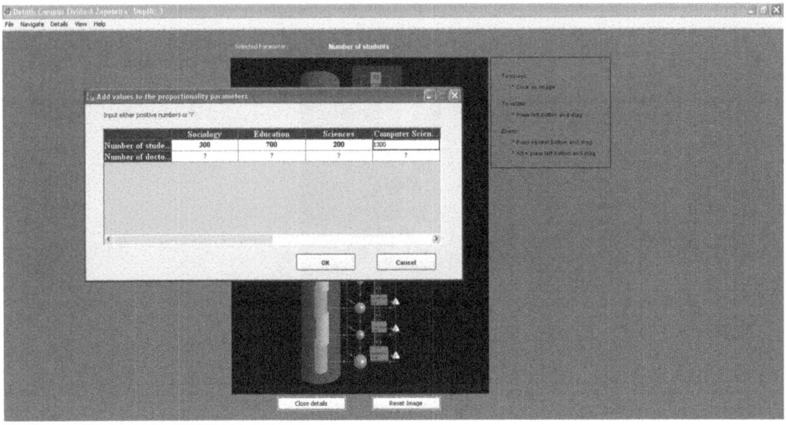

Fig. 4.36 Entering values in the parameters

a   b

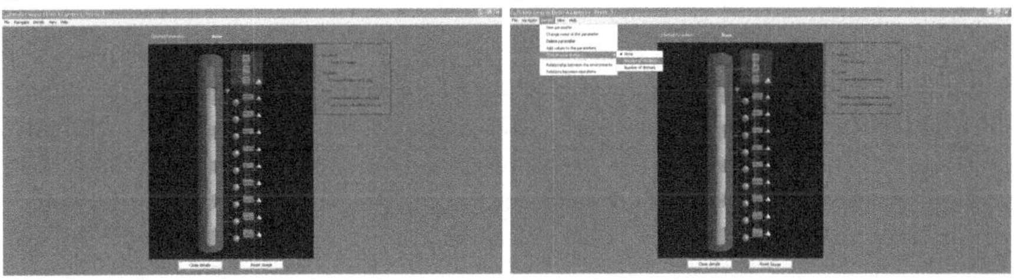

Fig. 4.37 Selecting parameters to represent System 1

that allows us to redesign System 1. We need to choose only the parameter in question in order to establish the comparison (Fig. 4.37). On making this selection we will see System 1 with its elements appearing according to their relative dimensions for the chosen parameter (Fig. 4.38). We can repeat this process with however many parameters we wish to include.

4.4.4.9 Changing the System-in-Focus

Once we have finished entering information in the system-in-focus (or simply visualising it), we can change the system-in-focus by moving to another subsystem, either within the same recursion level or within a different one. We can do this by using the navigation maps described above: Global Map, Map 1 or Map 2. We simply select the place we wish to move to, and the software application takes us there. The VSM map that will appear will correspond to the new system-in-focus we have selected. We can then continue in the way previously described to enter (or consult) information. This process may be repeated as often as we wish.

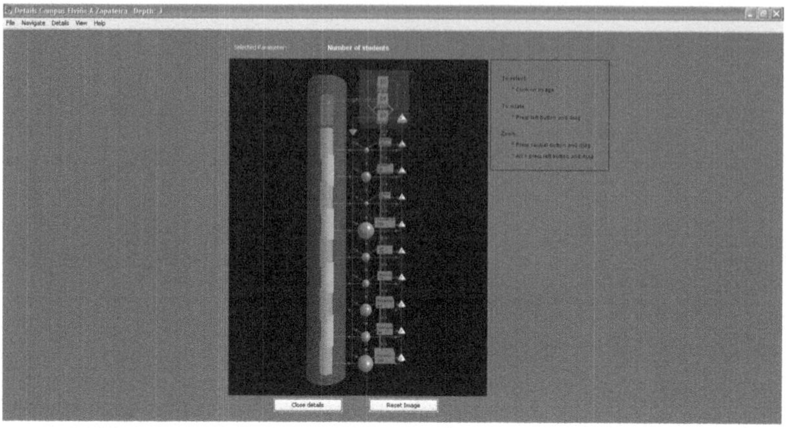

Fig. 4.38 System 1 elements showing their relative sizes according to the chosen parameter (number of students)

4.4.4.10 Visualisation Options

So far, we have seen the principal functions of VSMod® and the different screens allowing visualisation of the structure of the organisation we are studying, and how the pertinent information can be captured or shown. Regarding the visualisation method, I will make a final comment on the options offered here by the three-dimensional version of VSMod®. These include, on the one hand, the possibility of applying a zoom to the VSM image, with the result that we can either see the whole set of components, regardless of organization size, or bring the image closer in order to focus on a specific part we are interested in. In addition, we can rotate the image or shift it at will. By way of example, Fig. 4.39 provides an illustration of the diverse visual images we have spoken about by showing various screen captures.

4.4.5 Using the VSM in Conjunction with Other Methodologies or Tools

Just as we can enter all kinds of information in any of the VSM map elements, it is also possible to enter simulation models as well as website links which, via the Internet, allow us to access complementary VSM tools.

As regards simulation models, the possibility of including Systems Dynamics (SD) Simulation Models is particularly interesting. The advantages of the combined use of the VSM and SD were highlighted with the first appearance of the VSM. S. Beer himself, in the description he gives of the VSM in his book "The Brain of the Firm" (Beer 1981, p. 197), mentions the convenience of using Forrester's System Dynamics (Forrester 1958) together with the corresponding simulation software. The importance

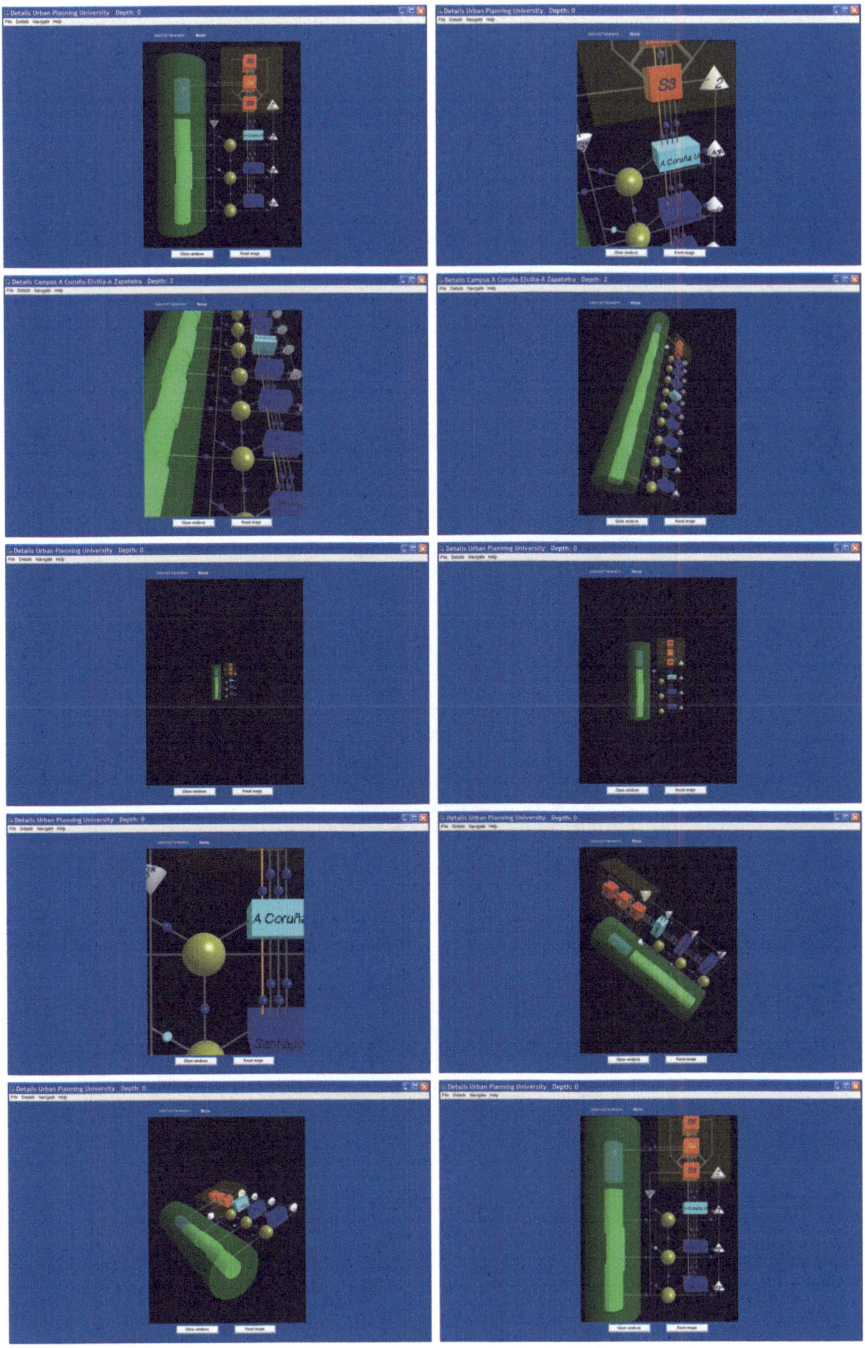

Fig. 4.39 Examples of different ways of visualising the three-dimensional VSM image

of employing SD and the VSM jointly has been stressed in further studies (Schwaninger et al. 2004; Pérez Ríos 2008d) and above all in Schwaninger and Pérez Ríos (2008a). A SD model makes it possible to perform functions peculiar to both System 3 and especially System 4, as well as facilitating interactions between System 3 and System 4 (System 3-System 4 Homeostat). As Schwaninger and Pérez Ríos maintain, the VSM is ideal for studying the context in which a complex problem shows up, whilst SD permits an analysis of its content and dynamic behaviour.

To insert a SD model within a VSM in, for instance, System 4, the only thing required, once we have constructed the model with any of the available software tools (Ithink, Powersim, Vensim, etc.), is to open the System 4 information-capturing screen (Fig. 4.40), select the SD model we wish to enter, and insert it directly (Figs. 4.41 and 4.42). This done, the SD model then becomes an integral part of our System 4.

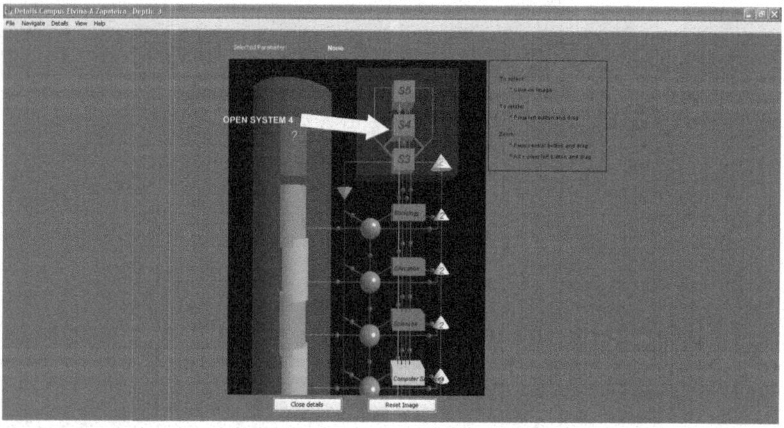

Fig. 4.40 Selecting System 4 to introduce (for example) an SD model

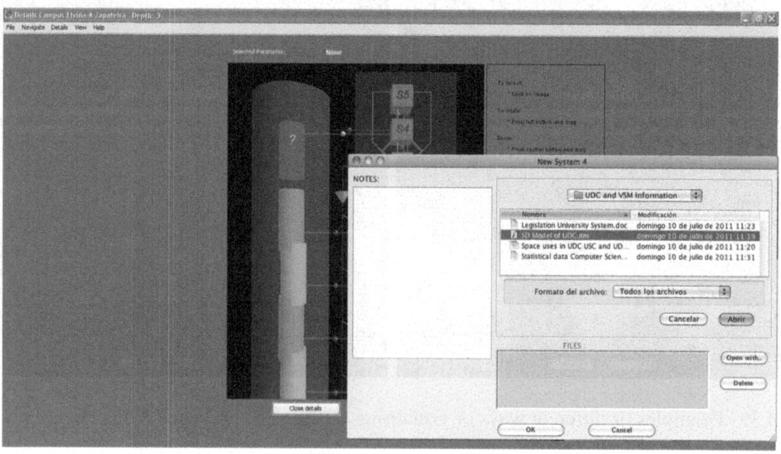

Fig. 4.41 Introducing an SD model in System 4

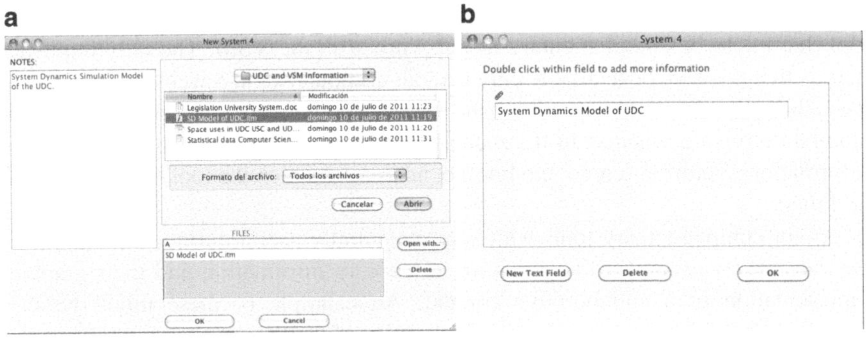

Fig. 4.42 SD model inserted in System 4

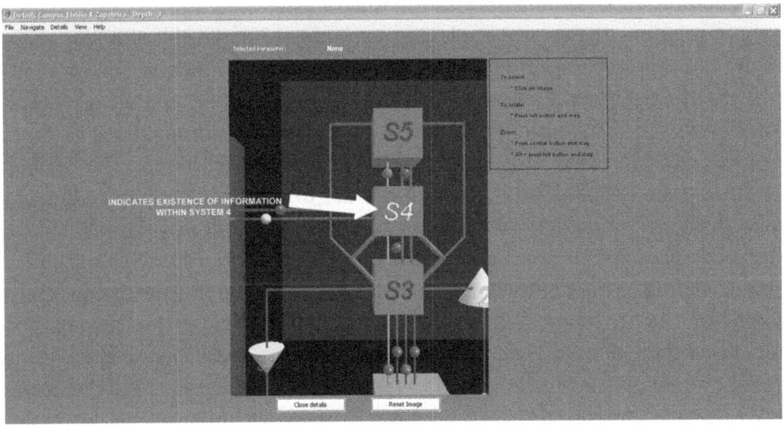

Fig. 4.43 Enlarged image of System 4 indicating that it contains information

In Fig. 4.43 we can see the screen showing how the file corresponding to the SD model is added as an information element to System 4. Once we have inserted it, we can use it by simply opening it and running it. After working with the SD model, we can save it again or modify it. In the latter case, when we close the model, the version that will be saved will be the modified one, which will then be available for future use. Therefore, the changes we have made in the SD model will, as a result of being used in our VSM study, be saved in our VSM model (in the case we are referring to, within System 4 of the system-in-focus). In this way, VSMod® permits the SD model to become an integral part of our study and VSM model.

When we are dealing with an organisation (or company) with many recursion levels, the representatives of the System 4s at their different recursion levels may likewise create and deposit their respective SD models within the VSM, and use them when needed.

In a similar way to the one we have just described for inserting a simulation model in our VSM study, which, as we have seen, is as simple as introducing the model by means of the information-capturing screen, it is possible to use any other tool that might be complementary in our work with the VSM. The only requisite here is that this tool be available either in our computer or at a website. In the first case, the operation would be exactly the same as that given above for introducing a simulation model, whereas in the second we would merely need to enter, via the information-capturing screen, the Internet address at which the tool in question can be found.

As for complementary tools which are potentially useful during a VSM study, we can cite as examples those helping to capture information and their graphic representation in a collaborative context. An example of these might be the so-called Col-KCap developed at the University of Valladolid within the Systems Thinking Group; this program allows several researchers or users to work via Internet, either synchronously or asynchronously, on the study of the same complex problem, helping them to construct causal diagrams as well as a certain preliminary analysis of relations between the relevant variables of the problem under study.

Another option of particular interest to the scientific community belonging to the domain of Organisational Cybernetics, is the possibility of accessing software tools specifically designed to facilitate the realization of Syntegration processes, or other tools (some of which have also been developed for specific purposes at Valladolid University), such as Interdelphi (created in order to carry out Delphi studies via the Internet) or the Systemic Meta-Tool (software developed to incorporate and facilitate the subsequent use of diverse systemic methodologies). Team Syntegrity is, as I mentioned before, a methodology (which is explained in the following Chap. 5) developed by Beer to make communication easier between persons responsible for the functions corresponding to System 3 and System 4. In this section, I simply comment on how the software VSMod® facilitates direct access to the instruments that may help us to apply this methodology. Access is similar to that we have just described for gaining access to any tool in general. We only need to introduce the Internet address where the tool is available.

4.5 Guidelines for Use and Future Developments

VSMod® software includes several documents that explain the procedure for installing it (Installation instructions) as well as a detailed operational guide (User's Guide). Both documents are accessible via the Internet at the VSMod® website.

As regards additional development of VSMod®, I have already spoken about the availability (although they are in a trial period) of a collaborative and also a more advanced version. These new versions of VSMod® incorporate, in addition to the necessary functions for permitting collaborative work (enabling various people to engage in working via the Internet, on the same VSM model and in both synchronous or asynchronous modes), additional functions related to advanced design and diagnosis of organisations.

Chapter 5
Team Syntegrity

5.1 Introduction

The need of a tool for facilitating communication between System 4 and System 3 in an organisation was made clear by Beer himself when the VSM was introduced. Its last innovation, termed Team Syntegrity (TS) (Beer 1994), was duly developed in order to help these two systems to communicate adequately and, as a result, to contribute to the smooth running of the System 4-System 3 homeostat, which, as we know, is critical for ensuring the organisation's adaptation and viability. In Chap. 1, Sect. 3, the necessity of such a tool is justified, and in this chapter I will attempt to explain its essential elements.

An observation I consider important with regard to TS is that, although this debate methodology arose, as noted, out of the need seen within the VSM to facilitate the interaction between these two systems, its conceptual worth and potential have caused TS to become one of the most powerful tools available today for helping people to carry out a joint study of complex problems. It permits them to extract the maximum amount of information brought by each party, thereby contributing to a very significant improvement in the quality both of the study relating to the problem in question and of the results obtained.

This is one of the reasons why the account that I give in this chapter, although of course it rounds off this explanation of the VSM, has a wider scope, making reference as it does to questions which affect not only organisations or companies but broader domains of decision-making (society in general).

The new frontier of humanity is, at the start of the twenty-first century, not so much scientific or technological development as an understanding of the complex social systems in which we are immersed. Such understanding is fundamental for our being able to deal effectively with the problems of social tension facing mankind. We must explore new ways to organise and engage in relations that will enhance the processes of communication and decision-making.

Making institutions more effective and democratic has been attempted from many different angles. Nevertheless, progress is still insufficient. This is borne out

J. Pérez Ríos, *Design and Diagnosis for Sustainable Organizations*,
DOI 10.1007/978-3-642-22318-1_5, © Springer-Verlag Berlin Heidelberg 2012

by certain fundamental challenges which still have not been resolved in a satisfactory way: for example, the development of group-decision processes which are at the same time democratic, creative and efficient, or the replacement of hierarchical organisational structures by other more democratic ones in which all points of view can be effectively taken into consideration, an aspect which is of particular importance in the case of decisions that affect groups of people or even future generations.

The problem of making organisational structures democratic is especially difficult for those organisations in which the number of members is large (Schecter 1993). In such cases, there is the huge problem of achieving the full participation of the group in discussion, information exchange and the taking of important decisions. With large groups, it is necessary to divide up the work; it is not possible for all the individuals to know one another directly, nor is it possible for all components to interact. Consequently, the organisation and its functional processes must be conceived as having multiple logical levels. In Chap. 1, Sect. 2, when we commented on the concept of variety (complexity), an example was given of how the latter grows depending on the increase in the number of components in a group, reaching truly enormous levels if the group is very large.

The discussion of these kinds of issues, referring to the structures of organisations, requires that new concepts become available that are suited to their complexity. It is necessary that the language we use will permit communication fully in line with the degree of complexity in what we will be studying.

The last few years have been characterised by a growing interest in the role that can be played by the new information and communication technologies, as a support for a higher level of participation in discussions and decision-making. Consequently, a wide range of technologies are nowadays available. Examples can be found in those generally known as "groupware", which include software for planning and programming in groups, conferences and computer-assisted cooperative undertakings, and the whole arsenal of tools that have appeared within the so-called Web 2.0 (Almuiña et al. 2008, pp. 253–265).

The conjunction of these two cornerstones – namely, on the one hand, the new conceptual framework for the design of organisational structures and decision processes, and, on the other, the availability of a technological support allowing remote collective inter-communication – opens up new horizons for relations between individuals and institutions.

The application of Beer's latest innovation, Team Syntegrity®,[1] is intended to make a contribution in this area. In this chapter, an analysis is made both of this methodology and of its application possibilities for designing organisation structures and communication systems, in accordance with criteria based on concepts such as de-centralisation, autonomy and participation. Among the reasons for using it, we will highlight the following; creating synergies among groups of

[1] Team Syntegrity® is a trademark for Team Syntegrity International Inc. (TSI).

individuals, making better use of advantages implicit in diversity and obtaining shared mental models.

Employing this methodology seems particularly suited to decision-making contexts in which the matter under consideration is complex, not well structured, knowledge-intensive and politically sensitive. It is also especially apt where the participants intervening in such processes are numerous, highly qualified, geographically dispersed, of different cultural backgrounds and with heterogeneous goals.

Once again, I insist that the reasons that motivated Beer to develop this methodology were derived from his intention to solve the communication problem between Systems 4 and 3 in organisations. For the System 4–System 3 homeostat to work properly, it is obvious that both systems must be able to communicate, although this has been seen to be difficult given the fact that both systems have such different interests. However, a proper functioning of the organisation's adaptation organ (the homeostat) is a must. For further information on Team Syntegrity (TS), Beer's book *Beyond Dispute* (1994) is recommended, in which the author explains in great detail both its bases and the application protocols.

The very potential of this methodology meant that, besides being used as part of the VSM application processes, it was also employed as an independent instrument for helping more or less large groups to discuss complex questions, and to provide all their constituents with a really profound understanding of both the problem in question and the perceptions held by other members of the group.

5.2 Conceptual Bases

Team Syntegrity® consists basically of a methodology developed by Stafford Beer with the aim of offering a creative, synergetic and participative platform for studying complex problems.

The concept of complexity and its relation to that of variety was discussed in Chap. 1, Sect. 2. For this reason, I will limit myself here to recalling the speed at which variety (complexity) increases in any situation as the number of those involved increases. Moreover, reference was made in Chap. 1 to the difficulty people experience in communicating. If we add to this the impact of delays in transmitting information, together with their effects, we have an idea of the size of the problem. In *Pensamiento Sistémico y Dirección Estratégica* (Pérez Ríos 1992), the concept of dynamic complexity is said to refer to situations in which cause-effect relations are not evident, as a result of the effects and their causes being separated in time and/or space. This is the complexity we are facing with insufficient means at the moment.

An additional inconvenience, aside from those inherent in a problem's dynamic complexity, is the difficulty in generating learning processes. If the individual, or their organisation, is incapable of associating effects with their causes, then learning is not possible, and both will go on repeating the same errors.

Systems Thinking, in its multiple varieties (Perez Ríos 2007a), attempts to a certain extent to deal with this type of complexity, thereby establishing the basis for making learning possible, for both the individual and the group.

This is the line of thought according to which S. Beer has developed, as we have already seen, his studies on the characteristics of viable systems, as well as the design of "Team Syntegrity", which we might regard as a structured means of creating and communicating a "group awareness".

The term "Syntegrity", included in "Team Syntegrity®" (and from which Syntegration®[2] derives), comprises the combination of the terms "synergy" and "tensegrity" (Beer 1994, pp. 12–14). The former refers, as is known, to the condition in which the properties of a whole are superior to and different from the combined properties of the parts. As regards the term "tensegrity", this derives from the combination of "tensile" and "integrity", and was created by Buckminster Fuller as an identification of structural strength resulting from tension, in contrast with that deriving from compression (Fuller 1979). Just as the molecules and cells which make up our tissues continually undergo a process of destruction and renovation, so that the existence of life is fundamentally linked, as Ingber argues (Ingber 1998), to the permanence of the architectural pattern, likewise in the case of structures designed according to the concept of tensile integrity, their mechanical stability derives not from the strength of the individual members, but from the manner in which the whole structure distributes and balances the mechanical tensions.

A characteristic of this type of structure is that the tension is transmitted uninterruptedly throughout all of its components, as a result of which an increase in tension in one of them will generate a subsequent increase in all other members of the structure. This global increase in tension is balanced by augmented compression in certain elements. This structural stabilisation mechanism is referred to by B. Fuller as uninterrupted tension and local compression. In buildings, stabilisation is generally attained by means of continual compression due to the force of gravity. An interesting property of "Tensegrity" structures is that they provide maximum strength for a given amount of building material.

The structural and communicative process that constitutes "Syntegration" is based on these types of structures, and its spatial reference (at least in its basic version) is the icosahedron. This regular polyhedron is made up of 20 sides (equilateral triangles), 30 edges and 12 vertices, on each of which 5 edges converge. As there is no upper or lower part, and neither left nor right, etc., we may consider that the configuration, as seen from the viewpoint of any of its aspects, whether edges, vertices or sides, is uniformly non-hierarchical. This is one of its many attractions.

---

[2] Syntegration® is a line of products registered by Team Syntegrity International Inc. (TSI).

5.3 Description of the Process

5.3.1 *Goals*

The goals sought via the application of the "Team Syntegrity" (TS) methodology can be summarised as follows:

- To generate a high level of participation among the individuals concerned.
- To provide a structure and a system of communication that guarantee the non-hierarchical nature of the process. For this purpose, access to information, opportunities for voicing ideas and position in the structure of the organisation are to be identical for all those involved. In addition, the structural design and the operational process are intended to be robust when faced with "non-democratic" actions, such as attempts to hide information or the exertion of pressure by certain individuals on others, etc.
- To benefit from the variety and wealth of knowledge supplied by each individual within the group, putting into practice the synergies derived from the interaction among all its members.
- To create a collective awareness, if possible shared among all the members of the group, regarding the central issue being considered and analysed.

5.3.2 *Phases*

The TS application process starts when a question is asked concerning the issue to be studied or discussed. This question is normally (though not necessarily) of a general, open nature. Its purpose is to serve as a focus for the entire process and to generate maximum variety in the resulting responses.

We base the following description of the process on the protocols designed by Stafford Beer and laid out in his book entitled *Beyond Dispute: the Invention of Team Syntegrity* (Beer 1994). Despite the fact that there are many types of application depending on the number of participants, I will restrict myself to explaining the phases of the basic method. Here the group involved in the process comprises 30 people. The term *infoset* is used to identify this set of individuals who sharing a common concern, have the pertinent information in relation with the issue of interest and are motivated to address it. This group (infoset) meets for a time which may vary according to the circumstances, but which generally ranges from 3½ to 5 days, during which it will endeavour to develop responses to the question posed.

Although initially the number of responses tends to be very large, application of the protocols dealt with below will finally reduce them to 12; thus, at the end of the process, we will have 12 considerably developed sides to the problem. Each will represent a matter to be discussed and developed at a later stage.

The reason for the number of group members and responses to the question being 30 and 12, respectively, lies in the geometric reference employed in the basic

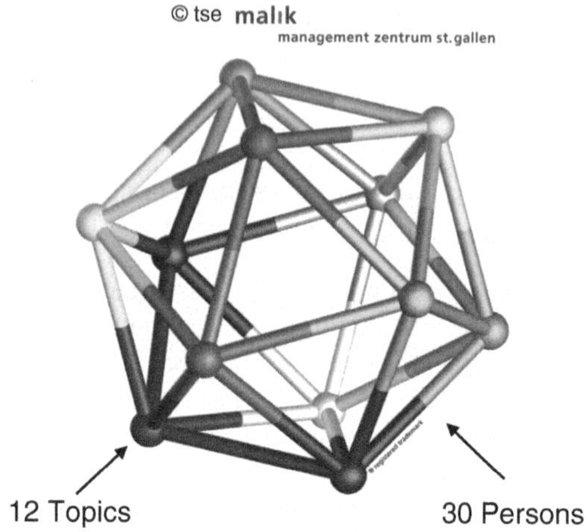

Fig. 5.1 Basic structure of a meeting (Syntegration) based on the icosahedron: 30 people and 12 issues (Courtesy of Malik Management Zentrum St. Gallen). Reproduced under authorisation

form of TS, which is, as I have said, an icosahedron (Fig. 5.1), with its 30 edges and 12 vertices. Each of the edges represents a group member and each vertex 1 of the 12 issues into which the response to the initial question has been broken down.

Nonetheless, I should point out that the features of the process described below are not restricted to a specific geometric form. I will later make reference to different methods of applying TS to groups containing other than 30 participants.

The stages characterising the application of TS can be summarised as follows:

5.3.2.1 First Stage: Statements of Importance

In this stage, each participant prepares statements they consider relevant (Statements of Importance/SI) to the central question. These statements are written down and pinned, for example, to vertical panels so that all members of the group can see them.

The only requirements regarding SIs are that they can be refuted and are not very extensive. In this way, SIs with a very general or trivial content will be avoided.

Once issued, SIs are discussed and grouped according to degrees of affinity. The aim of this is to identify issues which are dealt with by different SIs, so that they can be included within the same thematic group.

5.3.2.2 Second Stage: Complexity Reduction and Grouping

After issuing and grouping the SIs, we go on to generate Aggregated Statements of Importance (ASIs). Once the SIs have been examined, any member of the group can make one or several proposals as regards main issues to be discussed. For each proposal, the group member has to indicate the SIs that are related to the issue identified.

They will do this by writing on a clearly visible panel (poster) a brief text describing their proposal, and will then try to get people interested in the suggestion. The fact that an individual proposes an ASI indicates simply that they regard that question as worthy of debate.

The only requirement for an ASI to be admitted as a candidate for occupying 1 of the 12 positions, corresponding to the 12 issues that will be developed later on, is that it has the support of at least five people, who will express this support by putting their signature directly onto the panel where the proposal (ASI) is displayed.

Once the ASIs have been put forward by all members of the group who wish to do so, those ASIs that have gained the stipulated five signatures undergo a further process of aggregation. The idea is to group together those which deal with similar questions or which, even though not identical, may be integrated under the same issue for discussion.

This aggregation process usually named "Problem Jostle", is aimed at avoiding the loss of "variety", and thereby ensuring that the 12 issues finally selected incorporate all the possible information contained in the SIs and the ASIs. The overall purpose is to prevent as far as possible the application of selection methods based on "voting". The problem with those methods is that they exclude issues which are "losers", with the consequent loss of variety and wealth of information which they contain.

Although the objective behind this aggregation phase is, for the reasons I have just given, to reduce the number of ASIs to 12, if the final number is higher, because of the impossibility of combining ASIs or due to lack of agreement between the individuals who have proposed them, then the final selection is made by voting among the 30 members of the group. The 12 most voted ASIs, from now on referred to as Consolidated Statements of Importance (CSIs), will be the 12 topics to be debated.

5.3.2.3 Third Stage: Assigning Topics to People

When the 12 topics for discussion have been identified, it is necessary to determine which persons among the 30 in the group are going to take part in the debate on each of them. We need therefore to find out their preferences. This we do by asking every group member to indicate which topics interest them most.

Once these preferences have been ascertained, this information is processed with the aid of a computerised assignment algorithm, which tries to maximise the degree of satisfaction in the group. The maximum degree would be an assignment in which each individual was included in teams corresponding to their two favourite topics. This phase is usually named the "Topic Auction".

The distribution of individuals and the assignment of topics are performed with reference to the spatial structure of the icosahedron. Each person is represented by an edge and each vertex represents one of the 12 issues. The five edges that converge at each vertex are the members of the team responsible for discussing the topic. As each edge (person) is connected to two vertices, each person takes part in debating the two topics linked by the edge that he/she represents. The optimal situation would be that in which these two topics corresponded with the first two on the list of each individual's preferences.

The chance for conflicts and incompatibilities between diverse interests makes it necessary to employ a computerised assignment algorithm to search for the best possible solution.

5.3.2.4 Fourth Stage: Generating Contents

According to this structural disposition of the discussion process (Fig. 5.2), each topic (vertex) is consequently discussed by five individuals who make up a team (the five edges which come together at each vertex). To help organize and follow the meetings programme, each topic (and its corresponding team) is normally identified by a colour. Obviously, each person (edge) has two colours, corresponding with the two topics (teams) of which he/she forms part.

The function of each team is to explore and develop their topic, following a process whose aim is to produce a declaration which provides a response. Nevertheless, the teams are not made up solely of the five "members" indicated, but also of another five individuals who serve as "critics" (Fig. 5.3). Their task is to question

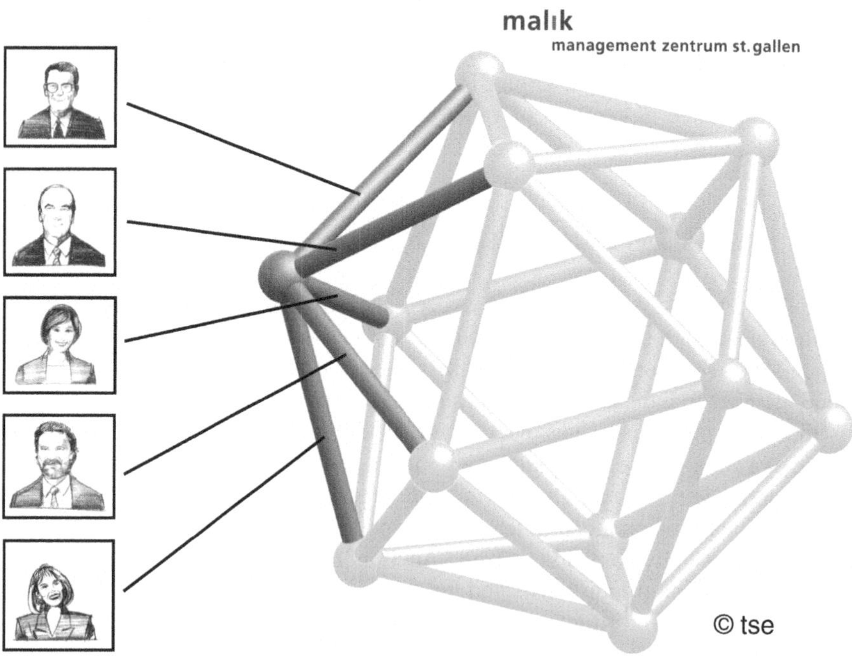

Fig. 5.2 A team: one issue and five members (Courtesy of Malik Management Zentrum St. Gallen). Reproduced under authorisation

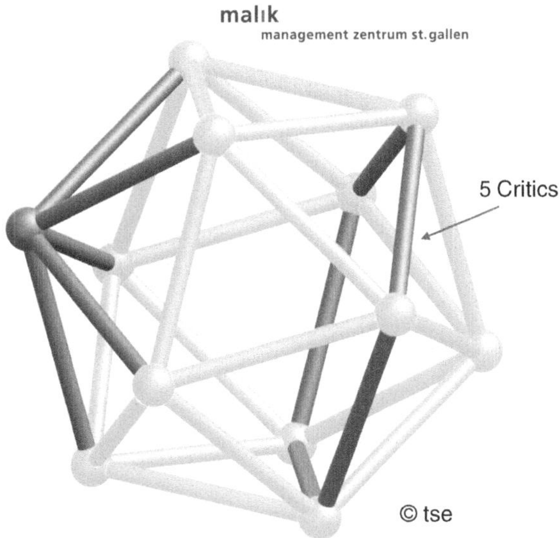

Fig. 5.3 A team: one issue and the five members with the role of "critics" (Courtesy of Malik Management Zentrum St. Gallen). Reproduced under authorisation

both the content of the discussion carried out by the five "members" of the team and the process employed.

The meetings corresponding to the 12 teams/topics are held in sequence, with 2 running simultaneously. In other words, during one day two parallel groups of meetings take place. Therefore, whilst the meetings are being held, there are ten individuals occupied as "members" of the two teams and another ten acting as "critics" within the same teams.

When meetings are taking place, then, 20 of the 30 individuals who constitute the group are occupied as members or critics, with the other ten doing nothing. The latter may devote this free time either to participating as observers (Fig. 5.4) at one of the meetings being held at that moment, or to any other activity they wish (exchanging information with other people who are also free, or simply resting).

The process involves a certain amount of organisational complexity, which is resolved with the aid of the available computer applications. These deal with the assignment of the topics, members and critics, as well as the corresponding time sequencing. Figure 5.5 shows the different groups and roles represented in a team responsible for discussing 1 of the 12 topics.

It is appropriate to bear in mind that the composition of the teams is different in each of the 12. Each person fulfils the role of "member" in two teams (topics) and that of "critic" in two more, and perhaps acts as an observer in another four (Fig. 5.5). As a result, each individual is exposed to the information generated in 8 of the 12 topics. The only topics inaccessible to them are those whose corresponding meetings are held concurrently with the ones in which they participate. All the same, this difficulty can be partially overcome with the organisation of specific encounters between people in positions exactly opposite one another (polar opposites) (Truss 1994b, pp. 296–297). Thus, in theory, each group member could have information on all 12 issues discussed.

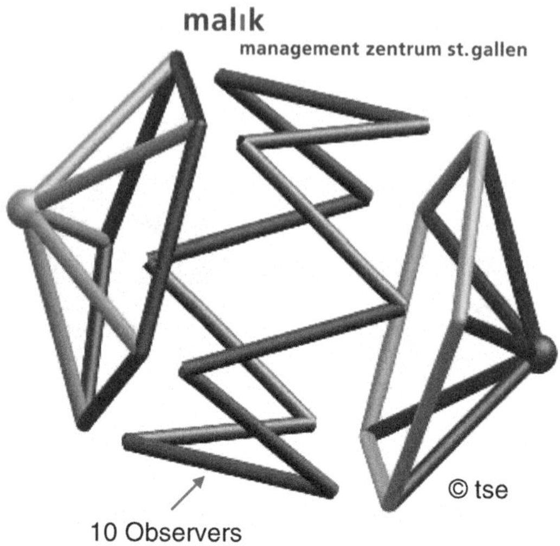

Fig. 5.4 A team: one issue and the ten possible "observers" (Courtesy of Malik Management Zentrum St. Gallen). Reproduced under authorisation

Fig. 5.5 A team: one issue, five members, five critics and observers (Courtesy of Malik Management Zentrum St. Gallen). Reproduced under authorisation

This sequence of six simultaneous meetings is repeated over 3 days. In this way there are three opportunities to discuss each topic (one per day), which allows a considerable degree of deep analysis. Besides, 3 days of discussion facilitates the exchange of information among people and teams.

This programming of meetings and variable team composition generate a "reverberation" effect, causing ideas to be transmitted via the "edges" (individuals) of the structure and to come together at the "vertices" (teams/topics), where they are subsequently digested and transformed, and so on and so forth. In this process of diffusing and transforming information, a key role is played by the teams' "members", "critics" and "observers". It should be remembered that the composition of these is different for each of the 12 topics.

This process guarantees the flow of information among all members of the group. What is more, the system of communication is robust, in the sense that one or various weaknesses in the structure's edges (individuals who do not transmit information or who try to distort it, etc.) are amply compensated for by the system's repetitive nature. Information circulates by a multitude of channels via the edges (individuals). It is worth recalling at this juncture what was said to be convenient for effective communication when we looked at the channels of communication (Chap. 1, Sect. 1.3), as well as the concept of redundancy of potential command and information in real time. So intense is the process of applying TS (the variable configuration of the different teams and the iterations in the debates, etc.) that, in effect, information is transmitted via multiple channels (the various individuals and the different discussion teams), and this fact in general ensures that the information reaches those concerned.

Through this sequence of formal and informal meetings, both individuals and the group take part in a learning process which, over the 3-day period, enhances both the level of discussion and the degree of maturity in the conclusions reached. Furthermore, the way the meetings are programmed ensures that each topic is directly influenced by the information and results generated as a consequence of the debates made on the other topics.

At the close of each session, every team has to produce a sufficiently detailed declaration, with the conclusions reached in all three sessions held over the first, second and third days. At the end of each of the first 2 days, the declarations of the 12 teams are publicly displayed for observation by the group, in order that any of the members may make whatever comments they deem appropriate. The use of a system to evaluate the quality of each group's work may act as an incentive.

Both the organisation of the sessions and the team members' work plan are normally facilitated by a colour code that allows the teams and their components to be identified.

The meeting (Syntegration) ends with a plenary session, during which each team puts forward the conclusions that have been drawn over the three iterations. These must be sufficiently developed that they give substance to each of the 12 topics, thereby also responding to the original question which, before it was divided into those 12, initiated the whole process.

Should there be enough time, it is possible to apply further designs oriented towards planning and implementing specific actions.

5.4 Results of the Process

The results and traits of a process such as the one we have described can be summarised as follows:

- The establishing of the agenda for the meetings by the participants themselves. This is made concrete in the 12 topics chosen for discussion.
- Generating responses that consider the issue under study from various perspectives, albeit grouped together in an integrating system.
- Involving the participants in a non-hierarchical discussion process, which activates both individual and group learning and enhances the quality of the responses to the issue studied. The identical character of the roles played by all individuals and teams guarantees the democratic nature of the process. In addition, the self-organising character of the way in which SIs are generated and complexity is reduced makes it more difficult for members to attempt to dominate others.
- The way the process is structured favours dialogue and community spirit. This is basically due to the diversity of roles played by every member throughout the various meetings and iterations, which inevitably leads to communication between the group members.
- An increase in levels of shared information (over 90% of the information is shared after three iterations, and this may reach 96% with a fourth iteration) (Beer 1994, pp. 223–224; Jalali 1994, pp. 263–280), and the chance to bring about a certain collective consciousness regarding the central issue debated (Fig. 5.6).

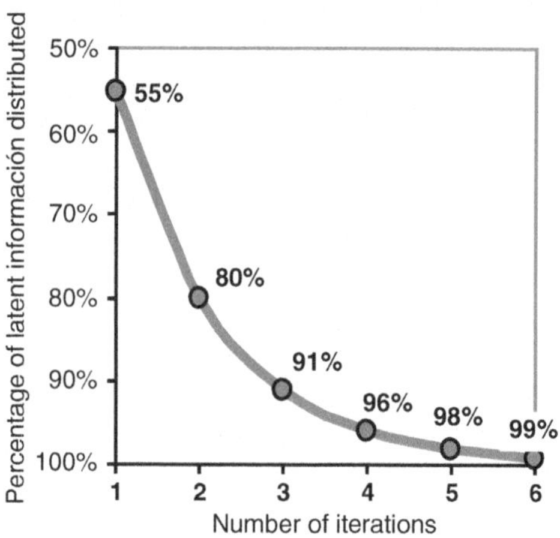

Fig. 5.6 Relation between the number of iterations and shared information (Beer 1994)

– Applying "Team Syntegrity" offers the possibility of achieving a context for personal inter-relations in which individuals can collaborate freely, within a creative, confidence-building framework, and where the wealth of variety contained in the group can bring forth benefits.

5.5 Complementary Forms and Uses

As I have previously pointed out, the process as described thus far corresponds to the basic form of TS (30 individuals, 12 topics). However, a wide variety of applications and forms exist, with implementation methods varying from the latter.

One of these consists of using groups not containing 30 members. In this context, the firms Team Syntegrity International Inc. and Malik Management Zentrum St. Gallen (Malik MZSG) have protocols facilitating its application to practically any number of individuals less than 30. In Fig. 5.7 the forms most commonly employed by Malik MZSG are shown. One can appreciate how participants in a "Syntegration" may be of almost any number. On the right of the figure we can see the duration of the different variants. In the case of groups of more than this number, the group could be divided into multiples of 30, or the number of

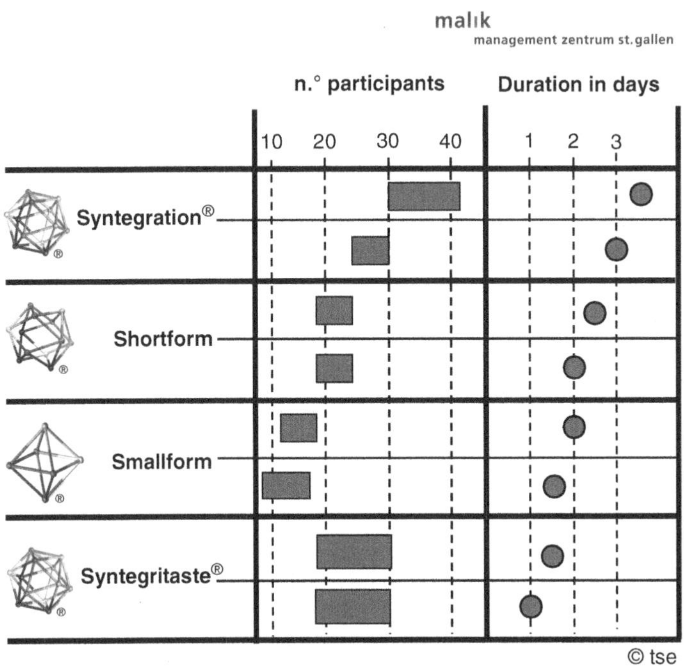

Fig. 5.7 Variants of Syntegration application (Courtesy of Malik Management Zentrum St. Gallen). Reproduced under authorisation

participants in each team increased. Nonetheless, this latter procedure has the drawback of augmenting the variety generated within each meeting, a limitation which, all the same, diminishes when distance-meetings (via the Internet) are held.

A further possibility for using TS, other than those listed, is as a backup tool for drawing up action plans. The protocols developed by Truss, for planning by sides, have such an aim (Truss 1994a, pp. 333–345). On each side of the icosahedron (basic form) three of the 12 topics are represented, via three of the 30 group members. Each of the three topics is shared by two of the three members of that side. This procedure ensures coherence among the diverse plans and their connection with the central question that started the whole discussion.

Finally, we will mention the option of extending the "Syntegration" process by integrating the results of different groups; in this way, the number of new participants could go on increasing exponentially. In *Beyond Dispute: the Invention of Team Syntegrity,* Beer offers an example of this expansion (Beer 1994, pp. 171–175).

5.6 Organisation and Information and Communication Technologies

Everything we have dealt with so far relates to organising encounters and exchanging information on a physical basis, involving members of the group in question. Nevertheless, the available current information and communications technologies open up new possibilities in this context.

Regarding TS, for instance, I can say that its use in situations where an actual physical encounter is not necessary ("virtual" meetings), it represents an open line of research offering results which, for the moment, are promising. Here, consultation of the book entitled *To be and not to be that is the system: A tribute to Stafford Beer,* CD ROM (Espejo et al. 1997) is recommended. This is the first application of TS using the new information and communication technologies. The purpose of the book was to set up a collective study in which over 30 cyberneticians from four continents and 16 countries could create a scientific work, revealing the usefulness of S. Beer's different theories for all kinds of organisations and for society in general. This work would be presented to Beer to celebrate his 70th birthday. The presentation in fact occurred on September 25th 1996, at John Moore's University in Liverpool.

The undertaking was carried out between October 1995 and July 1996. Almost all of the work, consisting of both identifying the chapters it would include (12) and drawing up the content (more than 600 pages), was done remotely via Internet. It should be pointed out that many members of the group did not know one another, and that the work was done from their different places of residence. Given the geographical dispersion, we should also not forget that there were even large time differences within the group.

The work was constructed according to TS protocols, and with the aid of the new technologies, particularly the Internet. In the above-mentioned CD ROM, documentation is included which is associated not only with the work itself, but also with the detailed construction process. As a member of the group which produced the undertaking and a participant in this experiment, I can vouch for the importance of employing TS in order that a project of this scope could be successfully completed in such a short period of time. In the book *Intelligent Organizations*, M. Schwaninger, co-director of the project (2006, pp. 123–128) talks about the elaboration process.

In addition to this experience, the combined use of information and communication technologies with new organisational methods, based on both TS as well as on other organisation designs, offers interesting possibilities. I will now comment on a few of these.

It would be possible, for example, to organise all kinds of conferences, meetings, debates, etc., amongst any number of members, with no limitations in terms of distance (or time). The agendas of the meetings could be worked out in advance by the participants themselves (thus ensuring the democratic, non-hierarchical nature of the meetings). Similarly, the content of the issues on the agenda could, to a large extent, be arranged prior to the actual meeting, which should mean a considerable improvement in the quality of the conclusions drawn from the encounters.

The meetings themselves could also be held without the need of any physical encounter, in other words "virtual" meetings (Almuiña et al. 2000). Despite the disadvantages of these, especially in aspects relating to personal interaction, they offer the advantage that they can take place over a longer time period, as a result of which, with more time for debating the issues, the conclusions could be better. In any case, current technological opportunities provide us with at least partial, although increasingly efficient and accessible, solutions to the problem of personal interaction (for instance, the use of "video-conferencing", etc.).

5.7 Final Thoughts on TS

As a final reflection on TS we can frame the following considerations:

- It is necessary to use alternative ways of organising meetings if we want them to be regarded as truly democratic and non-hierarchical.
- In addition, for an organisation's System 4–System 3 homeostat to function well, it is recommended that tools be used which facilitate conversation between the members of both systems.
- The methodology invented by S. Beer called Team Syntegrity® affords progress and opportunities in both aspects.
- The protocols regulating its application guarantee that information circulates among all members of the group. Furthermore, the structural design is robust when dealing with non-democratic or simply unsuitable actions.

- Another reason for recommending the use of TS is to assist people or managers in studying a complex problem which they are facing. TS provides us with an answer to both the initial explosion of variety (something which is most desirable if we wish to obtain as much knowledge as possible from those in the group regarding the issue being studied or discussed) as well as to its subsequent attenuation, with the assurance that the relevant information is not lost in the process. For this reason it is highly recommended in cases in which the question being dealt with is a complex or delicate one.
- Applying TS to its full extent leads to a better understanding of the problem under study by the members of the group who are taking part in the discussion. Likewise, it improves the chances of transforming and sharing different mental models, thereby encouraging a certain collective awareness regarding the central question under discussion.
- The recursive nature of both the VSM and TS itself signifies that the latter can be applied to a group of any size, practically without limitations. One essential issue can be debated in various groups, and each member of these can in turn organise another set of groups at the following level and so on. In view of the exponential way in which the whole unit increases in size as a result of the combination of the diverse groups at the different levels, the number of people may be unlimited. The organisation of the discussion process in each group is always the same, and consequently this is relatively straightforward. This is a further benefit of the recursive character of this tool in Organisational Cybernetics.
- The methodology described may be applied either in its basic form, that is, by physical encounters involving the group members, or remotely, making it unnecessary for them to leave their places of residence; the latter option, however, requires additional research.
- Application of TS is not limited to the field of business. In fact, it can be extremely useful for any type of organisation, and particularly for dealing with questions involving a great deal of complexity or difficulty, such as those relating to social, economic, political or ecological issues.
- As a final observation, I will mention the extent to which this sophisticated methodology has spread so far. Considering the number of syntegrations undertaken, I can say that, in spite of the short life of the methodology, the number of applications made since 1998 until the start of 2011 has, according to figures provided by the organisation Malik Management Zentrum St. Gallen, exceeded 600, of which Team Syntegrity Europa (Malik MZSG) has carried out over 500.

Acknowledgements I would not wish to end this chapter without giving special thanks to the firm Malik Management Zentrum St. Gallen for their collaboration, by supplying me with the images included in this chapter and giving me the authorisation to reproduce them in the book, as well as for information regarding the dissemination of the methodology and other aspects related with its use.

Chapter 6
Looking to the Future

Throughout these five chapters we have reflected on the complexity facing organisations and companies, and also society in general, as a result of the rapid, profound changes of all kinds (economic, political, energy, climatic, sociological, technological, etc.) taking place worldwide. In addition, we have mentioned the various schools which, within the framework of what is known as the systemic approach or Systems Thinking, have been springing up and evolving during the second half of the twentieth century and continue to do so today. Similarly, we have stressed the need to use this systemic approach if we wish to deploy tools with sufficient capacity to at least provide some comprehensive visualisation of the enormous complexity involved in such changes. We have also indicated some of the situations for which the different schools or systemic approaches may be of use.

The scientific field of Systems Thinking is enormously wide, and as a consequence it integrates such diverse methods or ways of studying complex problems, such as the following:

– One stream of Systems Thinking is that which looks at a system's elementary unit (the individual, the decision-maker, the individual firm, etc.). This is the case of Agents Based Modelling which, starting from the inclusion, in the model of the problem, of the population comprising its various individuals and rules or determinants of their individual behaviour, attempts to get the resultant of their interactions, in other words, the emerging behaviour (bottom-up approach).
– Another stream looks at problems from an aggregated point of view, taking as its focus the sets of actors and their inter-relations. The purpose is to study their dynamic behaviour and so obtain information on the potential trajectories of the system's critical variables (top-down approach), showing the possible effects of different intervention policies.
– Other focuses examine the complete structure of the systems being studied, with a view to assessing whether they meet the necessary and sufficient requirements for being viable.

In this book, I have had to limit myself to dealing with no more than a tiny subset of this veritable universe.

J. Pérez Ríos, *Design and Diagnosis for Sustainable Organizations*,
DOI 10.1007/978-3-642-22318-1_6, © Springer-Verlag Berlin Heidelberg 2012

Specifically, the book is devoted essentially to exploring the contents of Organisational Cybernetics and the Viable System Model, as methodologies that permit us to diagnose organisations or aid us in the design of other, new ones. The purpose is always to ensure that both of these are viable, that is, that they have the capacity to maintain a separate and long-lasting existence regardless of the changes that by necessity will take place in the environment in which they operate.

In the book, reference is also made to another widespread methodology which is absolutely complementary to Organisational Cybernetics, namely Systems Dynamics. Its integration with the former is not only possible but, in certain circumstances, to be highly recommended, as has been argued by Schwaninger and Pérez Ríos (2008a). A detailed description of SD and its integration with OC will be given in future editions of this book.

The principal purpose of the book is, on the one hand, is to contribute to a better understanding of the contents of OC, the VSM and TS, and, on the other, to provide orientation and guidelines both for the student of these matters and for those who wish to apply them in their firm or organisation. The chapters devoted to showing how the VSM can be used to diagnose or design organisations, as well as to aiding in the identification of those pathologies I consider most frequent, can, I believe, be useful in making these methodologies more accessible to managers of companies or organisations in general.

Our aim has been similar in developing the VSMod® software – in other words, we have sought to provide a medium that allows for both the creation of the structure of the organisation we wish to study and, once this has been created, the visualisation and input of information in all VSM elements corresponding to each of the constitutive sub-organisations. The user's guides accompanying the software may help to improve the understanding of the VSM itself as well as the method of its application.

The chapter dealing with TS is intended to familiarise the reader with this methodology, as well as with the areas where its use is pertinent.

Other aspects of the book are treated in a purely indicative way, but they represent enormously interesting lines of research. For example, those related with the design and development of "dynamic balanced scorecards" or the so-called "operations rooms", that is to say, decision environments in which a wealth of specific decision support tools (several of them related to systems thinking) are used. I have referred to these in Sect. 3 of Chap. 1 and Sect. 3 of Chap. 2, when commenting on the functions and activities of System 4 and System 3, and particularly on the System 4–System 3 homeostat. Regarding this matter, the joint use of Systems Dynamics and the VSM is of tremendous interest. This synergy, in combination with developments in software allowing access to information on both the past and the present (information in real time), and the availability of simulations results relating to consequences of different decisions regarding various future scenarios, together with their visualisation through the VSM prism, represents in my opinion a hugely significant challenge toward integration. Part of the software already exists, as in the case of SD (Powersim, Vensim, Ithink, etc.) and VSM (VSMod®), or the software facilitating access to various databases. What is needed is the integration of the diverse components in a coherent managing (governing) framework.

Further on-going lines of study in our research unit, apart from actually enhancing the current version of the VSMod® software by incorporating various additional modules (several of which are now being tested), are, among others, those concerning:

- Evolved versions of VSMod® that will allow it to be used cooperatively via the Internet. In this way, several researchers or managers will be able to work together, either synchronously or asynchronously, on the same VSM application.
- Constructing a software meta-tool permitting, via the Internet, both the uploading of different methodologies from the domain of Systems Thinking, and the availability of any of these to potential users (researchers or managers). By including the pertinent methodologies descriptions and users guides as well as complementary information in the meta-tool, we intend to assist their users in both understanding and applying them.

As a final reflection, I can say that, despite the enormous complexity of the problems affecting society nowadays, it is also true that we have never until now had such a wealth of conceptual, methodological and technological means with which to deal with them. These tools are becoming increasingly better known, better understood and more widely applied, serving the aim of future human betterment. With this book I have attempted to make a small contribution to that aim.

Appendices

Appendix I

INVESTIDURA DEL PROFESOR
DR. STAFFORD BEER
COMO "DOCTOR HONORIS CAUSA" POR LA
UNIVERSIDAD DE VALLADOLID

"LAUDATIO"
DR. JOSÉ PÉREZ RÍOS

26 de Octubre de 2001
VALLADOLID

J. Pérez Ríos, *Design and Diagnosis for Sustainable Organizations*,
DOI 10.1007/978-3-642-22318-1, © Springer-Verlag Berlin Heidelberg 2012

"LAUDATIO"

DR. JOSE MANUEL PÉREZ RÍOS

HIS EXCELLENCY THE PRESIDENT,
DISTINGUISHED AUTHORITIES,
MEMBERS OF THE UNIVERSITY SENATE,
LADIES AND GENTLEMEN:

I will begin by saying that it is an outstanding honour and privilege for me to to act as an investiture mentor for the Honorary Doctorate for one of the scientific personalities with a truly far-sighted and global vision of the world in the century which has just finished. I am referring to Professor Stafford Beer.

Therefore, I am deeply grateful to all the individuals and organizations of the University of Valladolid that have entered into the process of agreeing to award this Honorary Doctorate, for showing their interest in approaching a personality as difficult to classify as is Dr. Beer.

The study of his hugely extensive and profound output, as well as its application in various collaborative works undertaken with two of his main disciples, Doctors Markus Schwaninger and Raul Espejo, has allowed me to discover not only an eminent scientist but also an extraordinary humanist. His enormously original and innovative theoretical approach has always had man and the problems affecting human beings as his main focus and concern, as can be observed in his rich biography, some of whose main landmarks we will now describe.

Stafford Beer was born in 1926 in London. After his initial studies in mathematics, philosophy and psychology at Whitgift School and the University of London (University College), World War II saw him conscripted into the British Army; he became a company commander in the Gurkhas and finally a military psychologist with the rank of captain. Here he began to apply his inter-disciplinary approach to staff-selection processes and research into the relationship between psychopathology and illiteracy, being assigned to the area of human factors within Operations Research (OR) in the War Office.

Once back in civilian life he worked for 12 years for United Steel, in which he created and directed the first (civilian) Group of Operations Research whilst occupying the position of Production Controller. He is responsible for what was the first application in Europe of linear programming (around 1950). The OR group, which came to include over 70 professionals devoted to applying a multi-disciplinary approach to problem solving, was at the time the largest civilian OR group in the world.

During this period of Dr. Beer's activity, we see his innovations in cybernetic models of the corporation, massed batteries of charts for statistical quality control, mechanical simulation techniques, and the invention of the Stochastic Analog Machine which, with its complex series of interactions using ball-bearings, had great visual impact, currently surpassed only by the development of the digital computer and multimedia and graphic tools.

In 1956 at United Steel, he also installed one of the first computers (Ferranti-Pegasus) dedicated exclusively to management sciences, with applications to solving complex problems relating to production, finance, staff, marketing, energy, and the unprecedented development of simulation techniques applicable to steel production.

Dr. Beer's interest in experimenting with and researching into aspects of computing and control, as well as the material bases of computer hardware, led him to carry out experiments with Gordon Park on the use of microorganisms sensitive to light, which were "trained" to solve equations. We should bear in mind that in those years the development of computers was in its infancy and it was not clear which direction it would take in terms of digital or analogue computers.

During this period he also undertook his personal research concerning neurocybernetics and mathematical models of the nervous system, which resulted in the first formulation of the **Viable System Model**, used nowadays throughout the world. It was also during this stage that he invented various machines for studying processes of adaptation, homeostasis and human learning.

From 1961 to 1966, he did a great deal of work as a consultant at the firm SIGMA (Science in General Management), the first consulting agency in the United Kingdom devoted to consulting in operational research and specialised in applying scientific management techniques to the study of problems related to formulating high-level policies, strategy, developmental planning and cybernetics of organizations. Among SIGMA's clients were, in addition to six government departments, many of the leading companies in the UK.

In the period from 1966 to 1970, Dr. Beer became the Development Director of the International Publishing Corporation (IPC), at that time the largest editorial firm in the world; his intense involvement in Research and Development led, among other innovations, to the first automatic page composition. During this time, besides occupying several managerial posts, he created the company that he named International Data Highways, dedicated to the development of tele-publishing and tele-messaging, and in 1966 set up the Stockbroker Computer Answering Network (SCAN), which probably provided the first commercially viable service to remote terminals, serving over 100 stockbroker offices throughout the country.

In 1970 he retired from his managerial duties in IPC and returned to consulting, an activity to which he would devote the following 20 years. During this period he undertook a great deal of work as an international consultant, both for industry and for various governments. One of his best-known pieces of work was the one he carried out for President Salvador Allende in Chile (from July 1971 to September 11, 1973, when interrupted by the coup d'etat), the purpose of which was to develop a new cybernetic approach for organising and regulating a social economy.

Following this intervention, Dr. Beer was also a consultant for several ministers in Ottawa (Canada), New Delhi (India), as well as for the presidential offices of Mexico, Uruguay, and Venezuela (directly with the president in the latter two cases).

During the period from 1990 until the present, his fundamental area of activity has been research and development leading to the invention of the technique termed **Team Syntegrity**. This is a complement to the Viable System Model, which allows increased creativeness and communication among members of the management groups of organisations. Its scientific bases are to be found in the theory of group behaviour and the mathematical graph theory.

Apart from his role as manager and entrepreneur, Dr. Beer throughout his whole life has been very much engaged with university affairs. He was visiting professor at the Manchester and Durham Business Schools. Prior to that, he had been the first Professor of General Systems at the Open University and professor at the Wharton School of the University of Pennsylvania. More recently, he was professor at the universities of Swansea, Concordia Montreal, British Columbia and Toronto. Besides these, he has occupied positions as visiting professor in many other universities, 12 of which were in the United States. Currently he is engaged in teaching as visiting professor at the universities of Sunderland (since 1997), Newcastle (since 1998) and Stockholm (since 1999).

At this moment, Dr. Beer is President of the World Organization of Systems and Cybernetics, holds the Norbert Wiener Gold Medal, and is Governor of the International Council for Computer Communication. He has been President of the Operational Research Society and has been awarded the Lanchester Prize by the American Operations Society for Cybernetics, of which he is also "Trustee." Among the honours he has received we will mention: the "Freedom of the City of London," the Silver Medal of the Royal Swedish Academy for Engineering Sciences, the nomination as Honorary Professor by the John Moore University of Liverpool, honorary doctorates from the University of Concordia of Montreal and the University of St. Gallen, and a "Doctor of Science" from the University of Sunderland. In 1999, the United Kingdom Systems Society awarded him the "Lifetime Achievement Award Gold Medal" for his "outstanding contribution to systemic thinking."

After this necessarily rapid overview of Professor Stafford Beer's biography, let us take note of some of the most outstanding aspects of his monumental production, for which the recent comments made by Dr. Beer himself regarding his work in the Kybernetes journal will be very useful.

The upheaval facing humanity due to the dramatic events taking place and the multitude of problems affecting it (world terrorism, pollution, climate change, poverty, lack of equality among and inside countries, migratory movements, etc.) and growing economic globalisation, means that ever greater attention is being paid to the systemic nature of the world in which we live. There is a growing awareness, albeit dramatically, of the inter-relationship among such phenomena. Classical institutions are of no use for controlling the new state of affairs, by which is meant the appropriate functioning of the system. The problems are global but the institutions are not, or at least not global enough. The question is how to design them. It is here where we can best appreciate the work of Dr. Beer.

Following the success of the inter-disciplinary workgroups (eventually referred to as Operational Research groups) during the Second World War, in resolving problems transcending the particular area of each individual group, the employment of such groups extended, once this conflict was over, to dealing with non-military problems. One was created by Norbert Wiener in Mexico, which recognised the essential unity of a series of problems related with communication and control, both in the machine and in living beings. His work, as well as that of scientists such as Warren McCulloch, Walter Pitts, Ross Ashby and Grey Walter among others, gave rise to a new view concerning the interaction of complex systems and human responses to these. It was Wiener who gave the name *Cybernetics* to the new science, which he defined as the **science of communication and control in the animal and the machine**. In the post-war years numerous articles and books were published on this issue, and an international community began to develop an interest. During this period Stafford Beer comes into contact with the central group behind this trend, and in fact becomes part of it.

The ideas contained in Wiener's *Cybernetics* are put into practice by Stafford Beer in the British Steel company. Throughout the 1950s, he is responsible for several publications, seminars and talks until, in 1959, he publishes *Cybernetics and Management*.

With this book is born **management cybernetics**, that is, the application of the principles of cybernetic science to the study of organisations. In it Beer gives a historical review of the origin of cybernetics as a science, and proposes the system concept as an alternative to the reductionist approach then dominant in western culture. The description of complex systems as black boxes and the notion that systems with a purpose are defined by the product coming out of the black box (and not by desires or intentions) were responsible for Dr. Beer's famous statement: "the purpose of a system is what it does."

The book is a defence of "holism," through the study of whole systems, as opposed to the reductionism prevalent in the scientific method. Although nearly 50 years have passed since this call for applying a systemic approach to the study of complex problems, and despite the global nature of problems affecting humanity, the reductionist approach is still dominant in scientific, academic and medical environments as well as in the social sciences. Therefore, it is appropriate to remember what Dr. Beer proposes in the introduction to the book, when he argues that similarly to science's search for the original source of energy in the physics of the sun itself, that is, the liberation of energy in the basic process of transformation represented by the fusion of hydrogen-helium, science should now balance such findings by searching for the original source of control in the cybernetics of natural processes, in the evolution of the nervous system itself and the brain. The importance of research into control increases on a daily basis, as do the uncontrolled forces. This book sets out, for the first time, the possibility of scientifically designing an organisation as a system equipped with the capacity of learning, adapting and evolving.

In 1966, Dr. Beer publishes "*Decision and Control*," which deals with "management" and the way in which science may be employed to resolve problems of decision and control. "Management" is regarded as a profession responsible for the future of firms, countries and even the world, and one which requires a suitable language. Herein resides one of the book's chief aims. Old ideas and words are of no use when it comes to creating new approaches, and without these new approaches to new problems we will be condemned to suffer undesired consequences. For this reason, he once again proposes a holistic approach in contrast with the fragmented and partial nature of the then prevailing orthodoxy in the field of "management."

Since its origins at the start of the II World War, the aim of Operational Research was to be able to face extremely complex problems and increase the likelihood of effective decisions being taken in situations of extreme uncertainty. Hence, Dr. Beer has formalized the Operational Research approach with the following definition:

"Operational Research is the attack of modern science on complex problems arising in the direction and management of large systems of men, machines, materials and money in industry, business, government and defence. Its distinctive approach is to develop a scientific model of the system, incorporating measurements of factors such as chance and risk, with which to predict and compare the outcomes of alternative decisions, strategies or controls. The purpose is to help management to determine its policy and actions scientifically."

Decision and Control aimed to clarify these propositions in the context of "management". As Dr. Beer himself points out, the book is not the result of an academic research, but rather of real experience over more than 20 years in applying the principles contained therein whilst in charge of operational research activities in the then largest steel-producing company in Europe.

Stafford Beer considers this orientation towards problem solving to be vital for society, and he proposes cybernetics as the most powerful approach available for building multi-disciplinary models. The development of "academic" interests has, however, meant that operations research has become a type of applied mathematics, distancing it from creative problem solving. Although Professor Beer considers mathematics useful as a powerful language for discussing models and has, in fact, used them in some of his most innovative studies, he believes that models do not necessarily need to be mathematical. One of the most outstanding aspects of the book is precisely the way he deals with the appropriate methodology for selecting and using models.

The density of the book *Decision and Control* and the wish to render it more accessible to managers in general is what prompted the appearance in 1968 of *Management Science: The Business Use of Operational Research*. In this work he insists on differentiating between what is a scientific knowledge of "management" based on the theory of systems, and the consideration of the science of management as a collection of topics (an understanding of human factors, market research, cost analysis, balances, leadership, etc.) no matter how interesting and useful they might be, since its objects of study are complex, probabilistic systems considered as a whole.

The publication, in 1972, of *Brain of the Firm* marks the appearance of the first book in Dr. Beers' trilogy dedicated to explaining the Viable System Model (VSM). Employing the epistemology expounded in *Decision and Control*, the

VSM is conceived on the basis of the necessary and sufficient conditions that should be met by any system for it to be viable.

The book creates a description of the firm (or any other organisation) based on reflections deriving from the study of the human nervous system. The structures of the brain and "management" are continuously clarified and compared until they give way to a theory of effective organisation. This is not an analogy but rather a question of deducing the fundamental principles according to which viable self-organised systems are constructed.

The purpose of this book is stated by Dr. Beer when he maintains that the main discovery of cybernetics is identifying fundamental control principles applicable to all large systems. It is oriented towards a study of the contribution that cybernetics (the science of control) can make to "management" (the profession of control). Control is not something to be encountered in a place or a specific element of the firm (or organisation), but rather the function of control is shared by the whole of the firm's architecture. Control is what helps systems to go on functioning.

The model identified by Stafford Beer distinguishes five sub-systems, each of which carries out a systemic role. These are continually interacting so as maintain the system in a state of homeostatic equilibrium, in other words, under control. The entire regulatory process aims to ensure the system's survival, both in the short and long term, by means of learning, adaptation and evolution. Moreover, the five sub-systems cannot be isolated from one another because they form a whole in constant interaction.

In the second edition of *The Brain of the Firm*, published in 1981, Professor Beer adds a description of an application of the VSM and cybernetic principles to the case of Chile. It is tremendously interesting to see how in a short period of time it was possible to incorporate in the model two thirds of the country's social economy, as well as the diverse innovations that were applied to the system of control. More specifically, the orthodox information systems were replaced by a computerised system in real time, based on Kalman filters and Bayes' probabilities theory. Communications by microwave and automatic statistical filtering of information were used, and ergonomically designed operations rooms were created, as spaces for decision taking. Economic information at all levels, from production plants to the presidential cabinet itself, and which was never more than 24 h old, was filtered with a view to identifying the important aspects. In spite of the whole complexity of the control system, the informatics system was organised so as to decentralise authority.

After the work undertaken in Chile during the years 1971–73, Dr. Beer was sought after by a multitude of organizations and institutions in several countries. One of these was Canada, where as a consequence of intense activity for various organisations and governmental departments, the Canadian Broadcasting Corporation invited him to give the 1973 Massey Lectures. These were a series of talks broadcast on the radio each year to the whole country, and were given by an important person in the world of science or culture. All the lectures delivered by Professor Stafford Beer were included in the book entitled *Designing Freedom* published in 1974. The purpose of the broadcasts, as well as that of the book, was to explain to the general public some of the fundamental concepts of cybernetics. Emphasis is placed on the need to design new institutions that can make use of science as well as information and communication technologies for the benefit of mankind, in order that ongoing processes of instability may be controlled.

Dr. Beer's dedication to studying problems of a global nature affecting mankind and society increased in the 1970s. An indication of his intense activity during this period are more than 15 inaugural talks or plenary sessions he gave during the year 1970, to audiences as diverse as the Operational Research Society, the Pierre Theilard de Chardin Association in London, UNESCO, the Institute of Management Science, and the Society for General Systems Research in the U.S.A., etc. To prepare the content of such a wide range of activities, he decided to take on a more far-reaching project, namely, a book in which he would give his ideas on the relevance of this new science of cybernetics for holism, proposing it as a new world view. At the same time, whilst developing different concepts he would apply them to the pertinent problems of the various audiences. This context supplies the origin of the book *Platform for Change*, published in 1975.

It is a hugely original book in both form and content. Stafford Beer himself maintains that it is "a new kind of book for a new kind of world." It is structured around a thesis, named total system, which represents a world philosophy set forth in a simple systems diagram.

The main idea of the book focuses on the urgent need to reconsider all our social institutions, for which it offers a conceptual framework. Many questions are dealt with, such as global threats to humanity, overwhelming complexity, systems and meta-language, the use of science for studying organisations and society, and that of computers to manage information. Different colours and text layouts are employed to differentiate the arguments from the meta-systems in which they are included.

In 1979, he publishes *The Heart of Enterprise*. When Stafford Beer designs the neuro-cybernetic model of the firm as a viable system in *Brain of the Firm* (1972), he suggests that the human nervous system allows us to identify the rules according to which an organisation is able to survive, that is to say: it is regulated, it learns, it adapts and it evolves. Many considered the model to be an "analogy," in which case its validity on different specific occasions would be debatable. Nevertheless, as Dr. Beer himself has repeatedly argued, the model "is not an analogy." This signifies that it ought to be possible to identify the nature of viable systems and create this model from basic principles, regardless of the source from which the cybernetic considerations are drawn (in the case of *Brain of the Firm*, from neurophysiology). This is precisely the purpose of the book *The Heart of Enterprise*. The reason for including the term "heart" in the title is Professor Stafford Beer's awareness that man has to be placed in the centre of "management". In this work, he makes it clear that cybernetic concepts can be applied to all kinds of organisations (not only firms).

The book begins with a discussion regarding the meaning of the word system and its subjective and relative nature. After debating the question of measuring a system's complexity and how variety flux determines the latter's dynamic complexity, he considers how systems can be regulated. The answer constitutes the central axis of the book: by means of organisation. The book deals with organisational cybernetics: the science of effective organisation. Following the initial concepts he manages, by a deductive process, to identify the five sub-systems regarded as fundamental when it comes to guaranteeing the viability of any system.

The third book in the trilogy dedicated to the VSM is published in 1985 and is entitled *Diagnosing the System for Organizations*. Due to the complexity of the two previous books (*Brain of the Firm* and *The Heart of Enterprise*), Stafford Beer decides to write a book to facilitate the application of the principles contained in the VSM. All the same, this work is not restricted to aiding implementation but also constitutes the definitive formalisation, in graphic form, of this model. The origins of the VSM go back to a mathematical model of the brain published in 1960. Nevertheless, both the model, based on the theory of sets, and the mathematical notion of recursion, were not all that accessible to the general public on account of their difficulty. For this reason, he decided to represent the mathematical model in terms of rigorous diagrams, in this way fully maintaining the model's mathematical validity.

In 1994, he publishes his last book: *Beyond Dispute*. In all viable systems there are two sub-systems with very different functions, which he calls System Three and System Four. In simple terms, we may say that the former is responsible for the "here and now," that is, for ensuring functioning in present time, whilst the latter is responsible for the "exterior and the future," in other words, for trying to create the future of the organisation. Interaction between both is generally very conflictive due to diverse interests, but it is vital that they function properly for the system to survive as it depends on them for adaptation. This is one of the reasons why Dr. Beer has, throughout his last years, been interested in how to facilitate this interaction. The result of this is his invention of Team Syntegrity. We might say that this is a method designed to facilitate normative, strategic and operational planning, allowing us to capture the essence of an organization in a non-hierarchical and non-political way.

In its original format, it takes its inspiration from an icosahedron (a regular 20-sided polyhedron), in which each of the 30 edges represents a person and each vertex one of the topics into which the object of debate has been broken down; the latter could be symbolically situated in the centre of the icosahedron. All the edges are identical. There is no hierarchy. There is no top, bottom, right or left. Besides, the functioning protocols guarantee that the information circulates freely throughout the whole group, becoming more extensive and enhanced along the way until becoming totally diffused. Therefore, a group organised in this way is said to represent the greatest expression of participatory democracy, as each role is, structurally speaking, not distinguishable from the others. Finally, I will add that the agenda is not established previously, but that it is generated by the members of the group themselves whilst the progress is in motion.

Apart from the utility of this tool for guaranteeing that the homeostat formed by systems three and four works properly, it may also be extremely useful in the resolution of conflicts.

Following this overview of part of Dr. Beer's work, we will say a few things concerning its relevance within the systems movement and the theory of the organisation.

The success of the scientific revolution in the generation of knowledge and the development of world-transforming technologies is a fact, with the application of the "reductionist" method proposed by Descartes dividing a problem into parts in order to make it easier to study. However, the usefulness of this method can be questioned when we are dealing with real-world complex problems and particularly in social systems, which represent the main threats for our organisations and societies. Such problems are just the types that are examined by systems thinking. These thinkers espouse the use of "holism" – instead of "reductionism" – according to which attention is not on the parts but rather the inter-relations between them and the environment, and on how properties emerge that characterize the whole and which none of the parts possesses.

Ackoff describes this transition, maintaining that Descartes' reductionism was suitable for the "machine age" of the industrial revolution, and that systems thinking comes about as a response to the appearance of the "systems age" in which we are fully immersed. This is characterised by the complexity, turbulence and diversity of points of view regarding how to cope with the different kinds of problems facing us, at the individual level as well as in organisations, societies or the natural environment in which we live.

The appearance of a multitude of fashions, most of them ephemeral, focusing on partial aspects of these problems, such as Total Quality Management, Business Process Reengineering, Rightsizing, Knowledge Management, Learning Organization, Benchmarking, Empowerment, etc., reflect the importance of the problem as well as why we are looking to systems thinking as a global response, as opposed to this proliferation of recipes which are, in the best of cases, useful only for particular circumstances.

The tradition of systems thinking (holistic thinking) has a long history, but it was at the end of the 1940s and beginning of the 1950s when it took shape as a discipline, especially as a result of the work by Wiener and Bertalannfy. The decades of the 1950s to the 1970s marked the period of maximum influence of this trend in managerial sciences and many other fields. From the 1970s onwards, the traditional systems approach began to come in for growing criticism, above all in terms of its usefulness for dealing with loosely structured strategic problems, and situations in which it was not easy to determine a common goal or in ones with opposing interests.

As a response to such criticism there appeared, at the end of the 1970s and throughout the 1980s, alternative systemic approaches capable of dealing with problem situations like these. More recently, critical currents have emerged disapproving of the way the previous approaches and science in general have been used, giving rise to what is known as the emancipatory or critical movement.

We mention this so as to stress the amazing capacity of Dr. Beer to make valuable contributions in every developmental stage of systems thinking; such contributions justify his being regarded as one of the most relevant systems thinkers, and his work as an exceptional contribution to the study of organizations and their viability.

Systems thinking has undergone a development which parallels that of sociological theory. In this regard, the classification put forward by Burrel and Morgan, where they identify basically four large groups of schools – functionalism, interpretivism, radical humanism and radical structuralism -, allows us to throw light on the way in which Dr. Beer's work has developed.

As regards its areas of application, this evolution has been seen both in terms of the degree of complexity involved in the particular problem and also in the extent to which agreement exists on the intended objectives (situations: unitary, pluralistic and conflictive), as pointed out by Jackson and Keys.

Early systems approaches, such as Systems Analysis and Systems Engineering, were of use for examining simple unitary problems. However, excessive emphasis on the mathematical modelling of the systems studied showed how insufficient they were for complex problems (hard to model mathematically) and pluralistic or conflictive decision-making contexts. This caused a decline in the use of Operational Research and the appearance of new approaches which were more suitable for these problems, such as Dr. Beer's Organisational Cybernetics. This does not seek a mathematical model of the problem (although mathematics are also used) on the basis of superficial manifestations, but the identification of the profound fundamentals of viability. The positivist approach gives way to a structural one, and the focus of interest shifts from simple to adaptive complex systems. Interest in facilitating decision-making processes in pluralistic and conflictive situations gives rise to the emergence of systemic methods called "soft systems" and emancipatory methods. Dr. Beer´s contribution in this context is also very significant. Let us have a look at his work in the three systems approaches: functionalist, interpretive and emancipatory.

Within the functionalist systemic approach there is a wide range of schools and approaches, such as the contingent theory and socio-technical systems theory regarding the theory of the organisation, "Hard" systems approaches, Systems Dynamics, and many others. We will make special mention here of Dr. Beer's Organisational Cybernetics. This branch of cybernetics applied to management and organisation represents a break with the initial mechanistic and organicistic thinking behind cybernetics, making full use of the concept of variety. One of its great contributions is the construction of the Viable System Model on the basis of fundamental cybernetic principles totally disconnected from any reference to mechanical or biological manifestations. The other novelty is its incorporation into the scene of the observer, shedding light on what came to be known as second-order cybernetics.

The scientific superiority of Organisational Cybernetics compared with the traditional theory of organization is due to many reasons. First of all, its generality, as the recommendations emerging from the model do not prescribe a specific structure, but rather they are related with an essential organising of the system. Hence we find its application in such diverse domains as large companies, small organizations, industries, local or national governments, etc.

What is more, the model's recursive conception allows it to be applied to organisations with multiple interdependent parts (divisions, departments, companies, etc.), with an enormous economy of means for studying them.

The old dilemma of centralisation or decentralisation is determined scientifically within the VSM, which establishes that the subsystems must have the maximum amount of autonomy compatible with the global cohesion of the system. Control is shared throughout the whole organisation, making it easier to profit from the self-organising tendencies present in all complex systems. This enhances motivation and makes managers more willing to devote their attention to dealing with the boundaries of their organizations.

The VSM provides a solid foundation for designing management information systems. Most of these are based on preconceived, usually hierarchical, models of organisations. Organisational Cybernetics inverts the process completely, beginning by identifying the information processing needs in accordance with the law of requisite variety, and then going on to recommend the organizational design.

Dr. Beer's concern for increasing the organisation's efficiency is accompanied by his interest in contributing to the fulfilling of human potential. Both the adjudication of maximum autonomy to individuals and subsystems inside the organisation, together with a democratic establishing of its goals, are grounded in solid cybernetic arguments contained in the model. The only accepted degree of restriction is that deriving from the necessity of maintaining the cohesion of the global system. Efficiency and democracy are indissolubly bound within the model; hence the warning regarding the disastrous effects that may arise from the inappropriate use of power in organisations.

Organisational Cybernetics is far superior to the alternatives normally offered by organisation theory (classic, human relations and contingent), besides being capable of making sense of the latest findings in organisational theory and integrating them in an applicable management tool.

Its enormous explanatory power compared with the usual analysis carried out in organization theory lies in the science of cybernetics and the structuralist epistemology upon which it is based. Organizational theory (at least the theory based on positivism) generally bases its arguments on the relations observable among superficial phenomena, whereas cybernetics is able to explain these relations on the basis of functioning processes at the deep, structural level. As Jackson maintains, "It is not farfetched to see the whole history of positivist organization theory as an empirical commentary upon the cybernetic principles underlying the viability of systems as unearthed deductively by Beer".

We have seen the tremendous importance of Dr. Beer's work in the area of functionalist systems approaches. His contributions, however, do not end there. The interpretive systemic approach, also known as "soft systems thinking" as a result of its placing people at the centre of the study, and not the technology, the structure or the organisation, with the principal concern being for perceptions, beliefs, values and interests, starts from the premise that there are many perceptions of reality. It attempts, therefore, to help decision-makers to work in a pluralistic context. The important thing now is to identify the different "world views" (*Weltanschauungen*) or the "appreciative systems" that people use in order to understand and construct the social reality. The idea is to "accommodate" the different groups in this coalition, that is, the organisation itself. In this systems approach also Dr. Beer provides some really valuable tools. As Harnden points out, an alternative use to the one previously attributed to the VSM, as an expression of certain basic laws governing the organisation of complex systems (which we can only ignore at our peril), is as a "hermeneutic enabler", thereby ascribing it to interpretive thinking.

According to this particular use, organisational models are not seen as having captured an objective reality, but rather as being a support for conversations about complex social issues. The VSM can facilitate discourse on the emergence and evolution of appropriate organisational forms and provide a "consensual domain" in which to coordinate our interactions. Second-order cybernetics (that of observer systems), as defined by Von Foerster (1995), unlike first-order cybernetics (that of observed systems), shifts attention to the observers; this is what Maturana and Varela (1980, 1992) do when, as a result of their work on autopoiesis, they propose that the focus of attention should be moved to the observers and the distinctions these make. Dr. Beer's VSM is an excellent "hermeneutic enabler" as it helps to make such distinctions.

During the 1980s and 1990s, there was an increase in the number of systems thinkers who started to question the use of technical instruments without giving consideration to the interests these served. On the basis of the critical tradition in philosophy and sociology, there was an attempt to develop an emancipatory systems approach. In this line of development, we once again encounter some tremendously important contributions by Dr. Beer, particularly his relatively recent invention represented by **Team Syntegrity**. We have previously seen how groups organised in accordance with this approach are good examples of participatory democracy in which all the participants have identical access to information and absolutely equivalent roles. Under these conditions it might be possible to approach the ideal situation for communication without distortion proposed by Habermas.

Apart from the important contribution represented by **Team Syntegrity**, the VSM itself contains an emancipatory component. We mentioned above that Dr. Beer regards the decentralising of control as fundamental for the viability of any system. The parts of the system should be given autonomy so as to absorb some of the variety of the environment, otherwise the top managerial levels will be overwhelmed. If, however, the intention is that the parts make appropriate use of their autonomy, then they have to intervene in the process of setting the global objectives. For this reason, Dr. Beer argues that what he refers to as system five should embody the interests not only of the owners of the organisation, but also of the workers, suppliers, consumers and society in general. The board of directors, according to Dr. Beer, metabolises the power of all such participants in the organisation in order that it can survive. As a consequence, the VSM needs a democratic environment to function properly.

We have seen the enormous significance of Dr. Beer's work in the development of systems thinking and the theory of the organisation. Nevertheless, its importance is not restricted to academic or business domains, since it also provides a tremendously useful intellectual framework for dealing with the many problems affecting humanity nowadays (ecological aggression, unequal distribution of wealth, biological, chemical or nuclear terrorism threats, corruption, inexistence of an appropriate global judicial system, mass migration, assistance in cases of natural disasters, etc.). All these are manifestations of a huge increase in the complexity (variety) of present-day society, which has been rising exponentially during the last decades. However, the models we employ in order to make sense of them have not evolved in parallel. As Conant-Ashby remarked in their well-known theorem stating that "a good regulator of a system must be a model of the system", we need models of problematic situations with requisite variety. Yet very often the models employed are either lacking in sufficient variety or do not even exist.

Dr. Beer provides suitable elements for creating these models and for ensuring that interactions between the different parts of social systems, today the victims of growing oscillations that threaten to bring about their disintegration, can be stabilised so that a harmonious existence may be possible.

Many of the problematic aspects affecting us today were clearly identified by Dr. Beer:

Issues such as the "morality" of scientists and the function of science in contemporary society, or problems caused by an excess of data and information, which are indicative of the direction in which information technologies should be developing so as to permit the filtering of relevant information, previously identified thanks to the acknowledgement of the information required to guarantee systemic equilibrium.

Identifying the need of what Dr. Beer calls "meta-languages" to discuss a system's behaviour, the discovery of which he associated to Gödel´s theorem of incompleteness, and which gave rise to the "recursive methodology" permitting an explanation of the viability of systems.

A theoretical justification of the need for supranational institutions to define ethical, legal or ecological codes, among others, providing tools that enable rapid diagnosis of flaws in the design of international structures of governance.

Deducing the systemic requirement of decentralisation and autonomy within systems to guarantee their viability, thereby resolving the dilemma between autonomy and cohesion, which particularly affects systems such as organisations, firms, countries, supranational communities, etc.

The conception of communication systems among group members ensuring the complete distribution of information and participation, approaching what one might call "perfect democracy".

A reconsideration of the role of management in organisations as the creator of opportunities for conversations, where involvement should include, apart from the owners, all those affected.

The identification, more than 30 years ago, of the need for such conversations to break space and time barriers by means of information and communications technologies; this anticipated the emergence of Internet, computer-supported collaborative work, communications with sufficient bandwidth and the use of the computer as a complement to the capacity of the human brain (tools known nowadays as MIS, DSS, EIS, etc.).

Exploring the actual material components of computers, through experiments with living organisms, in search of ways to amplify human intelligence.

Countering decision-makers' short-term views by proposing measurement systems that consider, in addition to what systems already do, both their capacity and their potential; working also against the use of performance assessment parameters based on fundamentally (almost exclusively) economic aspects.

An exhaustive enumeration of Dr. Beer's contributions to scientific knowledge would make this overview much too long; so I will just end here by saying that the complexity of his personality goes beyond his different facets as a scientist, manager or consultant, since to this wealth of involvement we must also add those of painter and poet.

To conclude, I would not like to end this laudatio without making a brief reference to Dr. Beer's relationship with the Ibero-American world in general and with our university in particular.

Dr. Beer's relations with Ibero-America go back to the years in which he was professionally engaged as chief of the consulting company SIGMA through its operations in Chile. However, the first real contact came in 1971, when he was invited by President Allende to take responsibility, as Scientific Director, for designing a system for managing the national economy in real time. As a result of this work, he was invited to intervene as a consultant in other Ibero-American countries, such as Mexico, Uruguay, Venezuela and, more recently, Colombia.

Regarding his association with Spain, we must point out that so far this has been fundamentally through his scientific work.

Referring specifically to the University of Valladolid, first of all we will mention its participation in two actual syntegrations (the *First International Syntegration Conference* and the *I Sintegración sobre Ciudadanía Organizacional* and, above all, in the world's first electronic syntegration carried out in 1995 and 1996, in which 30 cyberneticians belonging to 16 countries and four continents were able, by means of tele-working via Internet, to prepare, over 8 months, a joint publication on Dr. Beer's work entitled *To be and not to be that is the system: A tribute to Stafford Beer*. A collaborative effort of this kind served to demonstrate the practical use of **Team Syntegrity**, and it led to the appearance of completely original lines of research in our university, which have been embodied in different research projects over the last few years.

Dr. Beer's work is also present in the University of Valladolid thanks to the incorporation of its theoretical corpus in the teaching material used in this institution. Moreover, we can mention the use of Dr. Beer's Organisational Cybernetics to conceive and design the system of communications and information exchange created by our university for Ibero-American and European academic communities; the intention here is to provide a tool in which cybernetic concepts are combined with the new information and communication technologies..

To conclude, I will use Dr. Beer's own words when he says: "A self-organized system must always be alive and incomplete. For completion is another name for death". We trust that Dr. Beer's work will continue unfinished for many years.

On Stafford Beer's agreeing to join as one of the doctors of the University of Valladolid, our institution is enriched with one of the most outstanding scientists in the field of systems thinking and organization theory, and whose lucid work contributes an essential reference framework, not only for students of industrial, telecommunications or computer engineering, but for all disciplines taught at our University.

Therefore, I proclaim and manifest:

His De Causis, Peto Gradum Doctoris Honoris Causa Domino Stafford Beer.

Appendix II

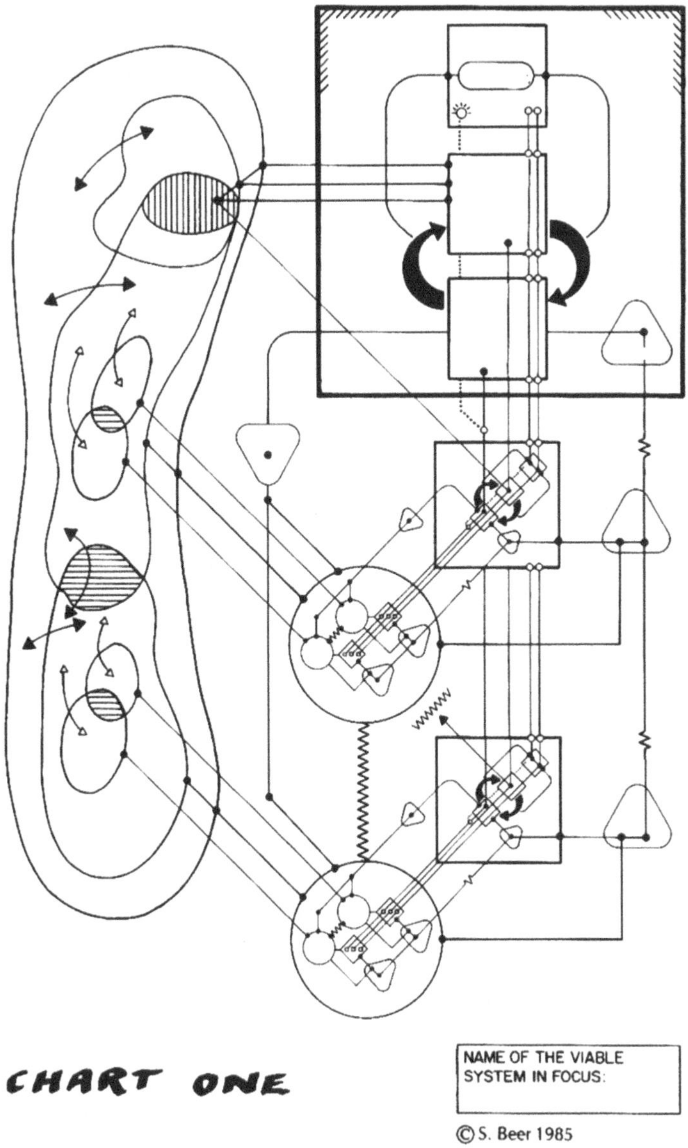

Fig. II1 Representation of the VSM showing its recursive structure (Beer 1985)

J. Pérez Ríos, *Design and Diagnosis for Sustainable Organizations*,
DOI 10.1007/978-3-642-22318-1, © Springer-Verlag Berlin Heidelberg 2012

Glosary of Rules for the Viable System

(After Beer 1979, *The Heart of Enterprise*. Reprint of 1994 "Stafford Beer Classic Library". Wiley, pp..: 565–567)

Aphorisms

The First Regulatory Aphorism

It is not necessary to enter the black box to understand the nature of the function it performs.

The Second Regulatory Aphorism

It is not necessary to enter the black box to calculate the variety that it potentially may generate.

Principles

The First Principle of Organization

Managerial, operational and environmental varieties, diffusing through an institutional system, tend to equate; they should be **designed** to do so with mínimum damage to people and to cost.

The Second Principle of Organization

The four directional channels carrying information between the management unit, the operation, and the environment must each have a higher capacity to transmit a given amount of information relevant to variety selection in a given time than the originating subsystem has to generate it in that time.

The Third Principle of Organization

Wherever the information carried on a cannel capable of distinguishing a given variety crosses a boundary, it undergoes transduction; the variety of the transducer must be at least equivalent to the variety of the channel.

The Fourth Principle of Organization

The operation of the first three principles must be cyclically maintained through time without hiatus or lags.

Theorem

Recursive System Theorem

In a recursive organizational structure, any viable system contains, and is contained in, a viable system.

Axioms

The First Axiom of Management

The sum of horizontal variety disposed by *n* operational elements equals the sum of vertical variety disposed on the six vertical components of corporate cohesion.

The Second Axiom of Management

The variety disposed by System Three resulting from the operation of the First Axiom equals the variety disposed by System Four.

The Third Axiom of Management

The variety disposed by System Five equals the residual variety generated by the operation of the Second Axiom.

Law

The Law of Cohesion for Multiple Recursions of the Viable System

The System One variety accesible to System Three of Recursion x equals the variety disposed by the sum of the metasystems of Recursion y for every recursive pair.

References

Ackoff RL (1999a) Ackoff´s best. John Wiley & Sons, USA

Ackoff RL (1999b) Re-creating the corporation. A design of organizations for the 21st Century. Oxford University Press, New York

Almuiña C, Martín R, Y Pérez Ríos J (eds) (2000) Las universidades iberoamericanas en la sociedad del conocimiento. Universidad de Valladolid, Valladolid. ISBN 84-8448-03-3

Almuiña C, Pérez Ríos J et al. (2008) *La relevancia de los medios de comunicación en Castilla y León*. Consejo Económico y Social de Castilla y León. ISBN: 978-84-95308-37-5

Ashby WR (1956) An introduction to cybernetics, vol 2. Chapman Hall, London

Beer S (1959) Cybernetics and Management. John Wiley and Sons, New York

Beer S (1966) Decision and Control: The meaning of Operational Research and Management Cybernetics. John Wiley and Sons, Chichester

Beer S (1975) Platformform for Change. John Wiley and Sons, Chichester

Beer S (1979) The heart of enterprise. John Wiley & Sons, Chichester

Beer S (1981) Brain of the firm, 2nd edn. John Wiley & Sons, Chichester

Beer S (1985) Diagnosing the system for organizations. John Wiley & Sons, Chichester

Beer S (1989) The viable system model: its provenance, development, methodology and pathology. In: Espejo R, Harnden R (eds) The viable system model. Interpretations and applications of Stafford Beer´s VSM. John Wiley & Sons, Chichester

Beer S (1994) Beyond dispute. The Invention of team syntegrity. John Wiley & Sons, Chichester

Cambel AB (1992) Applied chaos theory: a paradigm for complexity. Academic Press, New York

Checkland P (1981) Systems thinking, systems practice. John Wiley and Sons, Chichester/Great Britain

Checkland P, Scholes J (1990) Soft systems methodology in action. John Wiley & Sons, Chichester

Churchman CW (1968) The systems approach. Dell Publishing Co, New York

Churchman CW (1971) The design of inquiring systems: basic concepts of systems and organization. Basic Books, Inc Publishers, New York

Churchman CW (1979) The systems approach and its enemies. Basic Books, Inc Publishers, New York

Clemson B (1984) Cybernetics. A New Management Tool, Abacus Press, Philadelphia, USA

Conant RC, Ashby WR (1970) Every good regulator of a system must be model of that system. Int J Syst Sci 1(2):89–97

de Geus A (1997) The living company. Habits for survival in a turbulent business environment. Harvard Business School Press, Boston, Massachusetts

Drucker PE (1954) The practice of management. HarperCollins Publishers. Edición First Harper Business 1993, pp. 62–87

J. Pérez Ríos, *Design and Diagnosis for Sustainable Organizations*,
DOI 10.1007/978-3-642-22318-1, © Springer-Verlag Berlin Heidelberg 2012

Espejo R (1989) The VSM revisited. In: Espejo R, Harnden R (eds) The viable system model: interpretations and applications of Stafford Beer´s VSM. John Wiley and Sons, Chichester, pp 77–100

Espejo R (2008) Observing organizations: the use of identity and structural archetypes. In Special issue: organizational cybernetics in focus, Pérez Ríos J and Schwaninger M (Guest editors). *International Journal of Applied Systemic Studies* 2(1/2). ISSN: 1751–0589. ISSN (Online) 1751–0597

Espejo R (2009) Performance management, the nature of regulation and the Cybersyn project. Kybernetes 38(1/2):65–82

Espejo R, Bowling D, Hoverstadt P (1999) The viable system model and the VIPLAN software. Kybernetes: Int J Syst Cybern 28(6/7):661–678, ISSN 0368-492X

Espejo R, Harnden R (eds) (1989) The viable system model. Interpretations and applications of Stafford Beer´s VSM. John Wiley and Sons, Chichester

Espejo R, Reyes A (2011) Organizational Systems. Managing Complexity with the Viable System Model, Springer, Heidelberg

Espejo R, Schuhmann W, Schwaninger M, Bilello U (1996) Organisational transformation and learning. John Wiley and Sons, Chichester

Espejo R, Schwaninger M (eds) (1993) Orgnizational fitness: corporate effectiveness through management cybernetics. Campus Verlag, New York

Espejo R, Schwaninger M et al (1997) To be and not to be that is the system: a tribute to Stafford Beer. CD ROM, Carl-Auer-Systeme Verlag, Heidelberg

Espinosa A, Leonard A (guest editors) (2009) Action Research in Organizational Cybernetics. Systemic Practice and Action Research 22(4), ISSN 1094-429X

Flood RL, Jackson MC (1991) Creative problem solving: total systems intervention. John Wiley and Sons, Chichester

Forrester JW (1958) Industrial dynamics: a major breakthrough for decision makers. Harv Bus Rev 36(4):37–66

Fuller RB (1979) Synergetics: the geometry of thinking. Macmillan, New York

Hernández C and López A (1999) Beyond Experimental Economics: Trading Institutions and Multiagent Systems. Computing in Economics and Finance 1351, Society for Computational Economics

Hernández C (2004) Herbert A. Simon, 1916–2001, y el Futuro de la Ciencia Económica. *Revista Europea de Dirección y Economía de la Empresa* 13(2): 7–23

Hetzler S (2008) Pathological systems. In Special issue: organizational cybernetics in focus, Perez Rios J and Schwaninger M (Guest editors). *International Journal of Applied Systemic Studies* 2(1/2). ISSN: 1751–0589. ISSN (Online) 1751–0597.

Ingber DE (1998) The architecture of Life. Sci Am 278(1):48–57

Jackson MC (2000) Systems approaches to management. Kluwer Academic/Plenum Publishers, New York, pp 163–166

Jalali A (1994) Reverberating networks. Modelling information propagation in syntegration by spectral análisis. In: Beer S (ed) Beyond dispute. The invention of team syntegrity. John Wiley and Sons, Chichester, pp 263–280

Kaplan RS, Norton DP (1996) The balanced scorecard. Harvard Business School Press, Boston

Leonard A (1989) Application of VSM to commercial broadcasting in the United States. In: Espejo R, Harnden R (eds) The viable system model. Interpretations and applications of Stafford Beer´ s VSM. John Wiley & Sons, Chichester

López Paredes A, Hernández C (eds) (2008) Agent based modelling in natural resource management. INSISOC, Madrid. ISBN 978-84-205-4560-8

López Paredes A, Hernández C, Pajares J (2002) Towards a new experimental socio-economics. Complex behaviour in aargaining. J Socio-Econ 31:423–429

Maturana HR, Varela FJ (1980) Autopoiesis and cognition. The realization of the living. D. Reidel Publishing Company, Dordrecht

Maturana HR, Varela FJ (1992) The tree of knowledge. The biological roots of human understanding. Shambhala Publications, Inc, Boston
Morecroft JDW (1988) System dynamics and microworlds for policymakers. Eur J Oper Res 35:306–308
Pajares J, López-Paredes A, Hernández C (2003) Industry as an organisation of agents: Innovation and R&D management. JASSS 6(2)
Pérez Casares A, Hernández Iglesias C, y Pérez Ríos J (2008) An agent based model of firms' birth, evolution and extinction. In: López Paredes A, Hernández C (eds) Agent based modelling in natural resource management. INSISOC, Madrid. ISBN 978-84-205-4560-8
Pérez Ríos J (1992) Dirección Estratégica y Pensamiento Sistémico. Departamento de Economía y Administración de Empresas. Universidad de Valladolid, Valladolid. ISBN 84-604-7224-8
Pérez Ríos J (2000) Nuevas formas organizativas en sociedades complejas. In: Almuiña C, Martín R, y Pérez Ríos J (eds) Las Universidades iberoamericanas en la sociedad del conocimiento. Universidad de Valladolid, Valladolid, pp 291–317. ISBN 84-8448-03-3
Pérez Ríos J (2001) Laudatio de Stafford Beer. Investidura de Stafford Beer como "Doctor Honoris Causa" por la Universidad de Valladolid. Universidad de Valladolid, Valladolid, D. L. VA. 57.2002
Pérez Ríos J (2003) VSMod®: a software tool for the application of the Viable System Model, 47th Annual Conference of the International Society for the Systems Sciences (ISSS), Heraklion, Crete, Greece. ISBN: 0-9740735-1-2
Pérez Ríos J (2004) A self-organizing network for the systems community. Kybernetes: Int J Syst Cybern 33(3/4):590–606, ISSN 0368-492X
Pérez Ríos J (2006a) Information and communication technologies for viable organizations. *The WOSC 13th international congress of cybernetics and systems and the 6th international Conference of sociocybernetics*, Maribor, Eslovenia, 6–10 July 2006
Pérez Ríos J (2006b) "Communication and information technologies to enable viable organizations". *Kybernetes: The International Journal of Systems & Cybernetic* 35(7/8): 1109–1125, ISSN 0368-492X
Pérez Ríos J (2007a) Prologue of book: Herrscher E. El círculo virtuoso. Cambiar-Planificar-Aprender-Cambiar. Granica, Buenos Aires (Argentina), pp 9–14. ISBN 978-950-641-504-4
Pérez Ríos J (2007b) Viable System Modeling with VSMod®. *4th Metaphorum Conference "Evolution from and development of the work of Stafford Beer.* St. Gallen, Swizerland, March 2007
Pérez Ríos J (2007c) Modeling organizations for viability. *3rd National Conference of the Hellenic Society for Systemic Studies.* Piraeus, Athens, Greece, May 2007
Pérez Ríos J (2008a) Aplicación de la Cibernética Organizacional al estudio de la viabilidad de las organizaciones (Parte I). DYNA 83(5):265–281, ISSN 0012–7.361
Pérez Ríos J (2008b) Aplicación de la Cibernética Organizacional al estudio de la viabilidad de las organizaciones. Patologías organizativas frecuentes (Parte II). DYNA 83(7):403–422, ISSN 0012–7.361
Pérez Ríos J (2008c) Supporting organizational cybernetics by communication and information technologies (VSMod). Int J Appl Syst Stud 2(1/2):48–65, ISSN: 1751–0589 ISSN (Online) 1751–0597
Pérez Ríos J (2008d) Closing and enriching the loop. Comment on the paper by Kopainsky and Luna-Reyes. Syst Res and Behav Sci 25(5):487–492, ISSN 1092–7026
Pérez Ríos J (2008e) *Diseño y diagnóstico de organizaciones viables. Un enfoque sistémico.* IBERFORA 2000. ISBN: 978-84-612-5845-1
Pérez Ríos J (2010) Models of organizational cybernetic for diagnosis and design. Kybernetes: Int J Syst Cybern 39(9/10):1529–1550, ISSN 0368-492X
Pérez Ríos J, Martínez Suárez XL (2007) Applying VSM in the strategic management of A Coruña University in Galicia, Spain. In: Christopher WF (ed) Holistic management. Managing what matters for company success. John Wiley & Sons, Hoboken/New Jersey, pp 124–134. ISBN 978-0-471-74063-6

Pérez Ríos J, y Sánchez Mayoral P (2001) Gestión del conocimiento: un enfoque cibernético. *IV Congreso de Ingeniería de Organización: CIO-2001*. Septiembre de 2001, Sevilla

Pérez Ríos J and Schwaninger M (1996) "Integrative systems modeling: leveraging complementarities of qualitative and quantitative methodologies", *1996 International System Dynamics Conference,* Boston, EE.UU

Pérez Ríos J and Schwaninger M (Guest editors) (2008) Organizational Cybernetics in focus. *International Journal of Applied Systemic Studies* 2(1/2). ISSN: 1751–0589. ISSN (Online) 1751–0597

Reyes A (2001) Second-Order Auditing Practices. Systemic Practice and Action Research, Vol. 14, No. 2:157–180

Schecter D (1993) Beer´s "team syntegrity" and the challenge of democratic management. In: Espejo R, Schwaninger M (eds) Organisational fitness. Campus Verlag, Frankfurt

Schuhmann W (1997) Communication and information in society. In: Espejo R, Schwaninger M (eds) To be and not to be that is the system: a tribute to Stafford Beer. (CD-ROM), Carl Auer-Systeme Verlag, Wiesbaden. ISBN 3-89670-063-4

Schwaninger M (2005) "Design for viable organizations. The diagnostic power of the viable system model". In: Viable organizations. Matjaz Mulej, Eva Buchinger et al. (eds.). WOSC world organization of systems and cybernetics. 13th International Congress of Cybernetics and Systems and ISA International Sociological Association. Research Commitee 51 on Sociocybernetics. Maribor (Eslovenia), pp. 45–56. ISBN: 961-6354-58-2

Schwaninger M (2006) Intelligent organizations. Powerful models for systemic management. Springer Berlin, Heidelberg

Schwaninger M and Pérez Ríos J (1996) "ISM - Integrative systems methodology: a hybrid methodology for applying cybernetics cybernetically". In Espejo R and Schwaninger M. with Associates, *To be and not to be that is the system: A tribute to Stafford Beer*, Festschrift presented at John Moores Liverpool University, Sept 26, 1996; y CD ROM (1997) Wiesbaden; Carl Auer-Systeme Verlag. ISBN 3-89670-063-4

Schwaninger M, Pérez Ríos J (2008a) "System dynamics and cybernetics: a synergetic pair". Syst Dynam Rev 24(2):145–74, ISSN 0883–7066

Schwaninger M, Pérez Ríos J (2008b) Organizational cybernetics in focus (guest editorial). Int J Appl Syst Stud 2(1/2):1–5, ISSN: 1751–0589. ISSN (Online) 1751–0597

Schwaninger M, Pérez Ríos J (2010) A Manifesto for model-based management (Guest Editorial). *Kybernetes: The International Journal of Systems & Cybernetics*, 39(9/10):1414–1418, ISSN 0368-492X

Schwaninger M, Pérez Ríos J and Ambroz K (2004) "System dynamics and cybernetics: a necessary synergy". *International system dynamics conference*. Oxford, U.K. ISBN: 0-9745329-1-6.

Senge PM (1990) The fifth discipline. The art and practice of the learning organization. Doubleday/Currency, New York

Simon HA (1976) Administrative behavior. Free Press, New York

Simon HA (1981) The sciences of the artificial, 2nd edn. M.I.T. Press, Cambridge

Truss J (1994a) "About face. A turn for better planning". In: Beer S (ed) Beyond dispute: the invention of team syntegrity. John Wiley and Sons, Chichester

Truss J (1994b) "From prototype to protocol. Design for doing". In: Beer S (ed) Beyond dispute: the invention of team syntegrity. John Wiley and Sons, Chichester

Wiener N (1948) Cybernetics or the control and communication in the animal and the machine. MIT Press, Cambridge

Ulrich W (1994) Critical heuristics of social planning a new approach to practical philosophy. John Wiley and Sons, Chichester, First published 1983 by Paul Haupt

Von Foester H (1995) Cybernetics of cybernetics, 2nd edn. Future Systems inc, Minneapolis/ Minnesota

Yolles M (1999) Management systems. A viable approach. Financial Times, London

Index

J. Pérez Ríos, *Design and Diagnosis for Sustainable Organizations*,
DOI 10.1007/978-3-642-22318-1,

The manufacturer's authorised representative in the EU is Springer Nature Customer Service Centre GmbH, Europaplatz 3, 69115 Heidelberg, Germany. If you have any concerns regarding our products, please contact ProductSafety@springernature.com

Printed and bound by CPI Group (UK) Ltd, Croydon, CR0 4YY
22/09/2026
02221059-0006